Thunderous Tales: Zeus, Jupiter, and Tragedy

Bessie B. Anderson

ent ABSTRACT

This book is a study and comparison of the gods Zeus and Jupiter within various tragedies of Euripides and Seneca. It is concerned above all with the *tragic* representation of the two gods and the various levels of meaning that can be ascribed to individual references to each of them in a given play. The study furthermore discusses similarities and differences that exist between Euripides' representation of Zeus and Seneca's of Jupiter and how those changes affect the interpretation of the god and of each drama.

The study is comprised of three "Parts" each subdivided into chapters. Part I ("The Cosmos") is concerned with broad notions of fate, justice and nature, with a chapter devoted to each concept. Part II ("Family") analyzes Zeus and Jupiter's familial relationships with other deities and mortals in four chapters: two devoted to Zeus and Jupiter as "Father of Gods" and two to "Father of Men." Finally, Part III ("Challengers") discusses the potential for threats to Zeus and Jupiter's supreme position, by looking first at the early cosmogonic enemies of the gods (the Titans, Giants and Typhoeus) and two figures molded in their image (Capaneus and Ajax). The final chapter is a study of Seneca's Medea and Atreus as two opponents of Jupiter who are successful theomachists; Medea as a threat to Jupiter's world-order and Atreus as Jupiter's successor.

I demonstrate that while Zeus and Jupiter share many similar qualities and are represented as being concerned with the same issues in a general way, the two gods differ substantially in each playwright's corpus in specific situations. Moreover, Euripides' Zeus is shown to be far more secure in his position as Lord of Olympus than his Senecan counterpart. Jupiter, although he remains a sovereign deity, is plagued by threats to his *imperium*; indeed by the end of Seneca's *Thyestes* Jupiter is forced to leave the play-world and his own position in the heavens.

TABLE OF CONTENTS

vii

ABBREVIATIONS

A&A	*Antike und Abendland*
AHR	*American History Review*
AJA	*American Journal of Archaeology*
AJPh	*American Journal of Philology*
ANRW	*Aufstieg und Niedergang der römischen Welt*
CB	*Classical Bulletin*
CJ	*Classical Journal*
ClAnt	*Classical Antiquity*
Colby	*Colby Quarterly*
CPh	*Classical Philology*
CQ	*Classical Quarterly*
CW	*Classical World*
DHA	*Dialogues d'Histoire Ancienne*
EducTheatreJ	*Educational Theatre Journal*
G&R	*Greece & Rome*
GRBS	*Greek, Roman and Byzantine Studies*
Hellen.	*Hellenika*
HSCP	*Hellenic Studies in Classical Philology*
ICS	*Illinois Classical Studies*
IG	*Inscriptiones Graecae*
JAAR	*Journal of the American Academy of Religion*
JDTC	*Journal of Dramatic Theory and Criticism*
JFamHist	*Journal of Family History*
JHI	*Journal of the History of Ideas*
JHS	*Journal of Hellenic Studies*
Logeion	*Logeion: A Journal of Ancient Theatre*
Mètis	*Mètis. Anthropologie des mondes grecs anciens*
MD	*Materiali e discussion per l'analisi dei testi classici*
Mnem	*Mnemosyne*
NewTheatQ	*New Theatre Quarterly*
PCPS	*Proceedings of the Cambridge Philological Society*
PEG	*Poetae Epici Graecae*, ed. A. Bernabé
PMLA	*Publications of the Modern Language Association*
QUCC	*Quaderni urbinati di cultura classica*
REG	*Revue des études grecques*
RhM	*Rheinisches Museum*
RHR	*Revue de l'histoire des religions*
SO	*Symbolae Osloenses*
SyllClass	*Syllecta classica*
TAPhA	*Transactions and Proceedings of the American Philological Association*
TheatreJ	*Theatre Journal*
YCS	*Yale Classical Studies*

INTRODUCTION

Aims and Scope

Zeus, Father of Gods and Men, as he is dubbed in the Homeric poems, seems to be everywhere in extant Greek tragedy: the recipient of many prayers, as *supplicandus* to many suppliants, as the divinity whom all others, mortal and divine, fear and obey before all others. Yet, nowhere does Zeus appear in his own right as a character, fully epiphanic deity, *deus ex machina* or prologus; there is no *concilium deorum* as one sees in epic poems. But the *dios boulē* remains in force and Zeus retains his status and "ever-presence," while at the same time being (nearly) always remote and invisible. It is this pervasive, yet allusive, quality of the "tragic" Zeus, which formed the earliest seeds of inquiry for the present study. Any inquiry of Zeus, however, is surrounded not only by literally countless references to the god in every genre but also by the sheer magnitude of such a figure: a god whose domains encompass fertility, weather, law, order, fate, the family, the city, the protection of the weak and the disenfranchised, food and boundaries among many others; a god whose essence is paralleled by Jupiter and remains a vital force and no less prolific throughout Roman history. No inquiry of Zeus or Jupiter can hope to achieve totality, but within strictly defined parameters it may be, and has been, possible to highlight some common themes, offer analyses and contribute new interpretations concerning the complex and enduring figure that is Zeus.

Faced with the necessity for strict boundaries and a limited scope for inquiry, I have focussed my dissertation on the representation of a "tragic" Zeus: that is, Zeus, as interpreted within the genre of tragedy and, here, interpreted specifically by Euripides. For comparison, I am also treating the "tragic" Jupiter, as constructed by Seneca within his tragic corpus. Several implications arise from these decisions, but two are of vital importance: first, the adoption of tragedy as my genre of choice restricts my discussion of Zeus to *literary* representations of the god, rather than to philosophical or visual depictions, which, although valid and worthy of their own separate study, would necessitate a much longer dissertation and an entirely different approach.[1] The second significant implication is that the number of tragedies each poet produced (seventeen[2] extant tragedies by Euripides and ten by Seneca) far exceeds the space that could be allotted to any significant discussion for each play and, therefore, I have narrowed my discussion to approximately half of the Euripidean corpus and to all of the authentic plays of Seneca.[3] This means an investigation of a total of sixteen plays (eight tragedies per playwright), a number which, although it remains a large corpus, is sufficient for both drawing meaningful conclusions for each poet and for making fair comparisons between the two.

Choosing which plays to include was also given due consideration and, because of the need to be highly selective for Euripides, the choices were made with the entire Senecan corpus (not including *Hercules Oetaeus* and *Octavia*) in mind. Thus, the plays under consideration here are: Euripides' *Medea, Hippolytus, Hecuba, Electra, Trojan Women, Heracles, Phoenissae* and *Orestes* in addition to Seneca's *Agamemnon, Oedipus, Phaedra, Troades, Hercules Furens, Medea, Thyestes* and *Phoenissae*.[4] As there are so few one-to-one plays between the two poets and such comparisons are either already

---

[1] This is not to say that such interpretations do not also influence literary constructions, but they are not the focus and comments regarding such interpretations will remain peripheral.

[2] I have not included the disputed *Rhesus* or the satyr-play *Cyclops* in this count. *Alcestis*, although a fourth-position play, is part of Euripides' tragic *oeuvre* and is thus included. None of these plays, however, are included in the present study.

[3] The two disputed plays of Seneca, *Hercules Oetaeus* and *Octavia*, will be referred to throughout as Pseudo-Senecan.

[4] To facilitate ease in distinguishing plays with similar names, *Herakles* and *Trojan Women* will be used exclusively when referring to Euripides' plays (*Hercules Furens* and *Troades* for Seneca's). Seneca's *Phoenissae*, although included in the present investigation, is fragmentary and contains very few references to Jupiter and therefore generates very little analysis. Discussions focussing on *Phoenissae* will therefore refer to Euripides' version, unless otherwise specified.

available or offer little new analysis, the choices were made on a more thematic and character-based basis.

Due to the plethora of options for narrowing down the Euripidean corpus, the selection was as much choosing which plays to include as it was choosing which to exclude; and the desire to include as much as possible and therefore too much is always a danger. I will thus begin by defending the choices of *exclusion* rather than inclusion. The reasons for not including *Alcestis, Suppliants, Ion* and *Bacchae* should be evident: none of Seneca's plays deal with the death of Alcestis or the comic figure of Heracles; nor do any relate to the very Athenocentric play of *Ion* or the cult of Dionysus. Although Seneca's *Phoenissae* and Euripides' *Suppliants* both pivot on the Theban War, the focus of each is drastically different and they share none of the same characters. The remaining plays were rather more difficult to set aside and, indeed, had time or space permitted, I would have preferred to include them in the study. Euripides' *Heracleidae* does share with Seneca's *Hercules Furens* a significant suppliant scene; but it was decided that given the space restrictions, only one Heracles play would be included and I opted for Euripides' *Heracles* instead. *Andromache* focusses both on the aftermath of the Trojan War and shares various characters with Seneca's *Troades*, but again, it was decided that including *Trojan Women* and *Hecuba* were sufficient for fair comparison. It is recognized that such a choice is highly subjective and *Andromache*, in addition to both *Heracleidae* and *Helen*, would be among the first I would want to include in a future study or expanded version of the dissertation. The first reason for not including *Helen* here is the play's overall tone as a "melodrama" or "romantic tragedy" (or even "tragicomedy").[5] Seneca's plays are tragic and often quite dark and thus, although the Euripidean play does have in common with

---

[5] On "tragicomedy" and "melodrama" see Barnes (1964); Kitto (2011) 270-71; Michelini (1987) Appendix A; Mastronarde (2010) 61-62.

Seneca's *Troades* the character of Helen, it would not be a fair comparison for the present investigation based on the thematic interests of the two playwrights. Only the two Iphigenia plays remain: *Iphigenia at Aulis* contains so few references to Zeus (only two, all others are patronymics) that it was deemed to be too insignificant for investigation here. *Iphigenia among the Taurians* falls into the same category as *Helen*; as another "light tragedy" with few thematic connections to any of Seneca's plays, it fell outside the purview of the comparative aspects of this investigation. This leaves only *Thyestes* to be defended as a selected play as there is no extant "equivalent" for it. I include it here for its themes of cyclical violence and the inheritance of a curse, as well as its relevance for the portrayal of the Atreid family and its "favoured" position by Zeus and Jupiter.

Such choices have obviously limited my discussions in some ways,[6] but they have also broadened my discussions in others. Specifically, my selection of Seneca as my comparand of preference for Euripides, instead of Aeschylus or Sophocles, necessitates a comparison of cultures across many centuries. Choosing Seneca allows not only a comparison of Greek tragedy to Roman tragedy, but of Greek conceptions of deity to Roman. Of course not all conclusions presented here can be, or will be, generalized to such a degree, but there is nonetheless scope for a broader perspective on how Zeus and Jupiter can be represented in two, chronologically and geographically, distinct cultures.

The present investigation thus emphasizes three main areas of inquiry. The first is very localized: how is Zeus represented in each tragedy of Euripides? How is Jupiter by Seneca? In other words, can anything be said about the *function* of the god in a given play; could a reference to either god suggest anything about or provide nuance to a play's thematic interests? I would like to suggest that the answer is yes, each god contributes

---

[6] Although references to other tragedies and even epic poetry occur, they are generally very brief: the one exception to this is my extended discussion of the Titanomachy and Gigantomachy in chapter 8, where I rely heavily on Hesiod and Apollodorus.

something more to a play's meaning by virtue of what is either said about them or to them, as well as by any descriptions, objects or ideas that are associated with them. The second area of inquiry is more generic, that is, it focusses more on genre, but is related to the first set of questions. I am interested not only in specific resonances of Zeus and Jupiter in each play, but also in the overall representation of the deity in tragedy as conceived by each author. Does Euripides have a unified or consistent vision of Zeus across his plays? Does Seneca of Jupiter? Are such representations malleable, providing the author with the ability to shape a Zeus or a Jupiter for each play? Are they purely literary with no consideration given to contemporary politics, religion or history? Again, I would suggest an affirmative to each of these questions but the last. Both Euripides and Seneca do have specific ideas about their almighty god, but that is not to say that they are immutably fixed. Seneca in particular, I will argue, does present a shift in how he presents Jupiter to his audience and, such a shift I believe, is heavily influenced by his own personal circumstances and that of Rome. The final area of inquiry is much more broad and therefore the most tentative in its conclusions. Such a study would not be complete without also asking about the similarities and differences that become illuminated between the two gods and cultures. How do Zeus and Jupiter differ in their respective relationships to other gods and mortals? What do these differences suggest about their respective authors, or cultures? Admittedly, any responses to the last question must remain very generalized and tentative, but a few suggestions may be offered. That Jupiter can be characterized as more remote than his Greek counterpart is confirmed here, but such a statement offers nothing new. Significant changes across the two cultures can be seen most clearly, however, in the conceptions of Jupiter's relationships with nature; his relationships with some of the other deities, most specifically Juno and Dis, as well as the unrelenting furies; and his potential for being overthrown by mere mortals, a proposition that is never systematically articulated by Euripides, or in any other extant tragedy.[7] Such discussions will, I hope, offer new insights and avenues for further investigation, critique and consideration.

Past Discussions

I am not claiming that this is the first *ever* study of Zeus, only that it is the first one to focus exclusively and in detail on tragedy, specifically that of Euripides and Seneca. The first systematic study of Zeus was completed by A. B. Cook from 1914-1940. In this very large three volume set, Cook compiled evidence for rituals and shrines from archaeological remains of sanctuaries and temples. His concern was mainly the worship of Zeus as a weather deity, combining Greek and Italian material remains, as well as literary evidence. Although an extensive survey, its breadth of information is hampered by a lack of cohesiveness and any kind of systematic agenda. As a tool for gathering specific references or instances of particular epithets, Cook's work is significant. The lack of contextualization for much of his information, however, is a drawback for attempting to make any broad conclusions; and without any real thematic thread, it is difficult to ascertain or infer any meaning from the vast amounts of information he presents. In addition to these weaknesses, Cook's study also contains a few significant methodological faults. He, for example, will often use Roman evidence in order to discuss early Greek beliefs and practices, neither contextualizing the original evidence, nor discussing why

---

[7] In *Prometheus Bound*, the play's author (be it Aeschylus or someone else) presents a rather tyrannical Zeus, who responds harshly to Prometheus' challenge to his authority and punishes him without mercy. It is unclear, however, if such a depiction would have changed if the play was part of a trilogy. It is a problematic play for a number of reasons (authorship, dating, interpretation), but has been widely discussed: see, for example, Herington (1970) and Griffith (1977) on the isse of authorship; West (1979) on issues of dating and staging; Golden (1962), Yu (1971), Conacher (1980) and White (2001) on the role of Zeus. A recent overview of the play is in Ruffell (2012).

such a connection to earlier beliefs is warranted.[8] In spite of such shortcomings, the study remains quite useful as a compendium of information concerning material remains and artefacts which have some relevance to Zeus.

Since Cook's *Zeus*, there have been a number of other studies centred on the great god, the most significant theoretical work being that of Carl Kerényi. In 1972, he wrote a monograph on Zeus as the archetypal father where he attempted to trace the development of Zeus within Greek culture, from its hypothetical beginnings until the time of Homer and Hesiod. His study, while not directly related to my inquiry of Zeus within the realm of tragedy, does provide information concerning the early cult of Zeus within Greece, as well as a linguistic study of the word Zeus and its relationship to both θεός and δαίμονες. According to Kerényi, the word θεός can be understood linguistically without introducing any concept or idea of a god, if taken predicatively, and Zeus "has no other sense and no other currency than that belonging to the same category as the sense and currency of *theos*."[9] He further maintains that θεός and Zeus "are concrete" and that "Zeus was originally a definite event."[10] The event to which he is referring is the actual meaning of the word Zeus – that is "the *moment* of lighting up."[11] His continues his study along these lines, discussing the associations between the first light of day and Zeus' emergence as a sky deity. He is not so much interested in *how* a god of the sky becomes the god of Homer,

---

[8] As one example, Cook (1914) 33 cites Pompeiian wall paintings as evidence for Hellenistic portrayals of Zeus as a sky-god, evidently because the painter used blue dyes in association with Zeus. Why the paintings evoke Hellenistic ideas in particular is not discussed at all and while blue is a colour for the sky, Cook himself does note that other deities have their abode in the sky as well (40), but does not make it clear why here the colour is associated with Zeus, whereas it might be associated with another deity elsewhere.

[9] Kerényi (1976) xiii-xiv.

[10] Kerényi (1976) xiv.

[11] Kerényi (1976) 5.

who sits on a throne and becomes the father of men and gods, although he does briefly discuss this in passing; he is rather more interested in the idea of a sky god as a father and husband figure.

Kerényi's study is based on Jungian theories and his evaluation of Zeus concerns only the god as a father or brother figure in relation to Hera, with passing references to Dione and Leto as goddesses of earlier matriarchal societies. This type of investigation is beneficial for the study of early cults of Zeus and how they could have developed in Greece, but offers no interpretations of Zeus in tragedy. Kerényi then goes on to discuss how Zeus' appellation "father" could only have come about in a patriarchal society, for the father would have been the highest authority in the family.[12] He writes at length on the "divine triads" of patriarchal and matriarchal societies and suggests that Zeus, as head of a dynasty must have a "prince." Since, in Kerényi's estimation, neither Hephaestus nor Ares were suitable candidates, it was Apollo, whom he placed in a separate triad (Leto, Apollo and Artemis). While "divine triads" can be informative, Kerényi's discussion of how Zeus and Hera did *not* form one is rather unhelpful in providing positive evidence of their status as *archetypes*. In his final chapter devoted to Zeus (rather than to Hera) Kerényi also discusses the marriage between Zeus and Hera and the rituals involving their marriage rites. According to Kerényi Zeus' epithet "Teleios" originated from his marriage to Hera, as she attained "perfection" in her union to Zeus.[13] Marriage contracts are thus also within Zeus' realm of influence and protection as "Father of Gods and Men" and are not only in the purview of Hera. Such discussions, while useful for their broad insights into familial archetypes, offer little in terms of specific analyses of Euripidean tragedy.

The most influential study of Zeus as conceived by the Greek tragedians is

---

[12] Kerényi (1976) 47.

[13] Kerényi (1976) 98.

undoubtedly that by Hugh Lloyd-Jones; he has written several articles concerning the god as well as a collection of lectures, together comprising his book *The Justice of Zeus*. Lloyd-Jones' interest is in the concept of Δίκη as "a divinely appointed order of the universe"[14] found within the Homeric epics and he traces its history to the end of the fifth century. While his study of the Homeric epics and of the historians is quite useful in and of themselves, his chapters on the tragedians are, of course, the most relevant to the present study. Lloyd-Jones begins with Aeschylus and immediately dispels any doubt that the defining characteristics of his Zeus are found in Hesiod and Homer, especially as guardian of justice.[15]

According to Lloyd-Jones, Aeschylus fervently believed that the gods were "just and righteous"[16] and, moreover, that Zeus never punishes the innocent.[17] Zeus does, however, punish those who have committed a crime against the gods and if not the person himself, then his descendants. One might ask whether it follows then, that Zeus would punish a descendant of an evil man, just because their ancestor was an evil man, or does Zeus assume that "the apple doesn't fall far from the tree" and the descendant must therefore be a person guilty and therefore worthy of punishment? Lloyd-Jones does not question his assumption; in fact, he uses it in his discussion of Aeschylus' Danaid trilogy. His discussion of Zeus and Δίκη in the corpus of Aeschylus is summed up by asserting,

> beyond all doubt Aeschylus insists strongly in the value of the punitive element in the government both of the universe in general and of the Athenian state. . . Without the element which Aeschylus calls "the formidable," both the universal order and the order of the state of Athens

---

[14] Lloyd-Jones (1971) ix.

[15] Lloyd-Jones (1971) 85.

[16] Lloyd-Jones (1971) 109. He further maintains that anyone who believed that the gods even existed must have also believed that they were "just and righteous."

[17] Lloyd-Jones (1971) 87, 98.

would dissolve in anarchy.[18]

Lloyd-Jones also discusses the problematic *Prometheus* trilogy and argues for an Aeschylean authorship, which did not portray a "development" of Zeus, but rather a change in his attitude.[19] Zeus sent Δίκη to men as a security against anarchy, but also to maintain man's subjugation to the will of the gods and in particular Zeus.[20]

In the plays of Euripides, Lloyd-Jones sees a rather different sort of δίκη, one that is harsh and possibly at odds with a moral concept of justice. Zeus rules with his own concept of δίκη and concedes to punish the crimes of men, for he is not ruling for their sake and does not have any interest in their welfare.[21] This is a rather bleak portrait of Euripides' Zeus – especially since Lloyd-Jones asserted that anyone who believed in the gods, also believed in their justness. Lloyd-Jones does not discuss many of Euripides' plays at great length and perhaps, if he had done so, his study might have yielded a more nuanced view of the god. Lloyd-Jones attributes the change in attitude towards Zeus to the influence of the sophists and, indeed, they were quite likely to have influenced many aspects of Athenian life at the time. There is very little, however, in the way of contextualizing any of Euripides' plays, other than mentioning earlier plays versus later ones. His study is of great importance to this investigation from a literary perspective and especially because his work has been foundational for much that has been written since.[22]

---

[18] Lloyd-Jones (1971) 94.

[19] Lloyd-Jones (1971) 96.

[20] Lloyd-Jones (1971) 102.

[21] Lloyd-Jones (1971) 161.

[22] Connor (1972) 233 emphasizes "the importance of these lectures"; Oates (1972) 1420 describes Lloyd-Jones' book as "provocative"; Herington (1973) 395 refers to his work as "revolutionary; or perhaps *counterrevolutionary*" (*sic*). Whether or not scholars have agreed with the overall tenets of Lloyd-Jones' thesis or his specific arguments matters less than the fact that his work has

As a study of Zeus in Euripides, however, it is somewhat disappointing: he offers a paucity of analyses; a mere eleven pages are devoted to the tragedian at the end of a chapter on Herodotus. He leaves much undone.

One final study of Zeus in Greek literature that deserves mention is the most recent thematic investigation of the god by Noriko Yasumura. In her *Challenges to the Power of Zeus in Early Greek Poetry*, published in 2011, Yasumura discusses at great length the literary figure of Zeus in Homeric and Hesiodic poetry. One of her aims is to piece together fragments of other early poetry concerning the Titanomachy and Gigantomachy and to suggest, tentatively, a narrative which would make sense of the many references to an earlier set of stories as mentioned by Homer and Hesiod. Her work, although focussed on early poetry, has greatly influenced some of my own interpretations of Zeus and Jupiter in the final section of this dissertation.

Studies devoted to Jupiter are similarly infrequent. The foundational study of the Roman god would be Georges Dumézil's *Archaic Roman Religion*, written in two volumes and translated by Mircea Eliade in 1970.[23] Dumézil's study is certainly far removed from the present investigation of Jupiter in Senecan tragedy, but his comparative work on Roman and Indo-European religion has been influential in discussions of Roman religion and the cult of Jupiter at Rome. Dumézil discusses at length Jupiter's role in the religious lives of the Romans as well as his descent from earlier Indo-European sky-gods. Unlike Cook, Dumézil consciously describes Jupiter and his various cults with respect to historical events and incorporates archaeological material appropriately. He provides an excellent overview of the god's various roles and functions in society, but his work is

---

generated much scholarship since its publication and, in that respect, he has had great influence in discussions of Zeus and his "justice" ever since.

[23] Originally published as *La Religion romaine archaïque suivi d'un appendice sur la religion des Etrusques* (1966).

lacking with respect to discussions of the god's literary representations. It is in this regard especially that I find Dumézil's work less than satisfactory.[24]

One of the central tenets of Dumézil's thesis is his division of Roman religion into three functions (in very general terms): sovereignty as embodied by the king and priest, physical power embodied by the warrior and prosperity embodied by the farmer. He posits that this tripartite classification can been seen most clearly in the Archaic Triad of Jupiter, Mars and Quirinus who represent the three classes of ruler, warrior and farmer. Such a division is useful to Dumézil in comparing Roman religion to that of earlier Indo-European religions with similar structures, such as ancient Scandinavian and Vedic religion in India. His work is of interest for breadth of knowledge of other religions and their similarities to Roman religion and how the Romans could have conceptualized their gods; but it is rather less useful for any discussion of Roman religion after the advent of the Roman Empire and even less for any interpretation of Seneca's Jupiter.

For scholarship on Jupiter within the Roman Empire, we are indebted to the work of J. Rufus Fears, who has written two significant monographs involving close study of the god: the first was a book in 1977 entitled *Princeps a diis electus*, the second, a substantial article, "The Cult of Jupiter and Roman Imperial Ideology," published in 1981. In *Princeps*, Fears is concerned with the theory of monarchism in the Roman Empire and how it developed from the Greek Hellenistic period. He is interested in the relationship between the ruler and the god from whom he gains his right of imperium. Such a study has clear implications for any discussion of Jupiter and his favour of kings or emperors in Roman history. But while Fears' close examination of this relationship is thorough with

---

[24] This is not to suggest that Dumézil ignores literature in his scholarship, but that he engages with it only for the purpose of explaining certain religious rites or meanings of particular epithets. He is not interested, for example, in the presentation of Jupiter within Virgil's *Aeneid* or Ovid's *Metamorphoses*.

respect to the Roman emperors, he does not investigate such representations in literature and mythology of the same period. Thus any discussion of Seneca, while clearly of significance in the historical sense, is limited to his relationship with the Emperors and is not related by Fears to any of his dramatic works.

Fears' article on the cult of Jupiter is concerned far more heavily with coinage issues of Jupiter and how such images are used for the justification and validation of an Emperor's reign. Fears spends much time devoted to the reign of Augustus and the importance of Jupiter to the Emperor's Imperial ideology. He then goes on to discuss the reigns of other emperors, including an examination of the Julio-Claudians as a group and the ebb and flow of Jovian representations throughout their dynasty. Fears' analysis of Claudius' and Nero's reigns are of particular importance once again; however, the privileging of coinage over literature makes the study useful in general terms for my own treatment of Jupiter, but less so for any interpretations of the god within Seneca's tragedies.

Literary discussions of Jupiter have been reserved for the god's representation in epic; there is no examination of the god within Roman tragedy.[25] Scholars have treated his appearance, in varying degrees of detail, in Virgil's *Aeneid*, Ovid's *Metamorphoses*, Seneca's *Apocolocyntosis*, Lucan's *Bellum Civile*, Statius' *Thebaid*, Valerius Flaccus' *Argonautica* and Silius Italicus' *Punica*.[26] It is this lack of detailed study of Jupiter within the Senecan tragic corpus that this dissertation aims, at least in part, to address. Studies of Jupiter within epic are useful for literary representations, but epic, by its very nature,

---

[25] Boyle's (1985) treatment of Jupiter and *Natura* is one exception to this; but it is devoted exclusively to *Phaedra*, rather than to the whole of the Senecan corpus. Gilder's (1997) dissertation on Furies in Roman literature also discusses Jupiter in Seneca's tragedies to a certain extent, but only with respect to the god's relationship to the Furies. It is not an examination of Jupiter himself.

[26] See, for example, Feeney (1991) who treats Jupiter in various Roman epics.

presents the divine according to generic parameters (the use of the *concilium deorum*, for example, is an epic and not tragic device). Thus, such interpretations of an "epic" Jupiter cannot address specific nuances that are bound by a "tragic" framework. By convention, if nothing else, Jupiter does not appear as a character in tragedy; the same cannot be said for epic and such differences in genre necessarily effect the representation of the god.

Outline of Chapters

I have grouped my chapters into three "Parts" in order to emphasize both the inherent difficulty in attempting to separate the different realms of Zeus and Jupiter's influence, which inevitably are intertwined, and to bring discussions bearing similar themes closer together.[27] Such a division helps to give the smaller discussions relevance within a larger thematic framework as well as providing boundaries to keep the larger framework limited to a specific sphere of analysis. I begin the thesis by exploring Euripides and Seneca's portrayals of Zeus and Jupiter within their roles as guarantors of cosmic balance, inevitably a topic which will persist throughout my study, but I focus specifically on the gods' relationships with notions of fate and justice. Thus, the first Part, entitled "The Cosmos," consists of three chapters, "Fate and Fortune," "Justice" and "Nature and the Elements."

Chapter one begins with a study of the relationship between sight and knowledge and the importance of Zeus' "eye" with respect to how the god reacts to human situations. I investigate the various ways Zeus' "eye" is emphasized in each of the Euripidean texts with which I am concerned, before turning to an investigation of how that knowledge is used in the god's administration of life and death. The extent to which Zeus preserves or ends life is intimately bound up in notions of fate; and once again, I examine such notions

---

[27] I will be following the text of Murray (1966) for Euripides' plays and Fitch's Loeb texts for those of Seneca unless otherwise indicated.

in each of Euripides' plays, with the exception of *Orestes*. In *Orestes*, Zeus' administration of life and death is tied more explicitly to notions of *tyche* and the related concept of justice. I end the chapter with an overview of the same concepts in relation to Seneca's Jupiter. Only four of Seneca's plays receive attention: *Hercules Furens, Phaedra, Medea* and *Thyestes*.

Chapter two concerns the notion of justice as personified by the goddess Δίκη and her relationship to Zeus as well as other instances of δίκη in the plays of Euripides. I also discuss the goddesses Themis and Nemesis specifically in Euripides' *Medea* and compare their relationships to Zeus with that of Jupiter and Pietas in Seneca's *Phaedra*. The final section of the chapter is devoted to an examination of the goddesses of retributive justice, the Erinyes and Furies. Here I focus on examples from Euripides' *Electra, Medea* and *Heracles* as well as Seneca's *Hercules Furens, Medea* and *Thyestes*.

The final chapter of this first "Part" examines the connection between each god and elements of nature. In particular, I discuss Jupiter's relationship with the goddess *Natura* in Seneca's *Phaedra* and their respective roles as guarantors of cosmic balance. I go on to discuss Jupiter's use of the thunderbolt as an instrument of punishment in *Hercules Furens, Phaedra* and *Oedipus*. The wrath of Zeus is explored through his guise as *Horkeios* especially within Euripides' *Hippolytus*, but also briefly in *Orestes*. The final discussion of the chapter entails a consideration of the myth of the reversal of the sun as expressed in Euripides' *Electra* and Seneca's *Thyestes*. Although the motif remains the same in each play, the motivation for such a cosmic disturbance is greatly changed from one play to the next and is expressive of Zeus and Jupiter's respective abilities to maintain control over the natural elements.

I then go on to examine Zeus and Jupiter as mythological and literary father-figures within a complex family unit in the second Part entitled "Family." Here I take Homer's epithet of Zeus, "Father of gods and men," and discuss the implications of such a role in all of Euripides' and Seneca's tragedies. This Part consists of four chapters, the first being "Father of Gods I: The First Generation." I am concerned in this chapter to investigate the relationship Zeus and Jupiter have with their Olympian siblings. I begin with a detailed discussion of Zeus and Hera in Euripides' *Heracles* with a comparison of an equally detailed discussion of Jupiter and Juno in Seneca's *Hercules Furens*. I then turn to Hades and Dis as described once again in *Hercules Furens* and Euripides' *Hecuba*. I end the chapter with a brief look at Poseidon and Zeus in Euripides' *Trojan Women* and *Hippolytus* and Seneca's *Phaedra* and *Hercules Furens*. In each case I highlight the differences that are apparent between the respective relationships that Zeus and Jupiter have with their siblings and the impact of how co-operative or hostile each might be.

"Father of Gods II: The Second Generation" is the second chapter exploring the notion of Zeus and Jupiter as fathers of the other gods. Here I begin with the gods of love and procreation, starting with Eros and Cupid and Aphrodite and Venus in *Hippolytus* and *Phaedra*. The differences that begin to emerge when considering Eros and Cupid in particular emphasize the thematic interests of each playwright and their ability to manipulate myths to suit their own purposes. I then consider some of the children of Zeus and Jupiter, focussing on Dionysus and Bacchus in *Hippolytus, Phoenissae, Hercules Furens* and *Oedipus*. Here I focus on the similarities that Zeus and Jupiter share with this particular set of progeny: Dionysus and Bacchus are children of the thunderbolt and share many of the same qualities their fathers display. I emphasize especially the duality of divinization and death; that often one cannot occur without the other. I end the chapter with an extended discussion of patronymics as one potential way to emphasize particular traits or themes that are associated with Zeus and Jupiter. I begin with Ares in the *Phoenissae* as a child born of the conflict between Zeus and Hera and how such an identity is transferred into his patron city of Thebes. I give further examples from *Phoenissae* using Ephaphus and Apollo, before turning to two examples of Apollo and Athena in Euripides' *Heracles*. I end the chapter with a brief discussion of Helen and the Dioscuri as children of Zeus with dual paternity, a theme to which I turn in more detail in the following chapter.

Chapter six is devoted to Zeus and Jupiter as fathers of Heracles and Hercules in "Father of Men I." My investigation is strictly limited to representations of Zeus and Jupiter as paternal figures in *Heracles* and *Hercules Furens*. The implications of whether or not Zeus or Amphitryon is the hero's father are the underlying themes to my discussion of Euripides. Seneca does not question the paternity of Jupiter, but retains an interest in how the hero responds to such paternal authority in his life. Rather than accepting or rejecting the god as his father, Hercules' rejects the symbolic authority that is inherent in the figure of the *paterfamilias*. It is this tension which I investigate with respect to Seneca's *Hercules Furens*.

The final chapter of this Part, chapter seven, "Father of Men II: Other Progeny," is concerned with Zeus and Jupiter as the progenitors of mortal family lines and especially their own obligations to those more distantly related to themselves. The most favoured line is that of Atreus and Agamemnon, whose ancestor Pelops was given a particular sceptre with which to rule over all others. I begin the chapter with a discussion of the significance of this sceptre before moving on to examine Zeus and Jupiter's relationships with those who eventually inherit this emblem of power. I am concerned in particular with prayers made by Electra, Orestes and Pylades (or prayers made on their behalf) within *Electra* and *Orestes* as well as scenes from Seneca's *Agamemnon* which suggest Jupiter still favours the youngest generation of this line. I then move on to discuss supplication scenes from *Hecuba* and *Orestes* as illustrative of the efficacy of Zeus' status as a god who protects suppliants, before questioning the efficacy of his places of sanctuary, altars and temples which should offer similar protection. This discussion emphasizes the double-altars in *Heracles*, the temple of Zeus at Dodona in *Phoenissae* and the Temple of Zeus at Olympia in Seneca's *Troades*. The ambivalent protection offered by Zeus and Jupiter's places of sanctuary seems to be echoed by their roles as gods of victory in war. The final section of this chapter explores the relationship between the victorious general (king) and his defeated enemy (his equal). Often images of the two are blurred, especially in relation to the altar of Zeus and Jupiter *Herkeios*. In Seneca's *Agamemnon* and Euripides' *Trojan Women* this altar is the place of Priam's death and is linked to the future killing of Agamemnon. A similar scene is presented in Euripides' *Heracles*. In all three plays, the altar represents a place of death instead of sanctuary and Zeus and Jupiter's role as guardians of suppliants and of kings becomes rather ambiguous, an ambiguity which is furthered by a discussion of the trophy in Euripides' *Phoenissae*. Zeus and Jupiter require honour when a king defeats another king and yet when the victory that is achieved is accompanied by impiety it becomes impossible to honour the god properly. Neither Euripides nor Seneca offers any resolutions to such a paradox.

The final Part, "Challengers" is an analysis of those figures in the mythological tradition who may be characterized as "theomachists" and who can be classed either as potential usurpers or merely as potential threats. The first of two chapters included here is on "Unsuccessful Theomachists," where I discuss first the early cosmogonic wars with the Titans, Giants and the monster Typhoeus. I include a number of plays within this section: *Hecuba*, *Heracles*, *Agamemnon*, *Hercules Furens*, *Medea* and *Thyestes*. I investigate specific allusions to each of the early wars and how such allusions help to highlight particular themes of interest to each playwright and the impact of such allusions on our interpretation of Zeus and Jupiter in each play. I then go on to discuss two figures who are fashioned to become similar Titanic and Gigantomachic enemies of the gods: Capaneus and Ajax within Euripides' *Phoenissae* and *Trojan Women* and Seneca's *Agamemnon*.

The final chapter, "Successful Theomachists," is a detailed study of Seneca's Medea and Atreus as ultimate theomachic individuals who challenge Jupiter's authority. Although we do not see the aftermath of Medea's revenge – all we hear is that she will ride into the aether – we are left with an impression of a woman who has become a goddess, with the power to challenge Jupiter for his supremacy. Atreus takes up the task that Medea does not complete and is shown to displace Jupiter from his position as the ultimate source of judgement and authority.

At the end of each chapter, I provide a brief summary, highlighting some of the key ideas and my conclusions. These more brief conclusions are brought together in the final chapter, where I discuss in more detail some of the implications of my findings.

PART I

THE COSMOS

CHAPTER 1:
FATE AND FORTUNE

> For Fate alone with vision unconfin'd,
> surveys the conduct of the mortal kind.
> Fate is Jove's perfect and eternal eye,
> for Jove and Fate our ev'ry deed descry.
>
> *Orphic Hymns* 58.19-22[28]

The Orphic hymn addressed to the Moirai hits upon something fundamental in its description of the relationship between Zeus and Fate: they are at once inseparable entities bound together through the "eye" of Zeus and yet they are also clearly distinct beings who, although they share a common ability to discern the activities of all mortals, are each autonomous. Fate sees that which Zeus cannot, but through Fate, Zeus sees all. Zeus and Fate have always had an uneasy relationship with one another, but the one is unable to exist without the other, according to this hymn, because of their shared association with vision. Fate is unaffected by polluting visions, but Zeus is required to see all that transpires among mortals in order to maintain control over the cosmos and keep it in a harmonious balance. This connection between Zeus and what he sees through his "eye" is the subject of the first part of this chapter. Euripides, in several of his plays, emphasizes the desire on the part of human beings that Zeus see and take notice of what is happening in the earthly realm; but often their desire is quite at odds with what Zeus *ought* to see, the god preferring to avoid gazing upon polluting images. It is only through seeing such events and objects, however, that Zeus can become aware of them and take appropriate action.

The second part of this chapter then brings the idea of fate into the discussion, specifically fate as *moirai*: principles which determine the life span of each mortal rather

---

[28] Translation from Taylor (1792) 58.11-14:

Μοῖρα γὰρ ἐν βιότωι καθορᾶι μόνη, οὐδέ τις ἄλλος
ἀθανάτων, οἳ ἔχουσι κάρη νιφόεντος Ὀλύμπου,
καὶ Διὸς ὄμμα τέλειον· ἐπεί γ' ὅσα γίγνεται ἡμῖν,
Μοῖρά τε καὶ Διὸς οἶδε νόος διὰ παντὸς ἅπαντα.

than any specific event during that life span. Zeus has a duty to ensure that no person exceeds his or her allotted time on earth. This entails not only the cutting of their "threads" of life, but also ensuring they are not cut before their time. Although the personified Moirai traditionally enjoy this prerogative in myth, Euripides complicates the picture in a number of his tragedies by introducing the concept of "necessity" (ἀνάγκη). Zeus must contend not only with the proper life spans of mortals, but also of doing so within a larger framework which must take into account the requirements or rights of other deities, heroes and even other human beings. Such a discussion naturally turns to the concept of "fortune" (τύχη) and the events in one's life which may let anyone prosper or suffer. Only in Euripides' *Orestes* does this concept receive substantial attention, but its inclusion is worthwhile for the concept is one which becomes much more significant within the tragedies of Seneca.

Seneca's treatment of each of these topics in his tragedies is the subject of the final part to this chapter. The basic concept of the "eye" of Zeus carries into the Latin plays, but Seneca retains the framework only to manipulate the intended message. Jupiter's vision remains sacred but its vulnerability has less to do with potential pollution than it does with portraying an inherent weakness in the god. Jupiter's absolute power, although not contingent upon maintaining "clear" sight, does seem to be at least notionally affected by what he sees. Seneca's characters can also take advantage of Jupiter's panopticism to the detriment of others, precisely because of its recognizable and august authority. Jupiter's relationship to fate, although brief, follows the Euripidean emphasis on the aspect of life and death, but differs with respect to the inclusion of Venus as a significant factor. Fortuna, on the other hand, is a goddess about whom Seneca has much more to say. Her connection to Jupiter is portrayed as a relationship that maintains a precarious balance: like the Orphic Fate in relation to Zeus, one cannot exist without the other and each is a codependent. Jupiter and Fortuna stand almost in opposition to each other rather than working in concert for the greater good of the cosmos. In Seneca's tragedies the supreme god begins to descend from his lofty summit.

The Eye of Zeus: Sight and Knowledge

Sight and knowledge are associated, not only through their linguistic connections, where οἶδα means both "I have seen" and "I know," but also through their inherent semantic ranges: to witness something with one's eyes is to know that it occurred. As the human sense of sight is only partially reliable, like any other, it must be supplemented by one or more of the other senses. If one considers the structure of the Theatre of Dionysus and the relationship between the audience and the actors, it is immediately apparent that those sitting in the farthest seats must rely primarily on what they hear. The action is too far away to appreciate any subtle movements on the stage and, indeed, the theatre was built with acoustics in mind.[29] The only spectators with the ability to visually witness everything, or have "true" sight, are the gods (or those blessed with "second sight," often after being blinded). Thus, there is an implicit assumption that because the gods have this ability to see everything, they should also know everything; a prime example of this is, of course, Zeus. One of the most important attributes of the god would arguably be his omniscience: Zeus sees all and knows all, but he is himself inscrutable to others.[30] In

---

[29] As Rehm (2004) 38 states: "In Greek drama the primary acting tool was the voice, not the face . . ." Certainly the Theatre of Dionysus was not acoustically perfect, but such perfection was something for which the Greeks continued to strive and which they eventually achieved, at least at Epidaurus. See Hunningher (1956) for the seminal discussion of acoustics in the Theatre of Dionysus.

[30] Although he is referring instead to Artemis' eye in *Hippolytus*, Segal (1988) 268 states that it "is the outward gaze, the eye that is seen by others. It is objective rather than subjective; but its inwardness is problematical. One who sees this outward-looking eye has no certainty of

Euripides, the significance of this superior knowledge is brought to the audience's attention in several plays. Euripides accomplishes this foregrounding in such a way as to underscore the tension created by the god's awareness of events and the characters' often uncertain knowledge of, or confidence in, that awareness. Zeus is often questioned or even criticized for being unaware or ignoring incidents that happen under his gaze; yet these same characters who challenge Zeus' attentiveness are also the ones most likely to presume that he is aware of their need when they ask for his assistance. In *Hippolytus*, *Medea*, *Electra*, *Hecuba*, *Trojan Women* and *Phoenissae* the question of Zeus' knowledge as a reliable witness to events is a common thread and one which suggests that the "eye of Zeus" is a significant aspect of the god's characterization and deserving of attention.

The most explicit reference to the "eye of Zeus" appears in *Hippolytus*. After finding out that her nurse has betrayed her, Phaedra writes a letter to Theseus suggesting that Hippolytus has raped her and she then commits suicide. Upon reading this letter, Theseus denounces his son, believing that he has dishonoured Zeus and, more specifically, his eye: Ἱππόλυτος εὐνῆς τῆς ἐμῆς ἔτλη θιγεῖν / βίαι, τὸ σεμνὸν Ζηνὸς ὄμμ' ἀτιμάσας (*Hipp*. 885-86). The dishonour of which Theseus speaks refers specifically to Zeus' function as a god of marriage.[31] Theseus seems to take offence on behalf of Zeus as the act would have happened "under his eye" as it were; but, as the audience knows, Zeus could not have seen the act that Theseus believes the god to have witnessed as it never in fact happened. Furthermore, the audience also knows that what Zeus *has seen* is a woman

---

penetrating to any knowledge of the 'thought' or 'mind' (φρήν) within." Such a description can be applied equally to the eye of Zeus.

[31] Halleran (1995) 224 highlights the relationship of Zeus to Dikē but adds the aspect of marriage only as a possibility, whereas I would see Zeus' function as a god of marriage as primary here; see chapter 5 (under "Aphrodite and Venus," pp. 157-61) for a discussion of Zeus and marriage within *Hippolytus*.

refusing to succumb to incestuous feelings and a youth refusing to marry.[32] Although

Theseus is correct in his assumption that Zeus would be offended by Hippolytus' actions,

unbeknownst to the king, it is in Hippolytus' refusal to marry that he dishonours Zeus,

rather than some pseudo-incestuous violation of his father's marriage bed witnessed by

Zeus' "holy" eye (σεμνὸν, 886).

Referring to Zeus' eye as σεμνός ("holy") is also noteworthy, for it is an adjective

often used in describing the very nature of divinities.[33] Here, Euripides uses the word

(through Theseus) to suggest that Zeus' holiness resides specifically in his eye. While this

may be no more than a clear instance of metonymy where the eye represents Zeus,

Euripides seems to be suggesting something more: Hippolytus' supposed act has defiled

the *most* sacred aspect of Zeus' divinity. It is through his eye that Zeus witnesses all events

and accumulates his knowledge; thus, the god's ability to be fully aware of human events

is predicated on his ability to "see" clearly: in other words, with an eye free of pollution or

defilement. By underscoring Zeus' eye as "holy," Euripides is signalling the primacy of

sight over the other senses in a play where few characters really *see* the truth:[34] for the

---

[32] See below (pp. 159-60) for a discussion of Hippolytus' opinions on marriage and its place within
the world-ordering of Zeus.

[33] But in this play people and objects are also are referred to as such. The word occurs a further
fourteen times throughout the drama, the most of any extant tragedy: describing the Mysteries
(25); Artemis (61, 713, 1130 [as Dictynna]); Aphrodite (93, 94, 99, 103); the Corybantes (143);
Phaedra (490); the sky (746); words (957); and Hippolytus (1064, 1364). However, when *semnos*
is used as an adjective for Phaedra and Hippolytus, both mortals, there is an inherent negative
undercurrent, as if by elevating them with the use of this word, they are attempting to attain a
status which is beyond their reach and thus sacrilegious (Blomqvist [1982] 409; Luschnig [1980]
99; less explicitly, Berns [1973] 175-76; see also Kovacs [1980] for further general discussion of
the word). The same can be said to apply to the "words" of Theseus' speech at 957: while they
seem *semnoi*, they are in fact shameful. In this play at least, only those objects that are inherently
divine, or have inherently divine attributes (like the sky) can be truly *semnos*.

[34] An emphasis on sight in general is also important in the play as a whole, especially when few

tragedies of Hippolytus, Phaedra and Theseus result from their dependence on the less

reliable sense of sound, taking their cues from what they hear or assume to know.[35]

This emphasis on the ability of Zeus to see the truth is brought to the fore again in

the final scene of the play. After Hippolytus has been mangled by the bull sent by

Poseidon and his body is brought on stage once more, he cries out in agony and questions

Zeus: Ζεῦ Ζεῦ, τάδ' ὁρᾶις; (1363). It is important to Hippolytus, as he dies what he

believes to be a premature and unjust death, that he knows whether or not Zeus is aware of

his death and its circumstances. His underlying and unspoken question is whether Zeus

knows and understands everything that has transpired to create this situation (and even

whether he cares that it has happened thus), not merely whether or not he is watching.

Hippolytus wants Zeus to be present and to see the repayment he has received for leading,

what he assumes to be, a life of piety and is concerned over whether or not Zeus will take

any action to rectify the pollution the situation has caused (i.e. that the father has killed the

son). The problem arising from Hippolytus' question is that in order for Zeus to fully

comprehend the circumstances of his death, Zeus must look upon a sight which would

inevitably defile his vision.

Just as Hippolytus desires that Zeus be aware of all that transpires among men,

Medea too requests that the supreme god observe every detail in her own drama. After

Creon exiles Medea and expressly forbids her and her children to stay in Corinth, she calls

upon Zeus to ensure that the cause of all her present woes (i.e. Jason's behaviour toward

---

characters see the truth or see it too late; see Segal (1988); Goff (1990) *passim* and Luschnig
(1988) 3-15. It is perhaps interesting to note that Hippolytus finally understands ("sees") his
father only after he can no longer "see the light." As Avery (1968) 33 notes, "In this final scene
the father and son are brought together. They are no longer separated by confusion and
misunderstanding." Hippolytus gains true (in)sight only in blindness.

[35] On *hearing* in *Hippolytus*, see Roisman (1999).

her) does not escape his notice: Ζεῦ, μὴ λάθοι σε τῶνδ' ὃς αἴτιος κακῶν (*Med.* 332).[36]

There is an assumption on her part that Zeus should witness all events and while this outburst may be little more than a cry of anguish, Medea is calling upon the god to be "officially" present during her exchange with, and supplication of, Creon. Unlike Hippolytus, however, Medea does not just question whether or not Zeus sees what is happening; she almost demands it of the god in order to ensure that he sees all that takes place.

This early invocation by Medea to request Zeus' presence contributes to her later absolute conviction that the wrongs done to her have been witnessed by the lord of heaven. When Jason sees his children slain, he berates Medea for her actions; however, she refuses to recount all of his sins believing Father Zeus is fully cognizant of everything Jason has done to her and she for him:

> μακρὰν ἂν ἐξέτεινα τοῖσδ' ἐναντίον
> λόγοισιν, εἰ μὴ Ζεὺς πατὴρ ἠπίστατο
> οἷ' ἐξ ἐμοῦ πέπονθας οἷά τ' εἰργάσω (*Med.* 1351-53).

Although Medea does not emphasize sight, she presumes that because of Zeus' omniscience she has no need to tabulate each good deed done, or even each offence of Jason: she is certain that Zeus knows all.[37] Medea may be wrong in her assumption, but because this speech comes at the end of the play and she escapes without harm, there is nothing to suggest that she is anything but correct.

Medea's appeal to Zeus may be contrasted with the first and only invocation of the god made by Jason. When he sees both of his children dead and Medea is refusing to let him near their bodies, Jason questions whether Zeus is aware of their situation:

> Ζεῦ, τάδ' ἀκούεις ὡς ἀπελαυνόμεθ'

---

[36] For a discussion of the thematic importance of Zeus in *Medea*, see Kovacs (1993).

[37] Bongie (1977) 54; Kovacs (1993) 64.

οἷά τε πάσχομεν ἐκ τῆς μυσαρᾶς

καὶ παιδοφόνου τῆσδε λεαίνης; (1405-07).

What is significant about Jason's query is his choice of verb, ἀκούεις: he is relying on Zeus to *hear* events, while Medea relies on the god to actually *see* them. Given the important correlation between sight and knowledge there is something amiss in an appeal which does not ask the god to bear (visual) witness to an act which is obviously meant to be seen (the slaughter and the escape are surely meant as spectacle). Perhaps the murder is so atrocious that Jason does not wish the gods to see such pollution, but the text provides no evidence that this would be the case. Jason's appeal to Zeus is thus similar in structure to that made by Hippolytus: both men ask that the god pay attention to something that should be profane to see. But Jason's prayer differs from those offered by both Hippolytus and Medea because the hero does not wish to bring the full force of Zeus' eye on the situation, only the god's aural faculties.

Jason's appeal may also be compared to that of Orestes in *Electra*. After Orestes kills Clytemnestra, both her body and that of Aegisthus are brought out on the *eccyclema* and Orestes appeals to Earth and Zeus to witness the results of his revenge:

ἰὼ Γᾶ καὶ Ζεῦ πανδερκέτα
βροτῶν, ἴδετε τάδ' ἔργα φόνι-
    α μυσαρά, δίγονα σώματ' ἐν
†χθονὶ κείμενα πλαγᾶι†
χερὸς ὕπ' ἐμᾶς, ἄποιν' ἐμῶν
πημάτων . . . (*El.* 1177-82).[38]

As a pair, Earth and Zeus would normally be called upon together to witness oaths (and those who break them) rather than the results of ill-deeds such as murder.[39] But here, unlike Jason in *Medea*, Orestes invites the gods, and specifically Zeus, to look upon

---

[38] The remaining lines of this invocation are lost.

[39] Cropp (1988) 179 has noted that these deities would be the very ones who would be unable to look upon this kind of pollution.

(ἴδετε) the murders he himself has just committed in the name of revenge. Although Zeus should not be asked to witness such crimes, for doing so would defile his vision, he is here the most appropriate deity to be involved at this point: Zeus is the one to whom Orestes appealed before he set out to avenge his father (671-72) and, through Apollo,[40] the one who ordained that the murders should transpire at all. The bodies are thus both a testament of Zeus' will fulfilled and trophies of victory laid out for the god's honour (discussed further in chapter 7, 230-32).

This paradox of Zeus πανδερκέτα having to gaze upon that which would defile his sight is also emphasized by the specific epithet used by Euripides. It is a rare word and one wonders why Euripides would employ it, especially as it is not an epithet previously attested for Zeus.[41] That the word can be used both actively, meaning "one who is all-seeing" and passively "one who is seen by all"[42] could be part of the reason in choosing this particular phrase. Zeus, as all-seer from above, and Earth from below are able to observe all that has happened and Zeus also sees all that will happen in the future; the two gods are also the object of an audience who have seen all that has transpired (and so are "in the know"). Orestes is inviting the audience to witness what the gods have orchestrated, suggesting that both he and these gods are responsible for the murders that have occurred.

Euripides offers two further examples of characters commenting on what, if anything, Zeus sees. The first appears in *Hecuba* when Talthybius, who is presented as the

---

[40] Lloyd (1986) 18-19.

[41] This epithet is uncommon in Classical Greek literature: it is most frequently found in the Orphic hymns (six instances); there is one instance in *Bacchylides* 17.70 pre-dating Euripides' use here (referring to lightning) and three undated occurrences in the *Greek Anthology*, none of which refer to Zeus (9.363.24, referring to Dikē; 9.525.17, referring to Apollo; 16.303.3, referring to Helios).

[42] For example in Bacch. 17.70; see Maehler (2004) 182.

least offensive Greek in the play,[43] recognizes the wretchedness of Hecuba's current situation. Talthybius must deliver the news about Achilles' request to sacrifice Polyxena and he is quite critical of Zeus as he questions the god about his reputation for watching over the human race: ὦ Ζεῦ, τί λέξω; πότερά σ' ἀνθρώπους ὁρᾶν . . .; (*Hec.* 488). Talthybius' outburst is the only direct reference to a god by a Greek character in the play and one which has received much scholarly attention. Collard notes that Talthybius' initial question of whether or not Zeus watches over men is a paraphrase of the god's epithet "all-seer" and is one "which implies divine supervision, if not protection."[44] Talthybius goes on to wonder who is really "in charge," Zeus or Tyche;[45] but his question regarding the attentiveness of Zeus concerns more than merely how much the god sees. Talthybius is questioning not simply whether the god watches mortals, but whether the god really understands what is going on and if he even cares.

Talthybius' concern is much like Hippolytus' question as he was dying: Zeus might see everything that happens, but does he really comprehend the consequences? But the main difference between Talthybius' question and that of Hippolytus is that the audience has already been given a glimpse of further disasters to come. Neither Talthybius nor Hecuba is aware of the impending discovery of Polydorus' murder, nor are they aware of the gods' involvement in creating the situation.[46] Thus, while Talthybius' questioning of Zeus' concern and watchfulness is a valid response given the information available to him,

---

[43] Abrahamson (1952) 122: "In the characters of these two men [Agamemnon and Odysseus] Euripides represents two types of human viciousness which are the source of Hecuba's suffering: weakness and cruelty." Such a characterization is later contrasted with "the good Talthybius" (129); see also Conacher (1961) 5.

[44] Collard (1991) 156.

[45] Discussed below, pp. 46-49.

[46] Hades is clearly behind Polydorus' appearance in the play (prologue) and Zeus' involvement, or at the very least, approval, is implicit.

it is clear that his knowledge is only partial and incomplete, undermining the force and legitimacy of his question. But the question nevertheless carries importance for the tension Euripides creates between Zeus' sight and ability to maintain cosmic balance and the characters' belief in and reliance on, that ability.

Hecuba herself voices a very similar concern in *Trojan Women*, when at the end of the play another Talthybius announces that the women are to leave Troy as the Greeks set fire to their city. Hecuba, in despair, calls out to Zeus and asks whether he sees all that the women are suffering:

> Κρόνιε, πρύτανι Φρύγιε, γενέτα
> †πάτερ ἀνάξια τῆς Δαρδανίου†
> γονᾶς, τάδ' οἷα πάσχομεν δέδορκας; (*TW* 1288-90).

As Anselment so aptly puts it, "Hecuba is struggling for an elemental ordering force which might relieve the engulfing chaos" but "no answers are found."[47] Hecuba too wants to know that her suffering is not in vain and that something positive will happen after her expulsion from Troy and the annihilation of her city. She does not know, as the audience knows, that the Greeks will suffer casualties[48] in partial payment for wrongs committed while at Troy. The response Hecuba receives from the chorus is very disheartening; "He sees" (δέδορκεν, 1291) they say, acknowledging that while "Zeus is omniscient" he is also "callous enough to let this happen," at least according to Barlow.[49] The chorus believes that the god acknowledges their plight and the audience too knows that this is the case. But if Zeus is able to watch the suffering of these captive women, there must not be any pollution or defilement involved in their departure with the Greeks. Zeus is watching the women go to their deaths, but while he does not (and perhaps cannot) do anything to alter

---

[47] Anselment (1969) 413; Kovacs (1997) 164 also acknowledges that there is "a dim sense that there may be justice of some sort in the inscrutable workings of Zeus."

[48] Although so too will the Trojan women aboard the sunken ships.

[49] Barlow (1986) 227.

their situation he is at least witnessing the beginning of their end; a small comfort perhaps, but the lord of Olympus gives the Trojan women that comfort which many other characters request: that he *sees, knows* and *understands* their situation.

Whether or not Zeus sees events among men is an essential aspect of any character's comprehension of the god's control over cosmic order and adds to his or her own sense of self-worth. Euripides' characters cannot know what Zeus knows and yet they want to be reassured that they matter in some way to his overarching plan. Those who call him to witness achieve, at least in part, a further understanding of Zeus' knowledge and awareness of their own situation (for by calling upon the god's attention, they believe he must at least acknowledge their plea), although what Zeus may do with that knowledge is an entirely different question. It is clear, however, that the "eye" of Zeus plays a role not only as a tool by which the god accumulates his knowledge, but is also an assurance for humans to ensure that their own deeds and sufferings are being acknowledged. But there is also an assumption on their part that everything witnessed by Zeus will be repaid in kind; in other words, Zeus should not only see, but he should also take action.

This idea of Zeus acting upon that which he sees is cursorily explored in Euripides' *Phoenissae*, when Jocasta subtly admonishes Zeus about his wisdom concerning her sons. The audience has just heard Jocasta recount the events of Oedipus' life and explain how he laid a curse upon Polynices and Eteocles (67-68), when she prays to Zeus to establish peace once more in her family:

> ἀλλ', ὦ φαεννὰς οὐρανοῦ ναίων πτυχὰς
> Ζεῦ, σῶσον ἡμᾶς, δὸς δὲ σύμβασιν τέκνοις.
> χρῆν δ', εἰ σοφὸς πέφυκας, οὐκ ἐᾶν βροτῶν
> τὸν αὐτὸν αἰεὶ δυστυχῆ καθεστάναι (*Phoen.* 84-87).

This invocation contains two items of significance: first, Jocasta addresses Zeus in his cosmic element sitting at the apex of the heavens,[50] from which vantage point the god is able to witness all events. Secondly, the suppression of his name until the second line might have, at first, suggested to the audience another invocation to Helios, reminding them of Jocasta's opening prayer to that god ([Ὦ τὴν ἐν ἄστροις οὐρανοῦ τέμνων ὁδὸν / καὶ χρυσοκολλήτοισιν ἐμβεβὼς δίφροις] / Ἥλιε, 1-3). Euripides is here stressing the connection between Zeus and Helios as deities who witness all human affairs, although Jocasta is suggesting that Zeus should do more than merely witness events. She recognizes that Zeus can offer her sons salvation (the use of σῶσον perhaps hinting at the cult of Zeus Sōtēr) and believes that the god's wisdom (σοφὸς) would allow for this.[51] Unfortunately for Jocasta and her sons, it is because of her union with Laius, the begetting of Oedipus and his subsequent curse that the present woes are coming to fruition.[52] Thus, there are many other factors that are important to Zeus when he is deciding whether or not to answer

---

[50] Mastronarde (1994) 165; Amiech (2004) 258.

[51] The motif of wisdom is itself an interesting one throughout the play; it is applied initially to the Sphinx (48), an apt adjective for the beast who loves clever words, but equally apt as applied to one who destroys and is destroyed by them in turn. Results, advice, words are all described as *sophos* (453, 460, 1259 respectively) and Eteocles correctly identifies the problematic nature of the word as he states that not everyone defines it the same way, for if they did, there would be no strife (499-500). Describing Zeus with the same adjective places him within this semantic range; if *sophos* solutions are also the causes of eventual destruction, what does that imply about the god, except that he too is part of this continual ring of "destroy and be destroyed" – he is part of both the cause of the strife and the solution (which is itself only more bloodshed).

[52] The statement that Zeus ought to ensure one mortal does not have only misfortune in his life is a subtle yet disparaging comment (cf. *Il.* 24.525-28); however, as Craik (1988) 173 has said, this does not reflect a real disbelief in his justice or wisdom, only Jocasta's current pessimistic attitude (understandable given her circumstances). The concept of Zeus' justice is the subject of chapter 2.

a prayer such as Jocasta's. The specific connection, therefore, between Zeus, life and death is one worthy of further exploration.

Fate: Life and Death

Zeus' association with the administration of life and death is a complicated one. The god himself seems to represent life, as expressed in *Hecuba* where the fluidity of light, life and death is explored. Euripides also uses that play, as well as *Hippolytus*, to highlight the authority Zeus has over the length of one's life and his ability to extend or cut it short. In *Heracles*, the god's jurisdiction over life and death is complicated by the intervention of other divine forces like "Necessity;" even so, the relationship between the various entities and Zeus is obscure by human standards and the reasons behind Zeus' decisions remain mysterious. The god is clearly using his authority over life and death to maintain cosmic balance, as the chorus of *Medea* announces; but he also relies on humans to obey his will in order to achieve that balance, as in *Electra*, suggesting that while Zeus' authority extends over life and death, in a sense fating everything to happen as it should, not everything is predetermined. Homer's early image of the scales (*Il.* 8.69-74; 22.209-13) is thus an apt metaphor for the balancing act that Zeus must undertake in order to ensure that order is maintained in the world – his authority over life and death is but one aspect.

Of the Euripidean plays under consideration, *Hecuba* contains the most extended engagement with the link between Zeus, light and life.[53] Throughout this tragedy a sustained connection amongst these three concepts is implicitly and explicitly expressed. The first instance of the association between Zeus and light (meaning "life") is found in

---

[53] This is a link which dates from Indo-European conceptions of the god as the sky and is thus a very old and long-assumed association; see Cook (1914) 1-25.

Hecuba's opening monologue when, after waking from frightful dreams, she appeals to

Zeus and dark night and asks them why dark visions have appeared to her:

> ὦ στεροπὰ Διός, ὦ σκοτία νύξ,
> τί ποτ' αἴρομαι ἔννυχος οὕτω
> δείμασι φάσμασιν; (*Hec.* 68-70).[54]

Foreboding dreams are often "disclosed" to the sunlight in order to allay or avert what they

portend;[55] however, Hecuba appeals to πότνια Χθών (70) to achieve this goal, not the sun

or daylight. She questions Zeus and Night, but does not invoke them to allay her fears; nor

does she associate either deity with the sun. But Hecuba does appeal to the στεροπὰ of

Zeus – his flash or gleam. Commonly, when used in relation to Zeus, this word refers to

the god's lightning,[56] although some commentators have taken this instance as suggestive

of the light of Zeus, in the same manner Sophocles used when referring to Helios (*Trach.*

99).[57] Such a reading would suggest that Zeus is acting as the sun here, although there is

nothing else in the text to support this identification. Rather than equate Zeus with Helios

and his gleam as a physical manifestation of sunrays, we should perhaps interpret the

phrase as "the light of Zeus" in the metaphorical sense of the "light of life." Zeus'

association with light pervades the play and this light in turn is a metaphor for life;[58] night,

---

[54] See Bremer (1971) 235-40 for a discussion of this prayer in its entirety (68-89) in comparison to similar tragic prayers (for example, Aesch. *Pers.* 159-225).

[55] Collard (1991) 134.

[56] Hom. *Il.* 10.154, 11.66, 16.298; *Od.* 14.268, 17.437; Hes. *Theog.* 286, 505, 699, 707, 845, 854; Aesch. *Suppl.* 34, *PV.* 1084; Soph. *Ajax* 257, *O.T.* 470. It can also be used of the gleam of bronze weaponry or other metals: Hom. *Il.* 11.83, 19.363; *Od.* 4.72.

[57] Gregory (1999) 52, who goes so far as to say that this refers to the "first rays of the sun, which dazzle Hecuba." See also Collard (1991) 34 and Tierney (1979) 48, who also sees the rays of the sun as belonging to Zeus.

[58] Cf. 168, 248, 368, 435, 668 and 706. The references to light start and finish with references to Zeus, each having connotations of life and death. The only other mention of light in the play occurs when Polymestor's eyes have been darkened (1035), possibly suggesting a fate congruous

here associated with darkness, is thus a metaphor for death.[59] The juxtaposition of the dark of night to Zeus' light is not only the difference between night and day, but of life and death. Hecuba's prayer is thus to Zeus ("giver of life") and Night ("harbinger of death") in the hopes that they might prevent the ominous deaths foreshadowed by her dream.

Unfortunately, this particular prayer will not be granted to Hecuba; it is echoed, however, in the final direct reference to Zeus in the play. After an attendant returns with the body of Polydorus and she explains to Hecuba how he was found, Hecuba recognizes that her earlier dream, which she prayed to avert, was actually not predictive but descriptive. She now understands that what she saw (the death of her son) has already happened and that her trusted friend Polymestor has betrayed both her and Polydorus:

> ἔμαθον ἐνύπνιον ὀμμάτων
> ἐμῶν ὄψιν (οὔ με παρέβα φάντα-
>   σμα μελανόπτερον),
> ἃν ἐσεῖδον ἀμφὶ σοῦ,
> ὦ τέκνον, οὐκέτ' ὄντος Διὸς ἐν φάει (*Hec.* 703-07).

Whereas in Hecuba's earlier prayer the connection between Zeus' light and mortal life was only implicitly made, here it is made explicit in the expression of Polydorus' death as the loss of the light of Zeus.[60] And whereas her prayer to Zeus to preserve the life of her son could not be answered positively, the connection between Zeus, light and life is at its most successful here.

---

with Zeus' interest in light within the play.

[59] The goddess Νύξ is intimately connected with the Underworld: she resides in Hades and is the mother of Sleep, Dreams and Death (Hes.*Theog.* 221).

[60] Although audience members may not immediately be alert to the pairing of these two references to Zeus, Hecuba's own allusion to her earlier dream might have been enough to signal astute audience members to recall both it and her prayer to Zeus and Night to avert what the dream foretold.

The connection between Zeus and light/life also reappears during the choral ode after the departure of Polyxena. While musing on their futures as servants of Artemis or Athena once in Greece, the women recount the birth of Apollo and Artemis on the island of Delos (455-65)[61] and describe the *peplos* they might weave for Athena.[62] As they consider its design, they recall the Titanomachy and how Zeus defeated the Titans with his double-edged flame:

> ἢ Τιτάνων γενεάν,
> τὰν Ζεὺς ἀμφιπύρωι κοιμί-
> ζει φλογμῶι Κρονίδας; (*Hec.* 472-74).

A contrast is established within these details between Zeus' involvement in the birth of Apollo and Artemis and his ability to "put to sleep" the Titans. Zeus has the power to begin and end life: he provided the date-palm which enabled Leto to give birth (458-59) and ensured the Titans would remain entombed in Tartarus.[63] Euripides' use of κοιμίζει ("to put to sleep" or "to kill") is as double-edged as Zeus' flame: Zeus literally put the Titans "to sleep" in Tartarus, being unable to actually kill them (the Titans, being divine cannot die). But although the Titans are entombed alive, they no longer exist under Zeus' light, becoming metaphorically dead. Euripides thus blurs the meaning of κοιμίζει, foreshadowing its later use in the play when Hecuba refers to Cassandra "sleeping" at Agamemnon's side (826). While Hecuba does literally mean "sleep," the audience is fully aware that Cassandra will lie slain beside Agamemnon and thus κοιμίζει takes on this double meaning. The notion that putting someone "to sleep" or "to death" is ambiguous

---

[61] This ode may be in response to the purification of Delos in 426/5 BCE and the reinstatement of the Delian games, see Thucydides 3.104.

[62] On this ode in particular and the relevance of the *peplos*, see Rosivach (1975).

[63] This also serves to remind the audience of the on-going theme in the play of changing fortunes, see, for example, Segal (1990a); Reckford (1991).

may not be novel, but Euripides ties the idea specifically to Zeus' ἀμφίπυρος lightning.[64] His weapon may have flames at both ends, but it also seems to have a dual nature: with his lightning bolt, Zeus controls life and death, keeping people alive or sending them to their death by his will.

Zeus is thus clearly associated with the loss of life in *Hecuba*, but his double-edged weapon also preserves life in this play, especially that of the title character. After Odysseus explains the decision of the Greek army to sacrifice Polyxena, Hecuba addresses Zeus once more. She is in disbelief about Polyxena's fate, as well as her own and admonishes the god for keeping her alive only to witness misfortune upon misfortune: οὐδ' ὤλεσέν με Ζεύς, τρέφει δ' ὅπως ὁρῶ / κακῶν κάκ' ἄλλα μείζον' ἡ τάλαιν' ἐγώ (*Hec.* 232-33).[65] Segal considers this to be the "bitterest possible interpretation" of Zeus' interest in human affairs and Hecuba's expression incriminates the god as the cause of her troubles.[66] Although this is an especially pessimistic view of the gods and Zeus in particular, it is unsurprising to see sufferers indict the gods for their miseries. Of more interest is Hecuba's belief that she is being kept alive by the will of Zeus, rather than by the refusal of Odysseus to sacrifice her alongside her daughter (391-99).

Although Hecuba cannot understand why Zeus should deny her death, he is keeping her alive to be a witness to further atrocities for a reason. Had Odysseus given in to Hecuba's pleas to be killed instead of, or alongside her daughter, it is most probable that

---

[64] The verb κοιμίζειν is not widely used in Greek tragedy, appearing elsewhere only in Euripides' *Trojan Women* (594) and *Phoenissae* (184), the disputed *Rhesus* (669) and Sophocles' *Ajax* (832). In both *Phoenissae* and *Ajax*, there is an appeal to Zeus in conjunction with κοιμίζειν in its metaphorical sense of being "put to sleep;" in *Hecuba*, the same sense is maintained, but without the additional appeal to Zeus.

[65] The audience also knows of another impending disaster for Hecuba and this utterance makes her admonishment of Zeus all the more pitiful.

[66] Segal (1989) 16.

Polydorus would not be given the burial honours he so desperately wants and should in fact receive. Furthermore, the murder of Polydorus would not come to light and Polymestor's treachery would go unpunished. Polydorus' shade has been given the opportunity to visit his mother, while Zeus has ensured that Hecuba will eventually come to understand her son's fate and act as the instrument of punishment the god desires in the blinding of Polymestor and the destruction of his family. Hecuba's "extension of life" is here intimately bound up in both justice (discussed below, pp. 64-65) and what is "fated" to happen. Zeus is still clearly using his authority to take or preserve life as he wills, but there are also other facets of the cosmos to be considered and he will shorten or lengthen lives in order to maintain a balance of order. But, while in *Hecuba* the life of the title-character is lengthened, in other plays, lives are clearly cut short, as they are in *Hippolytus*.

The idea of shortening lives is clearly present in *Hippolytus*, for Aphrodite decides to take the lives of both Phaedra and Hippolytus in order to maintain her honour. But Aphrodite's plans are clearly made with the consent of Zeus, as Artemis articulates at the end of the play. When she appears to Theseus and offers him the truth behind Phaedra's suicide and the rashness of his own actions, Artemis also reveals the custom that gods do not interfere with each other's plans and admits her own reluctance to violate that custom specifically because of her fear of Zeus:[67]

> ἐπεί, σάφ' ἴσθι, Ζῆνα μὴ φοβουμένη
> οὐκ ἄν ποτ' ἦλθον ἐς τόδ' αἰσχύνης ἐγὼ
> ὥστ' ἄνδρα πάντων φίλτατον βροτῶν ἐμοὶ
> θανεῖν ἐᾶσαι (*Hipp.* 1331-34).

Aside from the obvious concept of "divine non-intervention," there could be a secondary meaning to be understood here. By naming her fear of Zeus as the reason Artemis will not aid Hippolytus, she implies Aphrodite's plans were made with the consent of Zeus. Thus,

---

[67] Halleran (1995) 261.

the death of Hippolytus was part of Zeus' larger cosmic scheme and the god had a hand in bringing all of the events to fruition: ensuring that Aphrodite maintained her honour; that Hippolytus received his due (with the promise of honour and tears); and that Artemis be at his side to reveal the truth. While it might be said that the hand of Zeus can be seen in every tragedy, there seems to be an implicit suggestion that something more is going on. This is confirmed by Artemis' final words to Hippolytus that his death was fated, ἔχεις γὰρ μοῖραν ἧι διεφθάρης (1436). Artemis understands that Hippolytus had to die at this time, although not necessarily under these circumstances; he fulfilled his allotted time and Zeus used his death as a means to bring the other events to fruition. Zeus and fate are thus connected by a larger cosmic order, ideas presented more clearly by events in *Heracles*.

This idea of "what is fated" in Zeus' world order finds further expression in *Heracles*, where the association between god and "necessity" is explored through a somewhat incriminating charge by Amphitryon against Zeus. Here, the two forces are differentiated, complicating this relationship between Zeus and "fate." The action of the drama is situated around Zeus' altar, but nearly 500 lines pass before any appeal is directed to the god; when one is finally made by Amphitryon, it is made out of desperation with little hope of fulfilment. He says,

> ἐγὼ δὲ σ', ὦ Ζεῦ, χεῖρ' ἐς οὐρανὸν δικὼν
> αὐδῶ, τέκνοισιν εἴ τι τοισίδ' ὠφελεῖν
> μέλλεις, ἀμύνειν, ὡς τάχ' οὐδὲν ἀρκέσεις.
> καίτοι κέκλησαι πολλάκις· μάτην πονῶ·
> θανεῖν γάρ, ὡς ἔοικ', ἀναγκαίως ἔχει (*Her.* 498-502).[68]

---

[68] The wording of the prayer suggests that Zeus has been called upon previously, although there is no evidence of such appeals: the audience has heard only a vehement criticism of Zeus' involvement with Alcmene and his subsequent abandonment of his purported (but not yet proven) progeny (339-47).

Fearing imminent death, Amphitryon appeals to Zeus with a note of resignation[69] and then accepts ἀνάγκη ("necessity) as the force calling for the demise of the family, as though the two cosmic forces (Zeus and ἀνάγκη) are separate and, possibly, opposed entities.[70] On the one hand, Zeus is being admonished for not coming to the aid of his suppliants even though their deaths here seem not to be controlled by the god; on the other hand, Amphitryon also seems to recognize that their deaths, should they happen now, are part of a larger cosmic order.[71] Amphitryon, of course, does not know that they are about to be "saved" by the arrival of Heracles; nor does he know that there are different fates in store for each member of his family. What is actually necessary for Zeus is that his suppliants be saved, that Lycus be punished and that Heracles finish his labours (all of which eventually happen). The family is not fated to die at *this* altar and Amphitryon's despair, while understandable given the circumstances, is based on partial (and mortal) knowledge. While this outburst could have incriminated the god, in the end, it only reinforces how little the characters comprehend about the overall working out of Zeus' order.

Amphitryon's partial understanding of "necessity" as an important part of Zeus' cosmic order, however, sets the scene for the Iris and Lyssa episode, when the two are discussing Hera's orders to destroy the house of Heracles. Lyssa is explaining that fate and Zeus were protecting the hero as long as he was completing his labours:[72]

πρὶν μὲν γὰρ ἄθλους ἐκτελευτῆσαι πικρούς,

---

[69] Bond (1981) 194 notes that his last words "undermine whatever force there is in the first three lines."

[70] For surely Zeus would be opposed to any force in the world which aims to harm his son and his son's family.

[71] Bond (1981) 194.

[72] Lawrence (1998) 144-45 notes that Lyssa does not say Zeus sent Heracles to save his family, only that he protected him while completing his labours; had the god sent Heracles to save his family only to kill them, he would not be indifferent but "viciously ironical."

τὸ χρή νιν ἐξέσωιζεν οὐδ' εἴα πατὴρ
Ζεύς νιν κακῶς δρᾶν οὔτ' ἔμ' οὔθ' Ἥραν ποτέ· (827-29).

Lyssa's explanation for the timing of Hera's intervention suggests two items of importance: first, Zeus cannot be said to have "abandoned his son,"[73] or his son's family, for Lyssa clearly states Zeus has been protecting Heracles while he completes his labours (including his current task of fetching Cerberus from the Underworld). Secondly, τὸ χρή νιν ἐξέσωιζεν (literally, "that which must be" and therefore, "necessity preserved him") implies that it was not only fated for Heracles to finish his tasks, but also that destiny is partially responsible for the hero's present madness, for his life has been preserved specifically for the present circumstances. In other words, Heracles was simultaneously fated to finish his labours and save his family, thanks to the protection of Zeus; but he was fated to save his family so that the will of Hera could be carried out and that his family die by his own hand.

The apparent discrepancy between the will of Zeus and the will of Hera raises the question of the nature of the relationship between these two deities (discussed in chapter 4), but also of how Heracles' slaughter of his family will affect his own relationship with Zeus (discussed in chapter 6). The murder is clearly a pollution, which necessitates immediate action: Heracles ought to be punished by the closest remaining kin (in this case Amphitryon) or be disinherited. Once again, the arrival of an outside character, here Theseus, provides a solution to the problem. Heracles will be purified at Athens, providing the necessary "loophole" for the hero to retain his status as a son of Zeus and ensuring that Hera's plan to disrupt Zeus' order is nullified. The competing strands of necessity and fate are so completely intertwined that for mortals they become indistinguishable from Zeus.

------

[73] Hartigan (1987) 127.

The god, however, is separate and uses each strand to maintain balance and order in his cosmos.

This emphasis on balance is brought out more clearly in the choral exodus of *Medea*. The chorus intimate that Zeus has brought all events of the play to pass, even though some things were perhaps unexpected. Most of these lines close four other plays (*Andromache, Alcestis, Helen* and *Bacchae*) and this has prompted some scholars to criticize them as unoriginal and superfluous to the action:[74]

> [πολλῶν ταμίας Ζεὺς ἐν Ὀλύμπωι,
> πολλὰ δ' ἀέλπτως κραίνουσι θεοί·
> καὶ τὰ δοκηθέντ' οὐκ ἐτελέσθη,
> τῶν δ' ἀδοκήτων πόρον ηὗρε θεός.
> τοιόνδ' ἀπέβη τόδε πρᾶγμα] (*Med.* 1415-19).

The difference between the closing lines in *Medea* and those of the other four tragedies is the specific reference to Zeus as being the instigator of what comes to pass.[75] Whereas in the other four plays the first line is πολλαὶ μορφαὶ τῶν δαιμονίων, here Euripides specifies Zeus as the instigator, likely a conscious choice to emphasize the god's role in the action of the play.[76] As Euripides may have invented the idea of Medea murdering her own children and escaping without punishment,[77] there would have been a need to place the tragedy of this play directly under the auspices of Zeus. Euripides accomplished this by naming Zeus explicitly, but also by the particular epithet he chooses for the god, ταμίας.

---

[74] See, for example, Dale (1954) 130; Dodds (1960) 240. For discussion, see Rees (1961) and for convincing arguments to the contrary, Kovacs (1993) 65-67.

[75] This specificity suggests that while Euripides may be using a stock idea to close the play he is not merely "copying and pasting."

[76] The role of Zeus in *Medea* is discussed by Kovacs (1993).

[77] For a discussion of the "invention" of Medea murdering her own sons and an overview of the primary sources and relevant scholarship, see McDermott (1989) 9-24; more recent discussions on the subject of Medea's children can be found in Segal (1997), Hopman (2008) and Holland (2009).

This epithet would have resonated quite emphatically with the audience, for many of the Athenian financial magistrates were ταμίαι, often in charge of temple revenues.[78] To refer to Zeus as ταμίας is to imbue him with connotations of collecting, dispensing and guarding money; the epithet thus meaning both, "Zeus as one who guards" or "oversees," and "one who dispenses" or "distributes." The former has obvious significance for the concept of Zeus' eye, while the latter suggests a god who controls what every person is allotted, or at the very least, that what one is apportioned is subject to his will. Zeus who "balances the books" (or indeed, the scales) is behind the events of *Medea* and those events were necessary in order for the god to ensure any breach of divine or religious law was met with appropriate punishment or action.

The final example of Euripides' exploration of the relationship between Zeus and fate is found in *Electra*, where the personification of fate (Moira) is explicitly acknowledged as joining forces with Zeus to ensure fated events will actually happen. At the end of the play, Castor and Polydeuces, the Dioscuri, arrive in order to share their own knowledge concerning the futures of Electra, Orestes and Pylades after the murders of Clytemnestra and Aegisthus. Castor announces that Zeus and Fate have ordained that Pylades marry Electra (1249) and that Orestes leave Argos to stand trial in Athens where he will be acquitted of murder by Athena (1264-66) before founding a city near the Alpheus River (1273): αἰνεῖν δ' ἀνάγκη ταῦτα· τἀντεῦθεν δὲ χρὴ / πράσσειν ἃ Μοῖρα Ζεύς τ' ἔκρανε σοῦ πέρι (1247-48). This pronouncement has been variously interpreted by scholars. Hammond, for example, believing that Necessity (ἀνάγκη) is the ruling force in the world, argues: "There is no partnership here of Zeus and Moira, no combined plan for

---

[78] *Tamias* "was a name given to any person who had the care, managing, or dispensing of money, stock, or property of any description confided to him . . . [They were] certain officers entrusted with important duties by the Athenian government; and more especially the treasurers of the temples and the revenue," Smith (1859) 1096.

benevolence toward man."[79] Taking a different stance, Cropp sees Zeus executing that which Moira apportions, but does not accept that the futures ordained for Orestes and Electra are predetermined: they are only a consequence of what has happened.[80] Both interpretations ignore the influence of Zeus throughout the play and especially the fulfilment of prayers made to the god.[81] Furthermore, Castor's explicit statement about what Orestes and Electra must undergo in no way suggests that these things were not part of Zeus' long-term plan. Assuming Orestes obeys the command of the god by standing trial at Athens, the other events will come to pass.

The suggestion that all of the outcomes may not be predetermined resides in the command that Orestes must accomplish the rest of his destiny: πεπρωμένην γὰρ μοῖραν ἐκπλήσας φόνου / εὐδαιμονήσεις τῶνδ' ἀπαλλαχθεὶς πόνων, 1290-91. This statement indicates that Orestes ought to comply with the orders from Zeus, not that that future will happen regardless of what he does next:[82] he still must go to Athens as directed by the gods. Castor reiterates the position of fate and necessity when Orestes asks him why he and his brother did not ward off the Keres. Castor responds by saying that fate, necessity and Apollo were responsible for leading events to their fulfilment: μοῖρά τ' ἀνάγκη τ' ἦγ' ἐς τὸ χρεών / Φοίβου τ' ἄσοφοι γλώσσης ἐνοπαί (1301-02). His words suggest that it was the combination of three forces (aside from Zeus) that brought about the present situation. The fate (or timing of death) of Clytemnestra, the necessity of her death and Apollo's directive to commit matricide together led to the presence of the Keres. While

---

[79] Hammond (1984) 385.

[80] Cropp (1988) 183.

[81] Such prayers to Zeus are discussed in chapter 7, pp. 208-11, 230-31.

[82] This dichotomy of necessity and personal will is nothing innovative, for the same "choice" can be found in Aeschylus' *Agamemnon*, when the king must sacrifice Iphigenia because of ἀνάγκη, although it does nothing to lessen his guilt (*Ag.* 218). See, for example, Lesky (1966), Edwards (1977) and Furley (1986).

Castor does not mention Zeus again, it may be understood that his own arrival with Polydeuces was orchestrated by Zeus to ensure Orestes complies with the god's order to stand trial and thus be free of his mother's avengers.

Tyche: (Mis)Fortune

The only tragedy under discussion here which does not have explicit references to the relationship between Zeus, life and death is *Orestes*, although that is not to say it does not engage with any of those concepts. For the play does explore the granting of fortune by Zeus, a notion crossing the concepts of both fate and justice, which will be discussed below. *Orestes* opens with Electra tending her brother on his sick-bed. She relates their ancestry, beginning with Tantalus, son of Zeus, one who was fortunate once, but is now eternally punished by perpetual fear from stoning:

> ὁ γὰρ μακάριος (κοὐκ ὀνειδίζω τύχας)
> Διὸς πεφυκώς, ὡς λέγουσι, Τάνταλος
> κορυφῆς ὑπερτέλλοντα δειμαίνων πέτρον
> ἀέρι ποτᾶται· (*Or.* 4-7).

Electra's account contains several items of interest: the (in)validity of Tantalus' descent from Zeus,[83] Tantalus' "fall from grace"[84] and the specific form of his punishment.[85] All three of these details involve Zeus: as father of Tantalus, as the one to be betrayed by Tantalus and as the one to choose and inflict Tantalus' penalty. West notes that the inclusion of ὡς λέγουσι does not in itself suggest Euripides was insinuating the story mentioned here is false (for Helen is proven to be a daughter of Zeus just as Tantalus was his son),[86] but Electra's belief or disbelief in the story does not really matter in the end.

---

[83] West (1987) 180; Kyriakou (1998) 292.

[84] Willink (1986) 81; Parry (1969) 340; Fuqua (1978).

[85] O'Brien (1988) *passim*; Hall (1990) 279-80.

[86] West (1987) 180.

What is significant is that Tantalus is symbolic of much more than the beginning of Electra's lineage; he is a prime example of the wrath of the gods against those who transgress their laws, but also as one whose fortunes were utterly reversed.[87]

Tantalus is characterized by the word μακάριος and as one who enjoyed τύχας, descriptions that clearly are not part of the lives of Electra and Orestes. These ideas are likely coming from the story that Tantalus once lived among the gods and also partook of their ambrosia, leading to his status as another "immortal" punished for eternity; Tantalus' crime, which is not made explicit, brought about his swift change in fortune.[88] The adjectives used to describe Tantalus, however, are shared not by Electra and Orestes, but instead by his other descendant, Menelaus (86). This is an apt characterization of Menelaus for he too will soon suffer a change of fortune as Tantalus once endured. Both the somewhat ambiguous portrayal of Tantalus (symbolizing Zeus' grant of good and ill fortunes in life, cf. Hom. *Il.* 24.525-28) and the inherited characterization of Menelaus point to the potential hazards of upsetting Zeus' order. Furthermore, as Zeus is the ultimate founder of Electra and Orestes' line he is the one ancestor able to make any change in

---

[87] Zeus' relationship to Tantalus (and thus to Electra and Orestes) is one on which scholars do not completely agree: the majority view Tantalus as the initiator of the curse which plagues the rest of his house (and is commonly used by poets), while a smaller group (for example, O'Brien [1988] 37) sees Tantalus as closer to the gods and Kyriakou (1998) 294 even refers to him as a "benevolent great-grandfather."

[88] In a fragment preserved by Athenaios (*Nostoi* fr 4 *PEG*), Tantalus enjoyed the company of the gods and was so favoured by Zeus, that the god offered to give him anything he wanted; but because Tantalus wanted to have a share in the gods' feasts always, Zeus was offended and in granting the wish of food and drink, he put a rock above Tantalus' head in order to prohibit him from enjoying any of those delights. A similar fate is mentioned by Pindar (*Ol.* 1.54-64) for the transgression of sharing the nectar and ambrosia which Zeus gave to Tantalus alone. In either scenario, Tantalus is first highly honoured by the gods before being swiftly punished for a hubristic transgression; Gantz (1993) 531-532.

(mis)fortune possible; ironically, however, he is the one god to whom the two pay the least attention.

Electra's account of Tantalus' punishment has also received much comment in this play, for it is not perpetual thirst and hunger which plagues Tantalus for all eternity, but rather the fear of a rock falling on him whilst suspended in mid-air (6-7). O'Brien has connected this image to a theme of "stoning" throughout the play[89] and, indeed, the principal characters are motivated to act due to their fear of death, which serves almost as a psychological punishment. The idea that Zeus has punished Tantalus by hanging him in mid-air also seems to be an invention on Euripides' part and provides a striking image. It is later recalled by Electra when she wishes to explain all of her woes to him; to do so she must travel to the place where Tantalus hangs between earth and heaven (982-88). We can imagine that Tantalus is caught between worlds: he is mortal and yet receives immortal punishment; he is not kept in Tartarus, where other "sinners" would be, but neither does he reside in heaven. Euripides has presented us with a Zeus who is able not only to reverse one's fortune, but one's status and identity.[90] As such, Tantalus has begotten a line of descendants who are favoured by the gods and yet will suffer much because of that favour.

It is clear that Zeus, as "overseer" of all human affairs, is not merely a figurehead; his duty to maintain order is predicated on his ability to "see" with an unpolluted eye. But it is not enough to acknowledge that certain events take place; it is expected that he react to what he witnesses. This prompts an assumption by mortals that the god will react in a manner they see fit, but not necessarily as Zeus sees fit. Because his authority extends over

---

[89] O'Brien (1988) *passim*.

[90] Problems of identity are common throughout the play and few characters adhere to their traditional roles – only Helen is referred to as being ever the "same woman" (129). For a full analysis of Helen's role in *Orestes* and especially the importance of lines 126-31, see Wright (2006).

the allotment of life and death, Zeus must balance what is fated, with what is necessary and with what ensures the stability of his own cosmic order. In order to accomplish this, Zeus must also rely on the obedience of mortals to comply with what he ordains, for the fortunes of men are not predestined; disobeying the gods or upsetting Zeus' order will ensure one's good fortune is utterly reversed.

Jupiter, Fate and Fortune

Seneca's Jupiter operates in a very similar way to that of Euripides' Zeus, although the emphases apparent in the Greek tragedies are less explicitly made in the Latin. The connection between sight and knowledge, for example, does not emerge to the same extent in Seneca's plays as it had in those of Euripides. In fact, there are only two references to be found related to that idea: one each in *Hercules Furens* and *Phaedra*. The concepts of fate and fortune, on the other hand, are more prominent, especially in *Phaedra* but also in *Agamemnon*. There are also two very explicit instances in *Medea* and *Thyestes* where Jupiter's authority over life and death is explored and these two examples differ the most from what one finds in relation to Zeus. What emerges from even this brief overview is that Zeus and Jupiter do not receive the same representation from their respective poets concerning their relationship to fate and fortune, although clearly some ideas do carry forward from Euripides to Seneca.

The clearest parallel to Euripides' ideas concerning sight and knowledge can be found in Seneca's *Hercules Furens*, although the play exhibits some intriguing differences. As discussed earlier, in *Hippolytus*, Theseus was concerned about his son's actions sullying the eye of Zeus and in *Hercules Furens* the title character is similarly concerned about Jupiter's eyes when he brings Cerberus up from the Underworld. The hero invokes the gods and warns them all to avert their eyes, before asking Jupiter to use his lightning to shield his own vision: *tuque, caelestum arbiter / parensque, visus fulmine opposito tege* (597-98).[91] Several significant details emerge from this brief address to Jupiter: first, Jupiter's lightning is here being used as a defensive rather than offensive weapon, as if this action of Hercules is somehow a threat to Jupiter's well-being; the risk of pollution implied in Euripides is brought out more explicitly here. Hercules is insinuating that Jupiter needs to prepare himself for what he is about to see. This suggests both that Hercules can witness something that Jupiter cannot, or should not (echoing the Euripidean notion that the eye of god is holy), but also that Jupiter needs to take precautions to ensure his own safety.[92] Furthermore, the phrase suggests that the only item capable of protecting Jupiter is his own lightning, this one item at once defining his immense authority, but also his vulnerability (for without it, the god is defenceless). The "eye" of Jupiter is thus no less important than Zeus', but Seneca introduces another element and changes the emphasis: here, it is not about ensuring Jupiter has sufficient knowledge, but rather about protecting his own *auctoritas* as well as avoiding pollution. For Jupiter, gazing upon something he should not would have repercussions for his ability to maintain cosmic control.

The second reference concerning sight is found in *Phaedra* and recalls the Euripidean invocations to witness the affairs of mortals. After her husband arrives, Jupiter is called upon by Phaedra as she is about to tell Theseus why she is intent on death. She invokes both Jupiter and the Sun, her two divine ancestors, as witnesses to her story: *Te te, creator caelitum, testem invoco* (888).[93] Phaedra's purpose in calling upon Jupiter is to

---

[91] The request, however, seems more of an order than an appeal.

[92] That the gods cannot come into contact with the dead or, presumably, denizens of the Underworld is commonplace (Fitch [1987] 278), but Seneca seems to be suggesting something more with his emphasis on Jupiter's lightning as an object of protection.

[93] The phrase *creator caelitum* is of importance here, for it is nearly unique in Latin literature, used previously by Cicero to refer to Romulus (*Pro Balb.* 31.10) and by Ovid to refer to Peleus (*Met.* 8.309); and the use of *creator* on its own to refer to Jupiter only occurs three times (in Cic. *de*

ensure that Theseus takes her words seriously and believes them to be truthful. The unspoken assumption is that the gods would only be invoked as witnesses to events which actually happened. Thus Phaedra's invocation of Jupiter gives her story credibility,[94] but she must then, of course, choose her words very carefully (indeed it has been noted how well she crafts her tale not exactly as a lie, but to give enough information leading to the wrong assumptions[95]). It is precisely because of this invocation that Theseus is led astray by Phaedra's carefully constructed story and why he immediately prays that his son be killed (903-04, 945-46.). Phaedra now remains silent until after Hippolytus has been pronounced dead and she never again invokes Jupiter. When she finally breaks her silence it is to tell her husband the full truth before killing herself and suggesting that Theseus do the same (1191-1200); no mention of the god or her earlier oath is made.

The invocation also provides Theseus the opportunity to invoke the wishes[96] granted to him by Neptune. It is because the gods were called to witness that Theseus believes the lie and does not hesitate to take revenge upon his son, using his father's benevolence. The invocation provides enough validation for him and the curse he places on his son is efficacious, essentially destroying his entire house. The death of Hippolytus, resulting from this curse, also prompts Phaedra's suicide. Again, because she called the

---

Div. 2.30.64; Luc. 10.266; and this instance in Seneca). Seneca's use here is an unconventional way to refer to Jupiter and while none of these previous usages corresponds to this Senecan phrase, there is a possible thematic link to Ovid. The mention of Peleus comes in the context of Ovid's tale of Meleager and the Calydonian boar, a story that has much in common with Seneca's *Phaedra*. There is the wrath of Diana and the use of her boar as a punishment for neglect and lack of honour; the boar itself shares a similar role in each; the death of a son, due to the wish of a parent; and finally a love which ends in disaster. That Seneca is choosing *creator* here may be a signal to look to Ovid for certain intertextual links.

[94] Segal (1986) 167: "she summons patriarchal authority for her false accusation."

[95] Davis (1983) 122-23.

[96] See Kohn (2008) for a discussion of the "three wishes" theme in both Euripides and Seneca.

gods to witness, they are aware of how her manipulation of words caused Theseus to kill his son and she must now make amends for her folly. Thus, the omniscience of Jupiter is used by Phaedra to hurt Theseus, but causes Hippolytus' downfall and eventually her own: the god's *auctoritas* as witness is thus a double-edged weapon employed by Senecan characters instead of a guarantee of cosmic order in Euripides.

The relationship between Jupiter and fate is referred to only once in Seneca's plays and it too emerges in *Phaedra*. When the Nurse approaches Hippolytus concerning his lack of interest in honouring Venus, she mentions Jupiter's involvement in procreation, suggesting that it is part of his "plan" to have humans create new offspring in order that the world not end up devoid of life:

> Providit ille maximus mundi parens,
> cum tam rapaces cerneret Fati manus,
> ut damna semper subole repararet nova (466-68).

This statement accords with the Nurse's beliefs that love is not a god (195-203), but there is a sense that she is making a distinction between amorous feelings and marriage for the purpose of procreation. The significance here is Jupiter's slight opposition to Fate. It becomes apparent that he saw a need to "undo" some of Fate's work (presumably that everyone must die) and to counter this, he made provision for the production of offspring. One wonders whether this "provision" was Venus herself, for the Nurse then asks what would happen if the world was deprived of Venus (*excedat agedum rebus humanis Venus*, 469), which suggests that both Venus and her son (who is himself a subject of much interest in the play) are ultimately under Jupiter's authority.[97] Jupiter and Fate are at odds here and the priority of one over the other is not clearly established. Jupiter is suggested to be the ultimate cause of life in the world, but there is an inherent tension here that does not

---

[97] Although, as Davis (1983) 121 remarks, both Venus and Cupid "connote a genuine power of universal significance."

seem to exist for Euripides. Seneca does not elaborate on this tension, however, and is, in general, more interested in the relationship Jupiter has with the personification of Fortuna.

Fortuna is the subject of the *parodos* in *Agamemnnon*. While the chorus sing of the goddess' fickle nature they muse on the preference of moderation to superiority, exclaiming that *feriunt celsos fulmina colles* (*Ag.* 96). Although this statement does not explicitly mention Jupiter, the lightning can be taken as an implicit reference to the god's interest in maintaining balance. Furthermore, it is reminiscent of a similar notion expressed by Aeschylus in his play of the same name (Aesch. *Ag.* 568-69) and one which is there inextricably linked to Zeus. In Seneca's *Agamemnon*, there is no mention of the god; only his lightning, the symbol of his power, is invoked. When we recognize that every other reference to lightning in the play is associated with the god's power,[98] with the possible exception of 829-30,[99] it seems probable that a mention of lightning would immediately bring Jupiter to mind. The reference at *Ag.* 96 to Jupiter striking down what is lofty indicates his wish for traditional hierarchy to remain unchallenged and respected, as well as indicating his continued interest in defending the rights of those at the top of said hierarchy. Fortuna and Jupiter are differentiated but clearly working together here to uphold the cosmic order.

A similar scenario can be inferred from another ode, when the chorus sing of longing for *libera mors* (591), a harbour of eternal peace (592), safe from the storms of Fortuna and the fires of Jupiter:

nullus hunc terror nec impotentis

---

[98] Cf. Sen. *Ag.* 334, 383, 495, 528, 535, 546 and 802.

[99] *Te sensit Nemeaeus arto / pressus lacerto fulmineus leo.* The Nemean lion is described as being lightning-like, referring to both its power and speed and thus not necessarily related to Jupiter at all; however, because it is the *Nemean* lion, there is an implicit reference again to Zeus (and thus Jupiter) as he was the chief god in the area, with both his temple and games linked to the site (Paus. 2.15.2-3); see Miller (2006) 107-12.

> procella Fortunae movet aut iniqui
> flamma Tonantis (*Ag.* 593-95).

Fortuna and Jupiter are again linked, in this case as evils with which one must contend until death. As Tarrant notes, the chorus is not speaking impiously against the god;[100] they are merely recognizing their place in Jupiter's cosmic order. The tone they use here, however, is quite negative, as *iniqui* retains an almost sinister sense. The chorus are assuming Jupiter to be "hostile" or "unfair" yet quite obviously the supreme authority. The more negative connotations here may be signalling the displeasure Jupiter feels for Agamemnon, who will be introduced during the next act, but it is worth noting the god's portrayal, especially in relation to Fortuna, who is also characterized quite harshly (as *procella*). It would appear that the two gods are acting as forces with which none should reckon, resulting in an image of a harmonious, but perhaps unsettling,[101] union of deities.

This "partnership" between Jupiter and Fortuna collapses in *Phaedra*, however, when the chorus in this tragedy question the integrity of the god while espousing his vast authority. They wonder why the supreme ruler takes such care of the cosmos, yet spurns the good and supports the wicked:

> sed cur idem qui tanta regis,
> sub quo vasti pondera mundi
> librata suos ducunt orbes,
> hominum nimium securus abes,
> non sollicitus prodesse bonis,
> nocuisse malis?
>   Res humanas ordine nullo
> Fortuna regit
> sparsitque manu munera caeca
> peiora fovens . . . (*Phaed.* 972-80).

---

[100] Tarrant (1976) 286.

[101] Having one deity who is hostile to the human race (Jupiter) in charge would be quite enough; adding another who is characterized as *procella* may seem like a disaster waiting to happen.

The chorus' final conclusion that it must be Fortuna ruling in Jupiter's stead when the cosmic balance is undermined suggests a rather different interpretation of the relationship between the two deities. Jupiter has either disengaged himself from being directly involved in human affairs and thus Fortuna is wielding authority instead, or Jupiter has allotted this particular portion to Fortuna as her realm of influence.[102] In either scenario the result is a poorly balanced cosmos and the chorus suggest that Fortuna must be the one in control at the moment because of the present circumstances (Theseus' curse and subsequent murder of Hippolytus, Phaedra's unnatural desire of her step-son and Hippolytus' unnatural celibacy).[103] They do not believe that Jupiter could be ruling the cosmos with all that has happened and, in either scenario outlined above, he is not shown to be particularly effective. Whereas in *Agamemnon* the two deities seemed to work in tandem with each other, here Fortuna is perceived to be the one in control and Jupiter either has no interest in what she does or has undermined his own authority by installing cosmic imbalance.

The two deities are mentioned together again in the final ode while the chorus muses, like their counterpart in *Agamemnon*, on the notion that those who are humble are rarely met with great misfortunes, whereas those in power are surrounded by them. The chorus notes how *minor in parvis Fortuna furit* (*Phaed.* 1124) before they describe Jupiter's relationship to the Caucasus mountains and Mount Ida, both of which Jupiter attacks because of their intrusion upon his realm:

> Raros patitur fulminis ictus
> umida vallis;
> tremuit telo Iovis altisoni
> Caucasus ingens
> Phrygiumque nemus matris Cybeles.
> metuens caelo Iuppiter alto

---

[102] Hill (2000) 572 asserts that the contrast is rather between the ordered governance of the physical world and the disordered governance of the human, only the latter of which involves Fortuna.
[103] Davis (1993) 150.

vicina petit.
non capit umquam magnos motus
humilis tecti plebeia domus;
   circa regna tonat (*Phaed.* 1131-40).

This ode might at first suggest that Fortuna and Jupiter are once again working together, for both divinities target the haughty and seldom attack the weak; however, the image of Jupiter striking out against the mountains and Mother Cybele has a different resonance. Jupiter is perceived as feeling threatened by those intruding upon his realm and his reaction is to assert his dominance, attempting to put those who would supplant him in their place.[104] The notion that Jupiter could feel threatened creates an unbalanced comparison between the two deities, especially after the mention of Fortuna reacting similarly against the weak, but without reference to any need to assert her own dominance. They behave in the same way against the modest, but only Jupiter reacts against the arrogant, as if Fortuna has no need to do the same. Only two lines later do the chorus then assert that *nec ulli / praestat velox Fortuna fidem* (1142-43). By implication, Fortuna's lack of loyalty to any other must extend to the lord of Olympus as well; this creates an uneasy disparity between Fortuna and Jupiter.

Finally, with respect to the granting of life and death, there is a striking difference between the ideas exhibited by Seneca from those asserted by Euripides. In both *Medea* and *Thyestes* Jupiter's authority in this area is claimed by other individuals, namely Medea and Atreus respectively. At least in the case of Medea, one can claim that she has some

---

[104] Mocanu (2012) 35-37 has recently explored the contrasting imagery of rural versus city as appropriate descriptors and symbols for Hippolytus and Phaedra respectively. She notes the image of the mountains and forests as particularly apt for a character that is portrayed as "cold" and "*durus.*" Such an interpretation of Hippolytus as embodying features of the mountains may support an interpretation of the choral ode on mountains as a far more specific commentary on the events of the play, rather than merely a more general observation about the state of human affairs in a wider context.

divinity about her, but the same cannot be said about Atreus and the obvious challenge to Jupiter's authority is quite apparent in each play (discussed in detail in chapter 9). In *Medea*, the eponymous character is depicted with certain qualities typically granted to Jupiter, suggesting that the latter may not be the sole or even the ultimate source of power. The first clear indication is provided by Medea's speech to the Nurse as she complains about Jason's disloyalty. Medea takes the credit for providing Jason not only with assistance, but his very life: *vivat tamen / memorque nostri muneri parcat meo* (141-42). While there is no question that Medea saved Jason's life, she is taking the stance that his life is at her disposal: she can give it or take it at will. This is not a prerogative associated with mere mortals, but rather the gods (or perhaps Kings and Emperors) and Jupiter in particular.[105] Medea is asserting herself with regal authority and claiming her (divine) inheritance.[106] Jupiter himself is not mentioned here, but the mere idea of a (female!) mortal taking on the qualities of the gods and Jupiter in particular, is something quite striking from that presented by Euripides. It could indicate a shift in ideology where the god is concerned and the example from *Thyestes* provides some corroboration of this interpretation.

In *Thyestes* it is Atreus who claims a very similar attribute to Medea, although not quite in the same way: here Jupiter has granted the tyrant the power to give and take life, *ius dedit magnum necis atque vitae* (608), a significant boon to Atreus, for it means Jupiter cannot punish him when he kills his brother's children. While this may, at first, be seen as an affirmation of Jupiter's *auctoritas*, the remainder of the play does not bear this

---

[105] Westbrook (1999), who has traced the literary life of the phrase *vitae necisque potestas*, notes that the exercise of such power occurs "primarily" between masters and slaves, rulers and subjects and fathers and children (203). Medea's connection to Jason cannot be reconciled with any of the relationships Westbrook has identified.

[106] Further examples and a discussion of Medea's relationship with Jupiter will be discussed in chapter 9, pp. 283-315.

interpretation out. Jupiter has given up one of his own spheres of authority and passed it to a mortal man to do with it what he will. There is no recourse of action and Jupiter must either stay and watch impassively what Atreus does with this power, or abandon the play altogether, because there is nothing more for him to do (which is, in fact, what occurs[107]). Whereas Euripides' Zeus retains such control over his authority and the lives of mortals, Seneca's Jupiter is unable to do the same.

Concluding Remarks

Euripides' Zeus is thus presented to his audience as being *potentially* omniscient; characters in his tragedies must request the god's presence in order to be assured that the god bears witness to their troubles. But Zeus is frequently requested to gaze upon actions and situations that no mortal should ever request a god to see: situations that are inherently impious and clearly polluting. Such requests, however, are often the only way to ensure that Zeus can take appropriate action or acknowledge that such situations arise. His presence (for example, at the departure of the Trojan women from Troy) implies not divine protection of those who call upon him, but divine recognition and understanding, if not support, of them in their time of need. The Orphic Hymn which opened the chapter found a way around this problem of Zeus seeing that which needed to be seen by bringing in Fate as an un-pollutable goddess who sees those events for the god. Euripides employs no such tactic, instead emphasizing this tension and dichotomy. For him the "eye of Zeus" is the sacred aspect of Zeus, inherently divine and inherently at risk, but decidedly an important aspect his overall characterization and the only sure way for the god to gain knowledge and take any further action.

---

[107] This is discussed in chapter 9, 315-33.

The actions undertaken by Zeus are often done in accordance with some idea of fate, be it μοῖρα or ἀνάγκη, but they are also often misunderstood by human reasoning. Zeus' motivations for his actions, while unclear to the mortal mind, are always working toward keeping the cosmos in balance; ultimately, this means that Zeus must ensure that each person fulfills their allotted time, not only for their own "fate" but in conjunction with others around them. He will preserve life or sentence death according to a larger scheme of knowledge of the cosmos. This does not equate to a predetermination of each person's life-course, but rather a force which ensures cosmic and religious laws are followed, with devastating results for those who choose to disobey them. Zeus also grants good fortune to those he particularly favours, but utter reversals of fortune await those who transgress against him.

Euripides' presentation of Zeus clearly has resonances with Seneca's own presentation of Jupiter, but the latter playwright includes a few variations in his depiction of the god that are particularly "Roman" and which offer a slightly different cosmic force than we find in Euripides. Seneca does not explore the divinity of Jupiter's eye to the same extent as Euripides does with Zeus, but he does take the idea that Jupiter's vision is at risk of pollution. But the risk for Jupiter is not wholly of a religious nature, instead symbolizing a far greater concern: Jupiter *must* protect himself and if he cannot his authority and *auctoritas* may be in danger. Jupiter thus relies far more heavily on other deities to keep the cosmos balanced, although occasionally these other deities can become quite powerful. While the personified Fate seems to accept Jupiter's authority, the personified Fortuna has far more potential to become a rival to the god. Her presence in Jupiter's order does not always seem to signify a harmonious relationship, but rather a fearsome combination where Jupiter may not always be dominant partner.

CHAPTER 2:
JUSTICE

A motif closely connected to the ideas discussed in the previous chapter concerning fate is that of justice, especially as personified by the goddess Δίκη. Often, what is fated or brought to pass is closely associated with Zeus' justice (or Justice), mythically interpreted as the daughter of Zeus and Themis (Hes. *Theog.* 901). Lloyd-Jones, when discussing the justice of Zeus within the plays of Euripides, asserts "Zeus and his justice either find no mention or are given only perfunctory notice."[108] This claim is an important one, for Lloyd-Jones' work is one of the few significant studies focussed specifically on Zeus and as such forms the basis for many investigations on the topic of the justice of Zeus.[109] An examination of the texts where Dikē and Zeus are invoked or mentioned together, however, would argue against Lloyd-Jones's assertion.

While notions of justice permeate every Greek tragedy and references to δίκη or any of its cognates are quite common, Dikē as a personification has significance in six of the plays under investigation here (*Medea, Orestes, Hippolytus, Hecuba, Electra* and *Phoenissae*)[110] and articulations of Zeus' justice are expressed in the other two (*Trojan Women* and *Heracles*).[111] Euripides uses both the concept of Dikē as a goddess, who supports Zeus and helps the god maintain order, and *dikē* as a moral notion to explore the

---

[108] Lloyd-Jones (1971) 145.

[109] A more recent overview of Zeus is found in Dowden (2006); among the handful of studies he directs his readers to is Lloyd-Jones: "But we learn more about the god and the Greek thought-world from the splendidly trenchant and faithfully grim volume of Hugh Lloyd-Jones on *The Justice of Zeus*" (14). Burkert (1983) 399 n. 41 also points his readers to Lloyd-Jones on the discussion of Zeus' justice.

[110] Not including references made in Euripidean tragedies outside the scope of the thesis: *Heracleidae* 941, *Suppliants* 564 and *Rhesus* 199.

[111] A very recent and welcome article by Papadodima (2011) investigates the concept of *dikē* in three plays by Euripides (*Heracleidae, Suppliants* and *Phoenissae*) and argues for a far more nuanced view of the concept within the Euripidean corpus.

sometimes unsettling execution of divine justice. In both forms (personification and concept) justice is served by Zeus according to his own understanding of appropriate punishment or reaction to a given situation. But such an understanding is often at odds with what humans might expect or desire. Euripides highlights the fallibility of mortal conceptions of justice within the larger framework of the cosmos, while at the same time revealing how harsh and rigid divine conceptions of "justice" can be. Of course Dikē is not the only goddess associated with the concept of justice and indeed both Themis and Nemesis are invoked alongside Zeus, revealing other occasions where Zeus' justice is brought to the fore.

Finally, a survey of justice would not be complete without mention of the Erinyes, goddesses who also play a vital role in maintaining Zeus' cosmic balance. For the Romans, Dikē's "equivalent" Iustitia did not develop to the same extent as her Greek counterpart and so Jupiter does not have a similar relationship to this particular personification. Instead, the goddess Pietas (being a good, though not exact, substitute for Themis) does receive a mention by Seneca and is given significance in *Medea* as one who also helps to maintain divine order. But it is the Erinyes who are most easily transferable to Seneca's tragedies as Furies and who receive the most attention by the playwright, one of whom even appears on stage. It is apparent from even this cursory summary that not only is Zeus' justice integral to the plays of Euripides, but also that there appears to be a significant shift in ideology when turning to Seneca. What this shift signifies is of course another matter entirely.

Zeus and Dikē

Euripides represents the relationship between Zeus and Dikē most explicitly in his *Medea*, where the goddess is not only invoked alongside the god, but is specifically made to belong to him, either as his daughter or as his "agent" (possibly even both). Medea calls upon Zeus, Dikē and Helios after Aegeus guarantees sanctuary for her in Athens upon her arrival. She is confident that those who have wronged her will pay for their crimes and asserts that she will be victorious over her enemies, insinuating to the audience that she enjoys divine support:

> ὦ Ζεῦ Δίκη τε Ζηνὸς Ἡλίου τε φῶς,
> νῦν καλλίνικοι τῶν ἐμῶν ἐχθρῶν, φίλαι,
> γενησόμεσθα κἀς ὁδὸν βεβήκαμεν,
> νῦν ἐλπὶς ἐχθροὺς τοὺς ἐμοὺς τείσειν δίκην (764-67).

This exclamation after the departure of Aegeus seems to suggest divine intervention in sending the king through Corinth[112] and also marks the point when Medea is convinced of her ability to exact revenge. Zeus is here clearly associated with Dikē and, although it is unsurprising the two would be connected, it seems significant that their relationship would be made so explicit at this particular juncture. Zeus and Dikē are linked specifically for the purpose of Medea's revenge against Jason and this provides evidence for the gods' support of her actions.[113] The additional invocation of Helios might also suggest that Medea is pledging an oath here to take revenge (although her descent from the god is an equally valid reason for the invocation); but even if the invocation is not also an oath, Medea is clearly associating her revenge with the justice of the gods and there is no indication that this association should not be considered viable. Medea will escape in a serpent-led chariot and will find safety in Athens: Zeus and Dikē are presented as part of this successful revenge, if not at least partially responsible for it.

The above quotation also contains only the first of two references to Dikē (as a personification) in the play, for when Jason curses Medea for the slaughter of their

---

[112] See Kovacs (1993) for a complete discussion of the idea that Aegeus is sent by Zeus.

[113] Mastronarde (2002b) 295, who also notes that the invocation "recalls Medea's cries mentioned or heard in the prologue and parodos (21-2, 148, 160, 168-69, 208-09)."

children, he calls upon the goddess to destroy her: ἀλλά σ' Ἐρινὺς ὀλέσειε τέκνων /

φονία τε Δίκη (*Med.* 1389-90). This second reference to Dikē refers far more to her

association with blood vengeance and her links to the Erinyes than to her connection to

Zeus, but it is nevertheless significant for ensuring the continuation of the god's "world

order." For Jason, Dikē is associated with blood-revenge and his choice of epithet for Dikē

is unusual; this is the only (as far as I know) instance of Dikē being awarded the epithet

φονία and, in the mouth of Jason at this point, it sounds almost profane.[114] He is obviously

feeling betrayed and wants to believe that the Erinyes and Dikē will exact (a fatal) justice

from Medea. Every indication is that this will not happen, rendering his outburst a

blasphemous remark against Dikē (and Zeus' idea of justice), rather than a defiant and

confident curse he has no means of achieving, which it appears to be at first. The two

references to Dikē as a personification are designed to impress upon the audience Zeus'

interest and control over "justice," which is at once comforting (because justice will be

served) and distressing (because the justice served is according to divine, not human,

law).[115]

This curse of Jason's may be contrasted to that of Pylades in *Orestes*, when he

appeals to Zeus and Dikē on behalf of Electra, Orestes and himself to grant the three

companions good fortune in the future: σὺ δ', ὦ Ζεῦ πρόγονε καὶ Δίκης σέβας, / δότ'

εὐτυχῆσαι τῶιδ' ἐμοί τε τῆιδέ τε· (*Or.* 1242-43). The two passages offer a number of

avenues for comparison as both men seeking aid are essentially requesting revenge in the

form of murder and appealing to the same deity; however, the two appeals result in two

very different outcomes. Pylades' request for good fortune is spoken in the context of

---

[114] Φόνιος is a more appropriate epithet for Hades (as, for example, at Soph. *OC* 1689).

[115] As Lloyd-Jones (1971) 154 remarks: "Zeus rules the universe in terms of his own justice; this is
not easily comprehensible to men, and may appear at variance with human justice."

planning the murder of Helen and the abduction of Hermione, both descendants of Zeus like themselves (although Helen and Hermione have much closer ties). To ask the gods for succour to accomplish such an act seems foolhardy at best, impious at worst and, of course, Zeus and Dikē will not grant such a request. On the other hand, the specific wording that Pylades uses suggests only implicitly that this is the precise good fortune the three youths seek; explicitly, he asks only that the gods grant good fortune and this can be interpreted by Zeus and Dikē (as well as the audience) as just that; eventually this is granted to each of them, for all three are saved at the end and provided with bright futures. Thus, the implicit request of Pylades to gain aid in murder and abduction is rejected, but the explicit request is granted and it seems it is for the audience member to decide how to interpret the gods' roles at this point in the play. Whereas for Jason, Zeus and Dikē were the means to achieve (and who were unsupportive of fulfilling) revenge against Medea, for Pylades, the two gods were objects of appeal for aid rather than pure revenge. The two invocations also provide an example of differing approaches to epithets: Jason's choice of φονία could not be more different than Pylades' choice of σέβας.

The importance of Dikē to Zeus' world order can also be discerned in other plays where the relationship between the two is not so explicitly mentioned. In *Hecuba*, when Polymestor has been lured into the tent with his sons, the chorus remark on his impending doom as the confluence of his debts to Dikē and the gods:

> τὸ γὰρ ὑπέγγυον
> Δίκαι καὶ θεοῖσιν οὐ ξυμπίτνει,
> ὀλέθριον ὀλέθριον κακόν (*Hec.* 1029-31).

Hecuba's revenge against her son's murderer is made in the name of justice and indeed *dikē* or its cognates appear often in this play.[116] Hecuba's punishment of Polymestor can be interpreted as divine punishment and Gregory has noted here that "the members of the chorus uphold the connection posited by Hecuba and Agamemnon (799-800, 852-53) between the gods and the cause of justice."[117] While Zeus is not named specifically, there is an inherent association made between Dikē and the gods, which would at least include Zeus. A similar connection is made in *Electra* when the messenger appears in front of Electra to relay the news of Aegisthus' death at the hands of Orestes: ὦ θεοί, Δίκη τε πάνθ' ὁρῶσ', ἦλθές ποτε (*El.* 771). The demise of Aegisthus is interpreted by Electra as an act of divine punishment by Dikē[118] and the other gods, again including Zeus.[119]

It is perhaps also worthwhile to note the Messenger's use of yet another epithet (πάνθ' ὁρῶσ') for Dikē, one which implicitly ties the goddess to Zeus, for "all-seeing" is not an uncommon epithet for Zeus, as discussed earlier. While this may not tie her

---

[116] *Dikē* is mentioned fifteen times throughout the play (271, 715, 801, 844, 853 [with two mentions], 1024, 1030, 1052, 1131, 1235, 1249, 1253, 1254, 1274), suggesting the ideas surrounding "justice" form an underlying motif. See Meridor (1978).

[117] Gregory (1999) 168; on divine punishment, Gregory has argued for a reading of the role of the winds as being a phenomenon of divine presence – they appear only after Polyxena's sacrifice implying divine displeasure and only blow again after Hecuba's act of revenge, implying approval (xxix-xxxi). Coo (2006) 107 discusses Achilles' supposed intervention of the winds and concludes that the hero must *not* be the cause of their disappearance, but does not go further in her analysis.

[118] As a personification Dikē is referred to at least twice more at 955 and 958; one further mention may be postulated at 1155.

[119] Again, a similar interpretation may be taken at 1169 when the chorus comments on Clytemnestra's death as the dispensation of justice: νέμει τοι δίκαν θεός, ὅταν τύχηι. It is not made explicit, but one can imagine an audience member as interpreting θεός as Zeus, especially considering the prayer made to the god at 671. See also Kells (1960) for a discussion of the cognate word δικάζειν and its importance throughout the tragedy.

specifically to the god here, it is nonetheless significant that the two share a common epithet, whose sense is also carried in a further mention in *Phoenissae*. Antigone, in response to Oedipus' wailing after he has been exiled, declares that Dikē does not suffer to see evil-doers go unpunished: τί τλάς, τί τλάς; οὐχ ὁρᾶι Δίκα κακοὺς / οὐδ' ἀμείβεται βροτῶν ἀσυνεσίας (*Phoen.* 1726-27). Dikē is not afforded an epithet as such here, but there is a strong indication that she is aware of all injustices and will not let them go by unnoticed. Although Zeus and Dikē are not explicitly connected through this statement, it nevertheless signposts the importance of Dikē in Zeus' world order in the plays of Euripides, at least as a personification.[120]

One further example underscores the inscrutability of precisely what the justice of Zeus' world order entails. In *Hippolytus*, when Theseus is informed that his son has suffered a fatal accident, he assumes that Hippolytus' death is an enactment of Dikē's wrath against him for dishonouring his father: εἰπέ, τῶι τρόπωι Δίκης / ἔπαισεν αὐτὸν ῥόπτρον αἰσχύναντά με; (*Hipp.* 1171-72). In fact, the death-curse cast upon Hippolytus by Theseus was an injustice and the apparent fulfilment of his call for justice an illusion. Theseus' curse served to satisfy a need for justice and a rebalancing of the cosmos of which he had no knowledge – the punishment of a violation of Zeus' cosmic order in Hippolytus' dishonouring of Aphrodite.

More explicit references to Zeus' justice (rather than Justice) occur in *Trojan Women* and *Heracles*, where a personified Dikē does not appear. Hecuba, in *Trojan Women* prays to Zeus just before the entrance of Menelaus and ends her invocation with what is probably one of the most positive affirmations of Zeus' justice to be found in

---

[120] As a concept *dikē* is also seen frequently throughout this play, appearing in thirteen other places (154, 452, 490, 492, 527, 548, 781, 1239, 1417, 1648, 1650, 1651 and 1654).

Euripides: πάντα γὰρ δι' ἀψόφου / βαίνων κελεύθου κατὰ δίκην τὰ θνήτ' ἄγεις (*TW* 887-88).[121] Lloyd's comments on this particular phrase by Hecuba are noteworthy:

> Her vision of the justice of Zeus is traditional, and her account of his silent tread resembles Solon's account of the movement of δίκη, but it more particularly resembles the views of some of the early philosophers and physical theorists who used hieratic language to describe their reductive versions of the divine. . . . Hecuba attributes impressive powers to Zeus to control human affairs in accordance with justice, and this means that some transcendent entity must be in question: she cannot, as is sometimes alleged, be expressing a view like that in fr. 1018 . . . where the existence of a transcendent deity, or at least its influence on human minds, is denied.[122]

There seems to be no doubt that for Hecuba at least, Zeus' justice is an integral part of the world. Amerasinghe would take this idea further and suggest that,

> We like to think of justice as operating through the exercise of human intelligence but in fact, says Euripides, it operates amongst us as a law almost of natural necessity. We are as much a part of nature as the elements and operate just as mechanically.[123]

While I would agree that Euripides is interrogating the relationship between Zeus and justice here, Hecuba's words do not immediately suggest that humans have no part in executing justice; for it is through mortals that Zeus and the other gods have a means of implementing it. Hecuba is hoping that Menelaus will be used for just such a purpose when he appears on stage and that through him (but because of Zeus) Helen will be punished.[124] That this does not transpire does not diminish the truth of Hecuba's words, it only suggests the fallibility of her comprehension of Zeus' justice.

---

[121] Gregory (1986) 6: "Her assumption that Zeus guides 'all mortal outcomes . . . according to justice' is hopeful and persuasive;" Croally (1994) 80: "Hecuba, at 887-8, seems to hold an exulted view of the goodness and the justice of the divine."

[122] Lloyd (1984) 310.

[123] Amerasinghe (1973) 104.

[124] Kovacs (1997) 174: "Her [Hecuba's] intervention ironically proves the truth of her statements about Zeus, for she fulfills Zeus' purposes in the very act of trying to thwart them."

On the other end of the scale one may place the view of Amphitryon in *Heracles*. Whereas Hecuba espoused a glorified vision of Zeus' justice, Amphitryon proffers one of the most negative views that can be found in the Euripidean corpus. Amphitryon first remarks on Zeus' "sense of justice" after Lycus has arrived and berated the old man about Heracles' supposed paternity and bravery. Amphitryon's response to the threats made by Lycus concerning the rest of Heracles' family is to claim that the tyrant deserves to be put to death if Zeus were just: εἰ Ζεὺς δικαίας εἶχεν εἰς ἡμᾶς φρένας (*Her.* 212). At this point in the play, there is no suggestion that Zeus has done anything thus far to aid Amphitryon and the rest of Heracles' family (they are still taking refuge at the altar of Zeus); however, Euripides is planting the seed for the future slaying of Lycus. Zeus *is* in fact just toward Amphitryon and he *does* send Heracles to rescue his family and kill the usurper. Zeus will answer this prayer, although it will eventually be to the detriment of Megara and her sons. Although this reference does nothing to guarantee (or hamper) the moral supremacy of the god, it does create the opportunity for the god to validate his righteousness.

It is Amphitryon's second admonition of Zeus' justice that has created the most discussion with respect to this question, for the old man's rebuke of the god is rather pointed and contemptuous:

> σὺ δ' ἦσθ' ἄρ' ἥσσον ἢ 'δόκεις εἶναι φίλος.
> ἀρετῆι σε νικῶ θνητὸς ὢν θεὸν μέγαν·
> παῖδας γὰρ οὐ προύδωκα τοὺς Ἡρακλέους.
> ....
> ἀμαθής τις εἶ θεὸς ἢ δίκαιος οὐκ ἔφυς (*Her.* 341-43, 347).

Amphitryon is making a moral judgement on the god's behaviour and Barlow notes that "humans emerge morally superior to the gods and Amphitryon in particular is superior to

Zeus in his loyalty to friends and family."[125] This type of personal attack on Zeus is surprising, for while it is not unusual for individual gods, or the gods in general, to be criticized, assaults on Zeus are uncommon and would almost necessitate immediate action on the god's part.[126] Gregory also notes that Amphitryon "seems in fact to be engaged in a perpetual and one-sided rivalry with Zeus; at every point he measures his own conduct against the god's and finds Zeus wanting."[127] Amphitryon is applying his own values to Zeus and believes that he is himself morally superior to the god because of them. Amphitryon's further comment about Zeus being either ἀμαθής or δίκαιος οὐκ suggests that he believes Zeus does not understand the gravity of his present situation, or that he simply does not care, implicating not only the mythological Zeus as father of Heracles, but also the cultic Zeus at whose altar he is supplicating.

It is clear that Euripides has an interest in examining the relationship between the justice of the gods, particularly that of Zeus and that of mortals; in the world of each play some form of justice is served, but it is according to Zeus' law. It is also clear that in most cases, while the characters do not fully comprehend the nature of the god's justice, they do believe in its efficacy and necessity. Even when Amphitryon decries the supposed unjust nature of Zeus, it is a statement made from utter desperation and one whose validity is ultimately undermined. It is precisely this apparent discrepancy between divine and human law which Euripides is scrutinizing and which makes his plays so tragic.

Justice Repaid: Themis and Pietas

The relationship between divine and human law receives its most extensive examination in *Medea*. Here, Zeus is very clearly associated not only with justice, but also

---

[125] Barlow (1996) 138.

[126] Barlow (1996) 138; see also Bond (1981) 144.

[127] Gregory (1977) 261-62.

with law and in very human terms. Euripides makes this connection even more complex, however, by introducing Dikē's mother, Themis, into the equation. As the female progenitor of Justice, as well as the goddess of wise counsel and divine law (Pind. *Ol.* 13.9-11), Themis represents the institution of Zeus' laws and is the convenor of councils for both gods and men (Hom. *Il.* 15.93-97; *Od.* 2.68-69). This goddess' importance in *Medea* lies within her close relationship to Zeus and the invocations made to her by Medea.[128]

The first appeal to the goddess is made in conjunction with Artemis when Medea asks the two deities to witness how Jason broke his oaths (160); the Nurse immediately reiterates this sentiment and refers again to Themis, this time in conjunction with Zeus, as one who oversees oaths:

> κλύεθ' οἷα λέγει κἀπιβοᾶται
> Θέμιν εὐκταίαν Ζῆνά θ', ὃς ὅρκων
> θνητοῖς ταμίας νενόμισται; (*Med.* 168-70).[129]

Both Themis and Zeus are named explicitly in the context of keeping one's oaths and, although this particular phrase reveals little about Zeus specifically, it does emphasize the relationship between the two deities. Zeus and Themis are assumed to be working together in order to ensure any impieties against the gods, here specifically oaths taken in their name, are punished.

---

[128] That there is a prayer to the goddess at all is uncommon in extant tragedy; only in *Eumenides* (2) is there another invocation made to her and in that play by the Pythia.

[129] Scholars have been divided over the apparent discrepancy between Medea's initial invocation to Themis and Artemis at 160 and the Nurse's response referring to Themis and Zeus. As it seems certain from ancient scholiasts that Zeus was not mentioned in Medea's cry at 160 but was invoked at 169, I am only concerned with the Nurse's response which includes Zeus. Walton (1949) and Willink (2003) provide synopses of the suggested emendations given by ancient and modern scholars.

Themis is not generally understood as a guardian of oaths, but by bringing Themis and Zeus together in this way, Euripides reinforces the implicit relationship between the laws ordained by men and the laws ordained by the gods. The course of events in the play is thus to be seen under the jurisdiction of both sets of law even though Medea's chosen mode of revenge will ultimately be a breach of both. There is also no immediate sense at the end of the play that Medea will be prosecuted for her actions: the only penalties are the knowledge (and guilt) she has of her actions and the infamy she gains as a filicide.[130] One would like to believe that the gods do not condone the murder of Medea's children and, indeed, it is expressly noted that the "sacrifice" of her children is not *themis* (1054); but Helios sends Medea her much-needed mode of escape and Themis and Zeus seem to be the instigators of the entire episode.[131] Themis was the one to have brought Medea to Corinth in the first place (209-12), presumably with the support of Zeus. But if Medea's actions are against the will of Themis, why does she succeed in her plans and receive no punishment?

One possible explanation for this may reside in the reference to Themis as Zeus' daughter. Immediately before Medea appears onstage for the first time, the chorus stress how Medea is calling upon the gods, specifically Themis as a goddess of oaths and as a daughter of Zeus: θεοκλυτεῖ δ' ἄδικα παθοῦσα / τὰν Ζηνὸς ὁρκίαν Θέμιν . . . (*Med.* 208-09).[132] If Themis is understood as the offspring of Zeus in this play, her authority and realm of influence would likely be placed under that of Zeus. In support of this view is the

---

[130] As Barlow (1989) 170 notes, "Medea may escape physically unpunished at the end, but there is irony because the mental and emotional punishment she has inflicted on herself more than counterbalances this apparent freedom."

[131] Foley (1989) 65.

[132] Referring to Themis as a daughter of Zeus also appears in Aeschylus' *Suppliants* (360), although Friis Johansen and Whittle (1980) have hesitated to take the genitive, without any specific word for child/daughter, to mean anything more than helper or agent, Mastronarde (2002b) 204.

later reference to Dikē as belonging to Zeus (*Med.* 764 and discussed above, p. 61-62); there is no specific word there for daughter, but it is assumed that such is meant. If Themis is also considered here to be a daughter of Zeus, she is thus on "equal footing" with Dikē and both are products of Zeus' will, creating an even stronger image of justice and divine law working together in the play and ultimately originating from Zeus.[133]

Aside from the various references to the personification Themis, Medea is also very conscious of her actions and whether or not they are *themis*: during the conversation between Medea and Aegeus when he is explaining the reason for his journey to the oracle and its reply, Medea asks if it is *themis* to know his purpose (676) and whether it is *themis* to know the oracle's answer (678). As Aegeus provides answers to both of these questions, it is obvious that Medea understands the importance of *themis* and, while the goddess is not being referred to here, the phrasing works as a reminder of the earlier invocations to her. The final reference to *themis* occurs immediately before the slaughter of Medea's children when, as a mother, she realizes that this action would offend both *themis* and Themis; she thus requests those who should not see such an act to leave (1054).[134] The goddess, until this point, has supported Medea in her quest for revenge, but will do so no further. Because Themis is understood in this play to be subordinate to Zeus, Medea is still acting under his guidance when she kills her sons and the act can still be considered god-ordained.

---

[133] Wildberg (1999) 241 offers the term *hyperesia* as one potential avenue of interpretation for Medea's acts of filicide: "What we encounter as dramatic subtext in this play, too, is the concept of 'piety as hyperesia,' that is to say of a willing and active service rendered to the gods and the moral code they stand for—irrespective of the crushing magnitude of the immediate consequences."

[134] Reinforcing the fact the Medea understands the concept of the "holy eye" discussed in the previous chapter and that she does not want to pollute the vision of those who have supported her.

That Zeus supports Medea can be inferred from the references to his potential role as Medea's advocate. At the beginning of the play, the chorus acknowledges Medea's right to be angry with Jason, but encourage her to leave the revenge up to the god who will act on her behalf:

εἰ δὲ σὸς πόσις καινὰ λέχη σεβίζει,
κείνωι τόδε μὴ χαράσσου·
Ζεύς σοι τάδε συνδικήσει (*Med.* 155-57).

According to Mastronarde, συνδικεῖν "is a technical legal term for the action of a third party who assists in a court case by delivering a supporting speech."[135] Here, the chorus urges Medea to let Zeus take action on her behalf; because of Jason's broken oaths, she has the support of the gods and Zeus will assume the role of σύνδικος in order to aid her in achieving justice. If we are to read Zeus' involvement in the play in this light, not only is it more likely that Medea will be successful in her revenge, but it also places the situation in a highly legal context.[136] This dispute will not stay private, but will become a matter of public interest and the chorus' identification of Zeus with law is significant. They have been persuaded to believe that Jason broke an oath to Medea[137] and thus are certain that Zeus will ensure Jason's punishment. When viewed from this perspective, Zeus is seen to be intimately connected with human justice and law and his association specifically as one

---

[135] Mastronarde (2002b) 197. He provides the example of Apollo at Orestes' trial in the *Eumenides* as someone fulfilling this role; however, although the word is used by Aeschylus, it does not refer to Apollo, but rather to Clytemnestra's supporters.

[136] See Luschnig (2001) 22-23.

[137] On the subject of oaths in *Medea* see: Burnett (1973) 12-14, Vickers (1973) 282-86, Flory (1978), Cowherd (1983), Schein (1990), Boedeker (1991) 95-96; Kovacs (1993); McClure (1999), Allan (2002), Fletcher (2003) 32-36, Holland (2003). Bowman (2002) 159-160 discusses Jason and Medea's "marriage" in terms of contemporary Athenian laws and notes that any oaths sworn to Medea by Jason would not be valid regardless of their nature. See Allan (2007) for a more recent discussion which argues against interpreting Jason's promise to Medea as a traditional oath.

who will be a σύνδικος (advocate/witness) for Medea brings the god a degree closer to the action than would otherwise be assumed. The cumulative effect of these references, evocative of justice and law, reinforces the real interest Euripides has in exploring what Zeus' justice means for the world of men. That Medea is both supported by Zeus, but ultimately abandoned by Themis, reveals the understanding of the poet of how blurred and ambiguous the definition of "justice" really was, for both gods and mortals.[138]

With no exact "equivalent" for Themis in Roman society, there is no real opportunity for comparison with Seneca's vision of Jupiter's relationship with this personification (at least in the tragic corpus). There is, however, one invocation to Pietas, whose identity is at least notionally similar to that of Themis. For the Romans, the goddess Pietas embodied reverence and justice for the gods (Cic. *ND* 1.116) and had received cult worship and even a temple since the Republic (Livy 40.34.4). In *Phaedra* Pietas is invoked by Theseus after Phaedra has informed him of Hippolytus' supposed "sin," and he wonders from whence the plague of the Amazons came:

> Pro sancta Pietas, pro gubernator poli
> et qui secundum fluctibus regnum moves,
> unde ista venit generis infandi lues? (*Phaed.* 903-05)[139]

Appealing to these three particular deities (Pietas, Jupiter and Neptune) in this way is novel and throughout the tragedy there seems to be little consistency in the construction of invocations, although each one attempts to reaffirm Jupiter's supremacy in the cosmos.

---

[138] Kovacs (1993) 69 comments that "the gods' rough justice rules the world, that the impious are punished – though sometimes by means of a criminal act far more ghastly than the offense – and that the confident expectations of blind mortals are often defeated."

[139] Theseus' concern about the origins of the Amazon women, although narrower in focus, is very similar to the view expressed by his son concerning the origins of the female race more widely. Theseus, however, couches his distress in a more religious fashion, suggesting that the Amazons as a race violate the natural laws of the entire world (symbolically expressed through the dual invocation of Jupiter and Neptune) and are opposed to the virtue espoused by Pietas.

What is significant here is the order of Theseus' invocation: Jupiter is placed second to Pietas, which does not conform to standard Roman formalities when addressing the gods.[140] The close juxtaposition, however, reaffirms the close ties between Pietas and Jupiter and her necessity in maintaining cosmic balance in both his realm and that of Neptune. Later in the speech Theseus refers to *pietas* once more (and incidentally the only other instance of the word in the play) remarking that those who appear pious are masking their immorality (921). Theseus, of course, does not realize how true his words are and yet how misdirected. By having Theseus call upon Pietas first, Seneca suggests that piety is an important motif throughout the play but that it is neglected everywhere else in favour of *nefandum*.[141] The neglect of such a seemingly important deity suggests a reason for the disturbance to the cosmic balance.

Pietas as a personification is mentioned in one other play, although not by means of any invocation. In *Thyestes*, as Atreus contemplates his revenge against his brother Thyestes, his assistant wonders whether the tyrant is not moved at all by piety. Instead, the *satelles* receives a very negative response, for Atreus deems the goddess' presence to be unwelcome: *Excede, Pietas, si modo in nostra domo / umquam fuisti* (249-50). Not only does Atreus not wish to consider or be moved by Pietas, he expressly demands her departure from his abode.[142] It is perhaps unsurprising in a tragedy as dark as *Thyestes* that

---

[140] Roman deities are often addressed in hierarchical order (with the exception of Janus as god of beginnings); thus, Jupiter and Neptune should both have preceded the invocation of Pietas.

[141] Sacerdoti (2008) 286-87, although discussing similar thematic interests between Seneca's *Phaedra* and Statius' *Thebaid*, notes that the idea of "universal *nefas*" is "clearly expressed" within Seneca's *Phaedra*.

[142] Association of Pietas with the emperor was commonplace during the early empire (as attested by the regular usage of her image on Imperial coinage, see Ulrich [1930]). But Manders (2012) 178 observes, "*pietas* can be described as a course of practices characterized by a sense of duty, devotion, and piety aimed at benefiting gods, people (mainly family), and homeland, and, during the Empire, the emperor. The emperor himself did thus not only express *pietas* himself, he was

Pietas would be forced to abandon the world of the play. Her relationship to Jupiter is not mentioned in this context, or at all throughout the drama, but it is apparent that her absence from earth signifies an imbalance in the world and portends problems in maintaining order[143] – problems which are rampant for Jupiter in this particular play.

Pietas and Jupiter are clearly linked in Seneca, although their relationship seems to differ from that of Themis and Zeus, at least in specific details. The absence of Pietas poses problems for Jupiter, for without her influence, his ability to rule effectively can be called into question; the same does not appear to be true for Themis and Zeus. Themis may also choose to abandon a particular mortal, as in the case of Medea, but this has no effect on Zeus' will or his authority. While these differences may be attributed to their slightly different realms of interest, it is nonetheless significant both that Jupiter appears to rely more heavily on other deities to maintain his control as well as the subtle hint that his control could be hampered in any way. The implications of such differences emerge more clearly when considering those deities whom both Jupiter and Zeus "employ" to dispense punishment on mortals.

Spirits of Vengeance: Erinyes and Furies

The Erinyes (Alecto, Megaera and Tisiphone) are the embodiment of blood-vengeance, goddesses who hound and exact retribution from those who have committed crimes against their kin. Most famously, they appear in Aeschylus' *Eumenides* as the

---

also its object." Atreus' vehement rejection of Pietas in *Thyestes* signals not only a moral deficiency, but would also have resonated with an audience who would expect a tyrant-emperor to maintain at least a political association with such a goddess.

[143] Although the chorus imagines a victory of Pietas in the third choral ode with the help of Mars (557-59), "when their words are juxtaposed with the realities of this play, what they offer as fact proves little more than pious hope," Davis (1989) 430. Pietas has indeed left the world of the play.

chorus, pursuing Orestes until he is acquitted at a tribunal. In an extensive examination of the Furies (their Roman equivalent), Gilder sums up the Erinyes' role in Greek literature before their transformation in later Roman works:

> the one lasting legacy of *The Eumenides* seems to be that the Erinyes in Greek literature finally recognize that their place is under Zeus' power, not against it, and that they are part of an order he rules. Along with that recognition is the uneasy feeling that the Erinyes still retain a power greater than their ruler's.[144]

This tension between Zeus and the Erinyes, underscored by Gilder, deserves attention. Gilder does not discuss the presence of the Erinyes in Euripides, but he does note the inter-changeability of their names with Eumenides, Semnai and Keires and he emphasizes how this "strengthens" their power.[145] The Erinyes' relationship to Zeus is not made explicit in any of Euripides' plays, but their description as goddesses seems to follow previous conventions. They do, for example, avenge the shedding of kindred blood (*El.* 1252, *IT* 79, *Her.* 1077); they cause madness (*Or.* 238, *IT* 299, as Poinai at *Her.* 886); they hate peace (as Poinai, *Supp.* 488-90); and they dwell in Tartarus (as Keires, *Her.* 870). An Erinys is also often said to belong to a wronged family member as in the Erinys of Oedipus (*Phoen.* 624, *Supp.* 836), Clytemnestra (*Or.* 255-56) and Agamemnon (*Or.* 582). Finally, there are a few examples of characters likened to the Erinyes, as if they embody their spirit of vengeance and/or destruction: Medea (*Med.* 1258-60, discussed below, p. 79), Cassandra (*Tr.* 457), Electra (*Or.* 264), Helen (*Or.* 1389) and the Sphinx (*Phoen.* 1029).

Zeus' relationship to the Erinyes emerges more clearly from specific references in *Electra, Medea* and *Heracles*. During the epiphany of the Dioscuri in *Electra*, Castor announces that it is fated that Orestes be hounded by the Erinyes as proclaimed by Zeus:

---

[144] Gilder (1997) 14.

[145] Gilder (1997) 13-14: "Euripides reappropriates every beneficent title in the name of the avenging Erinyes. Semnai and Eumenides become synonymous with Erinyes. Indeed, Euripides strengthens them, openly combing the Keires of Hesiod's *Theogony*, with the Erinyes."

αἰνεῖν δ' ἀνάγκη ταῦτα· τἀντεῦθεν δὲ χρὴ
πράσσειν ἃ Μοῖρα Ζεύς τ' ἔκρανε σοῦ πέρι.

....

δειναὶ δὲ Κῆρές <σ'> αἱ κυνώπιδες θεαὶ
τροχηλατήσουσ' ἐμμανῆ πλανώμενον (*El.* 1247-48, 1252-53).

Thus, according to the Dioscuri, Zeus lies behind the traditional role of the Erinyes in Orestes' story. From this perspective, it appears as though the Erinyes are clearly working as part of Zeus' world order; whether or not their power is as great as or greater than the god's is not an issue, nor is their activity as Zeus' agents or adversaries raised. When Orestes questions Castor as to why, as family, he is not preventing the Erinyes from pursuing him, Castor repeats that Fate, Necessity and the oracle of Apollo contrived to bring these events about (1301-02).[146] Castor does not mention Zeus here, but it is unnecessary as he had earlier stated this was Zeus' intention and furthermore, Apollo's oracles imply Zeus' implicit consent. In this play at least, Zeus appears to be using the Erinyes to further his own agenda and the Erinyes seem to be entirely subject to Zeus' will.

This power dynamic might be contrasted to that found in *Orestes*. When Orestes is beset by the Erinyes at the beginning of play, he indicates that he has a special bow, given to him by Apollo, with which to defend himself against harm (*Or.* 268-71). What is different about the Erinyes in *Orestes* is that they are specified as priestesses of the chthonic realm (ἐνέρων ἱέρεαι, 261). No mention is made of Zeus, but the need for a special weapon to protect Orestes alongside their ambiguous chthonic status suggests they may have a stronger "power" than those in *Electra*: it is not obvious they are acting on Zeus' order and it seems they could endanger Orestes were it not for the intervention of Apollo. It is made clear at the end of the play that Orestes is fated to win the vote at the Areopagus, but as judged by a council of gods, rather than a council of men (*Or.* 1650),

---

[146] A similar scenario is found in *IT*, when Athena announces that Apollo's oracles also foretold that Orestes would be hounded by the Erinyes (1438-41).

and to marry Hermione (1653-54). Thus, while the Erinyes may be fulfilling their allotted role, they seem to be taking it too far and it will take the cumulative authority of the gods themselves in order to defeat them, rather than a panel of mere *mortal* judges (with only Athena's vote necessary).

This tension found in *Orestes* may also be signalled by the references in both *Medea* and *Heracles*. There are two references to Erinyes in *Medea* and, although they are clearly connected to each other dramatically, they are also referring to very different concepts of an Erinys. These goddesses are first introduced by the chorus when they call upon Zeus to act in opposition to Medea. Immediately before Medea kills her sons the chorus appeals to the "light of Zeus" to stop Medea:

> ἀλλά νιν, ὦ φάος διογενές, κάτειρ-
> γε κατάπαυσον ἔξελ' οἴκων τάλαι-
> ναν φονίαν τ' Ἐρινὺν †ὑπ' ἀλαστόρων† (*Med.* 1258-60).

The chorus believes that the murder of Medea's children must be inspired by the Erinyes[147] and thus believes that Medea is acting as one of them. This is important for two reasons: first, if the chorus is right in their assessment and Medea is acting as though an Erinys, it would follow that the children's deaths are a punishment divined by the gods for a breach of one of Zeus' laws; Zeus would therefore not heed the prayer of the chorus to hinder her actions (which is, in fact, what transpires). Secondly, the involvement of the Erinyes implies that the offence committed was either against kin or involved blood-guilt, but does not rule out either Jason or Medea as the guilty party. Jason is implicated by his broken oath (necessitating the punishment of *exōleia*, an elimination of one's family[148]) and Medea has incurred blood-guilt in killing her brother (instigating a cycle of familial bloodshed); thus, the death of the children is a form of punishment that can be applied to

---

[147] Kovacs (2001) 397.

[148] Kovacs (1993) 59-60.

both parties.[149]

Jason, of course, does not believe he should have incurred any wrath and later calls upon the Erinyes of his children to avenge their own deaths (1389), which is the second important reference. Medea was initially likened to an Erinys, the one carrying out the punishment, but here Jason wishes her to be their prey. Medea, in embodying both the instrument of retribution and the one deserving of retribution, can only escape by the intervention of the gods, much like Orestes. In her case, salvation lies with her grandfather Helios, who intervenes to ensure her safe retreat from Corinth. When the chorus earlier called upon Zeus' light to stop Medea (which did not happen), they also asked that she be removed from the city, a wish that was eventually granted. Although it is by no means clear that the chorus was referring to Helios in their prayer, it is nonetheless intriguing that that particular prayer was granted in the manner that it was; the Erinyes clearly have a role to play, but without the intervention of Zeus, it seems their notion of justice, or revenge, would be a perpetual cycle of vengeance with no end in sight.[150]

One other reference which may shed light on the relationship between Zeus and the Erinyes is found in *Heracles*. After Lyssa has induced Heracles to madness and he has slain his children, the chorus call out to Zeus that Heracles will be ruined and childless because of spirits of vengeance:

ἰὼ Ζεῦ, τὸ σὸν γένος ἄγονον αὐτίκα
λυσσάδες ὠμοβρῶτες ἄδικοι Ποιναὶ
κακοῖσιν ἐκπετάσουσιν (*Her*. 886-87).

---

[149] This is to say nothing about the psychological effects of such a crime, which would inevitably be a punishment in and of themselves.

[150] The fratricide in *Phoenissae* is another example of the perpetual cycle of vengeance enacted by the Erinyes (1306) and in this instance it is even made clear that this is what they desire: the deaths of Jocasta, Eteocles and Polynices are considered "victories" (χάρματα, 1503) by the Erinyes.

Here personified as Poinai, these spirits of vengeance are blamed by the chorus for Heracles' actions and present misery, but their presence seems unjustified if they are exacting retribution for a familial crime, which is their usual prerogative.[151] What makes this situation even more complicated is that Lyssa, whose orders for inciting this crime came from Hera (855), was also reluctant to carry them out (858). Iris states that Hera's revenge is directed against Heracles (not Zeus, 840), but there is no evidence of Heracles himself committing any crime against his step-mother. There should not, then, be any spirit of vengeance plaguing the hero until after he has killed his children, but these very spirits vanish only when this killing is carried out.

The only familial crime committed and mentioned in the play is Amphitryon's murder of Alcmene's father (16). It is possible that the Poinai are visiting Heracles in place of his father, as Heracles made an offer to Eurystheus to expiate Amphitryon's crime (19). Thus, the Poinai would be taking the lives of Heracles' children in recompense for Electryon's death and not for any action Heracles himself has taken. This reading would at least allow the Poinai to remain operating within the laws set out by Zeus and under his authority; however, the intervention of Hera to beset the hero by these spirits and Lyssa's disinclination to see him harried by them suggests a rather different dynamic. Unless this is merely a case of "divine non-interference," the Poinai can be called to action by other deities for their own purposes rather than acting solely on their own auspices.[152] The cry to Zeus (886) might then be suggestive of a slight opposition between the god and these deities, or at least an assumption on the part of the chorus of his disapproval. The tension

---

[151] Visser (1984) 202 suggests that Poinai should be differentiated from the Erinyes in that the former avenge only family crimes, whereas the latter have a "civic responsibility." She does not, however, suggest their relationship to Zeus should be seen any differently.

[152] This may be corroborated by a reference in *Phoenissae* where the chorus sing of Ares bringing the Erinyes to Eteocles and Polynices (253-55).

that was underscored by Gilder is manifest in both *Medea* and *Heracles* and Euripides'
exploration of the nature of Zeus' relationship to these deities foreshadows quite well the
more sinister portrayals that are found in Seneca.

The Furies are mentioned frequently throughout Seneca's tragedies and, as in
Euripides, are called by various names: *Furia, Eumenides, Erinys, deae ultrices* and
squalidae sorores. In many ways they retain the same power they held in Greek literature,
for they are still vengeful goddesses of evil deeds (*Med.* 13), but they also seem to branch
out from merely hounding those who breached divine laws or shed kindred blood: the
chorus of *Agamemnon* sing of the Erinys who harries the arrogant (83) and attends the
houses of the excessive (84). While these qualities are not virtues, one might not expect to
be harassed by these terrible goddesses for exhibiting them. Gilder also sees Seneca's
Furies as "troubling,"

> because they reveal advanced powers not just over mortals, but divinities as
> well, including Jupiter and Juno. They appropriate formerly 'superal' [*sic*]
> attributes such as the power to direct the Fates; they lend power
> disconcertingly to superal gods who should not need such assistance; and
> they exhibit a fearful ability to drive away those superal powers at the point
> in the tragedy when the need for their presence is most acute.[153]

Three plays exhibit most clearly the relationship between these Furies and Jupiter:
Hercules Furens, Medea and *Thyestes,* the last of which presents a Fury on-stage, but in a
very different way than that of Aeschylus' *Eumenides*.

In *Hercules Furens,* Seneca takes the Euripidean idea of Hera mobilizing the
Erinyes to harass Heracles to the next level. Not only does Seneca remove the
intermediaries (Iris and Lyssa), but he brings Juno on-stage to elicit the aid of the Furies
and has the goddess open herself up to their furious energy, transforming her into another
pseudo-Fury. Juno makes it clear her anger is directed at her step-son for his supposed

---

[153] Gilder (1997) 54.

ambition to usurp Jupiter (65, discussed further in chapter 4, pp. 128-34) and for his triumph in completing the labours with which she tasked him (*HF* 58-63). When Juno decides that Hercules himself must become her weapon of victory, she rouses the Furies from Tartarus (86), calls them servants of Dis (*famulae Ditis*, 100) and invokes them to demand retribution for the violence committed against the Underworld (104). Gilder would interpret this invocation of the Furies as signifying her dependence on them to accomplish what she could not[154] and, indeed, they deliver precisely what Juno requests. While there is no specific mention of Jupiter's relationship to the Furies during Juno's monologue, two relevant points may be inferred. First, Juno makes it clear that the Furies are purely infernal beings belonging to Dis and not to Jupiter. The Erinyes of Euripides may also have resided in the Underworld, but they were under the authority of Zeus; here, control by Jupiter is less certain. Secondly, the power dynamic between Juno and the Furies is called into question. The goddess *requires* the aid of these deities in order to punish Hercules; she cannot do it with her own power alone, reinforcing Gilder's presumption that the invoked have more power than the invoker.[155] While it does not necessarily follow that the Furies have more power than Jupiter, they certainly outdo his sister's (1) and have the potential to rival his own.

Indeed, the Furies continue to rival Jupiter's power in *Medea*, whose title-character also invokes them in order to carry out revenge. Medea opens the play with a prayer addressed to the *di coniugales*, Lucina, Minerva, Neptune, Titan and Hecate (*Med.* 1-7); however, it quickly becomes apparent that she is not praying to these gods *for* anything, but rather to dismiss them with her words of ill-omen. Medea is speaking during the wedding of Jason and Creusa and it has been suggested that her invocation here is meant to

---

[154] Gilder (1997) 56.

[155] Gilder (1997) 55.

interrupt it with her *voce non fausta* (12).[156] Although she is not present herself at the wedding, in dramatic terms her words should be taken as a subversion of the ceremony. Medea is also not requesting that these gods take action against Jason, Creon or Creusa. It is at this point she prays instead to the Underworld deities to fulfil her wishes and for the Furies to be present again, as they were during her own wedding to Jason: *nunc, nunc adeste, sceleris ultrices deae* . . . (13-16). She asks them to grant death to Jason's new wife, father-in-law and any royal children (17-18). It would be expected that the Furies demand payment from Jason (but Medea reserves the punishment of life for him), but Creusa and her children are undeserving of this particular punishment (Creon's degree of guilt is open to interpretation). Medea's invocation of the Furies suggests that they not only avenge family crimes and blood-guilt, but that they are also inclined to be summoned for pure revenge (and Medea is granted precisely what she wishes for).

The Furies' relationship to Jupiter lies in Medea's opening words, where it is likely (but not certain) that he is invoked as one of the *di coniugales*, along with Juno[157] (although Venus and Hymenaeus have both been suggested).[158] As Medea does not call upon Jupiter elsewhere in her prayer, it most likely that he is meant as one of these marriage gods, for it would be unlikely that she would invoke these other deities and not the supreme god himself (and especially as oaths were involved). Because Medea calls upon Jupiter first and in his capacity as a god of marriage, she casts herself as a pious individual who wishes that her marriage pledges be protected and Hine suggests "this prayer powerfully expresses her feelings that her case is just."[159] There is nothing amiss in this prayer until she calls upon the deities of the Underworld; by invoking the Furies,

---

[156] Hine (1989) 414-15.

[157] Krill (1973) 199.

[158] Hine (2000) 111.

[159] Hine (2000) 165.

Medea has attempted to hinder Jason's wedding with words of ill-omen. This is Medea's first subtle dismissal of the gods: Jupiter and the other gods can no longer witness Jason's marriage with goodwill and, consequently, they will not take part in the ceremonies, even though the chorus will pray for just that (*Med.* 56-59). The Furies, although they can be summoned (and presumably dismissed) at will by mortals, are here being pitted against the gods, including Jupiter. As they once attended Medea's wedding, so they will attend Creusa's and the entire royal family will be at the mercy of these Underworld goddesses, while Jupiter and the other gods can do nothing to prevent it.

Medea, in a similar manner to that of Juno in *Hercules Furens*,[160] also opens herself to the will of the Furies and even takes on some of their features. When the Nurse is relating to the chorus all of Medea's actions and preparations for her departure, she notes that she has witnessed Medea *furentem saepe et aggressam deos, / caelum trahentem* (*Med.* 673-74). Medea is likened to a Fury who openly attacks the gods and brings the heavens down to her. More overtly, when Medea decides to kill her children in the manner of Tantalus, she witnesses the Furies' presence and willingly invites them to penetrate her body (965-66). It is made clear that the Furies are present because of Medea's fratricide and Medea recognizes that the slaughter of her first child is made in recompense for the murder of her brother.[161] Once again the image of a Fury being both a punisher and a punishment emerges. The absence of Jupiter may not have been cause for comment here, but in light of Medea's opening prayer dismissing the upper gods, including Jupiter, it is clear that her doubt in their ability to exact revenge was valid. The Furies may still be upholding their traditional role as avengers of familial crime, but their authority to do so no longer seems to be regulated by Jupiter.

---

[160] See Walsh (2011) 100-116 for an extended discussion of their similarities.

[161] Guastella (2001) 199.

The most explicit demonstration of this polarity of power is found in the opening of *Thyestes*. The play opens with a Fury (*Furia*) coercing the shade of Tantalus to do her bidding and wreak havoc upon his descendants. The Fury regales her audience with her vision of the manner in which his house (i.e. the Tantalid line) should exist and some of her statements are worth particular attention: *et fas et fides / iusque omne pereat* (*Thy.* 47-48a); *non sit a vestris malis / immune caelum* (48-49); *nox alia fiat, excidat caelo dies* (51). While one may fervently hope that these ideas of the Fury do not eventuate, and Tantalus tries in vain to hinder their fruition, there is no doubt that each of them will be realized. Not only is the Fury dictating how the descendants of Tantalus will live, but her ability to destroy this house has implications for the gods as well.[162] The evil about to be unleashed upon the world will affect the *caelum* and the sun will leave the sky – she is clearly intending to disturb Jupiter's natural order and cosmos.

Tantalus' response to the insistence of the Fury to carry out her orders is to call upon Jupiter for aid, even though he is currently in the realm of Dis: *magne divorum parens / nosterque* (*quamvis pudeat*) (90-91). He rejects the Fury's wishes to inflict madness on his descendants and calls upon Jupiter in distress, only remembering afterwards that he was punished by Jupiter for being too talkative (91-93).[163] Tantalus declares, however, that he will not stay silent about this treatment from the Fury either, apparently willing to be punished again for the same crime. He is suggesting that he would rather be tortured by Jupiter for having an "unchecked tongue" than by this Fury, for her punishment is much worse. Furthermore, Tantalus is asserting that he does not fear

---

[162] Rose (1987) 117 comments that the Fury's "catalogue of evils . . . reveals that what interested the poet in the myth was the cycle of crime and revenge perpetrated in the struggle for royal power." Although her statement is in response to the struggle between Atreus and Thyestes on the mortal plane, it is a sentiment that is equally apt for the battle between the Fury and Jupiter on the immortal plane.

[163] Cf. Diod. Sic. 4.74.

Jupiter's wrath, or at least that such fear is no deterrent. This is one of many examples throughout the play of one evil being considered good when faced with something even worse.[164] This polarization between Jupiter and the Fury is significant, for the god's initial introduction in the play suggests that his authority and power have been diminished by this infernal deity, which is further illustrated by the fact that whereas Jupiter was unable to silence Tantalus before, the Fury is now finally able to do just that.

Seneca's choice of phrasing also serves to highlight some other aspects of Jupiter's representation in the drama. The title and epithet, *magne divorum parens nosterque* (*Thy.* 90), at first seems to accord with the traditional name given to Jupiter (or Zeus) as "Father of Gods," which is normally followed by "and Men." The substitution of *nosterque* for *hominumque* is no accident. *Nosterque* could be taken in one of two ways: either as a reference to Tantalus himself, as a son of Jupiter and head of this mortal family line,[165] or as a straight plural, referring to Jupiter as a father of evils, for Tantalus is one of the *exempla* of those in Tartarus, punished for his sins. Such an implication is strengthened by Tantalus' qualifying statement: *quamvis pudeat* (91). Thus, not only is Jupiter father of the heavenly deities, but a father of the "lowest" forms of men – a disturbing initial image of Jupiter and one which does not sit well with what is expected.

The second observation to be made is that Jupiter is called *parens* here rather than *pater*.[166] Although they are metrically equivalent and the basic meaning of each is the same, the latter is more specific, emphasizing as it does the generative relationship of the male parent to his offspring. Jupiter *pater* is the "father" and "begetter" of his offspring. *Parens*, by comparison, can also refer to a female parent in addition to their role as a

---

[164] Meltzer (1988) 318.

[165] Fitch (2004) 237; Tarrant (1985) 101.

[166] References to Jupiter with either form occur only in half of the Senecan corpus (excluding the *HO* and the *Octavia*).

progenitor.[167] Jupiter as *parens*, apart from this single instance in *Thyestes*, occurs only in *Hercules Furens* (264, 517, 598, 1054),[168] although the use of *pater* in the latter play occurs almost twice as often. The specific use of *parens* by Tantalus here would suggest Seneca is employing this descriptor of Jupiter for a particular purpose. At Rome, one of the Emperor's titles is *pater patriae* and he is, of course, the representative of Jupiter on earth. This specific association between Emperor and deity is likely being scrutinized by Seneca in this scene. By introducing Jupiter as *divorum parens*, Seneca is distancing Jupiter from the Emperor (rather than highlighting their relationship, which would have been accomplished through the use of *divorum pater*) and therefore, as above, also from the human race in general. One may be tempted to see this phrase as an attempt to place Jupiter in a hierarchy above the Emperor; however, in consideration of the play's context, it is more likely that Seneca is using this less specific word to weaken the god's protective persona. Emperors were initially given the title of *pater* because of their duty in caring for Rome and because they were seen as a *paterfamilias* to all Romans. Instead, Seneca undermines the association of these ideas, for Jupiter, as *parens*, is merely seen as a begetter of Tantalus and his descendants, rather than a caring and dutiful parent.

One further point of significance may be found in Tantalus' use of the adjective *magne*. The most important aspect of Jupiter in cult in contemporary Rome was that of *Optimus Maximus*. It would have seemed more appropriate for Tantalus to have used *summe* here to grant Jupiter his rightful title, as he later does (*Thy*. 1077),[169] but instead of being considered the "greatest," Jupiter is merely "great" suggesting that the god's authority is being usurped and he is no longer to be seen as the ultimate authority. Comparisons with other uses of *magnus* in Seneca's tragic corpus reveal that most often

---

[167] Saller (1999) 185.

[168] In *Agamemnon*, it is Priam who is referred to as a *magne parens* (655).

[169] But which comes to naught.

the adjective is used in a negative sense: whatever noun *magnus* is describing will either be overcome or succumb to something *maior*.[170] Jupiter too, as *magne*, will not be great enough to overcome the *scelera* of the Tantalid family. Indeed, when Atreus invites the Furies to enter his home (in place of Pietas), he wishes to be filled with *maiore monstro* (254). Jupiter is not, and will not be, powerful enough to overcome the will of the Fury. Thus, not only do the Fury's own words (47-51) provide the basis for the opposition between the god and this Underworld power, Thyestes words too, although meant by him to glorify Jupiter, only serve to highlight the disparity between the two opposing immortals.

Concluding Remarks

Contrary to the view presented by Lloyd-Jones, Euripides does indeed include portrayals of Zeus' justice within his plays: he is concerned with presenting both Justice, personified by Dikē, and concepts of justice in relation to what is considered *themis* (and Themis) or violates divine and humans laws to the extent that pursuers of justice, the Erinyes, must become involved. Zeus and Dikē are clearly presented by Euripides as being closely connected to each other

Euripides illustrates in his *Medea* that Zeus and Dikē are a pair; they work together to ensure that their divine laws are upheld. But Euripides also emphasizes how difficult it is for humans to comprehend their justice, not necessarily because it is at odds with human justice, but because mortals need to have a moral code to abide by. Zeus and Dikē represent this moral code, but being divine, they are also unwavering. Jason both wants Zeus and Dikē to exact vengeance on Medea for her acts against himself and his children,

---

[170] Poe (1969) 363 notes the importance of comparative adjectives in this play, especially *magno*, *maiore* and *satis*. Such comparisons also tie into another theme of the play – hunger and appetite; see Boyle (1983) *passim*.

but it is the same justice that exacted vengeance on him in the first place. Zeus (and Dikē) sees all and because of that, his justice is not one-sided. Humans do not enjoy that privilege and so can only often see one side of his justice being implemented.

It is this misunderstanding, or perhaps fallibility, on the part of mortals that Euripides exploits in order to examine this relationship between the god and his working out of "justice." Even when he is discussing dikē, rather than the personification, Euripides is still concerned with illustrating both the close connection that Zeus has with justice and the expectation on the part of mortals that he will execute it accordingly. Both Hecuba in *Trojan Women* and Amphitryon in *Heracles* assume that in one way or another Zeus should be equated with justice.

Zeus is also shown to be particularly close to Themis and in *Medea*, perhaps even thought to be her father rather than her husband. Such a depiction inevitably leads to the suggestion that law is a product of Zeus, just as justice is a product of Zeus. And this law is both divine and human, for Themis is also associated heavily with the customs and laws of the mortal world. But in *Medea* she is also a guardian of oaths, tying her even more closely to both Zeus and the world of men. Themis almost becomes a link between the laws of heaven and the laws of humans, ensuring that Zeus' will and his laws are obeyed and only faltering with Medea's actions. Themis does not condone the heroine's actions, but rather leaves the ultimate judgement to Zeus.

Such a depiction of subordination is not at all what appears in Seneca's *Thyestes*. Although the comparison may not be precise in that the Roman goddess Pietas is similar to, but perhaps not quite the same as, Themis it is fair to suggest that the disappearance of Pietas which leads to cosmic unbalance is an image that would likely be very unfamiliar to Euripides. The disappearance of Themis only leaves Zeus to judge Medea or not; there is no sense that his authority or the cosmos has been damaged or is at risk. In *Thyestes* this is precisely the result of Pietas' exit from the world of the play. Jupiter's ability to maintain control of the cosmos is clearly diminished and the cosmic world of the play will be very disturbed indeed.

Thus Seneca's treatment of justice in relation to Jupiter is drastically different from that of Euripides in relation to Zeus. Although he may rely on other gods and expect them to help him maintain control, Zeus is never shown to be at the complete mercy of his inferiors. Should Jupiter lose those he counts on for help, he is instantly at risk. His position at the apex of the divine hierarchy does not seem to be quite as permanent and safe as that of Zeus. This becomes most clear in the difference between Zeus' relationship with the Erinyes and Jupiter's with the Furies. Zeus' Erinyes are clearly part of the god's order and under his control. They may be dangerous, as evidenced by Apollo's gift of a bow to Orestes in his play as a way to ward them off, but they do not pose a threat to the divine order. They do seem more powerful in *Orestes*, for the vote to acquit Orestes will take all of the gods to win against them, but Zeus' order still prevails. Seneca's Jupiter has no such luck against the Fury, just one, in *Thyestes*. It is by her will that the shade of Tantalus infects the mortal realm and incites his descendant Atreus to new evils. It is by the Fury's will that the cosmos be disrupted; her power and her will are enough to make Jupiter and the other gods flee the heavens.

CHAPTER 3:
NATURE AND THE ELEMENTS

Intimately bound up with the notions of fate and justice explored in the previous chapters are Zeus and Jupiter's roles as the guarantors of the natural world: they ensure that the sun remains on course, the stars do not fall from the sky and the seasons maintain their pattern. While Euripides' comments are slight on Zeus' connection to nature, Seneca explores the specific relationship between Jupiter and the personification *Natura* in more detail in his *Phaedra*. It is in this play that these two deities become polarized and, in some ways, inverted. Jupiter remains in control of the cosmos but is further removed from the lives of individuals, becoming rather more invested in state laws and ordinances of the larger cosmos. *Natura*, on the other hand, takes up the more familial role as *parens* and is the generative force in the world, who is concerned far more with human laws and morality.

It is also in this play that Seneca presents Jupiter's association with the natural elements in their role as instruments of his distribution of justice. While Jupiter is on occasion accused of using his lightning and thunder at random and without regard for human casualties, it is clear that Jupiter does not utilize his cosmic weaponry without need. Instead, Jupiter reserves his stores of artillery for use in extreme situations when no other option would present itself and usually in response to threats of a cosmic nature. Given the opportunity to create havoc at will, Jupiter clearly refuses to do so. This is made particularly evident through an examination of Zeus Horkeios, where a similar sentiment can be postulated for Zeus in *Hippolytus*. While Euripides also alludes to some of these ideas throughout his other plays, he more fully explores their connection in *Electra*, using the myth of Atreus and Thyestes as a manifestation of Zeus' will as reflected in nature. This particular treatment of the Thyestes myth is completely reworked by Seneca, to show, not how nature can be used as a tool by the god, but how substantial breaches to the cosmic order can virtually dissolve the god's *auctoritas*.

Jupiter and Natura

In *Phaedra*, the goddess Natura and Jupiter are invoked together after Theseus has cursed his son, believing that Hippolytus has raped his wife. The chorus call upon the two deities and wonder why they, but Jupiter in particular, take such pains to ensure the cosmic balance in the universe, preserving the seasons, in such a precise manner:

> O magna parens, Natura, deum
> tuque igniferi rector Olympi,
> qui sparsa cito sidera mundo
> cursusque vagos rapis astrorum
> celerique polos cardine versas,
> cur tanta tibi cura perennes
> agitare vias aetheris alti,
> ut nunc canae frigora brumae
> nudent silvas,
> nunc arbustis redeant umbrae,
> nunc aestivi colla Leonis
> Cererem magno fervore coquant
> viresque suas temperet annus? (*Phaed.* 959-71).

Some scholars have argued that Jupiter is here conflated with the personification of Nature, attributing this to Seneca's Stoic beliefs.[171] While Seneca as a Stoic philosopher may have interpreted the two concepts to be one and the same, that does not guarantee that such a belief is being portraying here, or that such a belief is the only valid interpretation of the passage. Seneca is clearly personifying nature as a goddess either in contrast to, or alongside, the god Jupiter. The use of *tuque* (960) by the chorus to introduce the invocation of Jupiter suggests a structure similar to that of a previous appeal where Theseus invoked the goddess Pietas first and then Jupiter (903-05, discussed above, pp. 74-75). There is no indication elsewhere in *Phaedra* that Nature and Jupiter are synonymous, although the word *natura* does occur on six different occasions (the most references to nature in any of

---

[171] Boyle (1985) *passim* and (1987) 195; Coffey and Mayer (1990) 173. For a discussion of the relationship between *natura* and the gods throughout the Senecan corpus, see Rosenmeyer (2000).

Seneca's plays[172]). Instead of an indication of Stoic teachings, the relationship between Jupiter and Nature may be productively interpreted as a far more complex relationship and perhaps even as a power struggle, where each deity tries to assert his or her respective influences over individual characters in the play.

Natura is presented in this choral ode as the generatrix of the gods (*parens deum*, 959), usurping an epithet most frequently associated with Jupiter; she is invoked alongside Jupiter in his guise as the fire-wielding lord of Olympus. Jupiter's realm is that of the starry heavens; he ensures that the physical momentum of the cosmos continues in perpetuity; he ensures the seasons maintain their schedule. Jupiter's control over these fundamental facets of the wider world, but not as the father of gods (as *pater* or *parens*), suggests an inversion of the traditional hierarchy. Natura (invoked first and thus given primacy of place) is here the mother of Jupiter (as one of the *deum*) and his realm of influence over celestial phenomena is his prerogative on Natura's authority, not his own. The emphasis placed on Jupiter's celestial responsibilities by the chorus also creates the impression that the god is somewhat removed from human affairs.[173] Here Jupiter represents cosmic authority, ensuring that traditional laws are maintained and exerting his power over other phenomena; in other words, Jupiter represents the cosmos and the laws of the human world on a larger scheme. In the world of the play, this set of priorities for Jupiter is emblematic of his association with laws of society and state and replaces his

---

[172] *Natura* is found three times in both *Phoenissae* (85, 273, 478) and *Oedipus* (25, 371, 943) and only twice each in *Agamemnon* (34, 250) and *Thyestes* (746, 834). Davis (1991) 156-161 discusses the thematic importance of *natura* in *Oedipus*, but without reference to Jupiter.

[173] Segal (1986) frequently uses the adjectives "distant" and "remote" to describe Jupiter (for example at 43, 118, 142 and 168).

connection to the issues of the individual as a father figure[174] (an interpretation which would complement the idea that Fortuna controls the affairs of men, discussed above, pp. 53-55). Natura takes on the responsibility as a mother figure, replacing Jupiter, and is the goddess of human affection and the bonds of kin[175] as Theseus will later remark (*O nimium potens / quanto parentes sanguinis vinclo tenes / Natura!* 1114-16).[176]

The chorus, however, finish an ode outlining Jupiter's immense authority by questioning the god's integrity:

> sed cur idem qui tanta regis,
> sub quo vasti pondera mundi
> librata suos ducunt orbes,
> hominum nimium securus abes,
> non sollicitus prodesse bonis,
> nocuisse malis? (*Phaed.* 972-77)

The chorus, at first, reaffirms Jupiter's vast realm of influence, but they then ask how he could maintain the balance of the universe while apparently letting imbalances occur amongst mortals. To place this in context, the chorus is reacting to the rampant deeds of lust, treachery and adultery taking the place of modesty and honour (981-88). The problem with their description of events is that it is ambiguous where they are aiming their criticism: Phaedra is of course guilty of lust and treachery for attempting to seduce her stepson, but Theseus is also guilty of adultery (91-92, 96-98)[177] and of being treacherous in

---

[174] Segal (1986) 117 notes "[t]he play presents a plethora of father-figures . . ." and "[t]he early dialogues between Phaedra and the Nurse discuss the struggle between . . . female desire [represented by Natura] and the Law upheld by Father Minos, Father Jupiter, and Theseus."

[175] Paschalis (1994) 112.

[176] One might think of Sophocles' *Antigone*, where there is a similar dichotomy of individual vs. polis; or of Aeschylus' *Eumenides*, where Natura could be seen as analogous to the Erinyes; a more relevant "equivalent" however, may be interpreting Natura as Aphrodite or Venus, an equivalent hinted at, but not made explicit, by Paschalis (1994) 110.

[177] Roisman (2005) 75-76.

his use of Neptune's wishes to kill his son.[178] Hippolytus, on the other hand, is culpable in refusing to marry and, in his initial monody on hunting, of trying to conquer nature itself.[179] All three characters are responsible for the imbalances the chorus seek to rectify and so the desire to see those who are *bonis* and those who are *malis* dealt with appropriately is complicated by the question of how those two terms should be applied and to whom they are applicable.

Phaedra, Theseus and Hippolytus are thus caught between Jupiter and Natura's respective laws. Phaedra's attempted seduction of Hippolytus clearly violates Jupiter's laws concerning marriage (as a societal law). But, by her attempt to satisfy her sexual needs because her marriage bed is empty (elsewhere in the play identified as honouring nature, 481-82),[180] she elevates Natura's laws over those of Jupiter. Theseus, on the other hand, places Jupiter's laws of atonement over Natura's laws of kinship when he rashly decides to kill his son for supposedly raping his wife. Hippolytus, however, does not elevate either set of laws over the other and instead tries to overpower each himself.[181] By asserting his preference for a "golden age" (*Phaed.* 483-564)[182] he shuns the existence of public life altogether, effectively placing himself outside of Jupiter's laws, as though they need not apply to him. Hippolytus also aims to control the wilderness and assert his dominance over the natural world (1-80), rejecting even close family contact, again as

---

[178] Kohn (2008) 387 emphasizes the impiety associated with a man asking his father to kill his own grandson.

[179] Davis (1983) 126; Crewe (1990) 110.

[180] Davis (1983) 125.

[181] On Hippolytus and Nature, Crewe (1990) 110 remarks: "By the same token, the fiercely defensive, self-sufficient, virginal youth is the play's universal, 'unnatural' love-object and thus Nature's rival;" Segal (1986) 126 suggests Hippolytus "is condemned to confront both parental figures [i.e. Natura and Jupiter]."

[182] See especially Segal (1983) 244-47; Hippolytus' "Golden Age Speech" is discussed in detail by Kirchhoff (2012).

though Natura's laws are not his own. The two gods, while operating in different spheres, nevertheless both need to be heeded and the downfall of each of the characters lies in their own inability to balance their obligations to each deity. Thus, the chorus' observation of an imbalance is not due to the god's lack of care or of a preference for *bonis* or *malis*, but to the errors of humanity.

Lightning as an Instrument of Retribution

Not only is Jupiter associated with notions of justice and punishment, but the ultimate symbol of his power, the thunder or lightning bolt, is one way the god can carry out his retribution. Indeed, Jupiter's fires are to be feared as much as sea storms and flooding for the havoc that they can create. Such an idea is furthered in *Hercules Furens* when Hercules prays to Jupiter after killing Lycus; instead of heeding Amphitryon's advice to ask for rest from toils, he asks that:

> nulla tempestas fretum
> violenta turbet, nullus irato Iove
> exiliat ignis, nullus hiberna nive
> nutritus agros amnis eversos trahat (*HF* 931-34).

Fitch suggests that there could be hubristic connotations here as the passage hints that Jupiter's lightning is as destructive and "wayward" as the other natural disasters.[183] The difficulty in accepting this interpretation arises when one also takes into account the adjective *irato*. These fires only occur when Jupiter is enraged; thus, Hercules is not suggesting that his lightning occurs haphazardly or, indeed, that it is not justified. Hercules is wishing that there be no *cause* for Jupiter to utilize his weaponry. This, of course, does not nullify the implication that his lightning is dangerous or the reason for Hercules' wish for its cessation. Thus, his prayer is evidence for the fact that only when Jupiter uses his

---

[183] Fitch (1987) 363.

lightning is he most feared and, further, that the god's use of it is not random, but rather methodical and deliberate.

It is only when Jupiter has sufficient cause that he utilizes his arsenal and is not, as Fitch suggests, wayward or random in his "attacks." A passage from *Phaedra* illustrates this argument well. When Hippolytus has been approached by his step-mother as an *amantis* (671) he calls upon Jupiter to witness Phaedra's crimes. He prays that the god witness these crimes both visually and aurally and he urges Jupiter to make it known that the whole universe acknowledges and reacts to what has occurred:

> Magne regnator deum,
> tam lentus audis scelera? tam lentus vides?
> et quando saeva fulmen emittes manu,
> si nunc serenum est? omnis impulsus ruat
> aether et atris nubibus condat diem,
> ac versa retro sidera obliquos agant
> retorta cursus (*Phaed.* 671-77).

Hippolytus' prayer to Jupiter that the god will hurl thunderbolts and collapse the sky, burying the sunlight in black clouds, so that even the stars turn away is more than an affirmation of the god's realm of influence. It is an expression of Hippolytus' belief that Jupiter should find Phaedra's act so threatening to the very fabric of the universe that the world should be engulfed by chaos; he cannot understand the god's inaction. While Jupiter may be able to do all that Hippolytus requests of him, there is no need for him to bring about such total devastation. Indeed, Jupiter has other plans in mind for restoring the balance of the cosmos.

Furthermore, the particular epithet Hippolytus uses to invoke the god (*regnator deum*) points to such an interpretation. The phrase (prior to Seneca) is very much a Republican poetic line;[184] more commonly found in Imperial poetry is the epithet *regnator*

---

[184] It is found in Accius (*Clyt.* 32), Naevius (*BP fr.* 15.1) and Plautus (*Amph.* 45); Virgil employs a variation of it (*ipse deum tibi me claro demittit Olympo / regnator, Aen.* 4.269).

Olympi.[185] On its own, *regnator* does not automatically signify a reference to Jupiter, although it frequently does; often it refers to Neptune as well and even occasionally to Dis.[186] Here it anticipates Seneca's second use of *regnator* in the play (945) which, together with the first, constitute the only two instances of word in the whole of the Senecan corpus. At 945, Theseus is requesting of Neptune (as *regnator freti*) that Hippolytus die for his crimes, using one of the "wishes" promised to him. Seneca is relating the two invocations by the use of the word *regnator* and indicating the relationship between the two gods. Hippolytus wants Jupiter to react quickly and destructively; but Theseus, in the end, is the one to react just as Hippolytus requests, having appealed to the same title of Neptune. Thus, Jupiter's answer to Hippolytus' appeal is brought about via this appeal to Neptune. While the entire cosmos may not be affected, Hippolytus' entire world (and Theseus and Phaedra's too) is certainly engulfed by darkness. Jupiter's apparent tolerance and tardiness by Hippolytus' standards is in fact a precursor to the god's restoration of order.

Hippolytus is not the only one to make reference to Jupiter's weapons of restoration. When the Nurse tries to reaffirm the authority of Jupiter in her discussion with Phaedra, she points to his status as a god of vengeance and retribution (or justice):

> quid ille, qui mundum quatit
> vibrans corusca fulmen Aetnaeum manu,
> sator deorum? (*Phaed.* 155-57).

The mention of Jupiter's thunderbolt is meant to scare Phaedra into submitting to the Nurse's pleas to refrain from impiety; but the added descriptive imagery is also worth noting. Jupiter is not just the father of the gods (*sator* being an attempt by the Nurse to place Jupiter in his proper position), but a god who menaces with his lightning bolts, made

---

[185] Used by Virgil on three occasions (*Aen.* 2.799, 7.558, 10.437); twice by Statius (*Theb.* 8.41, *Ach.* 1.588); and once each by Silius Italicus (10.350) and Martial (14.175.1).

[186] For Neptune as *regnator* see, for example, Virg. *Aen.* 8.77; Dis as *regnator*, Mart. 7.47.7.

from the forge at Aetna. The Nurse has no reservations as to his supremacy or his rule and she believes that there is no doubt as to his abilities to punish mortals. Jupiter's hand is *corusca*, as if he is "at this moment," shaking his bolts, making them shine and preparing to hurl them downwards.[187] In the Nurse's mind, Jupiter will no doubt punish Phaedra for her desires if she does not at once conquer them herself.[188]

Seneca's *Oedipus* also concerns itself with retribution and punishment, although the link to Jupiter in this respect is made from a slightly different perspective. The final reference to the god in the play is given by Jocasta when she has learned the truth concerning her relationship with Oedipus. In her final speech before her suicide, Jocasta asks that Jupiter punish her, but she claims that the god's lightning would be insufficient punishment as atonement for her crimes:

> non si ipse mundum concitans divum sator
> corusca saeva tela iaculetur manu,
> umquam rependam sceleribus poenas pares
> mater nefanda. mors placet: mortis via
> quaeratur (*Oed.* 1028-32).

The use of *corusca* here is significant; the word only occurs thrice in Seneca's tragedies (cf. *Phaed.* 156 and 889) and in each case is intimately connected to Jupiter. As in the above example in *Phaedra,* the usage of *corusca* here suggests that Jupiter is already brandishing his lightning and perhaps even preparing to strike.[189] Furthermore, that Jocasta does not believe his weapons are enough of a punishment or are strong enough to extract a

---

[187] Cf. Eur. *Hipp.* 683-84, discussed below.

[188] Segal (1986) 118 takes Phaedra's beliefs to the more accurate assessment: "The *maximum regnum* of Amor . . . implies another weakening of paternal power, the rule of Jupiter, highest father, now overshadowed by the 'greatest rule' of the impudent young god." I discuss the relationship between Jupiter and Cupid as well as Phaedra's disbelief in Jupiter's absolute supremacy in chapter 5, pp. 155-57.

[189] The use of the present tense here intensifies the immediacy of the action.

proper penalty for her crimes can be shown to be a false impression.[190] Jocasta's desire to find a way to die after suggesting that Jupiter's lightning is insufficient, does not accord with the earlier depiction in the play of lightning as fatal to Semele (501-02); indeed, Jupiter regretted its use. The god's ability to punish mortals is thus not at all diminished by Jocasta's claim. Upon the revelation of Jocasta and Oedipus' actions, Jupiter has decided to utilize the same element which destroyed Semele, knowing full well the repercussions. Although he is not shown to fulfil his intentions it does not detract from the representation of his power – Jupiter's lightning is enough to prove fatal to those it is directed against.

The Wrath of Zeus Horkeios

Zeus Horkeios, god of oaths, does not at first appear to have any explicit connection to the natural elements in any specific way, but he does play an important role in Euripides' *Hippolytus*, a play which brings to the fore aspects of this god which do seem inherently related to a more "elemental" Zeus. A line from *Orestes* spoken by the Phrygian slave as he runs out of the palace to relate what has transpired inside provides a basis for such an assertion. After explaining how Orestes and Pylades were carrying out their plan to murder Helen when she suddenly vanished, the Phrygian shouts ὦ Ζεῦ καὶ Γᾶ καὶ Φῶς καὶ Νύξ (*Or.* 1496) as though swearing an oath to prove the accuracy and reliability of his account.[191] The exclamation is neither a prayer nor a true oath, but the invocation of this series of deities (by a "barbarian" slave no less) not only emphasizes the impiety of the attempted murder, but also the futility of their earlier prayers to aid in its fulfilment. More

---

[190] A similar sentiment is expressed by Antigone in Seneca's *Phoenissae*: *non si revulso Iuppiter mundo tonet / mediumque nostros fulmen in nexus cadat / manum hanc remittam* (59-61). Antigone does not believe that Jupiter's fires are enough to make her forsake her father; and while such sentiments may be common in literature, the suggestion here seems incongruous. The one deity who should, before all others, protect the father would not blast Antigone for doing so.

[191] West (1987) 282.

significant for the current discussion, the deities are also all opposites as well as "elementals:" Zeus (sky/heavens) and Earth, Light (day) and Night. Although Willink notes that the inclusion of Night here signifies the presence of calamity (which is certainly true),[192] I would also posit that its inclusion in the two sets of divinities also establishes clear opposing dynamics. Zeus in his heavenly, celestial aspect certainly opposes Earth, just as Light or daylight opposes Night; but so too do Zeus and Light together oppose the pairing of Earth and Night. Such divinities were often called to witness oaths, possibly as a way to ensure that an oath is acknowledged in every "region" to ensure that it is upheld, with serious repercussions should it be broken.[193] Zeus Horkeios appears to be a god aligned most clearly with his celestial aspect, the one which oversees the cosmos, divine law and justice.

In *Hippolytus* this interpretation certainly holds true and Zeus as *Horkeios* dominates the second half of the drama. His significance first becomes apparent during the discussion between Phaedra and her Nurse after she has made a promise to Phaedra (although without explicitly making it an oath) not to tell Hippolytus about Phaedra's desire for him. Once Phaedra learns of the Nurse's exposure of her feelings, she denounces her Nurse and curses her with the punishment inflicted upon those who commit perjury: Ζεύς σε γεννήτωρ ἐμὸς / πρόρριζον ἐκτρίψειεν οὐτάσας πυρί (*Hipp.* 683-84). The common punishment for perjurers is *exoleia*, the utter destruction of the perjurer and his descendants,[194] precisely the curse Phaedra brings down upon the Nurse. Zeus is often invoked in these types of curses and the use of his thunderbolt to bring retribution is not unusual. As the audience hears nothing further concerning the Nurse's fate (but why should they?) we can assume that this curse comes to naught, precisely because the Nurse

---

[192] Willink (1986) 329.

[193] West (1987) 282.

[194] Mastronarde (2002a) 36-37.

did not make an *oath*, only a promise, not to reveal Phaedra's secret. Broken promises and oaths have very different consequences as Hippolytus well knows.

The second important feature of Phaedra's curse is in reference to the relationship she shares with Zeus. Phaedra refers to the god as her γεννήτωρ, suggesting that he is either her father specifically (which would not be true), the father of her specific line (which is true), or perhaps that he is her "creator" in the sense that Zeus created the female race, reminiscent of Hippolytus' claim (616-17). In the context of this play, Zeus as the father of Phaedra's line has little thematic importance, aside from emphasizing her noble genealogy.[195] That Zeus is associated once again with the female race seems more significant. This corroborates Hippolytus' view of the creation of women, but also signals that his disapproval of their existence would be an affront to the god and places Hippolytus in a less appealing light.

Hippolytus does, however, have reverence for the gods and Zeus specifically when he swears his famous oath and keeps it under trying circumstances. While the audience is not privy to the specifics of this oath, one may be able to assume at least some similarities with the oath he swears to Theseus that he did not touch Phaedra nor wished to do so:

> νῦν δ' ὅρκιόν σοι Ζῆνα καὶ πέδον χθονὸς
> ὄμνυμι τῶν σῶν μήποθ' ἅψασθαι γάμων
> μηδ' ἂν θελῆσαι μηδ' ἂν ἔννοιαν λαβεῖν (*Hipp.* 1025-27).

Unsurprisingly, Hippolytus swears by Zeus Horkeios and the earth that he did not violate Theseus' bed, conforming to the usual practices of swearing oaths. Presumably Hippolytus swore similarly to the Nurse and thus Zeus is now invoked formally a second time in the play to witness Hippolytus' oaths.[196] Unfortunately for Hippolytus, oaths are not believed

---

[195] Although Segal (1979) 157 attempts to link the "celestial fire" of Zeus with the destruction of Semele as a paradigmatic instance of "dangerous erotic passion."

[196] Fletcher (2003) 36-40.

in this play; neither Phaedra nor Theseus believes that Hippolytus will be true to his words and this disbelief casts a shadow of doubt over the efficacy of oath-swearing.[197] The audience will have witnessed real oaths being sworn by the judges on the day of the performance, made in the name of Zeus and these will be taken at face value.[198] The overt disregard for such a highly religious act in this play is worth commenting upon here. Theseus is especially guilty of disregarding religious rituals and traditions: he refuses to seek prophecy, omens or any other type of divination to cross-examine Phaedra's words[199] and is caught out by Artemis for doing so. Although Hippolytus can be viewed as immature for refusing to marry and participate in society, he is the only one for whom the religious sanctity of oaths means anything.[200]

Hippolytus goes even further, though, than merely swearing an oath in Zeus' name; he curses himself if his words prove to be false. He immediately makes a self-curse to remain an exile forever and to die without earth or sea as a tomb:

ἦ τἄρ' ὀλοίμην ἀκλεὴς ἀνώνυμος
[ἄπολις ἄοικος, φυγὰς ἀλητεύων χθόνα,]
καὶ μήτε πόντος μήτε γῆ δέξαιτό μου
σάρκας θανόντος, εἰ κακὸς πέφυκ' ἀνήρ (*Hipp.* 1028-31).

What is significant is the fact that only some, but not all, of these curses come true. Artemis ensures that Hippolytus does not die nameless and without reputation, but as he never underwent the transition to adulthood, Hippolytus does die ἄπολις after Theseus exiles him. As Segal has pointed out, the last curse also comes true in that Hippolytus dies

---

[197] The motif of oaths and curses is explored in detail by Segal (1972).

[198] Torrance (2009) 4; Sommerstein and Bayliss (2013) 44.

[199] Fitzgerald (1973) 32-34; Luschnig (1988) 47; see also Mitchell (1991) for the relationship between Theseus and Hippolytus throughout the play.

[200] Knox (1968) 106-07; Segal (1972) 169; Yunis (1988) 117. See also Goff (1990) 88-89 for a brief discussion of the implications of Hippolytus' reliance upon, and Theseus' rejection of, oaths and oracles.

neither on land nor in the sea but in between the two.[201] That some of these self-curses are heard by Zeus and do come true complicate the audience's perception of Hippolytus' guilt. This interpretation gains further credence during the Messenger's speech when he recites Hippolytus' second set of self-curses.

Even though the audience is not privy to the second oath, the wording is almost identical and should be taken as true:

> Ζεῦ, μηκέτ' εἴην εἰ κακὸς πέφυκ' ἀνήρ·
> αἴσθοιτο δ' ἡμᾶς ὡς ἀτιμάζει πατὴρ
> ἤτοι θανόντας ἢ φάος δεδορκότας (*Hipp.* 1191-93).

While in both of these examples εἰ κακὸς πέφυκ' ἀνήρ is generally taken to mean "if I am a guilty man" or "if I am a base man," the phrase could also mean "if I am an ill-born man." Because Hippolytus is praying to die if he can be proved guilty of dishonouring Phaedra and that is precisely what happens even though he is innocent, one can either assume that Hippolytus is dying not because of his curse, but because of Poseidon's promise to Theseus, or, because Hippolytus is in fact "guilty," "base" or "ill-born." Hippolytus is of course guilty of scorning Aphrodite and could be said to be base because of that, but he is also "ill-born," being an illegitimate child. Hippolytus also asks that his father come to know the truth whether he lives on or dies. This wish too comes to fruition through the presence of Artemis, which hints that the gods, Zeus and Artemis, are witnessing Hippolytus' tragedy.[202] What becomes apparent from such an overview of the role of Zeus Horkeios in this particular tragedy is that this aspect of the god is repeatedly associated with other "cosmic elements," specifically "earth" and "light." Both the gods by whom oaths are sworn, as well as the punishment incurred for perjury, involve "extremes:"

---

[201] Segal (1972) 170.

[202] This interpretation is not convincing to all scholars. Segal (1993) 118 suggests instead that the only response to the curse from Zeus is the roar from the ground.

the "highest" of divinities, Zeus and the "lowest," earth, witness oaths; perjurers find no rest in either realm, no longer able to see the "light" but also dying without earthly burial. Zeus Horkeios, god of oaths, is quite clearly a god who has the authority to make use of the natural elements in the restoration of balance.

The Reversal of the Sun

Jupiter's control over the cosmos, including the course of sun and stars and his identity as the god of thunder, lightning and rain, contributes to his use of these natural elements as weapons of justice. In addition to Jupiter's special weapon of the lightning bolt, the god is also believed to manipulate these celestial patterns to make his will known to mortals and any departure from his regulation of the cosmos indicates a breach in Jupiter's realm. The one myth where the cosmos is affected to this extent by human events is that of Thyestes. The treatment of this myth by both Euripides and Seneca offers some interesting points of difference: Euripides' version of the myth in *Electra* indicates that the changes in the cosmos were produced by Zeus and were manifestations of his will. Seneca's *Thyestes*, on the other hand, portrays human crimes as so abominable that Jupiter, unlike in *Phaedra*, has no recourse to administering justice. The reversal of celestial phenomena is literally caused by the events of the play and Jupiter is unable to use or even control weapons that ought to be at his own disposal.

During the so-called "golden lamb ode" in Euripides' *Electra*, Zeus is said to alter the course of the stars and sun in response to Thyestes' theft of Atreus' golden lamb, a manifestation of his wish that Atreus, not Thyestes, rule in Argos:[203]

---

[203] There are two standard versions of the lamb story: in one version, Atreus promises to offer his flock to Artemis, but when the golden lamb appears amongst the other sheep, he reneges on his vow, prompting the wrath of the goddess on his family (Apollod. *Ep.* 2.10); in the second version, the death of Hermes' son Myrtilus at the hands of Pelops angered the god (Apollod. *Ep.*

τότε δὴ τότε <δὴ> φαεν-
  νὰς ἄστρων μετέβασ' ὁδοὺς
Ζεὺς καὶ φέγγος ἀελίου
λευκόν τε πρόσωπον ἀοῦς,
  τὰ δ' ἕσπερα νῶτ' ἐλαύνει
θερμᾶι φλογὶ θεοπύρωι,
νεφέλαι δ' ἔνυδροι πρὸς ἄρκτον,
ξηραί τ' Ἀμμωνίδες ἕδραι
φθίνουσ' ἀπειρόδροσοι,
καλλίστων ὄμβρων Διόθεν στερεῖσαι (*El.* 727-36).

Thyestes was able to procure his brother's lamb with the help of Aërope, Atreus' wife, whom he had seduced. Both the adultery Thyestes committed and the usurpation of Atreus' right to rule Argos (as ordained by Zeus) were considered breaches to Zeus' world order, but as Rosivach has argued, they did not cause the natural phenomena to change course. Instead, this was "a divinely produced event which enabled Atreus to oust Thyestes and recover the kingship for himself."[204] According to Apollodorus, Zeus had sent Hermes to Atreus with a message to come to an agreement with his brother concerning the disputed kingship: whoever could exhibit the most spectacular portent would be awarded the throne by the people. When Thyestes brought out the stolen lamb, which should have been Atreus' portent, Zeus procured these celestial changes to "trump" the golden lamb (Apollod. *Ep.* 2.12). It is unclear whether these particular details would have been common knowledge for Euripides' audience, but it is certain that Zeus caused these natural phenomena to change course and that it was his will for Atreus to take the kingship.

2.4-8), who then placed the golden lamb amongst Atreus' flock to incite strife between the brothers and cause the eventual downfall of the house. Euripides chooses a previously unattested background story for *Electra* and has Pan bestow the lamb upon the house of Atreus as a symbol of his sovereignty. See Rosivach (1978) for a discussion of the implications for Euripides' choice in detail.

[204] Rosivach (1978) 192.

The chorus also dwells on the specific changes that occurred: the stars and sun reversed their natural paths and this resulted in significant changes to weather patterns from north to south and from east to west.[205] Rosivach connects this imagery of the sun and stars to Orestes and he interprets this story of kingship being stolen and returned as analogous to events in the play.[206] While the chorus is singing this ode, Orestes is off-stage killing his own usurper Aegisthus, corresponding to the removal of Thyestes' line in favour of that of Atreus.[207] The implication of this parallel between past and present, would indicate that Zeus brought about these celestial changes in order to "repay human misfortune on account of human justice" (ἀλλάξαν-/ τα δυστυχίαι βροτείωι / θνατᾶς ἕνεκεν δίκας, El. 740-42). In other words, just as Zeus ensured Atreus gained retribution from Thyestes, so he ensures Orestes gains retribution from Aegisthus.[208] Zeus' association with natural phenomena is thus not only a manifestation of his will, but it also has implications for his distribution of justice; and while the chorus is hesitant to believe

---

[205] It should also be noted that these celestial changes occur because of the disputed kingship, not because of Thyestes' later banquet, discussed in detail in chapter 9, pp. 329-332.

[206] Rosivach (1978) 193: [Orestes] "is like the sun and stars on Achilles' shield putting the enemy to rout and like the sun and stars in our ode causing the false king to lose his throne."

[207] This interpretation is also supported by Euripides' choice in placement: the ode occupies the centre of the play and is the turning point of the action. Given the centrality of its location and the emphasis on the myth, it is surprising that some scholars, such as Halporn (1983) and Morwood (1981), consider the myths of the house of Tantalus to have little bearing on the play.

[208] Rosivach (1978) 195. Orestes' murder of Aegisthus, who is acting as a host and in the midst of a sacrifice, would normally violate the laws of Zeus *Xenios*, but Aegisthus as a usurper has already proven that he himself is treacherous and thus he renounces any protection he may have otherwise received from Zeus. More troubling is the murder of Clytemnestra, who has come to the home of Electra as both a guest and in a religious capacity. While the murder of the former may have little consequence in terms of divine law, the murder of the latter is not so easily dismissed.

Zeus would affect such alterations in the cosmos,[209] they are also not entirely disbelieving

(737-38).[210] Euripides presents Zeus' powers as immeasurable and lasting; but perhaps

most significantly, when considered alongside Seneca's Jupiter, Zeus' control over the

elements is also clearly a tool for the god through which he can enact his will; the elements

are at *his* disposal rather than becoming a force of their own.

Seneca's *Thyestes* enacts the revenge Atreus takes on his brother for stealing his

wife and although there are different elements of the myth used in this version, the retreat

of the sun and stars is one that carries through. Seneca however does not use the golden

lamb as the impetus for Atreus' revenge, nor as a symbol of power; the sun and stars

changing their course is also not a manifestation here of Jupiter's will that Atreus remain

in power. Instead, it is Atreus' decision to slaughter his nephews as a meal for Thyestes,

subsequently consumed by his brother, which drives the sun to abandon its place in the

heavens and the stars to take flight from the sky. The motif recurs throughout the play,

with the most extended description given by the chorus after the messenger's description

of Atreus' sacrifice of the children (*Thy.* 789-884).[211] The chorus do not mention Jupiter

during their ode, but they allude to various items connected to him; in particular, they

wonder if the disappearance of the sun is somehow connected to the reappearance of

creatures once defeated by the gods, either the Giants or Typhoeus (805-13). They fear

---

[209] Zeus has altered the very basic elements of life, bringing rain to the north and drought to the south. The specific reference at 734 locates the south in Libya, at the site of Zeus' oracle in Siwa. Euripides is not only presenting a mythological story, but he is also bringing in cultic references which would resonate with his audience, perhaps to give further credibility to this particular myth. Kovacs (1998) 233 notes that it was this very event that caused the sun to travel from east to west (it was west to east before) and to alter the weather patterns, causing the dryness in the south.

[210] Willink (2005) 20.

[211] See O'Brien (2001) for an extended discussion of the political implications of the astrological motif.

chaos is about to return once more, as the planets and stars no longer orbit their usual paths (844-74) and the poles of the universe are overturned (877).[212] Even though Jupiter is not mentioned, it is clear that he is not the cause of the current events (880-81) and, given the close connection between Jupiter and these exact phenomena in other plays, it is clear he is also unable to control them.

The motif appears again just before Thyestes brings himself to eat the meal prepared by Atreus. Thyestes notes several portents, but without understanding their meaning: the ground shakes (989); the fire is dim (990); the skies have been abandoned between day and night (991); the vault of heaven is agitated (992-93); and stars are fleeing the skies (995). It is only after Atreus tells Thyestes precisely what he ate that he finally understands them: *hoc egit diem / aversum in ortus* (1035-36). Finally, Thyestes begins his appeal to Jupiter:

> Tu, summe caeli rector, aetheriae potens
> dominator aulae, nubibus totum horridis
> convolve mundum, bella ventorum undique
> committe et omni parte violentum intona (*Thy.* 1077-80).

This prayer, in many ways, parallels that of Hippolytus in *Phaedra* (671-7). Thyestes wants the universe and Jupiter in particular to react to the sacrilegious feast with a vengeance, calling upon the master of the skies (*caeli rector*) to bring chaos once more. Thyestes' choice of epithet, while seeming suitable here, is in fact, ambiguous. Jupiter is, of course, the ruler of the heavens, but Atreus had earlier announced the departure of the gods from the celestial sphere, including Jupiter: instead, Atreus has taken their place (887). Thyestes, invoking the highest power of the heavens to take action for the crimes of his brother, is in fact appealing to his brother, for Atreus has displaced Jupiter, who has

---

[212] On this ode, see especially Davis (1989) 431-34.

fled the skies, leaving Atreus to assume his position.[213] This does not lessen the association between Jupiter and his celestial elements, but it does raise the question of Jupiter's ability to maintain his control over them.

Thyestes finally comes to the end of his lengthy prayer and returns to the motif of the retreating sun, with an appeal that the god "avenge the lost daylight:"

           lumen ereptum polo
fulminibus exple. causa, ne dubites diu,
utriusque mala sit; si minus, mala sit mea:
me pete, trisulco flammeam telo facem
per pectus hoc transmitte. si natos pater
humare et igni tradere extremo volo
ego sum cremandus. si nihil superos movet
nullumque telis impios numen petit,
aeterna nox permaneat et tenebris tegat
immensa longis scelera. nil, Titan, queror,
si perseveras (*Thy.* 1086-96).

Even before Atreus had murdered his nephews, precipitating the flight of the sun and stars, the motif was introduced by the Fury in the prologue. Not only does she foretell that the sun will leave the sky, but that this will be the second time it has done so (51).[214] She is clearly alluding here to the earlier involvement of Jupiter in the kingship Atreus, which the god endorsed by directing the sun and stars to reverse their paths (cf. Apollod. *Ep.* 2.12). Now, however, it is the Fury who will inspire the celestial bodies to reverse their course yet again and, of their own volition, in horror at what they witness on earth. Jupiter has lost control not only of people and events on earth, but also of the denizens of heaven and their movements as well.

---

[213] Discussed in detail in chapter 9, pp. 330.

[214] *alia* found in manuscript *E*; *alta* and *atra* are also possibilities.

Concluding Remarks

The relationship between Jupiter and nature is thus a complex one. In *Phaedra*, Jupiter is conceived in contradistinction to the personification Natura; however, both are instrumental in keeping the order of the cosmos balanced. Jupiter is also in charge of the celestial bodies in heaven: the sun, the stars, the planets, the clouds all continue as per his directive. While it is tempting to impute morality into the essence of Jupiter's characterization, as the chorus does, it is perhaps not prudent to do so. In order for this cosmic balance to be achieved and maintained, Jupiter must remain an *impartial* judge of humanity and is thus "outside" of the law. Or, more appropriately, he *IS* the law and so by his very nature cannot do or be anything else. He represents law and justice for their own sakes. To put it another way, Jupiter operates in black and white when the human world exists in shades of grey. This is why he seems so remote and uncaring – it is not because he wishes to punish the good and reward the guilty, but because his role and essence prevent him from becoming invested in individuals. He keeps the world turning because if he did not, the world would descend into chaos. His black and white "poles" contain all the grey and keep it all in check.

Thus, Jupiter's immediate interest is the larger cosmic world and it is only when that domain is under attack or at risk, that Jupiter will utilize the barrage of artillery at his disposal. Although characters may wish that he use his weaponry in order to punish crimes of a human nature, Jupiter does not employ them thus, instead using other means to administer justice. This is not to say the god never uses these phenomena to illustrate his wrath or to punish the wicked, for the lightning bolt is his weapon of choice. But only when his cosmic authority is being threatened does Jupiter begin to wage war in this way. He is deliberate in his assaults on humankind, wreaking havoc only when necessary. Zeus also prefers to keep his thunderbolts in check unless they are absolutely required. His role as Horkeios in *Hippolytus* illustrates the god's involvement in the punishment of Hippolytus, but utter refusal to destroy Phaedra on the whims of a young man. Zeus maintains control without clouded judgement. Zeus is also able to use his cosmic elements for more positive actions, such as in the myth of Thyestes. In *Electra*, Zeus manipulates the heavens in order to manifest his will; the reversal of the sun is an indication of the god's favour. But such a depiction cannot be further removed from a similar event in Seneca's *Thyestes*. The same reversal of the sun is indicative of the moral bankruptcy of Atreus and Thyestes. That the heavens and sun move of their own accord in reaction to the events of the play, confirms an inherent inability on the part of Jupiter to retain control like his Euripidean counterpart.

PART II

FAMILY

CHAPTER 4
THE FATHER OF GODS I: THE FIRST GENERATION

Zeus is afforded the title "Father of Gods" for a reason: not only is he the biological father of many major and minor gods and goddesses, his place at the apex of the Olympian hierarchy also justifies this epithet. Zeus is the veritable father-figure and the one to whom all other deities, related or not, go for comfort, complaints and for the distribution of justice and *timē*. Zeus and Jupiter's relationships with the other gods are thus important considerations in teasing out further nuances in their representations by Euripides and Seneca. One of the most important, or at least most commonly, referenced relationship is that between Zeus and Hera. Given the numerous adulterous affairs by Zeus and the correspondingly numerous instances of revenge instigated by a jealous Hera, it is worthwhile to investigate the portrayal of their marriage, specifically within Euripides' *Heracles*. Seneca's version provides an interesting counterpoint that not only highlights the specific ideas illuminated by Euripides, but also offers a completely different way of portraying the divine couple. The tension between the respective pairs is also depicted in such a way as to suggest varying effects on the mortal sphere.

If one then compares these relationships to those of the gods' brothers, it is immediately apparent that not every relationship between the gods is the same. Zeus and Hades work together to ensure that justice is achieved among men, whereas Jupiter and Dis are presented within a less rigid hierarchy. In the plays of Euripides, a clear "chain of command" is established and Zeus is unmistakably superior to his brother; in Seneca, while this hierarchy might exist, Jupiter and Dis so closely resemble one another that it becomes difficult to distinguish who possesses absolute authority. The situation with Poseidon and Neptune is far less ambiguous; each god aids his respective brother to ensure his will is achieved, but neither strives, nor is shown to have any equivalency with Zeus or Jupiter. In both *Trojan Women* and *Hippolytus* Poseidon is clearly described as second to Zeus and as working in concert with him. Only in Seneca's *Phaedra* is there any hint that

Jupiter needs to respect the realm of his brother; but even here, Jupiter's supremacy remains intact. A final set of images from Seneca's *Hercules Furens* provides a far more succinct symbol of the inherent hierarchy of the three brothers: each brother carries his own sceptre, a physical emblem of their respective authority in their own realms, ostensibly creating equality among them. But this is an illusory equality, for Zeus' sceptre in the heavens still trumps Neptune's oceanic sceptre. Thus, the three male Olympians of Euripides seem to subscribe to a far more rigid hierarchy than their Senecan counterparts.

Marital Relations: Hera and Juno

πότερον ἀμείνον' ὡς λάβηι Διὸς πόσιν; (*TW* 978)
So that she [Hera] might have acquired a better husband than Zeus?

So says Hecuba to Helen in order to defend the goddess Hera from the slanderous suggestion that she took part in the "Judgement of Paris." Hecuba considers it outrageous that Hera would participate in such a trivial contest, as the goddess could not possibly gain anything by it being the spouse of Zeus, the supreme lord of Olympus. While Hecuba's attempt to place the goddess on a higher moral pedestal is commendable, her idealization of Hera's relationship with Zeus is problematic, for theirs is not a marriage to be emulated. Zeus' trysts with other women (both divine and mortal) are well-known, as is Hera's jealousy and penchant for vengeance against those (un)lucky enough to be the objects of Zeus' affections. But references to such trysts and plots of revenge are often seen as literary tropes to be understood purely in terms of their mythological frameworks.[215] Euripides, however, includes these seemingly trivial stories to depict the divine couple in a particular way and for a particular purpose. Euripides' *Heracles* is a case in point: a closer

---

[215] See, for example, Brown (1978) 26 who discusses the gods of *Heracles* and *Hippolytus*; on Hera specifically see Burnett (1971) 176 who cannot accept the idea of a sexually motivated goddess.

investigation of the dynamics between Zeus and Hera as presented in this play reveals that there is more to the relationship between god and goddess than would at first appear. This claim may be applied equally to Seneca's depictions of Jupiter and Juno. *Hercules Furens* is Seneca's version of the same myth, but Juno's relationship with Jupiter is not depicted in the same way as it was in Euripides. The dynamics of each pair as presented by the playwrights suggest not only that these divine relationships can be interpreted in different ways, but also that the stability (or lack thereof) between each couple can affect the other characters in their respective plays. In Euripides, when this stability breaks down, the disturbance exemplified by the immortal relationship is mirrored by other similar (mortal) relationships; in Seneca, the disruption to the couple's marriage results in a power-shift from Jupiter to Juno, temporarily threatening the cosmic order. Thus, the affairs of Zeus and Jupiter are far from being solely literary tropes and can instead point to significant changes in either the mortal or divine sphere.

Zeus, Heracles and Hera: A Family Model

Euripides does not waste any time when introducing the subject of marriage within his *Heracles*. It is clear from the very first line that this will be an important theme and that Zeus will be implicated in some way. Amphitryon introduces the play by describing himself as the one who shared his marriage bed with Zeus: Τίς τὸν Διὸς σύλλεκτρον οὐκ οἶδεν βροτῶν, / Ἀργεῖον Ἀμφιτρύων' (1-2). Although Alcmene is not mentioned by name, the explicit reference to Amphitryon's marriage bed is enough to bring her immediately to mind: in this drama, she is the mortal counterpart to Hera. It is this tri-partite relationship between Zeus, Hera and Alcmene which offers scope for an investigation of the dynamics which exist between the god and goddess. What is significant in *Heracles* is the extent to which Zeus' relationship with Alcmene is emphasized throughout the play and how it provides the counterpoint to Hera's later role in the drama: the privileging of the former relationship over the latter will lead to disastrous consequences and only when Hera is reinstated as Zeus' legitimate wife will there be any chance of normalcy being restored on earth.

Amphitryon's opening statement offers the first glimpse of these dynamics. As noted above, Alcmene is not the subject of his opening speech, but rather Amphitryon's own "participation" in the event: Zeus shared his marriage-bed (σύλλεκτρον) with Amphitryon, not Alcmene. This suggests two items of importance: first, Amphitryon and Zeus are almost equated with one another through their mutual relationship with Alcmene;[216] secondly, the reference to the bed, rather than to Alcmene herself, suggests a passive participation on her part although, as Bond notes, Amphitryon is mentioning this as something he can take pride in rather than offense.[217] This will become particularly important, for Amphitryon chastises Zeus for the same action later in the play (339-40, discussed below). Thus, the initial imagery as presented by Amphitryon is positive; Zeus and Alcmene's relationship is considered almost a blessing on Amphitryon, as if Zeus has honoured his house by sleeping with his wife. It is not, at this moment, considered a breach of marriage bonds for either party and the additional image of the *marriage*-bed enhances the legitimacy of the act, as if this were to be the first of several occasions.[218] Although Amphitryon may not have any motive for speaking of Hera at this point, her complete

---

[216] This is only the first of many instances where the two are portrayed similarly; further discussion of Hera's role with respect to Zeus' relationship with Heracles is discussed in chapter 6 (pp. 188-92). See Halleran (1988) 77-78.

[217] Bond (1981) 63.

[218] While the marriage-bed may be part of the myth in that Zeus supposedly visited Alcmene on the night of her wedding, it does not negate such an interpretation; in fact, it may bolster the argument that their tryst should be seen as a legitimate consummation of a marriage.

absence from this scene further contributes to the sense of lawfulness on Zeus' part (as we are not reminded of the god's own marriage).

Amphitryon's conviction of the factuality concerning the dalliance between Zeus and Alcmene is challenged, however, by Lycus, who uses this "boast" as something with which he can ridicule both Amphitryon and Megara:

> σὺ μὲν καθ' Ἑλλάδ' ἐκβαλὼν κόμπους κενοὺς
> ὡς σύγγαμός σοι Ζεὺς τέκνου τε κοινεών,
> σὺ δ' ὡς ἀρίστου φωτὸς ἐκλήθης δάμαρ (*Her.* 148-50).

Lycus presents Zeus and Alcmene's tryst as something of a fairy-tale, which no one should even believe, pre-empting Heracles' own moment of disbelief later in the play when he refers to these types of stories as "bards' unhappy songs" (1346).[219] The dalliance then, rather than being an event of miraculous proportions, precipitating the birth of the greatest hero, is considered a sham and an unlikely event. Zeus is, on the one hand, placed on a pedestal by Lycus – the thrust of his statement being that the god would never lower himself to such standards – and on the other, made into a potential philanderer if Amphitryon's tale is true. Whereas Amphitryon considered Zeus' interest in Alcmene as an honour, here it is presented in a far more disconcerting way. The status of Lycus as a tyrant does aid somewhat in dissipating the force of his challenge,[220] but it nevertheless serves as a caution to the audience concerning the validity of Amphitryon's words. Euripides is slowly preparing the audience for the coming attack on Zeus on account of his relationship with Alcmene, which has not yet been proven as fact, nor yet been shown to be reprehensible.

The change in perception of Zeus' relationship with Alcmene arises when Amphitryon despairs that he, along with Megara and the boys, will be slain with no aid

---

[219] Brown (1978) offers a discussion of this particular passage and the credibility of such stories.

[220] The "debate" of Lycus and Amphitryon is discussed in detail by Hamilton (1985).

from Zeus, both as a god of suppliants and specifically as the one with whom he shared his
wife:

> ὦ Ζεῦ, μάτην ἄρ' ὁμόγαμόν σ' ἐκτησάμην,
> μάτην δὲ παιδὸς κοινεῶν' ἐκλῄζομεν·
> ....
> σὺ δ' ἐς μὲν εὐνὰς κρύφιος ἠπίστω μολεῖν,
> τἀλλότρια λέκτρα δόντος οὐδενὸς λαβών,
> σώιζειν δὲ τοὺς σοὺς οὐκ ἐπίστασαι φίλους (339-40, 344-46).

This particular passage has been viewed by many as a denunciation of Zeus,[221] but the
concern here is the language Amphitryon is using to describe Zeus' partnership with
Alcmene. Amphitryon had considered Zeus to be his ὁμόγαμόν (almost rendering both as
equal husbands to Alcmene), but he now condemns him as an adulterer who should not
have been sleeping with his wife.[222] Euripides does not include any specific word to
describe Zeus, such as "adulterer," but instead expresses the god's actions in such a way as
to portray him in the least positive manner possible. Patterson defines what is commonly
rendered as "adulterer" (μοιχός) as "the nighttime sexual thief (a counterpart to other
thieves and nighttime criminals) who enters other men's houses and seduces the women
within." Patterson also highlights the one-sidedness of the act: it is the man who commits
this specific crime and the woman is the "passive object."[223] The description of the μοιχός
as given by Patterson matches Amphitryon's denunciation of Zeus as well as the emphasis

---

[221] See, for example, Barlow (1996) 138; Bond (1981) 143; Halleran (1988) 27; Rehm (2001) 366.

[222] The Athenians did not consider marriage to be a legal status as such, but rather a "social
process" including the betrothal, the "marriage night" and the acknowledgement of children,
Patterson (1998) 109; however, intrusions upon that socially-recognized relationship were
considered illegal and worthy of punishment.

[223] Patterson (1998) 123.

on the passivity of Alcmene.[224] Amphitryon's descriptive language invites the audience to think of Zeus in this way and while the god is often labelled as a seducer of women, it is usually in a choral ode (reducing the emotional intensity of the sentiment[225]) and not placed in such a significant position in the play.[226]

When the chorus sings of Zeus' relationship with Alcmene during their next ode, it reinforces the issues surrounding the legitimacy of Zeus' affair and, consequently, the paternity of Heracles (discussed in chapter 6). But rather than support Amphitryon's current perception of their dalliance, the language the chorus uses is far more suggestive of a marriage than an act of adultery:

> ὦ λέκτρων δύο συγγενεῖς
> εὐναί, θνατογενοῦς τε καὶ
> Διός, ὃς ἦλθεν ἐς εὐνὰν
> νύμφας τᾶς Περσηίδος· (*Her.* 798-801).

---

[224] Patterson (1998) 122. The term μοιχός was not acceptable to use in "polite society" and thus it is unsurprising that Euripides would not employ it here. Although Homer used a cognate term to describe the money that Ares was obligated to pay in recompense to Hephaestus (*Od.* 8.322), he stopped short of labelling the god an adulterer. The word is often found in Aristophanes, for example at *Lys.* 212, and is also used by orators, for example in Lysias 13.66.

[225] Calame (1995) identifies three different "voices" that a chorus can take, only one of which is connected to high emotional intensity; the other two are "explanatory" or "descriptive" and "ritual" or "cultic" voices. The context of the description of Zeus as a seducer of mythological women surely places this choral ode within Calame's "explanatory/descriptive" category.

[226] Halleran (1988) 27: "The stage in Greek tragedy was in general not very busy, with relatively few entrances and exits, and these rarely occurred in quick succession. Therefore, it is striking to find the successive exits of Lycus, Megara with the children, and Amphitryon within twelve lines of each other. As a result, emphasis falls on Amphitryon's final, brief and biting words against Zeus."

They sing of Alcmene as though she were a bride (νύμφας)[227] when Zeus came to her bed, again highlighting the possibility of a legitimate relationship. They place the emphasis on the marriage bed, just as Amphitryon had in his opening monologue; but now this serves as a reminder to the audience that Zeus was intruding upon someone else's bed and the illegitimacy of his actions. The cluster of words relating to the bed and marriage motif, (λέκτρων, συγγενεῖς, εὐναί, εὐνὰν, νύμφας) might also prepare the audience for the patroness of marriage, Hera, to finally enter the scene. Her total absence thus far from the discussion of Zeus and Alcmene's relationship corresponds to what has been, until now, an inability on her part to control or even temper the actions of her own spouse. This emphasis by the chorus on a marriage motif, but without any mention of the goddess with which it is most associated, underscores this tension and heightens the anticipation for her imminent arrival.

The first half of the play focussed on the affair between Zeus and Alcmene and the consequences of this for Amphitryon, but with no mention of the implications of their dalliance on Hera, and there are several. When Hera finally makes her will known to both characters and audience she confirms that Zeus should be seen as a μοιχός; but his infidelity is not merely a breach of marriage bonds. Zeus and Hera are the "perfect" (τέλειος) couple and as such are *the* gods of marriage. Thus, his act transgressed against both the goddess whose *timē* is marriage[228] and against his own obligations as the other god of marriage. This transgression becomes more apparent with the arrival of Iris and Lyssa, sent by Hera to incite madness in Heracles.[229]

---

[227] νύμφη "is used primarily of a young woman envisaged in relation to marriage," Seaford (1987) 123.

[228] Mikalson (1986) 95.

[229] See especially Lee (1982) and Provenza (2013) for a discussion of this scene.

When Lyssa attempts to dissuade Iris from their current mission of wreaking havoc

upon Heracles and his house, Iris explicitly mentions Hera as the legitimate wife of Zeus:

οὐχὶ σωφρονεῖν γ' ἔπεμψε δεῦρό σ' ἡ Διὸς δάμαρ (*Her.* 857). The use of δάμαρ to

describe Hera provides the goddess with her appropriate title, emphasizing exactly that

relationship which has hitherto been undermined in relation to Zeus' affair with Alcmene,

but which becomes increasingly important in the second half of the play. The emphasis on

Hera sending the two other deities on their mission also underscores her enmity toward

Heracles (as the product of Zeus' affair) and complicates the power-dynamic between the

two gods. The agenda to traumatize Heracles is an act of which Zeus would not approve,

as well as one that, apparently, he cannot stop[230] – both intimating the limitations of his

absolute rule.

This potential to see Hera undermining, or even limiting Zeus' authority, becomes

more pronounced after the goddess has succeeded in her plan to ruin Heracles' family.

Amphitryon, seeing the devastating results of Hera's designs, asks whether Zeus sees what

she has wrought: ὦ Ζεῦ, παρ' Ἥρας ἆρ' ὁρᾷς θρόνων τάδε; (*Her.* 1127). Amphitryon's

specificity of where Zeus is in relation to Hera is noticeable and is worthy of further

consideration, although scholars have taken different views of its significance. Michelini

observes that "the picture of Zeus as sharing his rule with his queen, who is enthroned

beside him, well expresses the essentially compromising effect of Hera on Zeus' status as

supreme god."[231] Bond, rather more cynically, suggests: "Zeus is not on his own throne,

ready to attend to his son's needs, but on the throne of Hera. The implication is clear: Hera

is seated on her throne, as deities are commonly depicted; with her is Zeus, engaged in

---

[230] Lawrence (1998) 143.

[231] Michelini (1987) 270.

some form of sexual intercourse."[232] Finally, Halleran's only comment is that "Amphitryon's remark suggests Zeus' subservience to Hera's wishes in this matter."[233] It is clear that the juxtaposition of a (likely) standing Zeus beside an enthroned Hera suggests a more complex dynamic between the two gods than is usually portrayed; however, there was also a temple of Hera at Olympia which depicts the same scenario (Paus. 5.17.1[234]) and could thus be influencing Euripides' choice of representation here. Therefore, even if the temple of Hera at Olympia were Euripides' source of inspiration, in the context of the play, the imagery and connotations of this arrangement would have suggested some kind of subservience on Zeus' part. At Olympia, they would have been occupying Hera's space (as it would be her temple) and Zeus would not be the dominant figure. This idea corresponds well to the action of the play, as the preceding scene is very much the product of her influence. Amphitryon's description of Zeus seemingly attending Hera indicates the goddess' dominance of the action and even over Zeus.[235] This suggests then, that even if he wanted to stop Hera from carrying out her revenge on Heracles, he would be unable to

---

[232] Bond (1981) 353.

[233] Halleran (1988) 60.

[234] Pausanias' description is not an exact match however: Hera is enthroned, sitting beside a standing Zeus, who is bearded and helmeted. They are accompanied by the Horai, also enthroned, and a standing Themis. There is no indication in Euripides that Zeus is helmeted, or that they are anywhere near Themis or the Horai.

[235] The juxtaposition of a seated Hera situated near a standing Zeus would at least be ambiguous for the ancient audience. On the one hand, being enthroned is a symbol of power, analogous to that of Zeus in his own temple at Olympia. On the other hand, females are often seated near their standing husbands to indicate their submissiveness and in Archaic Greek art this was a "perfectly ordinary" representation according to Bremmer (1991) 24. But around the beginning of the 6th c., the predilection for standing statues began to wane and reclining gods and goddesses became customary, Bremmer (1991) 25. In Roman statuary, the enthroned figure nearly always is the dominant figure (Davies [2005] 234), but whether this can be applied to 5th c. Athens is uncertain.

do so according to the "rule" that gods cannot interfere with the plans of other gods (cf.

Eur. *Hipp*. 1331-34).[236] The implication is that this rule applies equally to Zeus himself.

Indeed, Zeus did not stop Hera from her first attempt to destroy Heracles when the

goddess sent the snakes into the hero's bedroom, as the hero explains:

> ἔτ' ἐν γάλακτί τ' ὄντι γοργωποὺς ὄφεις
> ἐπεισέφρησε σπαργάνοισι τοῖς ἐμοῖς
> ἡ τοῦ Διὸς σύλλεκτρος, ὡς ὀλοίμεθα (*Her*. 1266-68).

Euripides has here used the same word (σύλλεκτρος) to describe Hera as he used to

describe Alcmene in Amphitryon's opening monologue (1); these are the only two

instances in Euripides' extant oeuvre (and neither Aeschylus nor Sophocles employs it),

making the usage even more significant. The effect is such that it would signal to the more

astute in the audience that Zeus and Amphitryon are once again being portrayed

similarly[237] and the earthly marriage between Amphitryon and Alcmene is almost a mirror

of their heavenly counterparts. Zeus is at once on the opposing side of Hera and yet also

her "other half" augmenting the complex power-dynamic between the gods, where Zeus

cannot interfere with Hera's designs, but also that Hera's designs only exist when Zeus

behaves contrary to his position as a god of marriage and as her husband.

As Heracles commiserates, he makes much of the relationship between Hera and

Zeus, insisting that Hera has contrived all of his misfortunes because of Zeus' infidelities

and that she is now celebrating her step-son's calamities: χορευέτω δὴ Ζηνὸς ἡ κλεινὴ

δάμαρ / †κρόουσ' Ὀλυμπίου Ζηνὸς ἀρβύληι πόδα† (*Her*. 1303-04). The image Heracles

presents of Hera leading a chorus in dance is striking and may bring to mind the choral

---

[236] This is *contra* Padilla (1994) 294 who claims that "Zeus has *permitted* Hera to attack Heracles
at his moment of greatest triumph" (emphasis my own).

[237] Although Padilla (1994) 295 interprets this second appellation as tying Hera to Amphitryon as a
connective between "Heracles' taskmasters."

dances in honour of Hera at Olympia (Paus. 5.16.1-8).[238] More importantly, however, is

that the theme of the legitimate wife returns with the reference to Hera as Zeus' δάμαρ.

While dancing, the goddess has the attention of all Olympus and, as the leader of such a

dance (if one takes it as part of the rituals celebrating the Heraia), can be interpreted as

finally being recognized as the rightful partner of Zeus, "becoming" once more married to

her spouse (as if re-enacting the annual marriage ritual where Hera "marries" Zeus).

The earlier suggestions that Hera is potentially the dominant partner in the

relationship, however, continue to be emphasized:

> ἢ γυναικὸς οὕνεκα
> λέκτρων φθονοῦσα Ζηνὶ τοὺς εὐεργέτας
> Ἑλλάδος ἀπώλεσ' οὐδὲν ὄντας αἰτίους (*Her.* 1308-10).

Zeus' ability to maintain his supremacy continues to be undermined by these references to

his spouse. The further suggestion that the play's disasters were initiated because of a

grudge (φθονοῦσα) against Zeus also undercuts the god's superiority, suggesting that

there is discontent amongst the gods and also that they have leave and authority to

undermine his will. However, because the words are coming from Heracles there is an

obvious bias against Hera and thus the hero's anger toward Zeus is expected. Euripides'

emphasis on the relationship between Zeus and Hera continues to evoke a sense of

discomfort at the power-dynamic between the two divinities for both inner and outer

audiences and, furthermore, creates uneasiness on the part of mortals to accept Zeus'

authority in Olympus, as they question his moral superiority and ability to maintain

control.

---

[238] According to Pausanias there were two choral dances instituted at the Heraia at Olympia, the
Physkoa and one inaugurated by Hippodamaia. Both were arranged by sixteen married women as
part of the festivities of the Heraia, begun by Hippodamaia out of gratitude to the goddess for her
marriage to Pelops.

Theseus makes the final reference to the relationship between Hera and Zeus when he responds to Heracles' criticisms of the gods. Theseus agrees that the responsibility lies with Hera, οὐκ ἔστιν ἄλλου δαιμόνων ἀγὼν ὅδε / ἢ τῆς Διὸς δάμαρτος· (1311-12), but suggests that the gods should not be looked to as role-models, for they do not live by mortal standards (1318-19).[239] The most pertinent aspect of Theseus' statement is the mention of the ἀγὼν, for he intimates that the contest is a struggle between Heracles and Hera. That the goddess has been Heracles' antagonist is without question, but a secondary reading might suggest that the contest is in fact between Hera and Zeus, for that is where the balance of power is most out of sync and is in most need of restoration. The disasters suffered by Heracles are a by-product of Hera's anger, but the goddess' enmity is actually directed at Zeus and not the hero himself (1308-10). The instability in heaven has resulted in a paralleled instability in the relationships which mirror those of the gods; and the relationships which should be sacred are undone: Heracles has killed his wife, sundering the sacred bond of marriage; he has killed his sons, an act of filicide; and he has abandoned his father out of need of friendship with Theseus, rejecting his duties as a son (discussed further in chapter 6, p. 192). Only when stability in the heavens returns, might it return to the human sphere.

In Euripides' *Heracles,* then, the arbitrary exercise of Zeus' power to do as he will creates the crack in the cosmic order that permits Hera to exercise, at least temporarily, authority over her husband and his progeny. The image of Alcmene as Zeus' legitimate partner in the beginning of the play displaces Hera from her proper place; such displacement prompts a sudden and swift reaction from Hera. Alcmene's replacement by Hera as Zeus' partner in the second half of the play thus corresponds to Hera's reclamation of her place as the wife of Zeus. The attainment of such heavenly accord (after reparations

---

[239] Halleran (1986) 174-75.

have been made) brings about a mortal accord once more. In Seneca, a similar scenario can be found, although there, Juno is not merely the displaced wife: she is also the displaced *sister* and her anger is directed more at Hercules than Jupiter and such anger is not solely about her husband's extra-marital affairs.

Jupiter, Hercules and Juno: Breaking the Model

In Seneca's *Hercules Furens*, Jupiter is no less of a philanderer than Zeus is in Euripides and Juno is no less angry. But what is at stake in this play is not only Juno's status as the legitimate wife of Jupiter, but also the future status of his son. Juno is far more concerned about the potential for Hercules to become a god and how that will affect her, than the trysts Jupiter has had with other women (although that is not to say she approves of them either). She also attributes some of her rage to her concern that Hercules will attempt to usurp his father (64-66)[240] and thus she is, in a sense, protecting Jupiter. The most significant change, however, and one which potentially alters the perception of the goddess, is that Juno herself appears on-stage. She does not use intermediaries to complete her task but instead uses the inspiration of the Furies to accomplish her revenge herself. Her presence as a character achieves two things: first, it dramatizes the diminution of her godhead; she cannot rely on others to do her work and must do it herself. Secondly, her appearance intensifies her anger and resolve, creating a "battle-scene" between goddess and hero: there is no doubt that Hera wants to destroy him and no doubt about whom he is battling against. Jupiter again does not interfere with Juno's attack, but her alleged concern for his supremacy is cause enough to reflect on the dynamics of their relationship and Jupiter's ability to maintain his position as lord of Olympus.

---

[240] Shelton (1978) 61.

The status of Jupiter and Juno's relationship is the very first piece of information provided in the play. Juno opens with a monologue and introduces herself as *Soror Tonantis* (*HF* 1).[241] As a sister, Juno renounces her status as Jupiter's wife, declaring that her godhead has been assaulted by the presence of Jupiter's paramours in the sky, leaving her with too little space. At first, this would seem to suggest that Jupiter's consorts (through the god's will) have more clout than the goddess herself.[242] This, however, is not the case. By referring to Jupiter as "Lord of the Thunder," she emphasizes his function as a god of retribution.[243] Juno as *soror Tonantis* is thus also linked implicitly with this function. By forsaking her status as a wife and taking up the title of a sister, Juno effectively replaces a position of potential subservience with one of potential equality; in doing so, she alters the power-dynamic between herself and Jupiter.[244] By declaring herself a *sister* of Jupiter, rather than his wife, she is attempting to equate herself with the god and his epithet and her actions will serve to question Jupiter's ability to maintain control over his "wife" and to protect his offspring.

---

[241] Lawall (1983) 6 notes Juno's monologue is clearly constructed in the Virgilian and Ovidian tradition, where in the former she declared herself queen of the gods as both wife and sister to Jupiter (*Aen.* 1.46) and in the latter declared that as queen she should be both wife and sister, but sister at the very least (*Met.* 3.266). Here, the titles of queen and wife both disappear.

[242] Shelton (1978) 18; Heldman (1974) 22 adds that Juno's descent to earth is made unwillingly, much like the ascent made by Thyestes and Tantalus in *Agamemnon* and *Thyestes* respectively.

[243] The connection between Jupiter's lightning bolts and the punishment of mortals is commonplace in Latin poetry; see, for example, Hor. *Od.* 1.3.37-40; Ov. *Trist.* 2.33-36, Luc. *BC* 3.317-20.

[244] Jupiter, as Juno's husband, ostensibly maintains control and absolute authority over his wife; as her brother, Jupiter has an obligation to defend her property and status. Juno, in return, would have an obligation to further her brother's interests as much as possible. See Dixon (1985) 361 for a discussion of the wife as *sui iuris* and still maintaining obligations to her natal kin.

Juno's hatred for Hercules stems less from who he is than from what he represents,[245] which is the usurpation of the heavenly abode by Jupiter's other amours, Alcmene in particular (21-22). Juno now dwells on earth (4-5), having abandoned *semper alienum Iovem* (2). That Jupiter is seen by Juno as forever belonging to another woman is unsurprising, although the specific word *alienum* could also have connotations of hostility.[246] Juno is aggrieved because of Jupiter's infidelities and hostility toward her, but more importantly, because she is losing honour in the heavens; her *vivaces iras* (28-29) will not dissipate and she threatens to pursue *aeterna bella* (29).[247] These threats are not yet specifically directed at Hercules; they seem rather to be the culmination of her grievances toward all of Jupiter's children (6-23).[248] Her immediate target, however, is Hercules, and Juno is using him as the means to her ultimate goal: she will set before him his final labour, to war with himself; the result of which she is hoping will be enough for Jupiter to reconsider his son's apotheosis, her "single-minded, monolithic" aim.[249] If she is successful, not only will she have conquered Hercules, but she will have regained some of her honour and made clear her grievance to Jupiter. While this obviously provides further insight into Juno's "psyche" as it were, it also suggests that Jupiter's actions do have negative consequences, given Juno's spiteful resentment and hostile reaction. Seneca's depiction of Juno further suggests that the goddess has the ability to undermine Jupiter's

---

[245] Taking the interpretation that Juno's persecution of Hercules is due to "what he is, not for what he does" (Motto and Clark [1981] 111) one step further; see also Lawall (1983) 6.

[246] Fitch (1987) 118.

[247] As Owen (1968) 303 notes, "Juno's opening *katabasis* . . . is provoked by a moral disintegration so pervasive as to make the heavens themselves uninhabitable, springing as it does from Zeus' marital delicts."

[248] Owen (1968) 303; see also Rose (1985) 104: "The starry spectacle, an aggravating reminder of Juno's rivals for Jupiter's affections, ultimately provokes her assault on Hercules, but, in addition, the astronomical catalogue anticipates the theme of cosmic disruption."

[249] Motto and Clark (1981) 115.

will. Hercules' eventual apotheosis is not treated during the play and we are left with no guarantee that it will occur. All we know it that he has been promised the stars (23, 959) and Juno wishes Jupiter to reconsider, leaving the audience with the suggestion that it may not happen after all. Indeed, at the end of the play, Hercules' only wish is to return to the Underworld (1338-39), not to the stars, awarding Juno at least a partial victory.[250] The audience would know Hercules is eventually granted apotheosis, but they also now know it almost did not occur, thanks to Juno's efforts.[251]

Juno acknowledges Hercules' divine conception when she declares her course of action against him to avenge his impiety against the Underworld (104). She will use Hercules' own parentage as her weapon, *hic prosit mihi / Iove esse genitum* (*HF* 117-18). As a son of Jupiter, Hercules has the potential to be brought up to heaven, but by staining the hero's hands with kindred blood, his divinity will no longer be secure. Indeed, when Juno refers to Jupiter as Hercules' father for the final time (four lines later), she refers explicitly to his potential divinization. She challenges Jupiter to accept his son after he commits such an offence: *scelere perfecto licet / admittat illas genitor in caelum manus* (121-22). Juno will cease her hatred only once the crime is complete and Jupiter will have leave to reconsider deifying his son. While Hercules' parentage will be questioned by other characters in the play, Juno acknowledges the god's role as the hero's father and she has (finally) found a way to accept it.

The relationship between Jupiter and Juno is given further nuance during the repartee between Lycus and Amphitryon. When Amphitryon is attempting to persuade Lycus of Hercules' divine birth, he uses the argument of Juno's hatred to prove the hero's divinity:

---

[250] Fitch (1979) 247.

[251] Lawall (1983) 7: "Juno knows that she cannot keep Hercules from his promised stars (23), but she will make it as difficult as possible for Jupiter to admit him into the skies."

Amph.:   mentimur Iovem?
         Iunonis odio crede.
Lyc.:   Quid violas Iovem? (*HF* 446-47).

Lycus of course does not consider Hercules to be Jupiter's son and believes it a profanity even to consider that Jupiter might consort with mortal women (much like Hecuba's belief concerning Hera's participation in the Judgement of Paris, Eur. *TW* 978). We know Lycus is wrong, given Juno's monologue at the beginning of the play, but the insistence by Lycus that Jupiter only associates himself with other deities provides another lens through which to interpret the god's representation. Jupiter's affairs are not always interpreted in the same way by the characters in the plays: Amphitryon is convinced of Hercules' divine ancestry and Lycus is certain Jupiter would never have a dalliance with a mortal woman – the former believing such an act perhaps extraordinary, but not impossible, the latter believing it an act of shame and disgrace.

Jupiter's relationship with Juno does receive further mention in the play however, and with intriguing implications. When Hercules is in his fit of madness, he believes at one point he is attacking the goddess, who in reality is his wife, Megara (1008-09). Hercules taunts his "enemy" and insinuates that by conquering Juno he will give Jupiter freedom from his wife: *sequere, da poenas mihi / iugoque pressum libera turpi Iovem* (*HF* 1018-9). The noun *iugo* here suggests that Jupiter is yoked by marriage as well as by humiliation or servitude[252] and this paints a very different picture of the relationship between the two deities. One could interpret Hercules' words as describing a pair of oxen, as if Jupiter and Juno are yoked to a plough together, a metaphor of their marriage. Hercules' offer to free Jupiter from his yoke would suggest that he sees his father as hindered in his exercise of authority by this plough-partner, a partner who often wants to pull in a direction opposite

---

[252] Fitch (1987) 381.

to his own. Only by being freed from the yoke can Jupiter exert his authority unencumbered. However, Hercules' desire to aid his father would throw the cosmos itself into chaos since Juno's own authority as goddess of marriage would be dishonoured, if not negated. Ideally, a way must be found for Juno to pull willingly in the same direction as her husband within the marriage yoke. In this play, that way is presented as the appeasement of Juno's wrath through the destruction of Hercules' family, Jupiter's descendants.

Upon the deaths of his wife and children, whom he now believes to be the family of Lycus, Hercules declares that all was done as a sacrifice to Juno[253] and he restores the title she had abandoned in the prologue: *tibi hunc dicatum, maximi coniunx Iovis, / gregem cecidi* (1036-37). Papadopoulou would see this "periphrastic reference to Juno" as "an offence against Jupiter"[254] and because Hercules has just committed murder and filicide in appeasement to Juno, such an interpretation is valid. However, having carried out Juno's will, Hercules has simultaneously fulfilled the wishes of the goddess, restored her honour and committed an impiety that will not easily be purified. Juno has proven that her will shall be done too and when her title is restored, she regains her place as Jupiter's wife, sharing now in his other title, *maximus*. She is no longer the sister, nor is she taking up the function of *tonantis*: she is, at last, wife of the supreme lord of Olympus. While Jupiter may (and would likely be) offended by the "sacrifices" made in his wife's name, Hercules is in fact admitting his own inferiority to the goddess, thus restoring to Jupiter his spouse and, as a by-product, putting an end to the cosmic turmoil created by his exploits.

The final two references to Juno in the play reiterate the goddess' interference in Hercules' return, although neither provides her with a title. Amphitryon lays the blame for

---

[253] Papadopoulou (2004) 272-73 discusses the sacrificial language Hercules uses to describe the murders, arguing its use underscores the atrociousness of the act against his family.

[254] Papadopoulou (2004) 273.

the hero's murders on Juno as Hercules' *novercae* (1201) and later reinforces the fact that it was *Iuno* who fired his bow, albeit with Hercules' hands (1297). Juno is not explicitly associated with Jupiter in either reference, although as a step-mother to Hercules, her relationship with Jupiter is implied.[255] What is clear, however, is the absolute conviction that Juno orchestrated these events and was able to achieve at least one of her objectives (that she regain some of her lost honour). In Euripides, the issue of the legality of Zeus' affair with Alcmene was of central importance and paved the way for interpreting the breach of heavenly marriage bonds as being reflected by a similar breach in the human sphere. In Seneca, there is no decision to be made regarding Jupiter's affairs and Juno is angry for losing honour to them. She is also concerned that Hercules will attempt to usurp her husband's place, a concern present, but not heavily stressed by Euripides.[256] Although each playwright emphasizes different aspects of the relationship between the two deities, it is clear that the uneasy tension between them is one which can be easily exploited by the tragedians.

Sibling Rivalry: Hades and Dis

Seneca's *Hercules Furens* portrays not only Jupiter's uneasy tensions with his sister-wife Juno, but also with his chthonic brother Dis and such tensions are highlighted from very early in the play within Juno's opening monologue. Juno is the first character to

---

[255] Juno took up the identification of a *noverca* at the beginning of the play (21) when she renounced her title as Jupiter's wife and wished to accomplish something *worthy* (112) of that name; the catalyst for her acts as a step-mother is Jupiter's infidelities, Fitch and McElduff (2002) 30.

[256] In Euripides, Hera is concerned about Heracles' success and its implications for the other gods (841-42), the chorus also sing of Heracles as if he were a god already (680-81) and Megara and Amphitryon look to him as though divine (520-22; see Papadimitropoulos [2008b] 133-34). The issue of bestowing divine honours upon Heracles before he is deified is thus present and the hero's relationship to Zeus will be considered in the next chapter.

allude to Jupiter's supreme (yet possibly tenuous) authority when she fears that Hercules is aiming to overthrow his father. The goddess goes so far as to suggest that Hercules might even be successful, *sceptra praeripiet patri* (*HF* 65). The fact that Juno herself has been pushed out of heaven by Jupiter's paramours (4-5), suggests that the gods can, in fact, be supplanted. Furthermore, while the idea of Hercules succeeding in an attack against Jupiter seems extravagant, that we are also told the hero conquered the lord of the Underworld (47-53) and, more specifically, Jupiter's own brother, makes it seem more plausible. Whether or not Juno is right to fear Hercules, that there is even the possibility of someone (especially a son) usurping Jupiter's place suggests that the god's control is not unassailable and this raises the question of Jupiter's relationship with his brother Dis, his counterpart in the Underworld.

The relationship between Jupiter and Dis becomes one of particular interest, as the two are compared several times in *Hercules Furens* and the hero's visit to the Underworld suggests Juno's fears about her step-son could be valid. During her monologue, Juno claims that Hercules visited the Underworld as a conqueror, returning to the upper world with triumphant spoils:

> effregit ecce limen inferni Iovis
> et opima victi regis ad superos refert.
> vidi ipsa, vidi nocte discussa inferum
> et Dite domito spolia iactantem patri
> fraterna. cur non vinctum et oppressum trahit
> ipsum catenis paria sortitum Iovi (*HF* 47-48, 50-53).

That Dis is referred to as the "infernal Jupiter" (*inferni Iovis*) is familiar enough, but the effect of introducing the scene by naming Dis a "Jupiter" reminds the audience of the similarities and kinship between the two gods. Hercules' triumph over this Jupiter (Dis) is suggestive of his potential threat to the celestial Jupiter.[257] Juno's description of the event

---

[257] Fitch (1987) 137.

also includes familial terms (*patri, fraterna*), which further augment the sacrilege committed against Dis.[258] Not only has Hercules defeated a god, and one who is described as another Jupiter, but a god who is his father's brother, making his so-called triumph that much more impious. Thus, Hercules' crime is committed on two levels: the first is impiety against the gods (descending to the Underworld and returning); secondly it is impiety against kin (stealing from and assaulting his uncle), verging on civil war. Whether or not Juno's description of the events is accurate (and in fact it seems not to be),[259] the description has succinctly linked the two gods in such a way as to suggest both their similarities and their weaknesses. If Hercules is able to defeat the lord of the Underworld, what is there to suggest he could not succeed against the lord of Olympus? This passage does much to undermine the certainty of Jupiter's continuing position as supreme ruler and suggests that there is the *potential*, at least, to be overpowered.

Theseus confirms Juno's suggestion of the similarities between Jupiter and Dis when he describes Hercules' visit to the Underworld. He gives an intriguing description of the infernal god and one which explicitly reveals the resemblance between the two gods: *vultus est illi Iovis, / sed fulminantis* (724-25). Theseus' description serves to equate Dis with Jupiter, but it also equates Jupiter with Dis. Jupiter as a god of lightning is thus equated with death, but it is even more than that – he is the *face* of Death. Furthermore, if someone deserving of punishment does not "receive his dues" in life (by Jupiter) he will

---

[258] Papadopoulou (2004) 275 notes how Hercules also refers to Dis periphrastically as the "infernal Jupiter" later in the play (608), reminding the audience of Juno's earlier expressed fear: that Hercules will become a threat to Jupiter himself. Hercules later admits that if he wished to rule in the Underworld, he could have (609-10), which further suggests that Juno's fears are not completely unsubstantiated.

[259] Although Shelton (1978) 17-25 has argued that Juno's monologue describes the events of the play as they happen, effectively compressing the play into her speech, before returning temporally to the beginning of the play.

receive them in death (a theme brought out by *Hecuba*, discussed below).[260] The grim and disconcerting portrayal of Dis can thus be transposed onto Jupiter as well. Theseus also relates that Dis' appearance *timet / quidquid timetur* (726-27). If Dis and Jupiter have a similar countenance, and Jupiter's face is the face of Dis, it should follow that Jupiter need not fear the sight of Cerberus when Hercules brings him up from the Underworld. This is not the case though, as Jupiter is instructed by Hercules to take a defensive position (597-98). Taken together, these parallels suggest that Jupiter is only feared when he is launching thunderbolts, or at least that he is feared less than Dis except when he is fulminating.

Jupiter's supremacy seems to be reinstated, however, when Amphitryon calls upon the god at the start of the second act to provide an end to his family's troubles:

> O magne Olympi rector et mundi arbiter,
> iam statue tandem gravibus aerumnis modum
> finemque cladi (*HF* 205-07).

Jupiter's place as a ruler of Olympus and of the cosmos is declared without hesitation and there is nothing unusual in the epithets used. Both *rector* and *arbiter* are elsewhere used in the play to indicate Jupiter's supreme authority (517, 597), but this confirmation of Jupiter's omnipotence is short-lived. When these titles are next used together, again by Amphitryon, they refer not to Jupiter, but to Minos, Rhadamanthus and Aeacus (730-34). Both of Jupiter's titles are usurped by the judges of the Underworld, suggesting again that his authority should not be seen as greater than that of Dis, or conversely that Jupiter's powers are arbitrary and that only in death will there be any real "end" (*finem*, 207) of disasters – essentially that which Amphitryon is requesting of Jupiter, but which will not be granted in the manner he expects.

---

[260] Henry and Walker (1965) 14: "Just as Pluto in a way mirrors Jupiter, so Hell mirrors Jupiter's kingdom of heaven . . . the total impression is not chaotic, but suggests that Hell has its place as part of a universal order.

The final allusion to Jupiter which equates the god with Dis is provided by the chorus. As the chorus sings of Hercules' trip to the Underworld, they give a description of the number of shades one meets while there. The chorus suggests that the number would equal that of a crowd in a city awaiting games, or as many as would attend the games of Olympian Jupiter: *quantus Eleum ruit ad Tonantem* (840).[261] While this is not a strict comparison between the two deities, it does imply that both gods draw an equal number of worshippers and even that there is no discernible difference between the two. The description the chorus provides of the shades could just as easily pertain to those attending Jupiter's festivals (845-54). The persistent comparisons and allusions to Jupiter and Dis as equals suggests that Jupiter's authority is not supreme, but that he shares his power with his counterpart, the nether Jove. Furthermore, the similarities found between the gods do not provide a jovial depiction of Jupiter, but instead imply that in many ways he is no different from his sibling.

Comparing Seneca's treatment of the relationship between Jupiter and Dis with that of Euripides' treatment of Zeus and Hades, suggests the above interpretation can be seen to signal a significant shift from the Athenian to Roman perspective. For, if one considers Euripides' version of the myth, the two gods are not at all contrasted in such a way. In fact, in *Heracles* the hero's *katabasis* to the Underworld is drastically downplayed and the capture of Cerberus is linked with Persephone rather than Hades (612). Furthermore, while the Underworld is acknowledged as the house of Pluto (Πλούτωνος δῶμα, *Her*. 808), the sceptre belongs not to him, but to his wife (1104). There is no impiety committed against kin as Seneca would have it and no reason to compare the realm of Hades to that of Zeus.

In Euripides' *Hecuba*, there is even a sense that the two gods work in concert in order to attain *dikē* for Polydorus. Here, there is no rivalry or strict comparison between

---

[261] Elean is often used to mean Olympic, Fitch (1987) 338.

the two gods, but rather a sense that the justice of Zeus is carried on into the afterlife, where one will receive "his dues" from Hades when not dispensed by Zeus, an idea that is picked up by Seneca, as mentioned above. In this play, there are no epiphanies of gods or goddesses, nor do any characters pray to or supplicate them – indeed Zeus is specifically *not* invoked (*Hec.* 345);[262] however, the gods do frame our reading of the play and how we interpret it.[263] When the audience is informed of Polydorus' murder and expulsion to the sea, the act would be understood as trespassing both societal and religious laws. Polymestor is presented as a murderer, as a breaker of oaths, as someone who broke his bonds of *xenia* and one who had ignored the rites of burial.[264] These offences are not only based on Athenian secular laws, but are offences against the gods, Zeus and Hades in particular.[265] That Hades is also the first deity mentioned in the play (2) and is mentioned more than any other, should be seen as a signpost for where to look for the presence of divine authority.[266]

Hades pervades the play from beginning to end and while some references signal the place rather than the god, they nonetheless encourage the audience to have the lord of

---

[262] Several scholars suggest the gods have little or nothing to do with the play; see, for example, the title of Hartigan (1997), Mossman (1995) 201 and Mitchell-Boyask (1993) 118; Segal (1990b) 125 and Zeitlin (1991) 55 do not go quite as far as "godless" but suggest the gods are "almost completely absent" and "seem to be absent" (respectively).

[263] Kovacs (1987) and Gregory (1999) both interpret the play as having important divine elements.

[264] Billing (2007) 53.

[265] Mitchell-Boyask (1993) 119: "to say that the *Hecuba* 'does not make use of gods as agents in the action' [Michelini 1987, 170] neglects the chthonic gods sanctioning Polydorus' appearance and misses one of the more distressing aspects of theodicy in the *Hecuba*." This statement, however, is made in reference to Achilles acting as a god, rather than recognizing the wider use and significance of the chthonic deities.

[266] Even more than Zeus, who is mentioned seven times (and is the only specific god referred to by a Greek – Talthybius, who disbelieves his cosmic authority and integrity, 488-91), Hades is referred to eight times.

the Underworld in their minds. Significantly, Hades is the god ultimately responsible for Polydorus' opportunity to appear to Hecuba in a dream and to be revealed on the beach as one in need of burial. The remaining references further encourage the audience to keep Hades in mind throughout the play. Polyxena is seen as a bride of Hades (218, 368) and the chorus explicitly mention leaving Asia and the chambers of Hades for abodes in Europe (479-83). These references serve to remind the audience of both Polyxena's and Polydorus' fate: each child now belongs to the realm of Hades, leaving the laws of Zeus for those of his brother. Hades does not reappear in the text until the choral ode preceding the mutilation of Polymestor and death of his sons. They sing of justice and that Polymestor's life will be forfeit to Hades (1033): a just reward for his actions against Polydorus.[267] Polymestor too sees Hades' hand in his fate, albeit in a somewhat different light, when he refers to the women as Bacchants of Hades (1076).[268] Polymestor also provides the final reference which is a question concerning his ultimate destination – up to the stars, or down to the ship of Hades (1102).

This emphasis on Hades is not without reinforcement in other ways as well. Persephone also receives a mention by the Chorus Leader when relating the decision by the Greeks to sacrifice Polyxena. It is reported that Odysseus refuses to let the Greeks in Persephone's realm, who died on their behalf, be without honours (136). This serves to highlight the fact that the dead belong to the gods of the Underworld and require certain rites once there; even though Odysseus is arguing from a political perspective, the religious undertones would not have gone unnoticed by the audience. Finally, there are further references to "powers below" which also highlight the importance of the chthonic deities in the play. Polydorus was given permission by these Underworld powers to let his

---

[267] Luschnig (1976) 277.

[268] The Dionysiac reference is obviously relevant, but so too is Polymestor's recognition that the women are dispensing the punishments of Hades.

plight become known to his mother (47); Hecuba prays to these same gods to spare her son's life (79); she is urged to pray to both the upper and lower gods to save Polyxena's life (147); Polymestor is said by Hecuba to fear neither gods above or below the earth (791); and finally Lady Earth (πότνια Χθών) is appealed to by Hecuba to cleanse her mind after her frightful dream (*Hec.* 70).[269]

In a play where Olympians seem to be absent, the presence of these chthonic deities serves to reinforce the importance of the rites of the dead and the inevitability of "justice" being enacted if not by Zeus, then certainly by Hades. Hades has allowed Polydorus' shade the opportunity to visit his mother and Zeus has ensured that Hecuba will eventually come to understand her son's fate and act as the instrument of punishment the god desires.[270] Thus, Segal's interpretation that Hecuba's prayer for a god to come to her aid does not eventuate[271] is not necessarily the case.[272] Instead, we should understand that Zeus and Hades work together to see "justice done," even if it is not always apparent that that is what is occurring.[273] Thus, in some ways, a very different picture emerges in *Hecuba* of the relationship between these two brothers from that proffered by Seneca. On the one hand, an obvious connection between the two gods and their ability to work together, or in Seneca their near uniformity, is clearly evident; on the other hand, however, Euripides emphasizes the dispensation of justice, whereas Seneca highlights their

---

[269] In this last example, it is especially relevant that Euripides chooses to use Χθών as opposed to Γαῖα, the former being explicitly related to chthonic powers.

[270] One parallel may be found in *Trojan Women* (887-88) when Hecuba prays to Zeus that Menelaus be the instrument of punishment against Helen, discussed above, chapter 2, pp. 67.

[271] Segal (1989) 16.

[272] Heath (2003) 258-59 presents the possibility that the gods have a hand in Polymestor's punishment.

[273] Kastely (1993) 1040.

similarities in terms of their deadliness. Once again, the comparison underscores important nuances of Zeus and Jupiter's relationships that each playwright wishes to manipulate.

The Other Brother: Poseidon and Neptune

There is, of course, a third brother and a third realm to consider, although there are fewer references to Poseidon and Neptune, who each are given little press by the dramatists. Poseidon does appear in Euripides *Trojan Women* and it is from this play and *Hippolytus* that one can discern the most about the god's relationship to Zeus (slight though it is). There is no such appearance of Neptune in any of the Senecan plays, although a few references in *Phaedra* and *Hercules Furens* offer at least a glimpse of this god's status is relation to Jupiter. Unlike Dis, however, Neptune's relationship with his brother seems to change very little from his counterpart in the plays of Euripides.

Poseidon provides the opening to Euripides' *Trojan Women*, explaining how Hera and Athena conquered Troy against his will and that he is now departing from Ilium (*TW* 23-26.).[274] Euripides does not provide any contrast between Poseidon and Zeus during this monologue, although the god does mention the atrocities committed at Zeus' altar (15-17). Instead, Poseidon is depicted much like Artemis in *Hippolytus*, where there is little he can do to thwart the will of the other deities. He is thus portrayed, in a sense, as an equal to the goddesses, but not to his brother. It is only when Athena makes her entrance that the audience receives any further information concerning the relationship between these gods.

---

[274] O'Neill (1941) 297; Scodel (1980) 66. Fontenrose (1967) has argued that Poseidon was only concerned about the physical city of Troy and not its citizens and furthermore that Poseidon was not a pro-Trojan deity. He does concede that the god was defeated by the goddesses at a council (137) and thus the interpretation that the rule of divine "non-interference" is at work remains valid. See also a reply by Wilson (1968) and a further response by Fontenrose (1968).

Athena's address to her uncle immediately undermines any connotation of equality between the two deities, for she humbles herself before Poseidon and signals his close connection to Zeus:

ἔξεστι τὸν γένει μὲν ἄγχιστον πατρὸς
μέγαν τε δαίμον' ἐν θεοῖς τε τίμιον,
λύσασαν ἔχθραν τὴν πάρος, προσεννέπειν; (*TW* 48-50).

It is clear that Athena is formally addressing Poseidon and the language she uses indicates both her status as kin to the god as well as the god's status as one ἄγχιστον πατρὸς ("closest to [my] father"). Athena is acknowledging the priority of Poseidon's relationship with Zeus over her own and, by implication, declaring Poseidon's status as second in the divine hierarchy only to Zeus. But not only is Poseidon second to Zeus in a technical sense, he is also greatly admired amongst the gods by his own *time*. It is clear that there is a hierarchy established, but unlike the relationship between Zeus and Hades (or between Jupiter and Dis) there is no sense of equality between the two brothers. This is further emphasized when Poseidon asks the reason for Athena's presence: μῶν ἐκ θεῶν του καινὸν ἀγγέλλεις ἔπος, / ἢ Ζηνὸς ἢ καὶ δαιμόνων τινὸς πάρα; (*TW* 55-56). He separates Zeus from both *daimones* and other *theoi*, thus acknowledging Zeus' superior status.[275]

In *Hippolytus*, Poseidon is invoked to fulfil one of the wishes he granted to Theseus as proof of his paternity. It is in the fulfilment of one of these curses that Poseidon and Zeus may be said to be working together. When Theseus learns that his wife was supposedly raped (an act that has dishonoured Zeus' eye), he calls upon Poseidon to kill Hippolytus, the god's grandson (885-90). Upon hearing the message that Hippolytus has been killed, Theseus again acknowledges Poseidon as his father and equates the event as a punishment of Dikē (1171). Indeed, when the messenger describes the advent of the bull from the sea, he likens the noise to Zeus' thunder: ἔνθεν τις ἠχὼ χθόνιος, ὡς βροντὴ

---

[275] Lee (1976) 74.

Διός, / βαρὺν βρόμον μεθῆκε, φρικώδη κλύειν· (*Hipp.* 1201-02).[276] This noise may be interpreted as a sign from the gods, although Segal does not interpret this particular sound as an omen from Zeus; he does, however, consider the bull itself as a manifestation of the divine and the "most powerful sign of successful communication in the play."[277] Rather than perceive the noise as solely belonging to one god or the other (and clearly it can be associated with both Zeus and Poseidon), it may be more prudent to understand it as a combined omen emanating from both deities.[278] The bull is simultaneously an answer to Hippolytus' earlier prayer to Zeus to strike him down if guilty (1191-3, and he *is* guilty), as well as a manifestation of the promise made by Poseidon to Theseus. Although not explicit, there is a sense that Zeus' will is being worked out with the aid of Poseidon, who is fulfilling his own pledge. This may liken their relationship to that found in *Hecuba* between Zeus and Hades, but once again, there is no evidence of any equality between the two.

---

[276] Berns (1973) 180-81: "In the following account of his death, *which might be understood as Zeus' answer* [my emphasis], one aspect comes to be pointed out as most terrible: that Hippolytos, who was so familiar with horses (1219-1220; cf. 110-112), should have been killed by his own horses, frightened by the appearance of the god-sent bull out of the sea (1204, 1218, 1229, 1240)."

[277] Segal (1993) 99.

[278] Such a description may fall under the category of Platt's "sonic epiphanies," for she notes that "[m]anifestations of divinity often involve significant crossover between the categories of 'vision' (*opsis*) and miracle (*aretê*), and have much in common with other forms of sacred semiosis, including oracles and portents" (2011, 10). See also Versnel (1987) 50 who observes that a "god manifests his presence not by his personal perceptibility whatever its nature, but by the signs or miracles he performs." He further states (51) that "[t]he presence of a god could be perceived by other means than visual or visionary illusions. Sometimes it is a mere awareness that the god is close by. One simply *knows* that he is there but language falls short in its task of providing an adequate description." Thus in Euripides' *Hippolytus* the visual manifestation of the bull from Poseidon in conjunction with sounds that are specifically linked to Zeus' thunder suggests that both of these gods are making their combined will known in the human sphere.

A similar scenario may be posited for the death of Hippolytus in *Phaedra*, which is a response to the youth's prayer that he be struck down with lightning, impaled and killed with fire:

> cur dextra, divum rector atque hominum, vacat
> tua, nec trisulca mundus ardescit face?
> in me tona, me fige, me velox cremet
> transactus ignis: sum nocens, merui mori:
> placui novercae (*Phaed*. 680-84).[279]

Hippolytus' death can surely be attributed to Theseus' wish that Neptune kill his son; however, the manner of his death indicates that Neptune may not be alone in ensuring the wish is carried out. When the messenger relates the tale of Hippolytus' death, he includes details of both the sea and the bull that has frightened the horses: the arrival of the bull is heralded by a "thundering" of the sea (*tonuit*, 1007) and as Hippolytus is being dragged along the ground, *raptum truncus ambusta sude / medium per inguen stipite eiecto tenet* (*Phaed*. 1098-99). Once again, the divine presence constitutes elements from both Jupiter and Neptune. The bull is clearly a manifestation of Neptune's pledge, but the manner of Hippolytus' death can also be attributed to Jupiter. Not only has Hippolytus been run down, but he was also impaled with a charred stake from a tree trunk. He has not been struck by lightning nor consumed by fire, but he has been transfixed and the stake itself was burnt, hinting at a reference to Jupiter's fires.[280] Given the fact that there are elements in the description of Hippolytus' death that are otherwise unnecessary, it is likely that Seneca is attributing at least part of his death to Jupiter's acknowledgement of Hippolytus'

---

[279] Coffey and Mayer (1990) 151 have suggested that Seneca could not "invent" any other "plausible" invocation for Hippolytus, suggesting that there is no dramatic or thematic reason for this prayer. But the details of how the prayer is fulfilled suggests that Seneca had a compelling reason to include it.

[280] Segal (1986) 58 associates fire with Jupiter and his governance of the cosmos.

prayers.[281] Again, the two gods are working in concert and, as before, there is here no discernible difference between the treatments of Euripides and Seneca.

One further reference in *Phaedra* offers the only real opportunity to question the hierarchy between the two siblings in the play, but it appears in a choral ode and has only minor relevance to the play's overall structure or themes. The chorus details Jupiter's theft of Europa, an episode of particular relevance to Phaedra's family history and her current plight, but one also of significance for the description of Jupiter traversing the seas with his newly-acquired maiden:

> fronte nunc torva petulans iuvencus
> virginum stravit sua terga ludo,
> perque fraternos, nova regna, fluctus
> ungula lentos imitante remos
> pectore adverso domuit profundum,
> pro sua vector timidus rapina (*Phaed.* 303-08).

Jupiter disguised himself as a young bull in order to make off with Europa and then made his way through the waves with her on his back. There are several striking images here, not least of which is the mention of his brother's realm, *nova* to Jupiter. It has been noted that this is indeed the first time Jupiter is *swimming* in the sea carrying Europa.[282] In Moschus' version, a similar simile is used of Jupiter's hooves as oars, but there the god walks on, rather than swims in, the water (Mosch. *Europa* 143). The sea, however, is no match for the god and Jupiter is able to conquer this realm, although not without some degree of danger, for Jupiter is *timidus*, an unusual adjective for the god. He fears that he may be unable to protect Europa, even though he has raped her. Why should this be so?

---

[281] Segal (1986) 126: "the answer [to Hippolytus' prayer] comes in the murderous apparition described later by the Messenger. The self-righteous appeal to the elevated Father of the Law, 'ruler of gods and men' (679), to 'transfix' him changes to physical impalement when the actual father returns."

[282] Boyle (1987) 156; Paschalis (1994) 108.

Simply put, although Jupiter remains superior in the grand cosmic hierarchy, he has trespassed into the realm awarded to his brother and this intrusion into his sibling's realm places him "on par" with other deities who need to respect the *auctoritas* of Neptune. Jupiter remains unparalleled in his sovereignty, but not without some apparent potential to come into conflict with the god whose realm he has penetrated.

The references in *Hercules Furens* support this view of a deity closely related to Jupiter and yet very firmly second to his authority. When Hercules arrives from the Underworld with Cerberus and instructs the gods (except Juno) to avert their eyes from beholding the creature, he addresses Neptune as *secundo maria qui sceptro regis* and suggests he *imas pete undas* (*HF* 599-600). As with Jupiter, Neptune needs to protect himself from an animal the mortal Hercules can look upon but which he cannot; more importantly, however, is how Hercules makes explicit the relationship between the two gods. Neptune is clearly second to Jupiter, just as Poseidon was to Zeus.

The final image to note here is that all three brothers carry sceptres.[283] While this is unsurprising, it does emphasize the ostensible equality among the three male Olympians, at least in terms of their traditional cosmic realms. But the emphasis on the sceptres not only signals this traditional division of the cosmos, it also stresses the individual *auctoritas* of each deity. While Jupiter remains symbolically superior to the other two (the heavens are above the seas and the Underworld), there is very little to distinguish between them. Thus, Seneca in *Hercules Furens* can describe Jupiter and Dis as nearly interchangeable and in *Phaedra*, Jupiter must *overcome* his brother's watery realm. Such "equality" is not

---

[283] Dis carries a sceptre at *HF* 707.

stressed by Euripides, although in his tragedies the brothers seem far more able to co-operate with one another, in contrast to the potential for friction as in Seneca's plays.[284]

Concluding Remarks

Zeus and Jupiter's title as "Father of Gods" applies only in a metaphorical sense to the deities discussed in this chapter, but it is nonetheless an important concept for the overall presentation of the two supreme gods. The three other Greek Olympians possess the most authority and potential to rival Zeus' *auctoritas*, but Euripides presents only Hera as a deity ready, willing and able to undermine his will. In *Heracles*, Zeus and Hera's "perfect" marriage is put to the test and the god's relationship with Alcmene is scrutinized in terms of its legality and appropriateness. When Zeus' tryst is given validation by other characters in the play, it causes a rupture in the heavenly marriage between Zeus and Hera, prompting the goddess to assert her godhead and demand reparations for the breach of her *timē*. This rupture of the divine marriage is then paralleled by a rupture in the mortal marriage between Heracles and Megara. The violent end to this mortal marriage is a reminder of the rights of Hera and the potential disaster that can befall those who

---

[284] The remaining siblings of Zeus and Jupiter (Demeter/Ceres and Hestia/Vesta) do not appear in the plays of either Euripides or Seneca. Although Demeter does have some significance in Euripides' *Suppliants* (referred to at 1, 34 and 173) and is mentioned by name once in *Bacchae* (275), she has no relevance to the plays under discussion here. Demeter's Roman counterpart Ceres is mentioned comparatively frequently by Seneca (*HF* 697, 845; *Phoen.* 219, 371, 608; *Med.* 761; *Phaed.* 373, 970; *Oed.* 49), but her name rarely signifies anything more than a symbol for grain and is occasionally used to refer to her Mysteries at Eleusis. Only Medea's reference to Ceres as forced by her to witness a winter harvest is suggestive of a deity who is at the mercy of this heroine. Her relationship to Jupiter is nowhere mentioned, nor is there enough information or description to offer any interpretation of significance. Hestia, as goddess of the hearth, is mentioned in Euripides' *Alcestis* (162) and *Heracles* (599, 715), but her presence is of little consequence and nothing is made of her relationship to Zeus. Vesta, Hestia's Roman counterpart, receives no mention at all by Seneca.

transgress her laws. That Hera was able to wreak such havoc on the mortal son closest to Zeus suggests that Hera is the most dangerous of Zeus' siblings in terms of maintaining his superiority. She is the only one with the potential to match his power and he is the only one able to control hers.

Seneca's version of the same myth in his *Hercules Furens* portrays a similarly powerful Juno, but the emphasis on the (il)legitimacy of Jupiter's tryst with Alcmene is lessened considerably. Instead, Juno's greater concern is to protect Jupiter from a potential threat by his heroic son, who, in her eyes, overpowered Jupiter's own chthonic brother. She is similarly concerned with regaining honour, but her assault on Hercules (and his family) is less a symbolic rupture of marriage bonds than it is a demonstration of her wrath and desire for dominance. Hercules' slaughter of his family becomes a sacrifice to Juno, confirming her divinity and providing just cause for Jupiter to reconsider offering similar divinity to his son. The transition from Euripidean to Senecan tragedy in terms of Zeus and Jupiter's supremacy over their wives changes little in the general depiction of their respective relationships. Both divine couples engage in "power-struggles:" for Euripides, Hera's displacement by Alcmene results in a devastating demonstration of Hera's demand for retribution; in Seneca, Juno's assumption of sisterly authority provides her with cause and means to conquer a potential cosmic threat. The motives for each goddess are different, but in both cases, Zeus and Jupiter are wed to considerably powerful goddesses who will assert their own godhead without mercy.

The relationships Zeus and Jupiter have with their brothers are drastically different for each playwright and differ considerably from this depiction of Hera and Juno as well. Zeus and Hades are not frequently compared, but in *Hecuba*, it is clear the two brothers, while operating in very different spheres, do work together toward the same end. What is not accomplished by Zeus will be accomplished by Hades; and while the two may be quite similar in terms of authority, there is no conflict or need to establish a clear hierarchy. This situation changes drastically in Seneca's *Hercules Furens* where Jupiter and Dis are not only compared, but seem to be almost interchangeable. This comparability, however, is not indicative of stability, but rather highlights the potential for friction. It is not clear who possesses more *auctoritas* between Jupiter and Dis and such uncertainty creates an ambiguous relationship between the two.

Poseidon and Neptune change the least between the Euripidean and Senecan tragedies. Both playwrights make it quite clear that these brothers are definitely ranked lower than their heavenly brothers and each works together with Zeus and Jupiter respectively to maintain the ultimate cosmic order. Although there is a hint in Seneca's *Phaedra* that Jupiter may come into conflict with Neptune, such an event would only occur when the god is intruding into the realm of his sibling. The three male Olympians have their realms and these realms are autonomous. As long as each respects the other, they seem, for the most part, to work together toward the same end.

CHAPTER 5
THE FATHER OF GODS II: THE SECOND GENERATION

For the most part, the second generation of gods prove far more benign in their relationships to Zeus and Jupiter: they rarely are given enough *auctoritas* to mount any kind of threat or disturbance to the power of the lord of Olympus.[285] As a prelude to discussing the offspring of these gods, it is perhaps prudent first to examine the gods' relationships to the deities of reproduction *par excellence*, Aphrodite and Eros (alongside Venus and Cupid). Both Aphrodite and Eros have complicated origins within the traditional accounts of their places within the cosmos: Aphrodite is either a goddess of the sea-foam, born of the severed genitals of Ouranos (Hes. *Theog.* 188) and thus conceived of as being "outside" Zeus' immediate family (at best, his "aunt"); or, she is a daughter of Zeus and Dione (Hom. *Il.* 5.370), placing her firmly within Zeus' ordered hierarchy. Eros too is conceived of as being "born" both prior to Zeus' existence (as the creative and generative force of the world, Hes. *Theog.* 120) and after Zeus' rise to power as the personification of love as a son of Aphrodite.[286] In both Euripides' *Hippolytus* and Seneca's *Phaedra* there are discussions concerning the power-dynamics between Zeus and Jupiter and these personifications of desire. Eros and Cupid in particular are portrayed by each playwright as powerful enough to make Zeus and Jupiter succumb to their will. On the one hand, it is quite obvious that Zeus and Jupiter would, by necessity, fall victim to the arrows of Eros and Cupid and, furthermore, it is clear that this idea is a favourite poetical *topos*.[287] On the other hand, neither of these

---

[285] Establishing a clear hierarchy with Zeus firmly at the apex was a theme of early epic poetry (especially in the *Homeric Hymns*). That hierarchy seems to be taken-for-granted by the time of Greek tragedy.

[286] The parentage of Eros varies substantially; while Aphrodite is often cited as his mother, Sappho calls him a son of Ouranos and Gaia (Frag. 198), Plato cites Poros and Penia (*Symp.* 178) and Pausanias relates another version where he is a son of Eileithyia (9.27.1). He was frequently said to have no father, although later tradition would make him the child of Aphrodite and Ares (Nonn. *Dion.* 5.88).

[287] Breitenberger (2013) 152.

151

reasons for including such a scene in a tragedy precludes the possibility that there may be more to be said about it. In *Hippolytus*, the relationship between Zeus and Eros is constructed for a specific thematic purpose, but one which differs vastly from the implications of a similar relationship depicted in *Phaedra*; each, however, is commenting specifically on the nature of the relationships between Zeus and Eros and between Jupiter and Cupid respectively.

Of the numerous children of Zeus and Jupiter that could be discussed in this chapter, I have selected only a few for in-depth investigation. The first is Dionysus/Bacchus, the child of the thunderbolt and Zeus' male "doublet."[288] Being conceived by a mortal, Dionysus can never challenge Zeus for his position as Father of Gods, but being "born of Zeus" makes him the most Zeus-like of the second generation of gods. Indeed, Dionysus inherits many of his father's qualities and it is this aspect of their relationship that will be the focus of my discussion. The various presentations of Dionysus' birth and Zeus' relationship to Semele (along with the highlighting or suppression of Semele's role in the birth) signpost specific thematic interests of the playwrights and colour the audience's interpretation of both father and son.

In opposition to Dionysus, I then discuss Ares as the son most alienated from his father. A child of Zeus and Hera, Ares is conflict personified and he exhibits the worst aspects of each of his parents. My investigation of Ares is conducted within a larger discussion of patronymics, the use of which by Euripides in particular, is meant to connect children of Zeus to their father in a specific way. The use of the patronymic in the examples I provide denotes more than mere lineage and a father-child relationship. The context of the

---

[288] Yasumura (2011) 95 uses the term "doublet" to refer to Athena's relationship with Zeus in Hesiod, emphasizing the goddess' representation as a weaker manifestation of Zeus himself. I am using the term here in a similar fashion for Dionysus, a god who shares a number of significant attributes with Zeus as I explain below, pp. 162-67.

patronymic enhances the meaning of the name and together it ultimately serves to highlight aspects of the god's importance to the plays in question, here specifically *Heracles* and *Phoenissae*. I also discuss the use of patronymics with respect to Epaphus, Apollo and Athena within these two plays and the potential not only to clarify one's lineage, but also to blur identities. Apollo and Athena are both "confused" with Heracles precisely because of the use of a patronymic. Thus, Euripides is able to manipulate a conventional naming device for different purposes, each revealing something about the child or father with whom it is linked.

The final section of this chapter is devoted to Helen and the Dioscuri within the plays of *Electra* and *Orestes*. The divinity of Helen and the dual paternity of Castor and Polydeuces are the focal points of this discussion.[289]

---

[289] The other second-generation Olympians receive much less press in the plays under discussion here. Artemis does, of course, appear at the end of *Hippolytus*, but the one instance where she mentions the "rule of non-interference" and her fear of Zeus was discussed above in chapter 1 (pp. 39-40). Artemis is also mentioned in *Medea* (160) in conjunction with Themis when Medea wishes that her suffering be witnessed by the gods; but no mention is made of her relationship to Zeus. The same can be said about the two references in *Hecuba* (464 and 935) and two of her three mentions in *Phoenissae* (152 and 802). She is significant in both of the Iphigenia plays, but neither of these is under discussion here; the same applies to *Suppliants* 958 and *Bacchae* 340. She is referred to as Zeus' "golden-haired offspring" at *Phoen.* 191, but again, this suggests nothing significant about her relationship to her father. Hermes receives no mention at all in the plays under discussion here (and only appearing in the *Ion* to deliver the prologue and mentioned by name in *Alcestis* at 743 and in *Helen* at 44 and 910). Similarly, Hephaestus is referred to in *Trojan Women* (220 and 343), *Electra* (444) and the *IA* (1072 and 1602) but with no relevance to Zeus. Diana, Mercury and Vulcan appear even less in Seneca's tragedies. Only *Phaedra* mentions the goddess once (72); Mercury is never mentioned by name and Vulcan is referenced only in the Pseudo-Senecan *Octavia*.

Euripides consistently refers to Eros as the offspring of Aphrodite, but he differs from the majority of sources when he describes the young god as a son of Zeus.[290] The chorus in *Hippolytus* sing an ode to Eros immediately after Phaedra agrees to go along with the Nurse's plan to aid her "love-sickness." The chorus express the power of both Aphrodite and Eros, going so far as to suggest that the god is in fact the son of Zeus:

> οὔτε γὰρ πυρὸς οὔτ' ἄστρων ὑπέρτερον βέλος
> οἷον τὸ τᾶς Ἀφροδίτας ἵησιν ἐκ χερῶν
> Ἔρως ὁ Διὸς παῖς (*Hipp.* 530-32).

Calling Eros a son of Zeus is significant, for it seems this parentage was an innovation by Euripides.[291] It has been suggested that by making Zeus the father of Eros the young god would be seen to be much more impressive[292] and given the context of the ode, this genealogy would add to the god's prestige. While this is a valid interpretation, it is not the only one possible. Eros had traditionally been acknowledged as a powerful deity in his own right and often the only one to make the other Olympian gods (including his own mother) successfully succumb to his powers; and this *without* being a son of Zeus. One might question then, how becoming a son of Zeus would make Eros even more impressive.

It is possible that Euripides is instead "reining in" the powers of Eros here by placing them under the authority of Zeus. This change in hierarchy (Eros is now a "lesser" deity and a son of Zeus) would thus create the opposite effect, for Eros is now subject to another god's will. One could argue, given the rest of the immediate context, that Eros' weapons are more powerful than both the weapons of fire and stars (both controlled by Zeus). However, the

---

[290] The author of the pseudo-Virgilian *Ciris* also adopts Jupiter as the father of Cupid (134) and while this obviously postdates *Hippolytus*, the author could be following Euripides.

[291] Halleran (1991) 111 notes that this is the first extant instance of Eros as a son of Zeus.

[292] Halleran (1991) 111.

weapons belong not to the young god but to Aphrodite;[293] Eros only sends the weapons, thus becoming an instrument for his mother. What then would be the significance of making Eros a son of Zeus, other than to see his powers as subordinate to that of his father? Euripides, by making Zeus the father of Eros, has subtly continued to illustrate a theme of marriage and of having *legitimate* children throughout. One of the play's themes, especially in relation to Zeus' significance to the tragedy, is the importance of procreating legitimately. Hippolytus himself is not a legitimate child of Theseus and therefore cannot fully partake in the society in which he is residing. Eros, as a child of Zeus and Aphrodite, while representing love and all of the other ideas associated with it, is presented as a god partaking of his father's authority and being granted his *timē* as a child of Zeus.[294] He is clearly accepted as fully divine and, with no mention of Hera, he is also legitimate and seemingly not born "out of wedlock." The second implication of this paternity is the potential for incest: Aphrodite is often thought of as the daughter of Zeus and, while this is not made explicit, it would likely be assumed by a portion of the audience. This would imply that Zeus has generated a child by his own child and, given the context of the play, it is unsurprising that this theme would be underlying part of the choral ode. Phaedra's desire for her husband's son, while not strictly incestuous, certainly invites such an interpretation.

In Seneca's *Phaedra*, the powers of Cupid go beyond those portrayed by Euripides. There, he was a son of Zeus fulfilling the portion allotted to him within Zeus' cosmos, but implementing it with his mother's weapons. Here, the way in which Phaedra and the chorus discuss Cupid's powers suggests something more is being revealed about Jupiter's abilities to

---

[293] Raising the question of Aphrodite's authority in relation to Zeus, to which I will return below, pp. 161-62.

[294] As Halleran (1991) 110 observes, the form of the choral ode on Eros (525-64) is in the traditional form of a hymn including the invocation, an outline of the deity's power and request. As such, the hymn follows the conventional pattern and perhaps should not be interpreted any differently than the *Homeric Hymn to Hermes* or *Apollo* in terms of a hymn which describes the *timai* of the gods.

maintain his dominant position. Phaedra openly questions Jupiter's supremacy as she believes Venus is continuing to curse her family with the help of her son Cupid (124). She further suggests that it is Cupid who has the most authority in life, for he is the only one who is able to conquer the gods, including Jupiter himself: *hic volucer omni pollet in terra impotens, / ipsumque flammis torret indomitis Iovem* (*Phaed.* 186-87). While the Nurse claims that Jupiter has the power to "shake the heavens" (155) and advocates for his ultimate supremacy, Phaedra insists upon his vulnerability to guard against Cupid and thus suggests a weaker authoritative persona for Jupiter. Furthermore, Phaedra is contrasting the flames of Cupid with the lightning bolts of Jupiter, which were forged in Aetna (155-56) and were divinely made (188-91).[295] She believes that Vulcan's fires are less effective than those of Venus' son. There is a possibility that Cupid's arrows were also forged by Vulcan, as mentioned in the *Anacreontea* (frag. 28),[296] which would perhaps explain the comparison and provide Cupid with an equivalent weapon. This additional information, however, may be later than our play,[297] and thus the question remains open as to whether or not Phaedra is correct in her assessment of the supreme god.

The chorus weighs in on the debate and it is obvious that they consider Phaedra's position to be correct. The chorus muse on the ability of Cupid to transform Jupiter into his various "beastly" manifestations:

> et iubet caelo superos relicto
> vultibus falsis habitare terras.
> ....
> Induit formas quotiens minores
> ipse qui caelum nebulasque ducit!
> candidas ales modo movit alas,
> dulcior vocem moriente cygno;

---

[295] Segal (1986) 120.

[296] The collection of poems attributed to Anacreon is dated to the 1st c. BCE through to the 6th c. CE.

[297] Coffey and Mayer (1990) 109 also note that the gods afflicted by Cupid's arrows are each carrying weapons of fire and thus should be expected to withstand the young god's attacks.

> fronte nunc torva petulans iuvencus
> virginum stravit sua terga ludo,
> perque fraternos, nova regna, fluctus
> ungula lentos imitante remos
> pectore adverso domuit profundum,
> pro sua vector timidus rapina (*Phaed.* 294-95, 299-308).

The chorus still maintain that Jupiter has supremacy in the heavens, but also that he has and can fall victim to Cupid's arrows. They remind us that Jupiter was transformed into a swan in order to pursue Leda[298] and of his theft of Europa, an episode of particular relevance to Phaedra's family history and current plight. One reason for portraying Jupiter and Cupid in such an episode is to highlight the limitations of Jupiter's authority and the vulnerability of the god to forces not under his immediate control. This differs substantially from the image gleaned from Euripides, where the activities of Eros are brought specifically under Zeus' influence. While both scenes may portray a traditional poetic *topos*, it is clear that the specific details of each imply a deeper significance. In Euripides, Eros is stripped of his autonomy and of his own weapons; as a son of Zeus he has been granted *time* by his father, who succumbs to love for the purpose of procreation. In Seneca, Cupid is aided by his own weapons which rival even Jupiter's; deployment of his weapons against Jupiter see the god succumb to frivolous affairs, leading not to legitimate children, but to dangerous situations.

Love and Marriage: Aphrodite and Venus

In Euripides' *Hippolytus*, Eros was said to use his mother's weapons against his "victims" and neither πυρὸς οὔτ' ἄστρων ὑπέρτερον βέλος (*Hipp.* 530) were a match against them. Both fires and stars are connected intimately with Zeus and the remark implies

---

[298] This may or may not evoke a version where Jupiter requests Venus to transform herself into an eagle and chase the god while he is disguised (Pseud-Hyg. *Astron.*1.8). The involvement of Venus in this tale would be well-suited to the chorus' purpose of insinuating the participation of the goddess with respect to Jupiter's paramours.

that the will of Aphrodite is stronger, or at least matches, that of Zeus.[299] The relationship between these two deities is of interest, especially with regard to this play, for the dynamics presented between them suggest that they are clearly working in concert toward a common aim. Secondly, Aphrodite's "domain" is presented as closely connected to marriage (properly belonging to Hera), not just procreation, effectively taking her place beside Zeus. This second idea begins to form quite clearly at the end of the choral ode to Eros. The chorus sing of the myth of Zeus and Semele to illustrate the dangerous side of love, countering the earlier version as told by the Nurse (453-54, discussed below):

> βροντᾶι γὰρ ἀμφιπύρωι
> τοκάδα τὰν διγόνοιο Βάκ-
> χου νυμφευσαμένα πότμωι
> φονίωι κατηύνασεν (*Hipp.* 559-62).

Whereas the Nurse chooses this myth to justify Phaedra's desire for Hippolytus and the futility of disregarding the will of the gods, the chorus emphasize the destructive nature of love[300] and the consequences of acting on impulse. The episode, however, is also framed in terms of a marriage. Aphrodite gives Semele to Zeus and acts as a *kurios* for the bride creating the image of a betrothal scene.[301] While it has been noted that Zeus is acting here in a passive capacity, rather than being the active partner as in the Nurse's telling of the myth, there is nothing to suggest this image weakens his persona.[302] Indeed, in a marriage ceremony the bride was "given" to her prospective husband and this telling of the myth would likely resonate with the audience in this way. Zeus' affair is thus being used to illustrate the

---

[299] Goff (1990) 28.

[300] Goff (1990) 53.

[301] Halleran (1991) 113-14.

[302] Luschnig (1988) 57: "In their song, the only active partner is Love itself (whether the Cyprian or her son). The humans and even the great Zeus are secondary."

important theme of marriage[303] and, in this play, it is being portrayed as a legitimate union. It could be interpreted that Zeus and Aphrodite are working together to procure proper marriages and legitimate offspring, which would incite the audience to have a ready response when Hippolytus questions Zeus specifically with regards to the place of women in society.[304]

Indeed, Hippolytus' famous tirade against women is the next time Zeus is mentioned in the text; up until this point the audience has been informed about two of Zeus' affairs (with Semele and with Aphrodite) in such a way as to see them in light of purposeful marriages rather than extra-marital affairs (even though that is exactly what they are). When Hippolytus hears that Phaedra desires him, his response is not merely an invective against the female species, but he begins by questioning Zeus' reasons for making women exist at all, even using language that would deny any female presence in the world:[305]

> ὦ Ζεῦ, τί δὴ κίβδηλον ἀνθρώποις κακὸν
> γυναῖκας ἐς φῶς ἡλίου κατῴκισας;
> εἰ γὰρ βρότειον ἤθελες σπεῖραι γένος,
> οὐκ ἐκ γυναικῶν χρῆν παρασχέσθαι τόδε,
> ἀλλ' ἀντιθέντας σοῖσιν ἐν ναοῖς βροτοὺς
> ἢ χαλκὸν ἢ σίδηρον ἢ χρυσοῦ βάρος
> παίδων πρίασθαι σπέρμα του τιμήματος,
> τῆς ἀξίας ἕκαστον, ἐν δὲ δώμασιν
> ναίειν ἐλευθέροισι θηλειῶν ἄτερ (*Hipp.* 616-24).

Hippolytus attributes the existence of the race of women to Zeus and recognizes that they exist to fulfil a purpose, which is propagating children, although he absolutely disagrees with

---

[303] Although discussing the theme of marriage with respect to the third choral ode, Swift (2006) identifies several features throughout the play which are inherently linked to this theme.

[304] See Breitenberger (2013) 28-32 for a discussion of Aphrodite as a goddess of marriage.

[305] Goff (1990) 19: "Hippolytus endeavours to speak as if from a time and a place before the creation of women when he uses *anthropoi*, the word for humans in general, to mean *Andres*, males, as if there were no women to complicate his usage (616); he denies sexual differentiation in language as he deplores it in life."

it. Luschnig sees his words as presumptuous in that Hippolytus believes he can reorder the cosmos and create a better system to produce offspring; furthermore, Hippolytus suggests that Zeus is more interested in propagation than the human race.[306] Zeus, however, is not merely interested in propagation for its own sake, but to produce legitimate children, among whom Hippolytus has no place. Hippolytus' wish to live apart from women and to stay chaste not only violates the (traditional) *timai* of Aphrodite, but also the will of Zeus; his specific denunciation of Zeus' cosmic order highlights this second offence. Such an interpretation could be taken even further; it is an indication that Aphrodite's plan to punish Hippolytus is in accord with Zeus' plan as well and this receives further corroboration at the end when Artemis expresses a fear of disagreeing with her father's will. A second point of interest in this particular passage is Hippolytus' wish to buy offspring from Zeus' temples (σοῖσιν ἐν ναοῖς, 620). One might wonder why children could not be bought from a temple of any god or goddess, rather than only from Zeus. Zeus is not only a god of marriage, but he also is the god to whom Athenian citizens swear an oath when introducing their children to their phratry,[307] thus it is no surprise that Hippolytus would associate children with Zeus, although again this would apply to legitimate children only.

What is perhaps interesting in the context of marriage is the obvious lack of any mention of Hera, who as the goddess of marriage would have no less a vested interest than Zeus in the matter. The one opportunity Euripides has to mention Hera is not taken up and he instead refers to Zeus alone. After Phaedra learns that the Nurse divulged her secret to Hippolytus, she immediately resolves to die and constructs a plan to ensure Hippolytus does not gain any opportunity to reveal what he knows. The chorus responds with dismay and sings another ode containing themes of love and marriage, including what is generally

---

[306] Luschnig (1988) 22.

[307] Lambert (1999) 132.

assumed to be a specific reference to the marriage of Zeus and Hera: κρῆναί τ' ἀμβρόσιαι χέον-/ ται Ζηνὸς παρὰ κοίταις, (*Hipp.* 748-49). According to Halleran, the audience is made to connect the place specifically with Zeus' marriage to Hera and yet the goddess has no place in the drama.[308] One explanation may be that by avoiding explicit references to her, Zeus' "marriage" to Semele appears that much more valid. One also might suggest that by only mentioning Zeus in this context, the reference is left to individual interpretation and does not necessarily imply Hera's presence at all.[309]

Furthermore, the final reference to Aphrodite in the play suggests that she, rather than Hera, may be inferred as the first of Zeus' loves. In the final ode, the chorus sing again of Eros and Aphrodite to highlight their power over all that the sun sees (earth, sea and mountains, 1272-80) and end it with an unusual descriptor of the goddess: συμπάντων βασιληΐδα τι-/ μάν, Κύπρι, τῶνδε μόνα κρατύνεις (*Hipp.* 1280-81). Not only is Aphrodite's domain essentially that of Zeus, but her power is also regal, βασιληΐδα. One may begin to wonder whether the Aphrodite depicted in this play should not in fact be seen as a primordial goddess who creates life alongside Zeus, rather than as a mere daughter of Zeus.[310] The total absence of Hera from this play and the continued presence of an Aphrodite concerned with marriage would suggest that the divine family here is not the one an audience would likely expect. Zeus' son is Eros and Aphrodite is at his side, creating an altogether different impression of the gods against whom Phaedra and Hippolytus both offend. The divine family

---

[308] Halleran (1985) 213.

[309] It has also been argued, by Padel (1974) 232 for example, that the marriage of Zeus and Hera depicted here parallels that of the marriage between Theseus and Phaedra; this interpretation would suggest either a happy marriage, which Phaedra certainly does not enjoy, or that Theseus is the ever-absent husband as Zeus is. However, the imagery of the scene does not suggest an absent Zeus but rather a place of wedded bliss and thus the argument does not seem convincing.

[310] See Segal (1965) for a comprehensive discussion of the various roles of the goddess in *Hippolytus*, both as "actor" and as a force of nature, but as especially related to the sea and water imagery.

here upholds the importance of having legitimate children and Hippolytus' refusal to marry and even his own status both condemn him to living outside of political life, whether he would wish to partake of it or not.

This depiction of Zeus and Aphrodite is not the one taken up in Seneca's *Phaedra*, for, as noted earlier with regard to Cupid, Venus' role seems even secondary to that of her son. Cupid uses his own weapons to bring down the other gods, including Jupiter, and Venus has little part in his activities. Indeed, Venus is associated more traditionally with Mars (125) and she is clearly not related to Jupiter, being born of the sea (274).[311] Seneca makes it abundantly clear that the goddess is not the one associated with shooting arrows of love: Cupid is dominant over even her and where Aphrodite was considered royal in Euripides, here her son enjoys that status (334).

The Child of the Thunderbolt: Dionysus and Bacchus

The depiction of Zeus and Jupiter's other divine children provide even more scope for exploring the implications of the title "Father of Gods." In the case of Dionysus (and Bacchus), there may be even more significance to be had, as his particular link to Zeus (and Jupiter) is made that much stronger because of his unusual birth. The recounting of his conception and birth by Euripides and Seneca offers a worthwhile avenue for interpreting the significance of the gods' relationship to Zeus and Jupiter in specific plays, in this case Euripides' *Hippolytus* and *Phoenissae* and Seneca's *Hercules Furens*, *Oedipus* and *Medea*. The various versions of the story offer some interesting insights as to why certain elements of the myth are highlighted at the expense of others.

---

[311] This is not to say that Venus is unimportant to Seneca's tragedy; she is mentioned as the origin of the curse of the House of Minos (124-28) and as the one whose "covenant" was broken when Phaedra fell in love with Hippolytus (910). See especially Davis (1983) 125-27.

Dionysus has strong ties to Zeus, not only as a son of the god, but because of the unique method of his conception and birth. He is literally a child of the thunderbolt, the most potent symbol of Zeus' authority and born (a second time) from the god's thigh. Only Athena's relationship to Zeus rivals this connection between god and child. The story of Dionysus and Semele is related in both *Hippolytus* and *Phoenissae*, with each recitation offering a particular and very different view of the event. In *Hippolytus*, the conception of Dionysus is introduced with the affair between Zeus and Semele. When the Nurse hears of Phaedra's love for Hippolytus, she attempts to soothe Phaedra's guilt by explaining how Zeus was struck by desire for Semele: Ζεὺς ὥς ποτ' ἠράσθη γάμων / Σεμέλης (*Hipp.* 453-54).[312] What the Nurse fails to include in her tale are the results of their union: complete destruction for Semele and the birth of Dionysus. The words the Nurse does use, however, are of particular importance. The juxtaposition of ἠράσθη and γάμων seems almost ironic given their definitions: the former meaning "eagerly desiring" or "lusting after" and the latter of course being the technical term for "marriage." That Zeus "lusted" after Semele is not uncommon or even surprising, but that the Nurse describes the god as desiring a "marriage" seems exceptional (and one might be reminded of the "marriage" between Zeus and Alcmene). The significance is that the union between Zeus and Semele, if portrayed as "lawful," would produce legitimate offspring and thus Dionysus would be considered a true son of Zeus, worthy of becoming a god.[313]

The chorus elaborate on this union in their second ode concerning Aphrodite and her son Eros. While much of the last stasimon reveals more about these two deities than it does about Zeus and Dionysus, it is nonetheless significant for its detailed description of the god's birth:

---

[312] A discussion of the rhetorical effects of this speech can be found in Pelling (2005) 89-92.

[313] Segal (1979) 161 reinforces the importance of legitimacy in his discussion of Semele and Phaethon as paradigmatic emblems for Hippolytus.

βροντᾶι γὰρ ἀμφιπύρωι
τοκάδα τὰν διγόνοιο Βάκ-
χου νυμφευσαμένα πότμωι
φονίωι κατηύνασεν (*Hipp.* 559-62).

The chorus, explaining Cypris' involvement, reiterate the Nurse's position that the affair of Zeus and Semele was a "wedding" (through the use of νυμφευσαμένα), but now they emphasize the disastrous end which befell Semele.[314] Zeus is described as βροντᾶι ἀμφιπύρωι, evocative of his immense power and potential for harm; it is also how Zeus was described in *Hecuba* when referring to his punishment of the Titans.[315] Here, as there, Zeus' double-edged flame is symbolic of both life and death: destruction for Semele, the genesis of life for Dionysus. It is clear here that the two events are intertwined; for the latter to eventuate, the former must occur. In effect, the ode highlights the dangerous power of love and the potential for harm if it is indulged.[316] The story, from the point of view of the chorus, should not be imitated but rather taken as a warning. Their interpretation, in contrast to that of the Nurse, is quite negative in tone. This has significance when turning to the second telling of the myth in Euripides' *Phoenissae* where it has a far more positive connotation.

In this play, the birth of Dionysus is related during a sequence of myths sung by the chorus to illustrate their own ties to the Theban people through their shared descent from Zeus. At the end of the first stasimon of the ode, they describe Dionysus' birth in the fields of Thebes:

Βρόμιον ἔνθα τέκετο †μάτηρ
Διὸς γάμοισι†,
κισσὸς ὃν περιστεφὴς
ἑλικτὸς εὐθὺς ἔτι βρέφος
χλοηφόροισιν ἔρνεσιν

---

[314] Halleran (1991) 115 emphasizes the role of Cypris in giving Semele to Zeus as a *bride*.

[315] Discussed above, p. 37.

[316] Goff (1990) 91.

κατασκίοισιν ὀλβίσας ἐνώτισεν (*Phoen.* 649-54).

The most striking aspect of this account is the suppression of the traditional story of the god's birth which precipitated the destruction of Semele and subsequent rebirth of the god from Zeus' thigh. None of these details are hinted at here; instead, the passage suggests that Semele herself delivered Dionysus, with misfortune playing no part at all.[317] The epithet of Bromios hints at the god's "wilder, thundering aspect"[318] but also ties him thematically to Zeus, as a child of the thunder god himself. The image of Dionysus is a rather pleasant one in contrast to that imagined by the chorus of *Hippolytus*. The allusion to Zeus' thunder here is also downplayed, again emphasizing the close tie between the god and Zeus, but without the destructive element. Instead, Dionysus is surrounded by greenery and foliage, connotations of life instead of death. This strophe provides a contrast to the following antistrophe which emphasizes the presence of Ares' savage dragon at Thebes rather than the mild and harmonious son of Zeus (cf. 784-85).[319] By the end of the ode, the dragon is overcome and the contrast between peace and strife is highlighted, foreshadowing events to come.[320] Zeus, as father of Dionysus as well as Ares, is the source of both the savage aspect of Thebes and the civilizing nature required to defeat it, at once the progenitor of the problem (Ares and his dragon) and the solution (Dionysus, who brings peace).

---

[317] Although the audience would undoubtedly be quite familiar with the Semele's fate, there is no suggestion from the text as transmitted that they should bring any of these details to mind: Mastronarde (1994) 338; Amiech (2004) 387, however, would suggest that the suppression of Semele's fate is because "Son union avec Zeus et la jalousie d'Héra l'ont immortalisée."

[318] Arthur (1977) 171.

[319] Arthur (1977) 171.

[320] As Arthur (1977) 169 notes, "Phoenicia is the past, Thebes the present, Delphi the future . . . Phoenicia and the chorus' journey are remnants of a peaceful prehistoric past, and Delphi is the locale of a *rapprochement* between opposing drives toward order and chaos. Thebes herself is a place of violence, and in subsequent odes the chorus explore the process whereby in Thebes the recurrent clash of forces ends, not in reconciliation, but in mutual slaughter."

Dionysus' status as Zeus' son is thus symbolic not only of Zeus' immense power but also his association with both life and death, reinforcing the arguments of the first chapter. The birth of Dionysus through the lightning bolt is predicated on the death of Semele (the lightning bolt thus a bringer of life and death). Dionysus is thus inherently linked to this duality of life and death through his connection to Zeus. But as Zeus' son, he also provides a genealogical link between Zeus and the Theban populace, allowing his descendants not only to strengthen ties between each other, but also to highlight the inherent dispositions of his various progeny. It is the former association, however, which Seneca adopts in his tragedies, specifically *Hercules Furens*, *Oedipus* and *Medea*. In all three cases, Bacchus' birth is associated with Jupiter's lightning and the destructive nature of his powerful essence, which is also seen as an important aspect of Bacchus' divinity.

When Amphitryon is defending Hercules' divine parentage in *Hercules Furens*, he begins by explaining to Lycus the difficulties accompanying those born of Zeus' ancestry. His first example is of the birth of Bacchus: *E matris utero fulmine eiectus puer / mox fulminanti proximus patri stetit* (457-58). The immediate point of Amphitryon's statement is to convince Lycus that Hercules is in fact Jupiter's son and to draw out the parallels between Bacchus and Hercules; but the entire reference also brings the unfortunate fate of Semele to mind. Seneca highlights the potential for Jupiter's destructive force, as *eiectus* has an implication of miscarriage,[321] and further highlights the significance of Jupiter's thunderbolt. The god's lightning is afforded a dual function: on one hand, it killed Semele, but on the other, it guaranteed Bacchus' divinity (perhaps also a foreshadowing of the unfortunate fate of Megara, who must die in order for Hercules to become divine). Furthermore, the description of Jupiter as *fulminatus* strengthens his association with each act. We also know

---

[321] Fitch (1987) 237.

from the prologue that Semele was eventually awarded deification herself (16), further emphasizing this connection between Jupiter's lightning and divinity.

A similar scenario is found in *Oedipus* during the choral ode devoted to Bacchus. They end their song with a reference to Bacchus' birth, hinting at the destructive force of Jupiter's weapon, which he himself hates: *telum deposuit Iuppiter igneum / oditque Baccho veniente fulmen* (501-02).[322] It is apparent that Jupiter would have preferred not to expose his lightning to Semele but he was obligated to do so because of the promise he made. In *Medea* too, the chorus refers to this unfortunate incident when comparing Jason to Bacchus as *proles fulminis improbi* (84). While the reference is brief, it still encapsulates Jupiter's violent force. In each of these plays Seneca chooses to emphasize the destructive element of the god's nature with respect to Bacchus, not highlighting the more positive representation in Euripides' *Phoenissae*, but underscoring Dionysus as a god intimately associated with the boundaries between life, death and divinity, inherited no doubt from his father.

Potential of Patronymics

Zeus' children, whether legitimate or not and regardless of their conception, are often associated with the god when introduced. For Euripides at least, genealogy is important and holds some significance in his plays; he uses it not only to establish who his characters are, but also to indicate to his audience specific relationships which help to shape the dramatic and thematic interests of a play. Given the importance of one's genealogy in the mortal realm and the prestige associated with being a member of a divinely-fathered bloodline, it is not surprising to find that Zeus (and Jupiter), as the supreme god, is credited with numerous offspring and that their connection to Zeus is clearly established through the use of a plethora of patronymics. The use of a patronymic, however, can signal more than just lineage; it also

---

[322] I follow Fitch (2004) 60 and Boyle (2011) 228 in the use of *oditque* over *conditque*.

serves as an indicator for an interpretation of the actions, abilities or motivations of a given character.[323] There are several examples of patronymics in Euripides being used to underscore certain thematic interests: in *Heracles* and *Phoenissae* references to Ares highlight the potential for self-destruction and familial strife; Epaphus is also mentioned in *Phoenissae* to illustrate the inherited bestiality of Thebes; finally Apollo and Athena, both mentioned frequently throughout the Euripidean corpus, are used for particular effect in *Heracles* when each god and the eponymous hero are blurred. Zeus as "Father of Gods" receives much attention from Euripides even if he never grants the god that title explicitly.

Ares

In opposition to Zeus' son Dionysus one might place Ares: whereas the former is associated with wine, ecstasy and embracing life as well as death, the latter is connected almost entirely with war, violence and the destruction of life. As the progeny of Zeus and Hera, Ares embodies the conflict between his parents and is thus a source of hostility for Zeus (one might bring to mind the god's words in Homer, that Ares is the most hated of the Olympians, *Il.* 5.699-700). Ares is also intimately connected to Thebes as the ancestor of the Spartoi, the Sown-men who fought amongst themselves until only a few brothers remained to populate the city. He is thus also the begetter of fratricide and civil war. These two markers

---

[323] Strauss (1993) 25-28 offers three functions or levels of meaning in the use of a patronymic: first, it "contains a wide range of connotative meaning . . . and might indicate formality or irony or the subject's youth or obscurity by his father's fame . . . More often, however, the patronymic connoted seriousness, manliness, and that combination of formality and intimacy that demarcates a moment whose symbolic is greater than its literal significance." Patronymics were also used to confer identity, legitimizing the birth of a child and asserting his or her social status. Third, their form indicated possession; the name of the child appeared in the nominative, whereas their father's name was in the genitive, thereby "limit[ing] a son's individuality." It is the first two categories with which I will be most concerned in this section.

of Ares' identity are alluded to in both Euripides' *Heracles* and *Phoenissae*, plays which have an inherent interest in the issues of problematic descent.

Ares' status as an ancestor of Thebes is mentioned only briefly in *Heracles*, but as great importance is attached to family lineage in this play, the god's role in the city's history is significant. Amphitryon explains in his opening monologue both his own and Megara's ancestries, including the fact that she and her sons are descendants of Ares (as the sower of the Spartoi, 5, 253) and, by implication, of Zeus and Hera as well.[324] Ares is the embodiment of the ("love-hate") relationship between these two deities and Heracles' "war" against his family is symbolic of both the war fought amongst the Spartoi, but also of the tension between Zeus' progeny with Alcmene and his offspring with Hera. Heracles' brutal actions are not only against his own family, but against Hera's family – the enmity continually reproduces itself and his own children are also a by-product of it. Heracles can only identify himself thus: Οὐχ οὗτος ὁ Διός, ὃς τέκν' ἔκτεινέν ποτε / δάμαρτά τ'; (*Her.* 1289-90). The acceptance of being a son of Zeus is inextricable from his acts against his family but accepting the former requires living with the latter. Euripides' inclusion of Megara's ancestry, while traditional, is also a reminder of Theban identity as self-destructive (or self-destroying); and Heracles is no exception.

It is in *Phoenissae*, however, that Ares' involvement in Thebes is more fully explored.[325] It is evident that the siege of Thebes can only be broken and the city safe from harm if the wrath of Ares is appeased; the god's sacred dragon had been killed by Cadmus and retribution for the impious act will finally be paid in full. It is the fate of Menoeceus to

---

[324] That Ares himself sows the teeth of the dragon is an unusual variant followed only by Euripides (at *Her.* 253) and Hellanicus (fr. 1a), according to a new monograph on the ancient dragon/serpent figure in myth by Ogden (2013b) 181. He discusses the dragon of Ares and the Spartoi in more detail earlier (48-54).

[325] Ares' thematic importance in Euripides' *Phoenissae* is discussed by Arthur (1977) *passim*; Papadopouolou (2001b) 23; and Lamari (2010) especially 2.4 and 3.2.

complete the cycle of violence that has disrupted Thebes, sacrificing himself to the god and thus terminating the savage element of Theban identity. Menoeceus invokes both Ares and Zeus after he convinces his father that he will go to Zeus' oracle at Dodona. He plans to sacrifice himself in order to save Thebes and swears by Ares and Zeus that he will never betray his family or fatherland: μὰ τὸν μετ' ἄστρων Ζῆν' Ἄρη τε φοίνιον (*Phoen.* 1006). Craik interprets Menoeceus's words as a verbal reminder of Jocasta's initial prayer to Zeus to save her family and to grant peace to her sons (84-87);[326] indeed, Menoeceus' oath is the answer to his aunt's prayer. Jocasta's plea to be saved will be answered through Menoeceus' self-sacrifice to Ares, but her wish for her sons to arrive at a peace agreement will only be met through their mutual destruction. Mastronarde's belief that Jocasta's plea was made in vain, "the first of three futile prayers for divine help in settling the dispute amicably"[327] is only partially correct. Her prayer was two-fold and Menoeceus' oath sworn by Ares and Zeus guarantees her wish for the salvation of Thebes. Menoeceus' promise of self-sacrifice to Ares sworn by Zeus assures the audience that both gods are aware of and have a vested interest in the current affairs. That Eteocles and Polynices kill each other is an indication that Jocasta's other wish is only answered in an ironic fashion; the brothers do reach an agreement, which is to fight one-on-one, leaving their respective forces out of it; the only outcome which would satisfy Jocasta's prayer (though not her actual desire) would be mutual slaughter. Thus, the sworn oath to Zeus among the stars and Ares of bloodshed is an apt one for Menoeceus to make, for it neatly encompasses the cosmic will of Zeus and the inevitable sacrifice to Ares, reminding the audience of the importance of past deeds, proper respect to the gods and the destructive force of fratricide.

---

[326] Craik (1988) 226.

[327] Mastronarde (1994) 165.

Epaphus, Apollo and Athena

Euripides' *Phoenissae* also includes a strophe that is concerned with another son of
Zeus, Epaphus, and is yet another attempt at linking the chorus to the people of Thebes
through the god. The chorus end their song with an epode calling upon Epaphus as a son of
Zeus and Io (as well as Demeter and Persephone) to protect the land of Thebes:

> καὶ σέ, τὸν προμάτορος
> Ἰοῦς ποτ' ἔκγονον
> Ἔπαφον, ὦ Διὸς γένεθλον (*Phoen.* 676-78).[328]

Io and Epaphus are appropriate ancestors for the chorus to call upon, for they link themselves
to the Thebans through their shared ancestry from Belus and Agenor respectively. The chorus
is invoking the most remote ties between themselves and the Thebans, reaching back to the
ancestors of Cadmus, about whom much of this ode is concerned. The purpose of reminding
the audience of Cadmus' genealogy is to highlight the bestiality of his heritage; as Epaphus
was the son of a bovine Io,[329] their descendants too will inherit this affinity for bestial
behaviour. Indeed, in the present generation this disposition can be seen to appear once again,
for both brothers are likened to beasts in the oracle given to Adrastus (411-12, 420) and again
when they fight to the death (1380-1). Thebes was built by Cadmus on the spot where
Europa, another Zeus-loved heifer, stopped as prophesied by an oracle. Dionysus too is
known to have the bull as one of his metamorphic shapes. The numerous allusions to bovine
and bestial aspects of the Theban household ultimately derive from both lines of heritage
originating specifically with Zeus. The emphasis first on Dionysus and Ares and now on Io,
Epaphus and Cadmus serve to highlight the inevitability of the present circumstances and
Zeus' place at the apex of the confrontation between the two lines of descent. Furthermore, it

---

[328] There are textual problems with this passage, but as they do not take issue with the general sense of
ode (but rather the specifics of phrasing), I am Murray's proposed text; see Willink (2002) for a
summary of the issues.

[329] Io's horned nature is referred to at 248 and 828.

emphasizes the familial destruction of the war: the brothers' duel is a potent symbol for the fratricidal nature of the Theban dynasty. The strife between Eteocles and Polynices is the result of a long-term and inherited form of conflict between the godlike descendants of Zeus and their bestial kin,[330] between the righteous and the base. The irony is that there can be very little difference between the two.

The final patronymic of importance in *Phoenissse* is provided by Eteocles (via the Messenger) just prior to the battle with his brother. Eteocles prays to Pallas Athena that she grant him the opportunity to kill his brother with his spear:

Ὦ Διὸς κόρη,
δὸς ἔγχος ἡμῖν καλλίνικον ἐκ χερὸς
ἐς στέρν' ἀδελφοῦ τῆσδ' ἀπ' ὠλένης βαλεῖν (*Phoen.* 1373-75).[331]

The relevance of Athena to Thebes is provided in the choral odes, for it is because of the goddess' guidance and advice that Cadmus was able to slay the dragon of Ares and sow its teeth to "beget" the Sown-men (667). Once more Athena's aid is invoked to prompt a fratricide and end the strife. But unlike the other branches of the genealogy, Athena is able to be both "just" and "warlike," understanding the need for balance between words and wars, a concept both brothers could not resolve for themselves (nicely summed up by Eteocles at 588-89).

Finally, one might consider the role of Apollo as Zeus' son and a medium through which his will is made known to men. One of the more interesting instances of blurred identity occurs during an ode to Apollo in *Heracles*. When Heracles arrives on scene, the chorus take his timely arrival as proof of his descent from the god and refer to him as such (Διὸς ὁ παῖς, *Her.* 696) in their paean after the hero plans to avenge his family. The chorus'

---

[330] Podlecki (1967) 362-67 discusses the significance of this animal imagery and stresses its importance to the overall themes of the play.

[331] As Mikalson (1989) 81 notes, Athena is particularly appropriate as the recipient of Eteocles' prayer, both in terms of "locale and function."

identification of Heracles as Zeus' son is the first since Amphitryon's "boast" at the beginning of the play and stems from his ascent from Hades and willingness to kill Lycus, punishing an unjust usurper and tyrant (700). The interest in this particular mode of identification lies in the immediate context of the paean – the chorus are singing of Apollo before they assert "he is the son of Zeus" and it is not clear until they then go on to refer to Heracles that the hero is the subject rather than the other divine son of Zeus.[332] This is only one among many examples of the conflation of characters, but it is unsurprising here given the number of similarities between the two sons of Zeus: both are renowned for archery, both have slain monstrous beings, both have been subjected to forms of slavery and both have saved someone from death; but only Apollo has been acknowledged by Zeus as his progeny.[333] The identification of Heracles with Apollo could suggest that the former will one day become immortal; alternatively, it could highlight the gulf that still exists between Heracles and his half-brother. Although they have accomplished similar feats, the fact that Heracles' mother is mortal means that his immortality, if it is to come, will come at a price not required by Apollo.[334] This reading becomes more apparent when the chorus once again reiterate Heracles' status as a son of Zeus after he has successfully killed Lycus and they sing of his strength and ability to return from Hades (805-08).

---

[332] Padilla (1992) 3.

[333] The chorus also refer to themselves as singing swans, birds who were believed to sing their own death dirge before dying; this reference would serve two purposes: it foreshadows imminent death, although whose death it would be is still unclear; secondly, it would bring to mind Apollo's act of saving Admetus from death along with the correlating notion that someone had to replace him. In *Alcestis*, the title-character went to Hades in her husband's place, but Heracles retrieved her. Here, Heracles has just brought up Cerberus and Theseus, suggesting that not one, but two are required to replace them.

[334] The slaughter of Megara and her three children would thus seem far more than necessary to appease Hades; on the other hand, Heracles has brought four heads up from the Underworld and sends four back, Megara in return for Theseus and the three boys in return for Cerberus.

There is one further occasion in the play where confusion of identities is used in relation to the use of patronymics. The chorus exclaim aloud their dismay at what is happening in the house and the turbulence which prompts the supposed arrival of Athena. The uncertainty arises when the chorus address the child of Zeus and ask what he/she is doing in the house:

τί δρᾶις, ὦ Διὸς παῖ, μελάθρωι;
τάραγμα ταρτάρειον ὡς ἐπ' Ἐγκελάδωι ποτέ, Παλλάς,
ἐς δόμους πέμπεις (*Her*. 907-09).

Kovacs assumes that the child of Zeus referred to here is Heracles and compares the hero to Athena when she defeated Enceladus.[335] Bond, however, believes the address is to Athena, "she is addressed first by a more general title, ὦ Διὸς παῖ; then as Παλλάς, which removes any doubt about her identity."[336] It is obvious from these two examples that it is not clear who is the referent at either point and the effect of ambiguity is clear. On Kovacs' reading Heracles is being assimilated to Athena in his destruction of the "enemy"; taking Bond's reading, Heracles is compared to the Giant Enceladus, as one disturbing the divine order. This dual identification builds upon the earlier duplicate readings of Heracles' identity and reinforces both the problems of patronymics as well as their inherent utility, being able to convey one, two or even several ideas at once. While this may suggest far more about the poetic ability of Euripides than it does about the characterization of Zeus, the discussion serves to highlight various aspects of the god which are passed down to his children and the impact these aspects have on the mortal plane.

---

[335] Kovacs (1998) 397: "Son of Zeus, what are you doing in the house? It is hellish confusion you send against it, as of old Athena did to Enceladus!"
[336] Bond (1981) 304.

Helen and the Dioscuri

In *Heracles* and *Phoenissae* especially, patronymics were utilized by Euripides to stress various inherited aspects of a god or a character's disposition as well as underscoring particular thematic elements important to the play. The significance of Zeus as "Father of Gods" in *Electra* and *Orestes*, however, relates to other children of Zeus, and with respect to Helen and the Dioscuri, to progeny with dual paternity. The most famous offspring of Zeus with this claim will be discussed in detail in the next chapter; for the present discussion, it shall suffice to look first at Zeus' (eventually) divine daughter, Helen, and then briefly at her brothers, Castor and Polydeuces. In *Electra*, we are informed by Castor that Helen never journeyed to Troy; instead, Zeus sent a phantom image with Paris and Helen herself was sent to Egypt. The reason Castor gives us is that Zeus wished to cause strife and bloodshed: Ζεὺς δ', ὡς ἔρις γένοιτο καὶ φόνος βροτῶν, / εἴδωλον Ἑλένης ἐξέπεμψ' ἐς Ἴλιον (*El.* 1282-83).[337] The idea that Zeus wished to rid the world of excess population can be found in the *Cypria*, although this may not be precisely the reason Castor hints at. Euripides takes this idea of a phantom-Helen further in his *Helen*, but here the idea is given no more than two lines. If the Trojan War was all about strife, Zeus obviously planned well and the death of Agamemnon may not have happened but for that; however, given the fact that the curse of Agamemnon's ancestor also has a part in this play, things may have come to pass as they did anyway. The only piece of information that is of real significance is that Helen is not to blame (for the war or anything else) – Zeus has ensured that all that has happened came to pass. Euripides leaves the audience with no doubt as to the god's interest in human affairs, only a question about his motives.[338]

---

[337] See Kovacs (1985) for the significance of the Dioscuri, especially Castor, in the play as whole.
[338] Thury (1985) 20-21.

While it may not be obvious in *Electra* that Helen is divine, there is no doubt about her status in *Orestes*. In this play, Helen is undoubtedly the daughter of Zeus and she is in fact the centre of much discussion (and spectacle) during the play's final scene. As the drama reaches a climactic point with Orestes holding Hermione hostage and ordering Electra and Pylades to set fire to the house, Apollo appears with Helen "on the machine" and announces that she has not in fact been murdered as Menelaus (and the audience) were led to believe.[339] Instead, as Zeus' daughter she was brought to safety and will now join her brothers in heaven, about to be enthroned as a saviour to sailors:

> ἐγώ νιν ἐξέσωσα χὐπὸ φασγάνου
> τοῦ σοῦ κελευσθεὶς ἥρπασ' ἐκ Διὸς πατρός.
> Ζηνὸς γὰρ οὖσαν ζῆν νιν ἄφθιτον χρεών,
> Κάστορί τε Πολυδεύκει τ' ἐν αἰθέρος πτυχαῖς
> σύνθακος ἔσται, ναυτίλοις σωτήριος (*Or.* 1633-37).

Willink and Kovacs note Euripides' use of word-play with Ζηνὸς and ζῆν to underscore Helen's immortality.[340] There is, however, another link between father and daughter in the new role Helen is about to take on as σωτήριος, one of Zeus' prominent epithets. In sending Apollo to save (ἐξέσωσα) Helen,[341] Zeus proves himself to be aware of his duties as a father (πατρός) to both Helen and her brothers Castor and Polydeuces. Furthermore, it is made clear that he also takes responsibility for ensuring the stability of the earth, for Apollo also states that Helen's beauty was used as the impetus for the Trojan War in order to relieve the world of excess population (1639-42), reminiscent of her role in *Electra*. While it seems a callous way to complete such a task, Zeus is shown to be at least aware of the need to protect

---

[339] See Arnott (1973) 56-59 for a discussion of Helen's "murder."

[340] Willink (1986) 352; Kovacs (2002) 599 n. 32.

[341] Apollo is clearly acting on behalf of Zeus and carrying out his will, suggesting, as Willink (1986) 352 has noted, that Apollo's "actions [are] beyond criticism."

not only the earth, but also its inhabitants, for all three of the Tyndarid children will now act as saviours to seafarers.

Apollo reiterates this last sentiment in his final words of the play and explains that he will be taking Helen to Zeus' house among the starry skies of heaven where she will be enthroned beside Hera and Hebe as a goddess, honoured with libations together with her brothers:

> ἐγὼ δ'
> Ἑλένην Ζηνὸς μελάθροις πελάσω,
> λαμπρῶν ἄστρων πόλον ἐξανύσας,
> ἔνθα παρ' Ἥραι τῆι θ' Ἡρακλέους
> Ἥβηι πάρεδρος θεὸς ἀνθρώποις
> ἔσται σπονδαῖς ἔντιμος ἀεί,
> σὺν Τυνδαρίδαις τοῖς Διὸς ὑγρᾶς
> ναύταις μεδέουσα θαλάσσης (*Or.* 1683-90).

There are two items of importance within this short speech of relevance to Zeus' significance in the play. The first is Apollo's specification that Helen will journey to the μελάθροις of her father; the second is the identification of Castor and Polydeuces as Τυνδαρίδαις τοῖς Διὸς. Taking the former first, it is perhaps intriguing that Zeus' home would be described as a μελάθρον, for it is a word used in the play to describe the Tantalid house and indeed, it is only used of that specific dwelling until this final instance.[342] I call this intriguing for the house of Tantalus is a significant focal point of the play, as the background in the action, but also as a house where ill deeds take place – a veritable symbol of the Tantalid line, for if the house should fall so would the "dynasty" of Tantalus (and when Orestes orders Electra and Pylades to set fire to the house, all the youngest descendants would be engulfed, including

---

[342] There are six such occurrences in the play: 378, 759, 1270, 1290, 1354 and 1547. The use of μελάθρον in tragedy is quite common as a word which can denote anything from a hut or cave to a palace of a king or a temple of a god. While it can be used to refer to the abode of a deity, this is the only instance in extant tragedy where it refers specifically to the house or halls of Zeus.

Hermione).[343] Thus by describing Zeus' halls as μελάθροις, Euripides is linking the Tantalid house to that of Zeus: it is a symbol of the relationship between Zeus and this particular family, but even more, the house of Zeus *is* the house of Tantalus. Each member of the play (with the exception of the Phrygian slave) is a descendent of Zeus and the μελάθροις of both Zeus and Tantalus becomes linked through the physical as well as the symbolic representation of the palace. Should the physical *domus* fall to flames, not only would it be the end of the Tantalid "house" but it would also endanger the "house" of Zeus. Thus does the god bring Helen to his heavenly abode. Helen is the "bridge" between the mortal and divine spheres by dint of both her genealogy (and semi-divine nature) and her relationships to each side. Through Helen's daughter, Hermione and her marriage to Orestes, the mortal house of Tantalus will live on. In bringing Helen to Olympus, Zeus saves the divine side of Tantalus' house.[344]

The status of Helen's brothers is far less ambiguous; the two sons appear together in an epiphany in *Electra*, but are introduced much earlier. They are called the sons of Zeus by the chorus when introducing their other sibling Clytemnestra. Helen is greeted as a daughter of Tyndareus and sister to the sons of Zeus:

> ἰώ,
> βασίλεια γύναι χθονὸς Ἀργείας,
> παῖ Τυνδάρεω,
> καὶ τοῖν ἀγαθοῖν ξύγγονε κούροιν
> Διός . . . (*El.* 988-91).

---

[343] As Fuqua (1978) 7 states, "the play is from first to last about the house of Atreus." He is referring both to the house as a physical domicile as well as the physical representation of the members of the Atreid line.

[344] Many scholars have noted the "Trojan" theme that runs throughout *Orestes* and the re-enactment of the war: see, for example, Fuqua (1978) 20-26; Falkner (1983) 297; Zeitlin (2003) 60-62; Wright (2006) 43-45.

The mention of the Dioscuri here foreshadows their later arrival, but the emphasis on Clytemnestra's lineage is intriguing. She is clearly being compared to her brothers, sons of Zeus, while she is merely the daughter of a mortal. The chorus goes on to praise Castor and Polydeuces as saviours of mankind and how they live among the stars in heaven before stating that they worship her just as they worship the gods (994). Clytemnestra, however, is not worthy of being honoured as gods would be and the emphasis on her lineage is a reminder that she is a mortal and should not strive beyond her station. Her death could thus be seen as a punishment for her hubris against the gods as well as her part in Agamemnon's murder, although this has not been made explicit.

As for the reference to Castor and Polydeuces, by naming them first as Tyndarids, Euripides is labelling them as the sons of Tyndareus; but then to say the Tyndarids are sons of Zeus, Euripides is not only calling them Zeus' sons, but providing them with a dual paternity. It is of course common for these two to be given this dual paternity, but in a play where identities seem to shift somewhat,[345] it is possible that Euripides is presenting us with a more nuanced patronymic. Not only is the dual paternity presented, but it is presented to us in such a way as to provoke questions about lineages and the favour of the gods. It is obvious that Tyndareus' family has been honoured by Zeus as much, if not more so, than the other branches of his family. Indeed, when Tyndareus first appears in the play, he is greeted by Menelaus as the co-partner in a marriage-bed with Zeus: ὦ πρέσβυ, χαῖρε, Ζηνὸς ὁμόλεκτρον κάρα (*Or*. 476). As West says, "Tyndareus is ennobled by Zeus' use of his wife."[346] It seems to be more than just "ennobling" Tyndareus, however, for it is as though his entire lineage is not only his alone, but that of Zeus as well. Just as Zeus was intimately connected with the earlier generations of the Tantalid line, so too is he now intimately

---

[345] Lush (2008) 62.

[346] West (1987) 215.

connected with the present generation. The difference is that where before Zeus ended up casting Tantalus into the atmosphere between worlds as punishment, he is now raising up not only Castor and Polydeuces, but Helen as well to the rank of divinities. The only child of Tyndareus who is not raised to such lofty heights is Clytemnestra, presumably because of her ill deeds against Agamemnon.

Concluding Remarks

In not one of the plays under discussion here is Zeus or Jupiter ever named as "Father of Gods" as he is in epic; yet their fatherhood of so many other deities is of considerable importance. It is specifically through tying Eros to Zeus as son and father that Euripides in his *Hippolytus* portrays legitimate unions in Olympus that ought to be mirrored by mortals. Eros is not traditionally thought of as a son of Zeus and yet such a relationship is given prominence in order to establish the young god's *timē* as granted by Zeus and to bring his "powers" under his father's control. Such an idealization of the roles of father and son are clearly problematized by the relationship exhibited by Theseus and Hippolytus. Seneca in his *Phaedra*, on the other hand, augments Cupid's *auctoritas* to become greater than his mother's and to rival Jupiter's own. Jupiter succumbs to Cupid's arrows, effectively bringing down the god to the level of a beast (turning him into a swan, a bull). In Euripides' plays such "trysts" were presented as legitimate unions, but in Seneca's they illustrate the immense power of a youthful god and the potential to humiliate the supposedly supreme Jupiter. Similarly, Aphrodite, who can be classed as either a first or second generation deity, is presented in relation to Zeus in a vastly different way from that of Venus to Jupiter. Aphrodite is a wife of Zeus and a legitimate one at that. She is a goddess of marriage and protects the household, usurping Hera's traditional role. Together, Aphrodite and Zeus are the divine couple against whose laws the three main characters of the play transgress. Seneca's Venus has no such importance in *Phaedra*, not only being eclipsed by her son Cupid, but reverting to her more traditional role as a paramour of Mars. In *Hippolytus* and *Phaedra* then, Zeus' and Jupiter's relationships to these "deities of love" differ markedly in order to further illustrate each play's main themes.

Zeus' connection with Dionysus is no less important, especially in Euripides' *Phoenissae*, but also in his *Hippolytus*. Dionysus' unique conception and subsequent re-birth from his father's thigh renders their relationship comparable only to that of Zeus and Athena. Dionysus is far more similar to his father in essence, however, than Zeus' daughter. He shares with his father the duality of bringing life as well as death through the symbol of the lightning bolt. It is through the lightning bolt that Zeus killed Semele, but through that same action that he gave birth to his son. The motif of Zeus and Semele's birthing of Dionysus is used by Euripides either to highlight the potential for destruction or to stress the true nature of Dionysus and to tie his own descendants in Thebes to his father. Seneca too utilizes the myth of Bacchus' birth in his *Heracles* and *Oedipus* to emphasize the destructive nature of Jupiter's thunderbolts as weapons which cause harm and which Jupiter would rather not use.

Whereas Zeus is depicted as close in nature to his (eventually) divine son Dionysus, he is generally represented as very much at odds with his far more legitimate son Ares. The product of Zeus and Hera's union, Ares is a god of conflict and the father of fratricide and civil war. His significance to the people of Thebes in most pronounced in Euripides' *Heracles* and *Phoenissae* where the god is linked to the dragon and the Spartoi. Euripides makes particular use of Ares as the ultimate ancestor of Megara in *Heracles* and as the antithesis to Dionysus in the *Phoenissae*. In both cases, however, there is a conflict between two lines of descent that ultimately lead back to Zeus. In *Heracles*, the hero wages war against his own family, symbolic of civil war, an act which is inherent in each member of Ares' family (which includes Megara and her sons). The Theban dynasty is prone to civil war and Heracles is no less immune from it. *Phoenissae* portrays precisely this aspect of inherent fratricide in the deaths of Eteocles and Polynices. Once again, descent from Ares' dragon is emphasized as the aspect of Thebes which needs to be "civilized." Descendants of Epaphus, another son of Zeus, arrive in the form of the chorus and they link themselves to Zeus through bovine images. Such bestiality is linked to Zeus though his own metamorphosis into a bull and his love for Io, but it also serves to highlight the bestial behaviour of the two Theban princes; their ancestry dooms them to their present circumstances.

Finally Euripides uses the device of patronymics not only in order to identify a clear blood-line to Zeus and establish an honourable lineage, but also to purposely "confuse" identities. Both Athena and Apollo are blurred with the hero Heracles when Euripides uses the phrase "child of Zeus" (Διός παῖ). It is not immediately clear to whom the patronymic refers and such blurred identification serves to equate the hero with each of Zeus' other divine offspring. Such potential confusion is also achieved by Euripides' emphasis on dual paternity (in the case of Castor and Polydeuces) and potential divinity (in the case of Helen).

The last two chapters explored the relationships of Zeus and Jupiter with other important gods and goddesses, focussing specifically on hierarchical power-structures and tensions. As "Father of Gods," Zeus is represented as the dominant deity in the Greek pantheon who relies on other gods and goddesses to uphold his divine laws; Jupiter is depicted as striving to maintain a delicate balance with other powerful deities who have the potential to disturb his world order. Even though there is a discernible difference in the way their relationships with other divinities is portrayed, they still have in common an innate patriarchal identity – that is, each god remains a symbol of the patriarchal order even though neither is literally a father in a biological sense to a number of the gods or goddesses discussed. In the divine realm the struggle for the kingship was over in the distant past and both Zeus and Jupiter are secure in their position; thus, their duties as a father-figure are limited, in many ways, to ideas and ideals associated with that position: as authoritarian, defender, guarantor of order, punisher of crimes, *et cetera*. This becomes difficult, however, when in both Greek and Roman society the father is eventually replaced by the son: an act which will never eventuate for either god. The implications of this tension can be articulated more effectively through an investigation of their relationships to one of their most ambiguous children: Heracles.

A complex and complicated figure, Heracles is an ambivalent character who is mortal and divine, an ideal role-model embodying many heroic attributes and yet inherently excessive and linked intrinsically with the bestial order; he is the ultimate civilizer, but often lives on the periphery of civilization; he is fatherless and of dual paternity. While the list could go on, it is the last of these that will be the focus of this chapter. Part of Heracles' complexity is due to his dual (perhaps triple) nature as a mortal who is semi-divine and who later becomes a god, receiving cult as both a hero and as a full-fledged divinity, making him a unique cultic figure. This exceptional status is accorded to him partly because of his dual parentage, being a son of both Zeus and Amphitryon (although he was not alone in having two fathers – the Dioscouri, Helen and Theseus could also make this claim). This double paternity is exploited by Euripides in his *Heracles* and by Seneca in his *Hercules Furens* where the hero is fully mortal throughout each play and the audience members' likely expectation (either at the end of the plays or beyond them) that he will be divinized, is neither realized nor confirmed in either tragedy. The hero's divine heritage, however, is a central problem in each drama and his dual nature cannot be denied.

In Euripides' *Heracles*, the question of the hero's paternity is a central concern and the identification of Heracles as either a son of Amphitryon or as a son Zeus results in serious repercussions. I discuss the issue of paternity with respect to the ritual *amphidromia* and how Heracles' identity as a(n) (il)legitimate son is linked to whether or not he undertook this initiation. The acceptance by Heracles of one or the other of his fathers results in an inverted *amphidromia* ritual which also has ramifications in both the divine and mortal spheres. Heracles' acceptance of Amphitryon forces the hero to undertake certain duties required of a son; but as soon as this father-son relationship is eclipsed by an acceptance of Zeus as the hero's divine father, Heracles must face the implications of being a son to Zeus. Thus, Heracles straddles the divine and mortal realms causing him to echo both divine and mortal responses to his father's reign: his heroic nature and completion of the Labours supports the rule of Zeus, but his destiny to become an Olympian also causes tension and creates the potential for hostility, especially with the goddess Hera.

A comparison with Seneca's treatment of the same theme will follow, for the Roman playwright does not follow Euripides in a number of important aspects. First, the divine paternity of Hercules is established from the beginning of the play and there is never any doubt about the hero's parentage. The interest for Seneca lies far more in the potential for friction between Hercules and his divine father. Juno's prologue suggests that the hero will attempt to displace Jupiter and thus the goddess plans to intervene. The divergent interests of both playwrights serve to highlight the various ways that Zeus and Jupiter's relationship to his heroic son can be presented and such interpretations of the relationship often reveal some of the other thematic interests in each of their plays.

Zeus and Heracles: Responsibilities and Expectations

The uncertainty concerning the paternity of Heracles is, of course, an inherent part of the "Heracles myth," but Euripides exploits this ambiguity from the very beginning of his *Heracles* and makes it an important issue for the duration of the play. The drama opens with Amphitryon introducing himself as the one who shared his marriage-bed with Zeus: Τίς τὸν Διὸς σύλλεκτρον οὐκ οἶδεν βροτῶν, / Ἀργεῖον Ἀμφιτρύων' (*Her.* 1-2). The statement is replete with ambiguity as Kraus has noted,[347] but it also clearly indicates one of the thematic interests of the play[348] – which of the two is the father of Heracles and what then are the implications for the hero's identity? The issue seems settled immediately, however, for Amphitryon goes on to say quite explicitly that Heracles is *his* son, πατέρα τόνδ' Ἡρακλέους (3). Therefore, the question of identity for all parties concerned remains thus until Lycus arrives and asserts that Amphitryon's boast about Zeus' shared paternity of Heracles is merely that: a boast (148-49). Amphitryon's only remark to counter Lycus' challenge is that Zeus will defend his own part in the begetting of Heracles: τῶι τοῦ Διὸς μὲν Ζεὺς ἀμυνέτω μέρει / παιδός (170-71).[349] Amphitryon offers neither proof nor further discussion on the matter, focussing instead on Lycus' suggestion that Heracles is cowardly.

---

[347] Kraus (1998) 145-46.

[348] Halleran (1988) 77; Barlow (1996) 125.

[349] Bond (1981) 113.

But his refusal to comment further on Zeus' supposed paternity indicates his presumption that the god will eventually claim the hero as his own progeny.

This initial questioning of Heracles' paternity at first appears to be a rhetorical exercise, for the audience knows that Heracles was indeed a son of Zeus; he received cult as both a hero and as an immortal god. One way of understanding Euripides' extended discussion on the matter is to interpret Lycus' opposition to Heracles' legitimacy as Zeus' son as a mythological expression of an Athenian political practice. Sons were presented to their father's demes and phratries to be accepted as legitimate children by the other group members; this was an opportunity either to accept or reject the son's status as a child born of both an Athenian father and mother (Arist. *Ath. Pol.* 42.1).[350] Rejection could ultimately lead to expulsion or even slavery (both of which Heracles has in fact suffered). Heracles' situation is obviously complicated by numerous factors (especially his dual parentage), but the fundamental question of his legitimacy and potential rejection does seem to be represented here, at least symbolically, suggesting that Euripides is exploiting this particular Athenian custom for a specific purpose.

Following this initial challenge to Heracles' paternity, the chorus, far from providing the audience with any closure on the question, heightens the uncertainty by asking whether they should refer to Heracles as a son of Zeus or Amphitryon: παῖδ', / εἴτε Διός νιν εἴπω / εἴτ' Ἀμφιτρύωνος ἴνιν (*Her.* 353-54). Lycus overtly voiced his scepticism concerning Zeus' paternity, Amphitryon refused to openly defend it and the chorus now add their voices to the growing sense of scepticism.[351] While this atmosphere of disbelief casts a shadow over Heracles' legitimacy and creates suspense about his identity (is he divine or is he mortal; is he dead or is he alive), it also, like Amphitryon's dismissal of Lycus' objection, provides an

---

[350] For an extended discussion of the father-son relationship, see Strauss (1993).

[351] Bond (1981) 152.

invitation for Zeus to settle the dispute, for at this point in the play, the god has not claimed

Heracles as his son in any way. It is precisely because Zeus does not provide evidence for the

hero's paternity that repercussions result for not only Heracles, in terms of his responsibilities

and duties, but also for Amphitryon and the hero's own sons. As Griffiths has articulated:

> a son's identity was formed though his father's identity, from the acceptance
> of the infant into the family shortly after birth, through the use of family
> names, and the assumption of adult status through admission to the father's
> community and the identification of a man as "X son of Y" . . . [but Heracles']
> social identity rests on an unsure foundation, which in turn raises questions
> about his own family links with his children.[352]

As long as Heracles has not been publicly recognized by his biological father and legally

incorporated into society, neither he, nor his sons, have claim to an ancestral line.[353] It is

possible that Amphitryon had carried out the ritual *amphidromia* for Heracles at the

appropriate time and thus incorporated the hero into his own *oikos* and society (discussed

further below, pp. 190-92). If this is the case, in doing so the act has proved problematic for

Heracles, for it is in upholding his own obligations as a son to Amphitryon that the hero

embarked upon his Labours in an effort to expiate the murder of Electryon (13-21).[354] This

filial piety to Amphitryon is admirable, but it ultimately creates the crisis situation to which

the hero returns: first, were it not for his absence, his family and even the city of Thebes itself

would not be in a dire situation with Lycus; and secondly, the very completion of his Labours

also provides the evidence of his divine nature which consequently spurs on the negative

attention from Hera. Thus in accepting his status as a son of Amphitryon, Heracles absented

himself from his familial obligations to his own sons, exposing them to potential disaster

when they were subsequently faced with the usurping Lycus. But, upon acceptance of his

---

[352] Griffiths (2006) 69.

[353] Palmer (1957) 52 discusses the implications of being an illegitimate son with regard to *Medea*, but
his comments can be applied equally to Heracles and his own sons.

[354] Indeed Heracles later comments (1258-60) that Electryon's murder is "part of his own inheritance"
(Shero [1956] 199).

status as a son of Zeus, his divine nature allowed Heracles to return from the Underworld and remove the threat to his family while simultaneously incurring a new threat from Hera. With these competing modes of identification it is not surprising that there would be much confusion when attempting to "pin-down" the true nature of this hero.

In spite of this initial confusion by other characters concerning Heracles' paternity, when the hero finally arrives on scene and reveals his plans to avenge his family, the chorus, in their paean, take his timely arrival as proof of his descent from the god and refer to him as Zeus' son (Διὸς ὁ παῖς, *Her.* 696).[355] Heracles, however, did not introduce himself as the son of Zeus when appearing for the first time, but rather claimed descent from Amphitryon when he remarked that his father was distraught (528). Thus, the chorus' identification of Heracles as Zeus' son is the first since the beginning of the play when Amphitryon "boasted" of sharing his bed with the god. Such identification of the hero is brought about by his completed *katabasis* (the literal and metaphorical conquering of death) and his willingness to kill Lycus, ridding the earth of one more "beast" (700). Both of these activities implicitly link Heracles to Zeus: only the son of a god could return alive from the world of the dead; and the dispatch of a usurper/beast places the hero in the role of defender of the city, defender of the rights of kingship and more broadly, defender of notions of justice. It is fitting that a son of Zeus returns from Hades in order to accomplish such acts.[356]

It is after the chorus hears the cries of Lycus as he is being executed by Heracles that they sing an ode which, by the end, brings the question of the hero's paternity full-circle. They praise Heracles as a son of Zeus and reiterate the same conception scenario which Amphitryon had "boasted" of at the beginning of the play. The chorus, using similar language to that of Amphitryon, now acknowledge without hesitation how he shared his wife with

---

[355] Bond (1981) 246-47.

[356] Gregory (1977) 266; Silk (1985) 12-13.

Zeus (798-804) and such acceptance echoes the Athenian practice of deme and *phratry* members legitimizing the status of another member's son. This affirmation by the chorus and the repetition of Amphitryon's claims suggests that the issue of Heracles' lineage has been settled – and indeed his descent from Zeus is clear; however, the chorus is oblivious to the implications of legitimately claiming such an illustrious father. As a son of Zeus, Heracles now gains a step-mother in Hera, whose presence in his life must now be acknowledged.

Thus acceptance of the fact that Zeus is the father of Heracles proves to be inherently complicated and ultimately disastrous; for immediately after these affirmations, Iris and Lyssa appear at Hera's behest in order to bring madness upon the hero and destruction to his family. Iris makes plain their mission: ἑνὸς δ' ἐπ' ἀνδρὸς δώματα στρατεύομεν, / ὅν φασιν εἶναι Ζηνὸς Ἀλκμήνης τ' ἄπο (*Her.* 825-26). While it may seem at first that Iris does not necessarily believe Zeus' paternity to be a fact (through the use of ὅν φασιν),[357] it is clear from her presence as an agent of Hera that Iris' anger is directed at Heracles for this very reason.[358] It is also clear that the entire δῶμα is in physical danger as a result of Zeus' relationship with Alcmene, as well as being in danger of disintegration through a breakage in family ties (discussed above, chapter 4, pp. 117-19). Now that the chorus has publicly acknowledged Zeus as the hero's father the repercussions are being realized and the social order will be overturned as Iris predicts: Ἥρα προσάψαι κοινὸν αἷμ' αὐτῶι θέλει / παῖδας κατακτείναντι, συνθέλω δ' ἐγώ (831-32). With Zeus established as Heracles' progenitor the chorus is now able to praise the hero not only as a son of a god but as though a god himself; this identification causes Hera to view her step-son as a potential usurper of and divine

---

[357] Barlow (1996) 16 notes that this phrase is more likely to be a common expression rather than an indication of disbelief or sarcasm at the thought of Zeus' paternity.

[358] Her words immediately following (828-29) also indicate Iris' acceptance of Heracles' descent from Zeus.

successor to her husband.[359] By accepting the paternity of Zeus, Heracles is now viewed as taking up the role of a divine son: traditionally that has resulted in the usurpation of the father (Kronos over Ouranos, Zeus over Kronos).[360] In order to prevent such a challenge to Zeus and the established divine order, Hera inverts the paradigm of the son replacing the father and instead causes Heracles to destroy his own progeny.[361] Not only does this cause Heracles to become a filicide, polluted with kindred bloodshed, but it also causes the hero to consider the ramifications of accepting such a role. Heracles does act out the tradition of eliminating threats from potential usurpers as Ouranos and Kronos had before him, but this will lead him to choosing Amphitryon as the father-figure from whom he constructs his future identity, effectively fulfilling the desired result of his step-mother.

After Heracles awakens from his madness-induced sleep and learns of the fate of his family he declares that he wants to commit suicide, believing his life is no longer worth living. He acknowledges the biological begetting of Zeus, but rejects the god as his father in every other sense, claiming Amphitryon instead as his "true" father:

πρῶτον μὲν ἐκ τοῦδ' ἐγενόμην, ὅστις κτανὼν
μητρὸς γεραιὸν πατέρα προστρόπαιος ὢν

---

[359] The declaration by Iris that Hera was not permitted to harm Heracles while undergoing his Labours suggests that her wish to harm him has nothing to do with the Labours themselves or Heracles' treatment of Lycus; instead, it must stem from something earlier and upon which she was prevented from acting until now. The only threat that Heracles poses to Hera which would also align with Iris' statement concerning a need to punish the hero in order to protect the gods from becoming "nothing" and curbing the power of man (840-43), is Heracles' identity as a human son of Zeus who has the ability to transcend that mortal boundary. We know that Heracles has that ability because we are told that he once fought alongside the gods (177-80; 1190-92) and thus his status as a favoured son of Zeus is clear.

[360] Ouranos and Kronos were both overthrown by their sons (Hes. *Theog.* 74, 175-83) and Hera fears history may repeat itself.

[361] Padilla (1994) 298 suggests that because Heracles cannot literally succeed Zeus, he attempts to become his father's equal by killing his own offspring and thereby ensuring his own god-like "permanence."

ἔγημε τὴν τεκοῦσαν Ἀλκμήνην ἐμέ.
ὅταν δὲ κρηπὶς μὴ καταβληθῆι γένους
ὀρθῶς, ἀνάγκη δυστυχεῖν τοὺς ἐκγόνους.
Ζεὺς δ', ὅστις ὁ Ζεύς, πολέμιόν μ' ἐγείνατο
Ἥραι (σὺ μέντοι μηδὲν ἀχθεσθῆις, γέρον·
πατέρα γὰρ ἀντὶ Ζηνὸς ἡγοῦμαι σ' ἐγώ) (*Her.* 1258-65).

This recognition of Amphitryon is suggestive of the Athenian *amphidromia* ritual, "a rite of integration within the family space and the paternal line of descent"[362] at which a father either accepted or rejected a child as legitimate. Padilla has used this ritual as a way of understanding the scene around the hearth and Heracles' relationship with his sons, prior to their deaths.[363] His reading of the ritual into that scene is quite perceptive, but it could also be used to understand Heracles' relationship with both of his fathers. Heracles was not accepted into Zeus' paternal line as he should have been and Amphitryon, in recompense for killing his father-in-law, is in exile from his native city of Argos, so even if Heracles had been accepted into Amphitryon's paternal line, he would still have no rights of citizenship until Amphitryon returns there. Heracles' crisis of identity has only been resolved through bloodshed which confirms his divine descent, but at a cost too high to accept willingly. Heracles cannot deny Zeus' part in his conception, but he can choose how he will live the remainder of his life and thus his acceptance of Amphitryon here could be read as an inverted version of the ritual. Now as an adult, he, as son, is choosing to accept Amphitryon as his legitimate father (instead of the normal practice where the father accepts the son); unfortunately, the pollution Heracles has incurred (reminiscent of Amphitryon's pollution and exile), prohibits him from taking up once more the duties that would normally accompany that relationship. Indeed, one such duty proves to be a concern at the end of play when Heracles is about to depart with Theseus for Athens and Amphitryon asks by whom will he be buried (1419). Heracles cannot

---

[362] Vernant (1983) 155.

[363] Padilla (1994) 282-86.

and will not be able to perform this task for the father he recognizes; the issue of burial is also important for his boys, for they will be buried by their grandfather, an inversion of the normal practice, where sons should bury their fathers (Dem. 24.107). Thus, the uncertainty surrounding Zeus' paternity and the lack of a secure lineage from which to create one's identity creates social problems for Heracles and his family, ultimately severing those relationships which it should have helped to protect. But when Zeus' paternity is finally confirmed, Heracles' relationship with Amphitryon is severed because of Hera's involvement and instigation of "madness;" the hero now must expiate the murders of his wife and children and leave the only father he ever knew. The only way forward for Heracles is thus to leave with Theseus and begin anew.

It is Theseus who provides the final image of Zeus in the play and it is one which picks up on many of the motifs that have been running throughout the tragedy.[364] Theseus reminds the audience of the time when Zeus bound his own father in chains and describes the god as a "tyrant," leaving the audience with a rather negative view of Zeus: οὐ δεσμοῖσι διὰ τυραννίδα / πατέρας ἐκηλίδωσαν; (*Her.* 1317-18). The two images are suggestive of "ancient history" as it were, but they also link the god to the tyrant Lycus and, inversely, to Amphitryon, for he had just bound Heracles, albeit not with chains but with rope.[365] Furthermore, Zeus is shown to be as poor a son as he is a father, for Bond notes that "any violence offered to a father may be regarded as defilement in a society where paternal authority is strong."[366] The irony, of course, is that Heracles lacked strong paternal authority which created even further problems. The picture as a whole suggests the cyclical nature of

---

[364] On Theseus' role in *Heracles*, see especially Conacher (1955) 148-50; Chalk (1962) 13-16; Robertson (1980) *passim*; Halleran (1986); Yoshitake (1994); Johnson (2002); and Holmes (2008) 263-73.

[365] On the theme of "bonds" in *Heracles*, see Worman (1999).

[366] Bond (1981) 394.

violence and instability,[367] as well as the fine line between strong paternal authority and none at all. The recurrent image of the bonds is symbolic of the inherent tension between fathers and sons, but such "bondage" can only occur where paternity is certain. Amphitryon inversely duplicates the binding of Kronos by Zeus solidifying his own position as a father-figure and prefiguring Heracles' acceptance of him as such. But this acceptance of familial roles is predicated both on violence and on the assumption of a (semi-) divine identity as a son of Zeus. Heracles depended on his mortal father to construct his identity, but such an identity *nearly* cost him his entire family; but when he attempted to construct an identity based on his divine father, it *did* cost him his entire family. Heracles cannot be a mortal son, but as a divine son, he can never replace his father. Only with Theseus is Heracles finally able to gain full control over his own affairs, but it means rejecting, in some way, both of his father-figures. For the hero, Zeus' paternity, although it cannot be fully denied, cannot be fully accepted.

Jupiter and Hercules: Like Father, Like Son

The question of Hercules' paternity is one with which the *Hercules Furens* is also concerned. Here this question is relevant to Jupiter's authority insofar as Hercules' actions reflect back on Jupiter as the god's son and as one attempting to "follow in his footsteps." Hercules' status as a son of Jupiter is asserted by Amphitryon after Lycus denies the hero's paternity:

> partes meae sunt reddere Alcidae patrem
> genusque verum ....
> ....
> nondum liquet de patre? mentimur Iovem? (*HF* 440-41, 446).

---

[367] Higgins (1984) 100, 103 and 104.

Lycus continues to disbelieve Amphitryon's assertions and the debate remains at a standstill. After Hercules' arrival and subsequent departure to conquer Lycus, Theseus relates Hercules' conduct in the Underworld and again stresses Jupiter's paternity of the hero as *Iove natus* (792). Thus, while Hercules is dispatching the one person who objected to their relationship, Jupiter is once again declared to be Hercules' father by Theseus, but it remains to be seen whether Hercules' actions are in accordance with what is expected of a son of Jupiter.

Hercules' slaying of Lycus is at once shown to be a pious act of vengeance and one in accordance with expectations.[368] The hero announces that he will make sacrifices to thank the gods for his victory: *nunc sacra patri victor et superis feram, / caesisque meritas victimis aras colam* (*HF* 898-99). Unbeknownst to Hercules, his sacrifice is the enactment of what Juno envisioned as the impious victory celebration earlier in the play (44-54). For the audience, however, it would be clear that Hercules, although acting as triumphant conqueror, is not laying down *spolia* from his conquest in the Underworld, but rather in thanks for the victory over Lycus and his associates.[369] They can be sure of this because Hercules made it clear that he was not showing his father that which he brought up from the Underworld: neither Cerberus nor any other form of *spolia* would serve for this sacrifice of thanksgiving. Thus, it is clear that Juno's first accusation against Hercules is shown to be false.[370] While Hercules did bring Cerberus from Dis, Hercules shows proper behaviour in sacrificing to Jupiter and the other gods for his victory over Lycus, not for any victory over Dis.[371] Hercules' invocation of Jupiter as his father suggests that he recognizes his authority not only

---

[368] Motto and Clark (1981) 110 argue for Hercules to be seen as functioning in a divine capacity and thus not acting impiously here. See also Rose (1979-1980) 136-37.

[369] *Contra* Henry and Walker (1965) 15 who state that the *spolia* of Hercules is Theseus and Cerberus. Shelton (1978) 54-56 discusses the Cerberus episode in detail and questions whether or not the nether dog should even be considered a worthy opponent of Hercules.

[370] As Motto and Clark (1981) 111 declare, "this is Juno's furious premonition and delirious vision."

[371] Motto and Clark (1981) 110.

as the supreme deity, but also as his *paterfamilias* and further acknowledges the support of the gods. This initial presentation of Hercules would suggest that the hero is in fact a "worthy" son of Jupiter.

This initial impression of Hercules does not remain unsullied, for there are two significant references to Jupiter as the "Thunderer," each made by Hercules and possibly linked thematically. After Hercules has slain Lycus, he returns triumphantly and wishes to make prayers and sacrifices to the gods and to Jupiter in particular: *Tonantem nostra adorabit manus* (914). Amphitryon suggests that Hercules pray to Jupiter to end his labours and give him rest, *Finiat genitor tuos / opta labores* (924-25), essentially asking that Jupiter uphold his responsibilities to his son and let Hercules quit labouring for others. Hercules does not adhere to Amphitryon's wishes and suggests instead that such a request is unsuitable and that he shall decide what the proper prayer should be: *Ipse concipiam preces / Iove meque dignas* (926-27). Hercules is implying that there is some element of comparability between Jupiter and himself.[372] That Hercules wants to offer prayers "worthy" (*dignas*) of both himself and Jupiter, the common adjective *dignas* serving to equate the two, intimates that the hero is, at the very least, elevating himself to divine status and likely to a status equal to that of his father.[373] Motto and Clark would take this even further and suggest that Hercules' prayer here is only the first step in *displacing* his father.[374] The only justification for such a step by Hercules is his earlier "conquest" over Dis (for executing Lycus is not an inherently divine

---

[372] Fitch (1987) 362; Papadopoulou (2004) 275.

[373] Fitch (1987) 362.

[374] Motto and Clark (1994) 271, emphasis added. They also see this line as the beginning of Hercules' madness and thus not part of what a sane Hercules would suggest.

action[375]); such a feat would place the hero in a similar situation to that of his father, the only god with any supremacy over the lord of the Underworld.

Shortly after this prayer to Jupiter, Hercules, while *furens*, refers again to Jupiter as "Thunderer," but this time there is no ambiguity over whether or not there is equality between the two; Hercules shows no fear, nor reverence, toward the god: *Licet Tonantis profuga condaris sinu, / petet undecumque temet haec dextra et feret* (*HF* 1010-11). At this point, Hercules believes his wife to be Juno and he fears neither the goddess, nor Jupiter's wrath when asserting that he will abuse the god's protection. The earlier reference to Hercules' own hands paying homage to Jupiter as *Tonans* (914) thus foreshadows the hero's present attempt to use his hands to violate the same aspect of the god; the pairing serves to emphasize Hercules' current rejection of Jupiter's *auctoritas*. Both of these references refer to Jupiter as a god of retribution, an ironic epithet given Hercules' position: he is a pawn of Juno's wrath, while believing he is punishing those who threatened his family (and thus taking on a similar persona to that exemplified by the epithet *Tonans*). That Hercules offers a sacrifice to Jupiter Tonans is appropriate, at least initially, for the victory over Lycus. But the explicit assertion that Hercules is no match for Jupiter as Tonans (and that anyone taking sanctuary with him will perish by Hercules' hands) not only reiterates the comparability that the hero earlier professed, but is also inherently ironic. The counterpart of Jupiter Tonans is Juno and she is the one currently carrying out her own retribution against Hercules. Thus, any suggestion by Hercules that he can overcome a god of retribution is patently false. It was precisely when Hercules instead announced that he would make prayers "worthy" of both Jupiter and himself (926-27) and began to equate himself with Jupiter, that he was beset by madness. The rejection by Hercules of his place as a *son* of Jupiter (a perversion of familial status) and

---

[375] Although Hercules' subjugation of various beasts and his "civilizing" role might be worthy of other divine children of Jupiter, even these feats are not enough to suggest an equality with the supreme god.

subsequent self-elevation to a status equivalent to a Tonans (a perversion of cultic status)

precipitated the onset of Juno's furies.

When Hercules again refers to Jupiter as his father – while influenced by the furies –

it is as a potential enemy, for Jupiter rules the heavens, which Hercules has yet to conquer

(957). Hercules wants to see Jupiter as his father for he promised him divinity and voices a

belief that he deserves to become a god himself: *astra promittit pater* (959).[376] But ultimately,

Hercules envisions Jupiter as an impediment to his succession and this scene is the enactment

of Juno's earlier visions.[377] Hercules announces that in order to achieve those stars, he will

unleash Saturn and command an uprising against Jupiter:

> vincla Saturno exuam,
> contraque patris impii regnum impotens
> avum resolvam (*HF* 965-67).

The problem with this scene is whether Hercules' aspirations to usurp Jupiter's authority are

genuine, or merely the result of his furial madness. There has been no indication in the text

up to this point that Hercules would actually stage an uprising against his father,[378] although

the incident in the Underworld is cause for concern. Juno's prologue indicated that Hercules

would attempt this – but not while "mad," and this would suggest that she could only procure

his rebellion through such orchestrated means.

It is also worthwhile to note some of the language used by Hercules during his

"uprising." Hercules refers to Jupiter as *impii* and this is an unusual adjective for the god, as

it carries with it many connotations – including being sacrilegious and an enemy – and indeed

variations of the word occur frequently throughout the play. Here, Fitch suggests that the

---

[376] Henry and Walker (1965) 21; Papadopoulou (2004) 274.

[377] Rose (1985) 119.

[378] Indeed, as Fitch (1987) 369 notes, such an assault goes "against that very cosmic order for which
H. prayed so recently (927-28)." It is thus unlikely that Hercules would attempt any uprising against
Jupiter under any other circumstance.

primary meaning intended by Hercules is "unpaternal."[379] Whether this suggests that Hercules is simply critiquing Jupiter's performance of his paternal responsibilities or that he has rejected the notion that Jupiter is his *paterfamilias*, the term is one of censure, implying that Jupiter is "undutiful." Because Hercules believed that Jupiter was not forthcoming with his promise of the stars, he thus saw him as neglecting his duty toward his son (and is perhaps referring to Amphitryon's plea for rest). The attack on Jupiter then is not so much to usurp Jupiter's authority as to gain that which Hercules desires most – acceptance into the heavens.

When Hercules recovers from his fit of madness, his acknowledgment of his relationship to Jupiter reverts to his initial stance – that Jupiter is his father and *paterfamilias*. Hercules refers to his conception, as well as to his unique status as someone whose life affects the very fabric of the universe. When he sees his weaponry is missing, he demands to know what other son of Jupiter could have conquered him: *quem novum caelo pater / genuit relicto?* (*HF* 1157-58). Hercules also poses the question, *cuius in fetu stetit / nox longior quam nostra?* (1158-59). Clearly he does not believe that there is any enemy able to conquer him except another son by his divine father and, furthermore, that his existence was brought about through cosmic alterations.[380] Jupiter is recognized by Hercules as his father without question, as well as being able to control the elements of nature, such as the rising and setting of the sun (1158-59). Nevertheless, recognition does not necessarily imply deference and thus Jupiter's authority is far from secure; Hercules, although unsuccessful in launching an attack on the god, is nevertheless presented as someone with the *potential* to be triumphant. Jupiter remains in control, but not without many doubts being raised.

---

[379] Fitch (1987) 370.

[380] Rose (1985) 120 expresses Hercules' thought process well: "in keeping with his growing awareness of the truth, he senses that the culprit must be another self, born under similar circumstances (1157-59) and wearing the Herculean armor (1172) which he knows well no-one could take from him (1153-55 ; cf. 1197f.)."

The final reference made to Jupiter as Hercules' father is when the hero wishes to be blasted by Jupiter's thunderbolts as punishment for his impiety. Hercules refers again to Jupiter's neglect of duty, but requests that he remember his grandchildren, even if he refuses to remember his own son:

> Nunc parte ab omni, genitor, iratus tona;
> oblite nostri, vindica seru manu
> saltem nepotes (*HF* 1202-04).[381]

Jupiter does not answer Hercules' requests, likely because he recognizes that Hercules does not *actually* pose a threat to his regime. This could reflect the absence of thought for Hercules by Jupiter, or his disregard for the affairs of men. The emphasis placed on Jupiter's paternity, however, would seem to tell against these interpretations. Much is made of their relationship and it is unlikely that Jupiter would completely abandon his progeny, although it is not assured that he will favour him with divinity either.

While the hero in this play is explicitly connected to Jupiter, the other mortals involved are separated as much as possible from the divine. In the majority of the following examples, it is the prayers the characters make which ultimately serve to confirm, or wholly destroy, any sense of Jupiter's presence or thought for the affairs of humankind. Seneca's Megara and Amphitryon both pray to the gods and to Jupiter in particular for assistance, but both in the end acknowledge the futility of such prayers. Lycus does not pray to Jupiter and instead compares himself to the god, only to realize such actions have lethal consequences.

In Megara's opening monologue (279-80), she calls upon Jupiter and the other gods to restore Hercules to the upper world, but her last words confirm her belief that her prayer is futile. Although this is not the first prayer to Jupiter in the play, it is the first to reject

---

[381] The knowledge of his own actions suggests that Hercules is cognizant of his crimes and deserving of punishment; it also implies that Hercules believes the only proper, or suitable, punishment is one dealt out by Jupiter's most potent weapons.

explicitly Jupiter's ability to fulfil what is requested. Megara pleads to Jupiter and even offers him a hecatomb, if only Hercules will be returned to her:

> tibi, o deorum ductor, indomiti ferent
> centena tauri colla.........................
> ....
> ....nec ullus eriget fractos deus (*HF* 299-300, 308).[382]

The initial prayer would seem to confirm Jupiter's ultimate authority, for *ductor* can have a sense of *dominus*, but this is the only passage cited by the *TLL* for *ductor* used of a god.[383] One wonders why Seneca would choose this particular epithet for Jupiter, when there is no precedent and, furthermore, no metrical reason for doing so. The word carries military connotations as well as imperial resonances. It may be tempting to see a correlation between Jupiter and the Emperor, but if that were the case, why then end the prayer with the notion that the gods (including Jupiter) are ineffectual and that prayers made to them are futile. If we were meant to see a link between Jupiter and the *princeps,* this would be undermining the imperial authority. If *ductor* is meant to be taken militarily, Jupiter is being presented as a commander of an army, perhaps to allude to the primordial battles between the Olympians and Titans (or Giants). This would then foreshadow Hercules' visions while *furens,* for he seems to recreate this war, with himself leading the opposition against Jupiter (965-66). The god's authority remains intact then, but is not necessarily secure; Jupiter is on the defensive.

This ambiguity is more apparent during Amphitryon's final plea to Jupiter to prevent Lycus from carrying out his malevolent threats. The prayer is similar to previous mentions of Jupiter in the play (205-07, 249; 299-308; 440-48; 457-61) in that immediately following an assertion of Jupiter's supreme authority, such authority is then diminished; here Jupiter's authority is not merely questioned but exclaimed to be inadequate:

> Pro numinum vis summa, pro caelestium

---

[382] But as Fitch (1987) 210 comments, "Megara implicitly rejects as useless her appeals to Jupiter . . ."
[383] Fitch (1987) 208.

rector parensque, cuius excussis tremunt
humana telis, impiam regis feri
compesce dextram! – quid deos frustra precor? (*HF* 516-19).

Jupiter is referred to as the "highest power" among the gods and thus he should be able to stop Lycus. Amphitryon recognizes that Jupiter will help neither him nor Megara and he confirms Lycus' assertion that "no god" will come to their rescue. What is significant here is that Amphitryon ceases to pray to the gods and turns instead to his son for help, as if Hercules were a god already. That Amphitryon rejects the gods in favour of his son has an element of impiety about it and Fitch has noted that this is a new twist in Seneca.[384] The only character in this play who does not question Jupiter's authority is Lycus and, in fact, he appears more god-fearing than any of the other characters.[385] As he leaves the scene, he announces that he is departing to prepare sacrifices to Neptune (514-15). Amphitryon, on the other hand, attempts to beseech Jupiter, but in the end turns to Hercules for aid. This may speak more to the short-sightedness of mortals than to the failings of Jupiter's guidance and protection, but in context, it does serve to undermine the god's authoritative position, suggesting he cannot offer any assistance or comfort to those seeking his aid.

Lycus' view of Jupiter differs from that of both Megara and Amphitryon and his function as the "villain" of the play affects our interpretation of his philosophies and ideology

---

[384] Fitch (1987) 250.

[385] Lycus is the only one who prays and sacrifices to the gods. While Megara does offer a hecatomb to Jupiter, she immediately declares that there is no god who can answer her prayers and help her family (308). Amphitryon also prays to Jupiter then believes such prayers are futile (519). In light of both of these reneged prayers to the gods, Lycus' departure to sacrifice to Neptune seems all the more pious, even though his current actions are inherently impious. But the sacrifice to Neptune also implicitly suggests that the sea god may be more receptive to prayers than Jupiter, or perhaps more reliable in answering prayers. The potential dichotomy is not, however, developed any further.

of the god as he espouses them.[386] Nevertheless, a negative view of Jupiter is also conveyed, if ironically, through Lycus' positive view of the god. This emerges most clearly when Lycus is attempting to persuade Megara to marry him. Amphitryon and Megara, in order to dissuade Lycus from such an act, attempt to persuade him of Hercules' divinity and thus of his eventual return. In response, Lycus uses Hercules' divine paternity (in which he does not actually believe) as a precedent in order to achieve his goal of marriage: *Quod Iovi hoc regi licet: / Iovi dedisti coniugem, regi dabis* (*HF* 489-90). Lycus compares himself to Jupiter, suggesting that he is somehow worthy of the same "privileges" as the god;[387] it also serves to link the play to contemporary Rome, where the Emperor is seen as Jupiter's representative on earth. The effect of this scene, however, is to challenge Jupiter's entitlement to have access to any female he chooses. Although comparing a mortal to a divinity is not necessarily appropriate, the association between Lycus and Jupiter remains explicit and perhaps does more to suggest the god's abuse of power, which augments his authoritative position, but diminishes his integrity.

Concluding Remarks

Zeus, as a literal father to Heracles, is portrayed somewhat ambiguously with respect to his paternal responsibilities. Euripides questions whether or not the god is truly the father of the hero in order to highlight the ramifications of illegitimacy and the lack of having a strong father-figure from whom to construct one's identity. Zeus, as father to Heracles, is not confirmed by Euripides until half-way through his play at which point Hera directs her

---

[386] As Shelton (1978) 32 comments, Lycus is one of Seneca's "shrewd realists" who can "employ any means toward a given end. Often we cannot argue with the 'end.'" Lycus is thus both the tyrant in his actions, but a cunning politician in his words. The audience is thus emotionally dismayed by him, but cannot help but agree with the pragmatism of his rhetoric.

[387] Such an act was precisely how the conception of Hercules came about. Lycus is attempting to duplicate with Megara Jupiter's act with Alcmene and produce his own version of Hercules.

intermediaries to send the hero "mad." In such madness, Heracles acts out the traditional divine conflict between fathers and sons when he kills his own children. Zeus cannot and does not intervene, causing other characters in the play to question the god's moral integrity, especially when Theseus recounts the time when Zeus bound his own father in chains. As a father-figure to this particular hero, Zeus remains an important part in Heracles' identity, but the god cannot truly have a relationship with his son. He must remain aloof and leave Heracles in the care of other foster-fathers.

Seneca's Jupiter and Hercules have a similarly difficult relationship, but in this Roman incarnation, their kinship status is never questioned. The interest for Seneca lies in Hercules' acceptance of Jupiter's status as *paterfamilias* and all that that role entails. While the hero remains "submissive" to his father and respectful of his *auctoritas* and *imperium*, Hercules is able to function as a hero and as a son. But as soon as he rejects that role and begins to equate himself with his father, essentially rejecting Jupiter's authority, Heracles is beset by Juno's furies. Jupiter's paternal responsibility to Hercules is never questioned, but his ability to carry out retribution as *Tonans* is portrayed as potentially inadequate. Several characters question his authority and capabilities and, while such speculation is eventually shown to be unwarranted, Jupiter's *auctoritas* is nevertheless challenged. While *furens*, Hercules is shown to have the potential to usurp his father, creating an impression that the continuation of Jupiter's reign is somewhat reliant on his son's ultimate acceptance of their respective roles.

The title "Father of Gods" is awarded to both Zeus and Jupiter due to their roles as literal and metaphorical father figures within their divine pantheons; they are also given the epithet "Father of Men" because of their similar roles among mortals. Not only do they have illustrious offspring, Heracles and Hercules being the prime examples, but various other heroes and kings also trace their ancestries back to these gods, making Zeus and Jupiter quite literally fathers of mankind. These gods also epitomize the patriarchal order to which both Athens and Rome subscribe: they are the ultimate symbols of the hierarchies imposed upon domestic and political life for both Greeks and Romans, the latter eventually going so far as to link explicitly the person of the emperor with the supreme god Jupiter. Such links between ruler and god are not, however, unique to Rome and can in fact be traced back to Homer and his representation of the Atreid line as particularly linked to Zeus.

The relationships between mortals, the royal houses in particular, and their divine ancestors offer different insights than those discussed in relation to Zeus and Jupiter and their divine kin. In the celestial sphere, those subordinate to Zeus or Jupiter either make an effort to support the god's rule or exhibit varying degrees of hostility, creating an environment of tension. In contrast, mortal kin (either children or descendants that are more distant) rarely have the ability either to help or to hinder their progenitor's authority. Instead, they rely on Zeus and Jupiter's goodwill and, in particular, their favour and protection because of their familial ties. There are exceptions to this generalization, one of which, Heracles, was discussed in the last chapter (the other exceptions will be examined in the next section focussing on "challengers" to Zeus and Jupiter). The final chapter of this "Part" examines both favoured, close kin (the Tantalids and Heracleids), and more remote descendants (the Labdacids, Theseus and Hippolytus, Hecuba and Polyxena, and Achilles), concentrating on the various modes and contexts for communication between mortal and god. Such modes and contexts for communication are generally "religious" in nature: prayers and appeals, supplication and sanctuary, sacrifices and offerings. Finally, a discussion of Zeus and Jupiter as recipients of trophies, indicating their requirement for honour while emphasizing impieties that often accompany that honour, completes the chapter and section.

Zeus, Jupiter and the Atreids: A Favoured Family

> εἷς βασιλεύς, ᾧ δῶκε Κρόνου πάϊς ἀγκυλομήτεω
> σκῆπτρόν τ' ἠδὲ θέμιστας, ἵνά σφισι βουλεύῃσι
>
> (Hom. *Il.* 2.205-06)

The Tantalid line is favoured by Zeus, not only because of its close kinship ties through Tantalus but also because it was chosen by the god to be the one family that ought to reflect and symbolize the will of the gods and Zeus' in particular. The fact of the Tantalid line being chosen by Zeus to be honoured above all other men was established as early as Homer's *Iliad*. The favour shown to Agamemnon specifically is emphasized through the symbol of the *skeptron*, a divinely-wrought family heirloom passed down through the generations after being presented to Pelops by Hermes as a gift from Zeus himself (Hom. *Il.* 2.100-08[388]). The *skeptron*, much discussed with respect to its significance in the *Iliad*,[389] not only endows Agamemnon with authority to give counsel and make judgements, but it also symbolically ties himself and his family (for it will presumably be passed on to his own son) to Zeus. Furthermore, because the *skeptron* is no ordinary

---

[388] Hom. *Il.* 2.100-108: ἀνὰ δὲ κρείων Ἀγαμέμνων / ἔστη σκῆπτρον ἔχων τὸ μὲν Ἥφαιστος κάμε τεύχων. / Ἥφαιστος μὲν δῶκε Διὶ Κρονίωνι ἄνακτι, / αὐτὰρ ἄρα Ζεὺς δῶκε διακτόρῳ ἀργεϊφόντῃ· / Ἑρμείας δὲ ἄναξ δῶκεν Πέλοπι πληξίππῳ, / αὐτὰρ ὁ αὖτε Πέλοψ δῶκ' Ἀτρέϊ ποιμένι λαῶν, / Ἀτρεὺς δὲ θνῄσκων ἔλιπεν πολύαρνι Θυέστῃ, / αὐτὰρ ὁ αὖτε Θυέστ' Ἀγαμέμνονι λεῖπε φορῆναι, / πολλῇσιν νήσοισι καὶ Ἄργεϊ παντὶ ἀνάσσειν.

[389] See, for example, Combellack (1947); Mondi (1980); Thalmann (1988) 10-14; Easterling (1989).

object, having been made by Hephaestus, Agamemnon is doubly honoured: first by Zeus' act in giving the Tantalid line honour above all others and, secondly, by giving the Tantalids honour through a divinely-made *skeptron*. This object possesses a divine element or "aura" that bestows upon its wielder a similar defence as a divinely-wrought shield, protecting its wielder from all but the strongest judgements. This is not to say that Agamemnon, for example, can never be defeated, just as Achilles' shield cannot protect its bearer from death; but it does offer a level of divine assistance that is not otherwise offered to those who carry ordinary staves or sceptres.[390]

This particular *skeptron* is indeed unique and, as can be gleaned from an example by Seneca, it expressly associates its bearer with the god from whom it was given. In the second choral ode of Seneca's *Agamemnon*, Juno is invoked as sister and wife of the *magni sceptri* (*Ag.* 340-41), metonymically referring to Jupiter. Here Jupiter *is* the sceptre; and this is not the only reference to *sceptra* in the play: from the beginning of the play, the sceptre is a symbol which is intimately connected to the Tantalid family. When describing the ancient house of Pelops, Tantalus mentions the throne whence *hoc sedent alti toro / quibus superba sceptra gestantur manu* (9-10). In the first choral ode thrones and sceptres are again joined, although more obliquely: *numquam placidam sceptra quietem / certumve sui tenuere diem* (60-61); and later Clytemnestra contemplates her role as regent of Agamemnon's authority and sceptre (110-11), but fears that it will be passed on instead to wives of Trojans (194). It is with such associations in mind that Jupiter is then referred to as a *sceptrum* himself. Although it is possible to separate the object of the sceptre from the power which it represents, it is unlikely in this case for such an object as Agamemnon's sceptre to be viewed without the inherent association with Jupiter. Thus, when Jupiter is

---

[390] Van der Mije (1987) 262 discusses Agamemnon's sceptre as both a "material gift" and "pseudo-material gift," referring to its importance as an emblem of Zeus' vested interest in the safekeeping of the political and social orders.

referred to *as* the sceptre, the sceptre itself takes on that association and vice versa. Agamemnon wields the authority of Jupiter; Clytemnestra is guarding the authority that will be passed on to her son;[391] and conversely, Juno is not married to a physical sceptre, but to what that sceptre represents.[392]

The authority of Jupiter is thus invested in the sceptre and because he gave a particular sceptre to Agamemnon's family, that sceptre carries within it the divine law and authority of Jupiter and represents the god's will. Such a sceptre sets the Tantalid family apart from all other families and connects each member to the god in a way that no other family can claim. It is this added layer of association that lends an almost protective essence to the entire House of Tantalus. Its members are favoured above all others and although that cannot guarantee their ultimate survival, it provides a gravitas to their connection with the god and a stronger bond upon which any one member may wish to draw when invoking the gods or appealing for aid.[393]

The reason for beginning with this brief discussion of the sceptre is to establish a continuum from Homer to Seneca focussing on the symbolic potential of the sceptre as an

---

[391] The association between the sceptre and Orestes becomes more clear at the end of the play when Electra invokes the *sceptra terris nota* and implores Strophius to take Orestes away (930). Strophius does so with a further mention of Pisaean Jupiter who will keep his charge safe (938-39). The directive to Strophius to steal away the future bearer of the sceptre while invoking the authority of the family heirloom intensifies the association between the god and the last member of this family line. Strophius' acceptance of the task and belief that Jupiter will protect Orestes further emphasizes the familial bond between the two.

[392] Nagy (1999) 179-180: Agamemnon's sceptre "is a thing of nature that has been transformed into a thing of culture."

[393] References to sceptres are quite frequent in Senecan tragedy appearing nine times in both *Hercules Furens* (65, 272, 331, 342, 399, 430, 502, 599, 707) and *Oedipus* (12, 105, 241, 513, 635, 642, 670, 691, 705); 6 times in *Phoenissae* (57, 275, 584, 599, 615, 648), *Agamemnon* (10, 60, 111, 194, 341, 930) and *Medea* (59, 143, 205, 252, 529, 982); 5 times in *Thyestes* (229, 341, 532, 604, 971); 4 times in *Troades* (152, 271, 728, 771); and twice in *Phaedra* (217, 868).

object as well as the elevated status of Agamemnon's family in relation to Zeus. It is this relationship which has a particular bearing on the subject of familial prayers to Zeus in Euripides and, indeed, in Seneca. Prayers to Zeus occur frequently throughout the plays, but the examples chosen for the present discussion all share the commonality of having an emphasis placed on the Atreids as having a "special" or somehow distinct relationship with the god.

The first example, from Euripides' *Electra*, is significant more for what it does not explicitly express than for what it does. It is also, in fact, the first reference to Zeus in the play; but rather than adhering to a straightforward formula for a prayer, Euripides has Electra's "plea" to Zeus appear more as an interjection than a proper invocation. Electra is merely expressing a desire for her brother to come to her aid:

ἔλθοις δὲ πόνων ἐμοὶ	you, come, be my deliverer,
τᾶι μελέαι λυτήρ,	a wretched girl, from my pains,
ὦ Ζεῦ Ζεῦ, πατρί θ' αἱμάτων	O Zeus, Zeus, and be my father's ally
αἰσχίστων ἐπίκουρος, Ἀρ-	after his shameless murder, put into
γει κέλσας πόδ' ἀλάταν (*El.* 135-39).	Argive shore, your wandering feet.[394]

Although the context makes it clear that Electra is appealing to Orestes for his imminent arrival, the apostrophe to Zeus at first appears to make this plea an appeal to the god, rather than her absent brother; it is not until she mentions his wandering feet that the focus is directed once more to Orestes. In fact, it is only the context and Electra's earlier address to her brother (130-34) that suggests this is anything other than a real prayer to Zeus.[395] The pleas Electra makes could suit either Orestes or the god and even the reference to wandering feet could imply Zeus' prolonged absence from Argos (given the usurpation of Agamemnon's throne by Aegisthus and Clytemnestra, the forsaking of Argos would not be

---

[394] The translation here is my own and I have included it in order to emphasize the ambiguity of the apostrophe to Zeus.

[395] Indeed Roisman and Luschnig (2011) 115-16 do refer to this as a prayer to Zeus.

uncharacteristic of Zeus). According to Pulleyn, "the most basic pattern for a Greek prayer . . . is an invocation and request,"[396] two elements which are clearly part of Electra's plea. Furthermore, "Greek prayers, and Greek hymns, commonly contained imperatives telling the god to come or listen,"[397] again an element clearly part of Electra's address. What is significant, is that although the address is structured as a prayer and spoken in a context where a prayer would be expected and by one who ought to pray, is it nonetheless marked before and after as an address to a mortal (rather than divine) agent.

The expectation that Electra would call upon the gods and especially Zeus to come to her aid and send Orestes as her saviour, is thwarted here. Instead, Electra later explains that she has appealed to the gods in the past, but believes they do not heed her prayers for assistance (198-99). The audience knows, however, at this point that Electra's assumption is wrong and that Orestes is now in Argos, ready to fulfil those desires Electra earlier specified. It is thus reasonable to suggest that those previous prayers, presumably to Zeus (as he is the god of whom we hear first), have in fact been heard by the god and Orestes' arrival is the result. Such an interpretation is strengthened when considering the later reception of Orestes by Electra and her immediate acknowledgement of the gods' involvement. When Electra learns that Orestes is alive, she asks the Farmer to bring the news to the Old Man who saved her brother, for she believes that he will want to offer prayers to the gods for saving him (415). Indeed, when the Old Man recognizes Orestes himself, he asks Electra to pray to the gods for delivering her brother (563) and she dutifully complies (566). Orestes' arrival is considered above all to be divinely inspired[398] and given Electra's initial request to Zeus in all but name, one might interpret her wishes

---

[396] Pulleyn (1997) 7.

[397] Naiden (2013) 53.

[398] Orestes also tells us that his presence in Argos happens after leaving the "mysteries" of a god, which is interpreted as being Apollo, the god who gives prophecies on behalf of Zeus.

as heard and answered by the god himself, although such direct confirmation is not made explicit.

That Electra ought to pray to Zeus is confirmed after the recognition scene, when the god does receive a proper invocation after the decision to kill Aegisthus has been made. Before Orestes leaves to carry out his task, he prays to Zeus, Hera and his father to be victorious against his enemies; Electra echoes his pleas. The prayers they make to Zeus are personal; they are uttered, not by any unknown person, but by individuals tied to Zeus in a familial manner: ὦ Ζεῦ Πατρῷε καὶ Τροπαῖ' ἐχθρῶν ἐμῶν / οἴκτιρον ἡμᾶς· οἰκτρὰ γὰρ πεπόνθαμεν (*El.* 671-72).[399] This is followed by Electra's οἴκτιρε δῆτα σοῦ γε φύντας ἐκγόνους (673). There are two elements of importance here: the religious aspect of the prayer and the familial. Although Cropp would argue that the religious emphasis here is cursory in comparison to the treatment in Aeschylus,[400] there is no doubt that the religious element is important. Orestes is calling upon Zeus in his capacity as a god of the household (Zeus Patroös), a very appropriate aspect of the deity to which to appeal, but also as a god intimately associated with his family. Zeus, as father of the Tantalid line and as the one who gave Agamemnon the sceptre with which to rule (*Il.* 2.100-08) and his goodwill are of the utmost importance to Orestes, and the hero recognizes this fact. The main difference between the appeal here and that in Aeschylus is the motivational aspect Orestes uses to gain the god's good favour. Here, Orestes is not reminding Zeus of past favours or sacrifices given by his father; instead, Orestes and Electra both appeal through οἶκτος or a sense of pity.[401] Zeus, for Orestes and Electra, has a responsibility beyond

---

[399] I am here following Kovacs' (1998) proposed text.

[400] Cropp (1988) 146.

[401] It has been noted by Konstan (2001) 53 that "appeals for οἶκτος are uncommon in Greek literature generally." Johnson and Clapp (2005) 154 suggest that instances of *oiktos* cognates in tragedy are used to indicate "a sorrowful, sympathetic emotion" and "a sympathetic emotion that

being a god associated with justice and maintaining the cosmic order – he is the patron god

of their family and thus they offer a very personal plea rather than the conventional *da-

quia-dedi* or *da-quia-dedit* prayers, such as the one used by Aeschylus' Orestes (*Choe.*

246-63).[402]

In *Orestes*, rather than any appeals to the gods from Electra and Orestes

themselves, it is the chorus who prays to Zeus on their behalf, again with an emphasis

placed on the pair's justified reliance on the gods for aid. The prayer comes when Helen is

supposedly being murdered by Orestes and Pylades; the chorus takes up the cause of the

trio and specifically asks that Zeus comes to their aid: ὦ Διὸς ὦ Διὸς ἀέναον κράτος, /

ἔλθ' ἐπίκουρος ἐμοῖσι φίλοισι πάντως (*Or.* 1299-1300). Although it is perhaps surprising

in this play that neither Orestes nor Electra pray to Zeus themselves,[403] the most significant

element of the prayer is in the language that the chorus uses. In particular, it is the chorus'

choice of the term ἐπίκουρος (which, incidentally, was also used by Electra in the above

example, *El.* 138), a word of some significance in the play.[404] It appears several times

throughout the drama, is connected to ideas of *philia*[405] and, in some cases, divinity.

Orestes first uses the word when he awakens from his slumber and exclaims how sleep is

an ἐπίκουρος against disease (*Or.* 211); Electra wonders how she can gain an ἐπίκουρος

with the divine as her enemy (266); Orestes counsels Electra on what being ἐπίκουρος

---

arouses a behavioral response." Orestes and Electra are thus asking Zeus to act based on an
emotional response to their situation, stemming from his familial relationship to them.

[402] See Pulleyn (1997) 16-38 for a discussion of these prayer-types.

[403] Prayers are only made by Pylades, at *Or.* 1242-43 and by the chorus here at 1299-1300.

[404] ἐπίκουρος is an epic word, more specifically Iliadic (34 occurrences) and while it is not
uncommon in extant tragedy and comedy (occurring 17 and 6 times respectively), it appears
more often in this play than in any other (6 occurrences compared to once or twice in any other
play).

[405] Rawson (1972) discusses the importance of *philia* in *Orestes*.

means (300) and then states that she is the only ἐπίκουρος on whom he can count (306); and finally Orestes calls upon his dead father Agamemnon to be an ἐπίκουρος to those who are in need (1226).

It is clear that there is an inherent association between ἐπικουρία and *philia*,[406] but there also seems to be an undercurrent of divine association as well. It was a concept heavily used in the *Iliad* to refer almost exclusively to allies of the Trojans, specifically Lycians under the command of Sarpedon.[407] According to Lavelle, Homer used the word to mean a "*fighting* ally"[408] (emphasis mine). Someone who was to be an ἐπίκουρος had to fulfill his duty in both word and in deed. The Lycians under Sarpedon, who was a "paragon" of Greek *aretê*, were ἐπίκουροι *par excellence*, coming to the aid of their friends and allies.[409] It is thus in Homer a very *human* adjective; gods have no need to be ἐπίκουρος to each other and after Homer they seldom appear alongside their human favourites, let alone to actually and physically *fight* as their ally. In *Orestes*, that Sleep (or sleep) can be said to be an ἐπίκουρος is understandable given the "enemy" (disease) is invisible and divine aid in this context is perfectly understandable. But the chorus has asked that Zeus be ἐπίκουρος in a similar way that Electra asked Orestes/Zeus in her play. To ask such a favour from a god, especially Zeus, is surprising, but Euripides makes it

---

[406] Lavelle (1997) 236-37.

[407] Lavelle (1997) 232-33.

[408] Lavelle (1997) 231: "in the *Iliad*, *epikouroi* are, for the most, mature males: seasoned warriors who fight for others as their allies; they are neither 'youths,' 'youthful fighters,' nor 'armed youths who act as servant-protectors for Zeus or other gods.'" The word *epikouros* referred to the "more restricted military sense of a 'fighting ally.'"

[409] Lavelle (1997) 233.

quite clear that such a sense of ἐπίκουρος is intended,[410] for Zeus is also ἀέναον κράτος (*Or.* 1299), "forever strong" or "with ever-lasting power." The chorus is underscoring Zeus' *physical* might, thus the desire for him to become a true ally to Orestes and Electra as an ἐπίκουρος. Such a request also comes in the context of the kidnapping of Helen, who has been taken into a besieged palace. The epic resonances are not to be underestimated. As the Trojans had called upon Sarpedon and the Lycians, the Atreids (or their supporters) call upon Sarpedon's father and the Atreid's most esteemed and powerful ally. That the chorus can call upon Zeus in such a manner can only be due to the family's very close connection to the god. None other can claim the bonds that tie the Atreid line to Zeus and get away with it.

Such favour bestowed upon the Atreid line is also clearly at work in Seneca's *Agamemnon*. Once again, it is the chorus who prays on behalf of the Atreid family, although here the desire is for Agamemnon's safety rather than his children's. We do not yet know that the Greek fleet has returned; only that Aegisthus and Clytemnestra have begun to plot the demise of the king. The chorus is thus hoping that Jupiter will turn his attention and protection to one of his own descendants:

> Tuque ante omnes,
> pater ac rector fulmine pollens,
> cuius nutu
> simul extremi tremuere poli,
> generis nostri, Iuppiter, auctor,
> cape dona libens
> abavusque tuam non degenerem
> respice prolem (*Ag.* 382-87).

---

[410] Contemporaneously, both Thucydides and Herodotus use ἐπίκουρος in the sense of "mercenary" (LSJ s.v. ἐπίκουρος), but such a connotation instead of "fighting ally" had not yet become dominant even in the late fifth century, Lavelle (1997) 258.

The chorus not only calls upon Jupiter's authority and responsibility as one who controls the entire cosmos, but also very specifically as the great-grandfather of Agamemnon (*abavus*). They appeal to his duty as the ultimate *paterfamilias* of the Atreid line: he should not ignore the safety of one of his own kin, especially not one who is *non degenerem*. Such an appeal underscores the elevated status that Agamemnon's family enjoys, one that surely also extends to the next generation. The chorus ask that Jupiter accept their gifts with goodwill and the very mention of *dona* here could foreshadow the *donum* granted to Orestes by Pisean Jupiter at the end of the play.[411] When Orestes arrives in the final act with Electra, he is handed over to Strophius and placed under his protection: *et ista donum palma Pisaei Iovis / velamen eadem praestet atque omen tibi* (*Ag.* 938-39). The phrase evokes victory and is obviously meant to foreshadow the eventual return of Orestes.[412] Orestes is thus not only under the protection of Strophius, but also of Jupiter and the familial bloodshed will end with him. Seneca seems to be downplaying the future murder of Clytemnestra, focusing rather on the fact that Orestes will bring the cycle

---

[411] Wilson (1985) 137 has suggested that *dona* could be understood in conjunction with the choral ode to Juno (*tu nunc laurus Agamemnonias / accipe victrix*, 346-47) and proposes that the laurel is presented to the god for destroying Agamemnon, rather than as a thank-offering for Agamemnon's victory. Such an interpretation would imply that Jupiter is being offered Agamemnon's life as a sacrifice, an appropriate description of his demise, which is likened to a bull at an altar (898-99). Although this is a reasonable conjecture and one that works on many levels, it is not the only level of meaning possible. The emphasis the chorus places on *future* protection certainly favours an interpretation focussing on the safeguarding of Orestes.

[412] Boyle (1997) 38: "Strophius, equipped with the palm of victory around which the whole scene revolves, responds to Electra's prayer . . . and, handling the palm, 'gift of Pisaean Jove', to Orestes as veil and *omen* (938-39), prefigures Orestes' triumph and the regicides' defeat. The Strophius scene not only underscores the pattern of crime and retribution, but, associating with the foreshadowed victory the *pietas* (931) and *fides* . . . seems to offer the possibility of (ambiguous) moral hope. The act's final scene does nothing to dissipate this promise."

of revenge to an end. Thus, the choral prayer that Jupiter *respice prolem* (386)[413] may in fact be answered by the actions of Strophius. He may not be able to fulfil their desire to keep Agamemnon safe, but Seneca suggests that the god is not unwilling to fulfil their other desire to keep the next generation safe.[414]

Divine Protection: Supplication and Sanctuary

Zeus and Jupiter's protection of their family members and others who seek their help is related to, but quite distinct from, other forms of divine shelter that they offer, in particular, their roles as guardians of suppliants (in any context) and as guardians of those who seek their places of refuge (altars and temples). Once again there are plentiful examples of suppliants throughout the tragic corpus and I will focus here on a number of very specific examples: Polyxena's "supplication" scene in *Hecuba* and Orestes' extended supplication in *Orestes*; the role of Zeus Sotēr and the double altars in *Heracles*; and the importance of Zeus' temples in Dodona and Olympia in Euripides' *Phoenissae* and Seneca's *Troades*.

Euripides' *Hecuba* contains three scenes of supplication and while all are significant and integral for a thorough understanding of the play, it is Polyxena's non-supplication directed toward Odysseus that will be the focus here. After Hecuba makes her plea to Odysseus to save the life of her daughter, a plea which is utterly rejected, Hecuba urges Polyxena to do the same, using whatever means possible to avoid becoming an

---

[413] Wilson (1985) 138 suggests that this phrase echoes that of Thyestes' ghost in the prologue, where he addresses Aegisthus and urges him to *respice ad matrem* (52). There is an emphasis throughout the play on honouring familial relationships, although the actions of the characters are generally anything but honourable.

[414] Indeed, it may even be possible to suggest that the choral recognition of Jupiter's nod (383), an indication of a promise or vow, foreshadows the god's assent to their request, although such an interpretation may be stretching the textual evidence a bit far.

object of sacrifice. Although Hecuba does not mention Zeus explicitly during her supplication to Odysseus, she does invoke past favours and suggests that she and Odysseus share a bond of *philia* (239-48).[415] Such a suggestion, in addition to the supplication act itself, would have resonated with the audience and brought Zeus to mind. If it did not, the mention of Zeus *Hikesios* by Polyxena immediately following her mother's plea certainly would have done so: πέφευγας τὸν ἐμὸν Ἱκέσιον Δία (*Hec.* 345). As Odysseus would only save Hecuba's own life for saving his during the war (272), Polyxena is left to fend for herself. Surprisingly, however, Polyxena instead tells Odysseus not to fret as he has escaped her suppliant status and she will not invoke the god.

Even though Polyxena expressly denies her right of petitioning the god (at a point where such a petition would be most expected by both inner and outer audiences), she understands that Zeus would be important at this juncture and she relieves Odysseus of the possible religious complication.[416] Furthermore, when Odysseus sees that Polyxena has an opportunity to supplicate and invoke this right, he immediately shies away and fears her touch (342-44). This automatic reflex suggests that Odysseus understands a religious obligation to Zeus *Hikesios* would be necessitated at this point if not for the fact that Polyxena chooses to abstain from using this right. A further significant point noted by Segal is that it is not Odysseus, but Polyxena who refers to the "efficacy of the suppliant gesture and to 'Zeus god of suppliants.'"[417] The Greeks do not refer to their gods in this play – the Trojans do. Segal makes the observation here in order to support the notion of Odysseus' godlessness and Heath comments on how Odysseus' evasiveness is a foil to

---

[415] For discussions of the theme of *philia* throughout the play, see Adkins (1966) esp. 196-208; Croally (1994) 62-63; and Stanton (1995) *passim*.

[416] Discussions of supplication can be found, for example, in Gould (1973), Vickers (1973) 438-94, Naiden (2006) and Tzanetou (2011).

[417] Segal (1989) 12.

Polyxena's nobility.[418] The fact that Odysseus and the Greeks in general do not speak of their gods at all could suggest a certain degree of impiety on their part, except that this does not correspond to Odysseus' reaction to Polyxena. If Odysseus were not a god-fearing man at all, he would not fear Polyxena's invocation of Zeus and his movement away belies this interpretation.

A more nuanced interpretation may be found in Polyxena's choice of phrase that Odysseus has escaped *her* Zeus (ἐμὸν Ἱκέσιον Δία, *Hec.* 345). Although both Hecuba and Polyxena would be under the guardianship of Zeus at this point, Hecuba's life is not in danger and therefore Odysseus need not be concerned about any violation of Zeus as *Hikesios*. Only by Polyxena's rejection of Zeus, does Odysseus escape the obligation a second time. Both Polyxena and Odysseus recognize the religious consequences of her (potential) supplication and although a second supplication is rejected, it is the suppliant who does so, ensuring her death is neither a violation of Zeus *Hikesios* nor of Zeus *Xenios*[419] and further that as a sacrificial object her death adheres to the moral (and heroic) code.[420] Zeus is as significant here for not being invoked as he would be otherwise.

The supplication scenes in *Orestes* are no less complex, although in an entirely different manner. Whereas in *Hecuba* Polyxena expressly rejects Zeus' protection (and through mentioning him, relieves him of duty), in *Orestes* the god is conspicuously absent from both past and present suppliant acts.[421] Here, there is one act of supplication by Orestes of Menelaus, interrupted by Tyndareus, who mentions a past supplication of

---

[418] Heath (1987) 146.

[419] As Daitz (1971) 220 remarks, Polyxena "has decided to walk freely and in freedom to the sacrificial altar."

[420] Gregory (1999) 87.

[421] Goslin (2006) 186-246 discusses supplication in the *Orestes* more generally.

Clytemnestra to Orestes. The present supplication is initiated at 382 and proceeds as expected, although Orestes does acknowledge his lack of a bough as he requests aid:

> τῶν σῶν δὲ γονάτων πρωτόλεια θιγγάνω
> ἱκέτης, ἀφύλλους στόματος ἐξάπτων λιτάς·
> σῶσόν μ' (ἀφῖξαι δ' αὐτὸν ἐς καιρόν) κακῶν (*Or.* 382-84).

Orestes is clearly supplicating Menelaus and continues to grasp his would-be rescuer's knee until 544. Aside from the bough which Orestes admits he does not have, he also does not call upon any god to come to his aid or as a witness as one would expect in such a situation. The addition of σῶσόν με could bring to mind the absence of the one deity associated with supplication as one of Zeus' primary epithets and although this need not be the case, it is not an impossibility that at least some members of the audience would make this connection and perhaps even ponder its significance. Be it due to improper ritual ceremony (either the absence of the bough, or the lack of divine witness) or merely the disinclination of Menelaus to help his nephew, the first supplication scene ends without the grant of aid.

With the arrival of Tyndareus the supplication ends, but the theme does not dissipate, for he recalls a similar act by Clytemnestra to supplicate Orestes, which also leads to an unfruitful request:

> ἐπεὶ τίν' εἶχες, ὦ τάλας, ψυχὴν τότε,
> ὅτ' ἐξέβαλλε μαστὸν ἱκετεύουσά σε
> μήτηρ; (*Or.* 526-28).

This supplication too is problematic, for a mother should never have to ask that her son not kill her and the scene is even more emotional because she had bared herself to him. The supplication thus did not only fail, but was then turned into murder and could almost be described as a perverted sacrifice. Orestes' dismissal of his mother's plea could also play a part in his own lack of pity from Menelaus and thus the past is returning to play itself out once more.[422] It is perhaps somewhat ironic that when Orestes turns to supplicate his uncle

for a second time, he does so in the name of Helen, his mother's own sister (and also the

daughter of Zeus who will eventually become a *sōtēr* of a sort), and then to Menelaus as a

brother:

> ταύτης ἱκνοῦμαί σ' – ὦ μέλεος ἐγώ, κακὸν
> ἐς οἷον ἥκω. τί δέ; ταλαιπωρεῖν με δεῖ·
> ὑπὲρ γὰρ οἴκου παντὸς ἱκετεύω τάδε.
> ὦ πατρὸς ὅμαιμε θεῖε . . . (*Or.* 671-74).

Orestes asks for aid in Helen's name, having murdered her sister, and also asks that

Menelaus remembers his brother, also murdered by that sister. Again, no gods are called

upon to witness this supplication; for although Helen will become divine by the end of the

play, she is not a deity yet and the supplication is thus again doomed to failure. Instead,

family violence begets family violence, rituals are ignored or perverted and the place of

Zeus is overshadowed by the aggression and sacrilegious acts of each member of his

lineage, except for the only descendant whom he raises to divinity.

Zeus as *sōtēr*, hinted at in *Orestes* but ultimately ignored by all in that play,

becomes a focal point in *Heracles*, both as deity and through the physical presence of his

altar. The play opens with Amphitryon, Megara and her three sons supplicating at an altar,

which is almost immediately revealed as an altar set up by Heracles to Zeus Σωτήρ (48).

This type of opening scene would have signalled to the audience several important pieces

of information: this play is a suppliant drama (evoking similar plays such as *Suppliant

Women*, but perhaps more poignantly, the *Heracleidae*); Zeus will have a stake in the

outcome, both because of the fact that the suppliants are at his altar, but also by virtue of

their being suppliants and, furthermore, because they are his immediate family. Each of

---

[422] Greenberg (1962) 160, Burnett (1971) 210-11 and Porter (1994) 93-95 discuss the cyclical
nature of Orestes' attempt on Helen's life as a re-staging of his murder of Clytemnestra.

these pieces of information contains religious associations and involves Zeus in a familiar cultic context. The Athenians in the audience would have recognized Zeus Sōtēr as the "proprietor" of their Stoa in the Agora, built to recognize his involvement in delivering their ancestors from Persian slavery.[423] Far from suspecting that Zeus will not save Heracles' (and his own) family,[424] the audience would, at this point, be fully convinced that the god will intervene in some fashion and deliver the suppliants from harm.[425]

Almost immediately after Amphitryon's formal prayer to Zeus for safety (497-500), Megara announces that she sees Heracles approaching and urges her sons to seek shelter with their father, implying they should forsake the "safety" of the altar in favour of the "safety" of Heracles. As she says this, Megara also explicitly makes the comparison between Heracles and Zeus, referring to both as saviours: ἐπεὶ Διὸς / σωτῆρος ὑμῖν οὐδέν ἐσθ' ὅδ' ὕστερος (*Her.* 521-22). This comparison serves two purposes: first, it suggests to the audience that Heracles' arrival is due to Zeus' intervention (and this is further suggested by the fact that Megara at first believes Heracles to be a dream and therefore sent by the gods, 521),[426] rendering Amphitryon's criticism and doubts invalid.[427] Secondly, the comparison suggests a close affinity between Zeus and Heracles and, at this juncture at least, creates the (illusory) impression that Heracles should be seen as an equivalent of Zeus Sōtēr. After Heracles has been subjected to Lyssa's stings of madness and destroys his own family as Lycus himself had intended to do, the audience will be left to reconsider Megara's comparison of the two "saviours." Heracles, who should have been

---

[423] Mikalson (1986) 90; Vickers (1995) 55.

[424] Bond (1981) 74.

[425] Although both Bond (1981) 74 and Barlow (1996) 127 believe the supplication at the altar of Zeus Sōtēr to be ironical; Bond going so far as to suggest "we" would not expect Zeus to save the suppliants.

[426] Contra Halleran (1988) 81: "Zeus did not save them . . ."

[427] Barlow (1996) 148; Lawrence (1998) 142.

the one to save his family, proved to be their destroyer and Zeus, who was believed to send

Heracles to save them, will also be implicated as a guilty party; however, the visual

significance of the suppliants forsaking Zeus' altar in favour of Heracles may also have

served to mitigate the impression that Zeus was complicit in Heracles' subsequent actions.

For in abandoning the altar, the suppliants revoke their suppliant status in favour of relying

solely on Heracles to save them. It is also somewhat ironic that when Lycus takes

sanctuary at the altar within Heracles' home, also dedicated to Zeus, his supplication is

rejected by the god.

The idea of the altar or sacred space of a god offering protection to those who seek

out those spaces is brought to the fore in Euripides' *Phoenissae* and is also briefly alluded

to in Seneca's *Troades*. Although the temple remains in the background of *Phoenissae*,

Zeus' temple at Dodona remains a focal point for the choral members of the play, whose

ancestors were supposedly the ones to build it, and for Menoeceus, who is urged to seek

sanctuary there, rather than become a sacrifice for Theban victory. Zeus' temple is thus

always a place "to go to" but never fully becomes a place of sanctuary, the purpose for

which it is intended.

In Euripides' *Phoenissae*, Teiresias explains to Creon the best method of rescue for

Thebes and the requirement of Menoeceus' sacrifice; but rather than accept Tiresias'

advice, Creon attempts to persuade his son to leave Thebes and travel to Thesprotia (982).

Menoeceus understands immediately that he is meant to seek safety at the sanctuary of

Zeus at Dodona: σεμνὰ Δωδώνης βάθρα; (*Phoen.* 982). Zeus is not explicitly mentioned,

but the audience would associate a religious place in Dodona with Zeus' sanctuary.[428] The

---

[428] The role of Zeus' temple at Dodona is discussed in comparison to Apollo's temple Delphi by
Castrucci (2012), esp. 20-23 for this particular scene. She examines both sanctuaries in terms of
their opposing functions, emphasizing the connection between Dodona, the *oikos* and the hero's
final destination (Apollo's temple, by contrast, is where a hero begins, often necessary for

reference to the oracle serves a two-fold purpose for Euripides. First, it establishes the sacred authority of Zeus, by whom Menoeceus will later swear an oath (discussed in chapter 5, pp. 169-70). The faith that Creon holds in the sanctuary of Zeus is also emblematic of the reliance on oracles in general by the Theban populace, even though oracular responses are often ignored by them to their own peril.[429] Menoeceus also disregards his father's advice to seek sanctuary at Zeus' oracle and instead stays to fulfil his fate at Thebes in order to save his country from harm. Secondly, Zeus' oracle is also portrayed with a dual function: it has the potential to safeguard one's life (if Menoeceus went as a suppliant), but should Menoeceus rely on the sanctuary to protect him, the oracle becomes a symbol of the destruction of Thebes (by leaving his fate unfulfilled in refusing to become a sacrifice, Menoeceus would guarantee the demise of his city).

Rather than the Dodonan temple of Zeus, it is the Olympian temple at Elis which becomes important for the chorus members of Seneca's *Troades*. The significance of the temple here is not as complex as that in *Phoenissae*, but once again, the idea of sanctuary as destination becomes notable.[430] After Ulysses takes Astyanax in order to be sacrificed, the chorus wonders where they themselves will be taken as captives. They surmise that one of the possibilities will be Pisa or Elis, known as the site of the games and Jupiter's

---

expiation of crimes). Such a function for the Dodonan temple is clearly illustrated by Creon's desire to send Menoeceus there in order to keep his *oikos* safe.

[429] Creon would have his son ignore Teiresias' prophecies, thus repeating once again the inherent distrust of the gods' will (as Jocasta and Laius had ignored Apollo).

[430] Lawall (1982) 249 discusses the site (and others) in terms of distancing the chorus from their present situation both temporally (they will go there in the future) and geographically (the temple is some distance from Troy). While this is certainly true, the knowledge of what going there will actually entail only intensifies the emotional impact of their present situation. The temple of Zeus *ought* to be a place where one can escape from their troubles, but in this situation, the chorus can only hope (at best) to be treated well as slaves; certainly a situation far worse than the one they are currently experiencing.

temple: *Pharin an Pisas Iovis et coronis / Elida claram?* (*Tr.* 849-50). On the one hand, this allusion to Jupiter's temple at Olympia suggests that the Greeks (and in historical context – the Romans) will always be victorious over their enemies; but in the mouths of the chorus, the reference has a more sombre note, for they will not be going there to compete for garlands, but to become enslaved. The one place where safety and sanctuary should be the dominant force instead emphasizes the dangers which make the idea of sanctuary necessary.

The Victors and the Vanquished: Sacrifice and Trophy

This dual function of sacred spaces, particularly altars, as places of sanctuary and of destruction will be the focus of this final section. Temples and altars symbolize a place of safety but also a place of death, of sacrifice and of (ritualized) murder. Sacrifices are made to honour the gods and trophies are often set up in place of, or to mark, other forms of death carried out at places other than an altar. The altar of Zeus and Jupiter Herkeios will form the bulk of the present discussion, followed by a discussion of tropaic imagery in *Electra* and *Phoenissae*.

One of the most poignant images of the Trojan War is often a description of the death of Priam at Zeus' altar; it is also an image which reappears and continues to resonate in both Euripides and Seneca, whose use of the image in both his *Agamemnon* and *Troades*, I will discuss first. While Priam's death at Zeus' altar is also mentioned in Euripides' *Trojan Women* (16-17; 481-82), I will instead discuss a similar image of death at an altar in Euripides' *Heracles*. The motif of the murdered suppliant remains, but Euripides' emphasizes the familial aspect, taking the murder out of the arena of war and inserting it into a domestic scene of the *oikos*.

At Rome, the Emperor was the representative of Jupiter on earth as well as the chief priest. In the world of the *Agamemnon*, this relationship between god and king is maintained, but there is inherent tension, for there are not one, but two kings of importance: the returning and triumphant king, Agamemnon, and the murdered king, Priam. Both would have had links to Jupiter by dint of their political/regal position, but Agamemnon is also Jupiter's favoured king, or at least, he should be. Instead, because of Agamemnon's actions at Troy and against his daughter, the king is portrayed as a defiler of Jupiter's bestowed power. In the end, he is offered as a sacrifice to Jupiter in recompense for Priam's death.[431] Seneca has the messenger describe Priam's slaughter at the altar of Hercean Jupiter: *sparsum cruore regis Herceum Iovem* (*Ag.* 448). Such a reference foreshadows the death of Agamemnon, for this is a play where history repeats itself, and by placing Priam's death in this context, Seneca is explicitly linking his fate with an impious action on behalf of Agamemnon.[432] When the king is about to pray to Jupiter (793), Cassandra's foreshadowing of the king's death could be read as Jupiter's punishment for Agamemnon's disrespect of the god's altar. Agamemnon has not only dishonoured Jupiter as the one responsible for a king's death at his altar (448),[433] but has

---

[431] Calder (1976) *passim*; Boyle (1983a) 201-02.

[432] Fantham (1981-1982) 120: "Seneca goes further, artificially enhancing the king's offences toward the vanquished to suggest that he has brought on himself, by his responsibility for Priam's death, the same fate as his Trojan counterpart." See also Shelton (1983) 169 who notes that "Agamemnon, as leader of the Greek expedition against Troy, must assume a major responsibility for his soldiers' abuse of victory (as Priam assumes a major responsibility for Paris' breach of good faith)."

[433] The impiety of Priam's death is also emphasized in the familial terms that Seneca employs; for example, having Clytemnestra point out that Agamemnon returns as Priam's "son-in-law" (191). Although the audience would know, and indeed is reminded later on (658), that Pyrrhus was the one to kill Priam, Agamemnon remains responsible for the actions of his soldiers (*miles*, 444), who have just been mentioned in the context of Priam's death. Agamemnon is thus directly responsible for the death of his daughter and indirectly for the death of his "father-in-law."

acted impiously against the specific aspect of the god who protects the family – and this is precisely the aspect of Agamemnon's life which is in the most turmoil and in need of divine support, given that having sacrificed his daughter, he is now returning to a wife who is plotting to kill him. Jupiter, as a god, requires due compensation and in this instance he will extract Agamemnon's debt from his family in blood, until enough blood has been paid back. Furthermore, Seneca omits any word to refer specifically to Jupiter's altar, creating a sense that Jupiter is almost physically present and that the desecration by the Greek army was much more "personal"[434] and thus his anger that much more violent (and warranted).

Once Agamemnon appears, he announces the day of his arrival as a *dies festus* and his prisoner/concubine Cassandra engages him in dialogue revealing the similarities between Troy and Argos. Agamemnon suggests that they pray at Jupiter's altar, *Iovem precemur pariter*, only to be reminded by Cassandra of Priam's fate, receiving the reply, *Herceum Iovem* (*Ag.* 793). This exchange is meant to foreshadow Agamemnon's death as well as the irony of praying at the altar of a god whom Agamemnon and the Greeks dishonoured.[435] Furthermore, Cassandra would be disinclined to pray to the god who did not protect her father while at his altar and so would have little comfort in praying to him now. That Jupiter is again called *Hercean* emphasizes the death of Priam, an event which is inherently linked to this aspect of the god, but it also has connotations of the cultic aspect of Zeus *Herkios*. That Agamemnon should pray to Jupiter in his guise as a god who protects households is evident, for the king needs such protection now more than ever. It is precisely this aspect of the god who is about to wreak havoc on the family through the actions of Aegisthus and Clytemnestra. Cassandra knows what is in store for Agamemnon,

---

[434] Wilson (1985) 149.

[435] Boyle (1983a) 201.

but as her fate is always to remain the ignored-prophetess, her hints to Agamemnon lead to naught.[436]

In *Troades* Jupiter receives much less attention than in *Agamemnon*, but he is introduced into the play with reference to the slaughter of Priam at the Hercean altar: *magnoque Iove victima caesus* (*Tr.* 140). The chorus is here speaking of Pyrrhus, Achilles' son,[437] when he killed Priam who was taking sanctuary at Jupiter's altar. The killing of Priam was of course not a proper sacrifice, but a perversion of one, and the reference here precipitates the later "sacrifice" of Polyxena to the shade of Achilles (1132-64). The correlations between the two deaths do not concern the victims only, but also the recipients. Seneca is almost recreating Achilles to be a type of god, who is demanding worship as if he were another Jupiter.[438] Such an interpretation is brought out further when Talthybius reports the delay of shipping out. The fleet cannot take sail until they have appeased the shade of Achilles, whose off-stage appearance is described in a manner that would invite thoughts of Jupiter: *fragore vasto tonuit et lucus sacer* (174). Achilles' shade causes the sacred grove to thunder as though it were the supreme god himself who was approaching. The word *tonuit* is often associated with Jupiter (reminiscent of his epithet *Tonans*) and while Achilles' shade should be insubstantial, it is here given weight and substance through the use of such a verb. Thus, Achilles' shade, although in a grove rather than an altar, is given the same respect offered to any celestial deity.[439]

---

[436] Fantham (1981-1982) 120.

[437] Also known as Neoptolemus.

[438] Although it was not Roman practice to offer human sacrifice.

[439] Achilles is also referenced with respect to the gods when Pyrrhus is demanding that his father's shade be appeased. Part of the argument Pyrrhus uses against Agamemnon is the fact that Achilles is near to the gods in every region *Illo ex Achille, genere qui mundum suo, / sparsus per omne caelitum regnum, tenet / Thetide aequor, umbras Aeaco, caelum Iove* (344-46). Achilles was a great-grandson of Jupiter, but Seneca here dispenses with particulars and the wording

The altar of Zeus Herkeios becomes the focal point in the second half of Euripides' *Heracles*, not through the reference to Priam's death at a similar altar, but as the location of a sacrifice even more heinous than a slain king during battle. In the first half of the play, the altar of Zeus Sōtēr is made to become a physical locus of suppliant activity; in the second half, it is mirrored by the unseen altar of Zeus Herkeios, an altar which every Athenian would have recognized as being part of their everyday experience. The imagery begins when the Messenger arrives to report Heracles' acts against his family: the hero starts by directing the children, Megara and Amphitryon to stand near the altar of Zeus Herkeios in order to purify the house after killing Lycus. Euripides complicates this picture, however, by introducing the scene using ambiguous language when referring to the victims awaiting sacrifice:

> ἱερὰ μὲν ἦν πάροιθεν ἐσχάρας Διὸς
> καθάρσι' οἴκων, γῆς ἄνακτ' ἐπεὶ κτανὼν
> <ἐξέβαλε> τῶνδε δωμάτων Ἡρακλέης·
> χορὸς δὲ καλλίμορφος εἰστήκει τέκνων
> πατήρ τε Μεγάρα τ', ἐν κύκλωι δ' ἤδη κανοῦν
> εἵλικτο βωμοῦ, φθέγμα δ' ὅσιον εἴχομεν (*Her.* 922-27).

The Messenger commences with the image of sacred victims standing before the altar, but does not describe them in any detail; instead, he then describes where Heracles' family is situated, subtly blurring the images of sacred victims for sacrifice and those who will

---

brings him ever closer to the god. Pyrrhus sees his father as a kind of god and Jupiter's importance in the play is diminished through Achilles' significance. Jupiter's presence is brought out through the shade of a hero who acts as if he were a god. Achilles' actions are not presented as being pious and his association with Jupiter is presented not to give the hero greater status, but to show the senselessness of the god's will. In both the *Troades* and the *Hercules Furens* Jupiter is associated with heroes who do not act with honour, but who desire glory for glory's sake, making it all the more difficult to interpret Jupiter as a god who is guiding and controlling the cosmos with the interests of men at heart.

become the actual sacrificed victims.[440] The family was huddled around an altar of Zeus while outside and now stands at another of his altars within the house. Where before they were supplicating for fear of their lives, they now stand believing themselves free of danger; the irony is of course explicit.[441] As the audience is invited to visualize this scene around this altar hidden behind the *skēnē*, they can also actually see the stage altar around which they had witnessed Heracles' family gathered as suppliants and from which the family had been granted freedom by Heracles' return. The altar thus stands as a concrete reminder of both the earlier danger and their present salvation. The visible and now-empty altar provides symbolism of the house now empty of its patrons. According to Rehm, the internal, unseen altar functions as a "centrifugal force that keeps what is dangerous out, beyond the perimeter;"[442] however, while that is what it *should have done*, the opposite occurred, in fact, twice. The first danger which breached the home was when Lycus threw Amphitryon from his bed (555) and this undermines the confidence in the ability of the altar to "keep what is dangerous out." In both the earlier scenario and the present slaughter of Heracles' family, the house's altar represents precisely the opposite of safety; it was only when the family was outside, that they were in fact safe.

The altar of Zeus Herkeios continues to provide a focal point for the audience while the Messenger describes the eventual slaughter of Megara and the boys and Heracles' transition from a pious man purifying himself in front of Zeus to being supplicated by his own son to avoid becoming the victim of filicide. Heracles does not finish his purification; instead he addresses his father and asks why he is not now killing Eurystheus: Πάτερ, τί θύω πρὶν κτανεῖν Εὐρυσθέα / καθάρσιον πῦρ καὶ πόνους διπλοῦς ἔχω; (*Her*. 936-37). Euripides is blurring the distinction between Zeus and

---

[440] See especially Foley (1985) 155-62 for a discussion of the family as sacrifice.

[441] Barlow (1996) 166.

[442] Rehm (2001) 369.

Amphitryon and it is not absolutely clear which "father" Heracles is addressing at this point.[443] One might expect his words to be directed at his divine father at this moment, thus making this the first time Heracles recognizes himself as a son of Zeus. The alignment with Zeus at this point is significant, for not only does it require the god's attention as part of a "ritual," but it also ensures that Zeus will be witness to Heracles' filicide and the murder of his own grandsons. The alignment with Zeus also serves to highlight the inherent tensions between fathers and sons in the play as a whole. After Heracles has shot his first son, he hunts down the second and finds him taking shelter at the very altar of Zeus Herkeios. The boy then supplicates Heracles and pleads with him to cease his slaughter (988-89), a plea which is made in vain. For Heracles' family neither the altar of Zeus Herkeios, nor the son of Zeus himself affords them the protection they seek.

Zeus Tropaios[444]

The sacrificial act is meant to honour the god who is to be the recipient of the offering, but it is not the only symbol of "honourable" bloodshed. The *tropaion* or "trophy" was an item set up, often on battlefields but also dedicated in temples, which serves not only as evidence of a victory over an enemy, but also as a way to honour the god(s) who helped achieve that victory.[445] The imagery of the *tropaion* occurs especially in *Electra* and *Phoenissae*, but also in *Agamemnon* in honour of Jupiter Feretrius. Such imagery is significant for acknowledging the involvement of the divine in each instance of "victory" as well as for examining what notions of "victory" are at work in each play.

---

[443] *Contra* Papadopoulou (2004) 236 who suggests, without question, that Heracles is addressing Amphitryon.

[444] The title of Zeus Tropaios was also known from Athenian cult; it was instituted after the victory over the Persians and based at Marathon (*IG* I3.255.11).

[445] Trundle (2013) offers a very recent overview of the *tropaion* in Classical Greece.

Zeus in his tropaic aspect is a recipient of prayer in *Electra*. When Orestes appeals to Zeus he does so in two ways, first as Patroös and secondly as Tropaios (*El.* 671-72). This second aspect of Zeus is associated above all with war and this drama is replete with just such imagery, even though neither the death of Aegisthus nor that of Clytemnestra occurs in any battle. The word *tropaios* specifically occurs in two other instances in the play: the first is during the "Achilles ode" when the shield of Achilles turns Hector's eyes to rout (469) and the second when the chorus is describing the bodies of Aegisthus and Clytemnestra as trophies from a battle (1174). Both of these images relate well to Orestes' original appeal to Zeus as Tropaios: Orestes wishes to replicate the routing of Hector and to ensure that Aegisthus suffers the same fate;[446] and later, the two bodies represent the results of this wish. Both murders can thus be seen as "sacrifices" in honour of this aspect of the god. Furthermore, the messenger relates that when Orestes and Pylades approached Aegisthus at this sacrifice, the pair revealed that they were on their way to sacrifice to Zeus Olympios (781-82). It makes sense that Orestes would not say Zeus Tropaios here, for such a statement would incur suspicion. Given that the audience would know that Zeus Olympios often received trophies, it is possible to hear an oblique reference to Orestes' request to the god as Tropaios in his naming of Zeus.

When we finally receive word from the messenger that the deed is done and Orestes has been victorious against Aegisthus, we are also told the tale that Orestes spun in order to gain access to his enemy's sacrifice, which is that he and Pylades were on their way to the Alpheus River to make a sacrifice to Olympian Zeus: Θεσσαλοί· πρὸς δ' Ἀλφεὸν / θύσοντες ἐρχόμεσθ' Ὀλυμπίωι Διί (*El.* 781-82). Kovacs would see this ruse as

---

[446] King (1980) 204-05; see also O'Brien (1964) and Porter (1990) for their discussions of Orestes' murder of Aegisthus.

a way for Orestes to present himself as an athlete going to the Olympic games[447] and there are, to be sure, many references to athletics in the play.[448] The story, however, would only make sense if the games were in fact about to be held, otherwise the ruse would not work. The audience would likely understand the story in relation to the earlier prayer to Zeus Tropaios, for the sacrifice Orestes is about to offer Zeus is the head of a usurper. The sacrifice to Zeus Olympios works for both on the level of tropaic imagery and as an offering to the god of a murderer of the legitimate king;[449] as god of the Olympic contests, this Zeus often receives trophies as thank offerings from victorious athletes. Military combat and athletic contest were thus considered parallel activities for the Greeks, as both were tests of strength, agility and skill. Orestes' combat/contest with Aegisthus, if successful, would demand a corresponding tropaic offering to Zeus.[450]

The image of the trophy is also significant in *Phoenissae*: it is a motif which runs throughout the play and constitutes one element in the larger theme of the perversion of traditional roles and rituals. The first image occurs during the truce when Polynices has

---

[447] Kovacs (1998) 239.

[448] On the topic of athletics in *Electra*, see Myrick (1994) esp. 135-44.

[449] Arnott (1981) 189 also notes this imagery in particular as illustrative of his "double view" reading of the play: "In the view particularly of Electra, but also of the chorus and of Aegisthus' retainers as described by the messenger, Orestes is a great victor and his killing of Aegisthus a heroic feat superior even to victory in the Olympic Games. At the same time and on a less subjective level the murder is brutal, sordid, and cowardly. The two views, ironically juxtaposed, are not mutually exclusive."

[450] Orestes and Pylades would appear too young to be approaching Zeus Olympios as warriors and thus they must present themselves as athletes. It has been noted by Papadimitropoulos (2008a) 122 that Aegisthus shows some scepticism as to Orestes' identity and asks him to flay the calf and prove the truth concerning the pair's famed ability in that area. This may suggest that Orestes' story is not believable to Aegisthus because Orestes and Pylades have no plausible reason which they can share with their enemy, to be travelling to Olympia, and thus this has put him on his guard.

arrived at Thebes and is conversing with his mother and brother. Jocasta asks each son in turn why they should wish to settle their dispute by the sword and specifically how Polynices could honour the gods after winning such a war with his own kin: φέρ', ἢν ἕληις γῆν τήνδ', ὃ μὴ τύχοι ποτέ, / πρὸς θεῶν, τροπαῖα πῶς ἄρα στήσεις Διί . . . ; (*Phoen.* 571-72).[451] It was customary after a battle to erect a trophy as an offering to Zeus to honour the god for supporting the victory. As the general for the Argive army, this responsibility would lie with Polynices; however, in this case it would dishonour the god to set up a trophy after sacking one's own city and would be impious after committing fratricide (although Jocasta would not be considering that potential outcome here).[452] As ever, Zeus provides the locus for the prospect of both victory and defeat, the trophy a source of both pride and of shame. Even though the erection of the trophy is still a future event, the discussion of it here emphasizes not only the problematic nature of the war, but also the complex relationship Zeus has to the Theban dynasty. The victory in the war would not only entail the honouring of Zeus Tropaios, but would also lead to the sole kingship of Thebes (assuming a different end result). Polynices rhetorically suggests that he proceeds justly and that he honours the gods (469-96) while Eteocles openly declares Tyranny the highest divinity instead of Zeus (506); the former could not possibly erect a trophy to Zeus without dishonour, and Eteocles, should he remain king, has already shown

---

[451] Amiech (2004) 156 disputes the accepted emendation of this second line and instead renders it thus: πρὸς θεῶν, τρόπαια πῶς ἀναστήσεις δορός;. She notes that the manuscripts almost unanimously give δορός and that not one has Διί (368). Whether or not Zeus is specifically named does not preclude there being a reference to him; implicit in the erection of trophies is the dedication and as the dedicatee is specified twice later in the play as Zeus (and these are the only other references to trophies), it should not be impossible that there is also an implicit assumption here that the god is meant as the recipient of this trophy too.

[452] Craik (1988) 199.

his own arrogance and impiety.[453] Zeus Tropaios thus is an aspect of the god which should have no part in this play and his presence here only emphasizes this incongruity.

The concepts of victory and kingship are both brought to the fore when this prospect of setting up a trophy to Zeus arises again. At the end of the first messenger speech, the messenger describes to Jocasta how the two camps encouraged each brother to go to battle, Polynices to honour Zeus Tropaios and Eteocles to wield the sceptre:

> Πολύνεικες, ἐν σοὶ Ζηνὸς ὀρθῶσαι βρέτας
> τροπαῖον Ἄργει τ' εὐκλεᾶ δοῦναι λόγον·
> Ἐτεοκλέα δ' αὖ· Νῦν πόλεως ὑπερμαχεῖς,
> νῦν καλλίνικος γενόμενος σκήπτρων κρατεῖς (*Phoen.* 1250-53).

Mastronarde remarks that, "the two exhortations effectively display a dissonance between the enthusiasm of the warrior comrades and the shock and revulsion that an audience will imagine to be felt by Jocasta."[454] These "exhortations" also reaffirm the earlier connections made between Polynices and the raising of a trophy and between Eteocles and kingship. The former has been urged to honour Zeus, while the latter urged to maintain his unjust hold on the sceptre of Thebes, essentially maintaining the broken oath made to alternate the throne between the brothers. Polynices, while also committing an injustice, at least attempts to keep the gods on his side, whereas Eteocles disregards them completely in his quest for power. The honouring or lack thereof of Zeus Tropaios signals the difference between the two brothers, but this is not enough to acquit either of their "sins;" each will suffer the same deadly recompense, the only difference being the decree to leave Polynices unburied – a further indication of Eteocles' godlessness.

The final reference to raising a trophy to Zeus occurs at the very end of the second messenger speech. We are informed that after Jocasta commits suicide, both armies

---

[453] Saxonhouse (2005) 483-85.

[454] Mastronarde (1994) 495.

declared victory for themselves and the Thebans attacked the Argives while unprotected, leading to the destruction of the enemy. The messenger reports that some men did honour Zeus Tropaios while some stripped shields for war booty and others helped bring in the dead: ὡς δ' ἐνικῶμεν μάχηι, / οἱ μὲν Διὸς τροπαῖον ἵστασαν βρέτας (*Phoen.* 1472-73). Finally the foretold trophy to Zeus is raised, but the men who take on this responsibility are nameless, suggesting that victory belongs not to the generals themselves, but to all those who fight for it, every soldier.[455] Zeus can be honoured, but there is no mistaking that this remains a bittersweet victory, for it comes on the heels of fratricide and suicide. This final reference to Zeus in the play reveals the realities of war, the god's requirement for respect and honour and the hollowness of a victory won through destruction of family and kin.

At Rome, it is Jupiter Feretrius who is traditionally associated with receiving trophies of war. This aspect of the god was considered one of the oldest at Rome and the historical tradition suggests the act of a victorious general dedicating triumphal spoils of the enemy's general to the god was quite rare.[456] Having defeated Priam during the Trojan War, Agamemnon has earned this right to bring back spoils and dedicate them to Jupiter Feretrius in his temple, marking himself as victor.[457] But significantly, when he prays to the god, he also rejects the rights of Hercean Jupiter at whose altar Priam fell:

---

[455] Trundle (2013) 138 asserts the "the trophy – the *tropaion* of victory – was really only possible when a state could dedicate some of the stripped armor itself in the wake of a battle and individuals did not steal . . . all the metal for themselves. Individual greed and desire was submerged beneath the state's political interest to demonstrate its own victory on the field over a neighboring state and the state's ability to redistribute and so dedicate the spoils of war itself as the community rather than as a group of aristocratic individuals. . . The state and not the individual assumed credit for winning battles."

[456] According to Livy, only three generals deposited spoils at this temple, Romulus (1.10.7), Aulus Cornelius Cossus (4.20.5) and Marcus Claudius Marcellus (*Periocha* 20).

[457] Tarrant (1976) 322.

> At te, pater, qui saeva torques fulmina
> pellisque nubes, sidera et terras regis,
> ad quem triumphi spolia victores ferunt,
> et te sororem cuncta pollentis viri (*Ag.* 802-05).

As previously indicated, Agamemnon should be praying to Hercean Jupiter if only because this aspect of the god is the one most in need of appeasement. Yet, this prayer not only emphasizes the arrogance of Agamemnon, but also places the king in a coveted position. Few generals can claim the right to deposit spoils in the temple of Jupiter Feretrius and such an honour should be celebrated and welcomed by all. That such an honour is therefore darkened by the shadow of the nature of Priam's death and is a foreshadowing of Agamemnon's own demise, suggests that perhaps such a coveted honour is really a double-edged sword: it is not the nature of Jupiter Feretrius or Zeus Tropaios to be "honourable" only to be honoured; and such "honour" for men is often only achieved by dishonourable means.

Concluding Remarks

As "Father of Men" Zeus has a myriad of responsibilities to all mortals, especially in his roles as a protector of guests and hosts, suppliants and the household. And Zeus' responsibilities to those who claim descent from him are no less important, especially when such progeny appeal to him in his guise of one of these roles. Zeus is shown as particularly vested in the interests of the Atreid line, as descendants of Pelops, who was favoured with a sceptre from Zeus. The god is shown to be far more responsive to the prayers of this family, when its members are shown to offer the proper respect to the god. In Euripides' *Electra*, both siblings offer prayers to Zeus and are rewarded with favour from the god; when the siblings ignore or otherwise disrespect Zeus in *Orestes*, the god is less likely to intervene on their behalf. Euripides' presentation of Zeus in this respect is fairly straightforward and unambiguous. A similar scenario can be found in Seneca's *Agamemnon* where Jupiter, although he is mentioned less frequently, is also shown to favour his more distant progeny. He punishes Agamemnon for the death of Iphigenia and the fate of Priam, but ultimately saves Orestes' life.

More problematic is the representation of supplication scenes and temples as places of sanctuary. Zeus as god of suppliants does have efficacy in that he instils fear into those who may have to abide by his laws (such as in *Hecuba*), but such fear is not always enough of a deterrent, as shown in Euripides' *Orestes*. This disregard for Zeus as a god of suppliants is shown far more clearly in Euripides' *Heracles* when the hero's family are at risk of being burned alive at Zeus' altar. While the family members were saved by Zeus Sōtēr, they were not so lucky when at the altar of Zeus Herkeios. The one place in their home which should afford the family safety was the one place where they were in the most danger. Zeus' places of protection are not presented by Euripides as fulfilling their allotted duty; far more often, they are places of crime and impiety. A similar situation appears in Euripides' *Phoenissae*, where Zeus' temple at Dodona is believed to be a source of safety for Creon's family; but if Menoeceus were to use Zeus' temple for that purpose, he would be ensuring the destruction of Thebes. Less violent, but no less illustrative of this dual nature, Jupiter's temple at Olympia is also described as a place of entertainment and victory, but is ultimately the destination for a group of women about to become slaves and trophies of war.

It is this uncomfortable duality of Zeus and Jupiter as gods of victory (and thus also of defeat) that is also explored by both tragedians. Zeus Tropaios expects to be honoured with trophies of victory, but as Euripides' *Phoenissae* demonstrates, the nature of victory is such that it also requires defeat, destruction and death. It is most problematic when two brothers vie for occupation of one city: victory of one or the other will result in impiety and honour to the god will in fact, by default, be dishonour. Seneca's *Agamamnon* illustrates this dichotomy through the deaths of Priam and Agamemnon. Agamemnon has conquered the king of Troy and thus returns home triumphant and ready to honour Jupiter with spoils; but Agamemnon is responsible for the death of Priam at Jupiter's own altar and thus will become the spoils of victory for the god. Zeus and Jupiter require honour in victory, but the nature of such "honour" is presented as problematic from the human perspective.

PART III

CHALLENGERS

CHAPTER 8
UNSUCCESSFUL THEOMACHISTS

The previous six chapters have focused primarily on Zeus and Jupiter as guarantors of a stable cosmos after they have established their ultimate sovereignty – in other words, the chapters were concerned with each god as firmly in control and without facing any real threat to their authority. In contrast, this chapter will address references to events set in the cosmological past, in particular to the Titanomachy, Gigantomachy and Typhonomachy, in which Zeus was required to either gain his supremacy over his father (and his father's kin) or maintain it in the face of potential usurpers. Such overt attempts to overthrow Zeus seem to disappear once his absolute rule has been cemented, but references to these events occur in the plays of both Euripides and Seneca and are worth discussion, for such episodes become paradigmatic for later mythological representations of similar theomachic individuals. Zeus was, of course, ultimately successful in quelling these early efforts to displace him, resulting in severe punishments for the offenders; but these past victories were no guarantee that future attempts to usurp him, though futile, would not be forthcoming.

Such futility can be seen in two similar though distinct characters as portrayed by both Euripides and Seneca, namely Capaneus and Ajax. The second part of this chapter explores these two figures, who are clearly modelled on the early adversaries of Zeus but are also definitely differentiated from them: whereas the Titans, Giants and Typhoeus were overtly attempting to overthrow Zeus, Capaneus and Ajax can only threaten and boast – there is no potential for either to supplant the father of the gods. In many ways the treatment of Zeus and Jupiter is quite similar with respect to these mortal "threats" and the extent of the gods' personal engagement in their punishment is an indication of both their own powerful abilities and the real magnitude of either man's challenge to their *auctoritas*.

Overt Usurpers (Unsuccessful): Titans, Giants and Typhoeus

Although often conflated by both modern and even some ancient authors,[458] the

Titanomachy and Gigantomachy were two separate events according to authors such as

Hesiod (*Theog.* 617-735) and Apollodorus (1.2.1, 1.6.1-2).[459] In essence, the Titanomachy

was a generational (and familial) war fought between Kronos and his siblings (collectively

called the Titans) on one side and Zeus and his siblings (the Olympians) on the opposing

side. The feud apparently lasted for ten years and ended with two decisive battles: one

involved the Hecatoncheires (Hundred-handed sons of Kronos, *Theog.* 671-686 and 713-

735) and the other involved Zeus himself (*Theog.* 687-712).[460] Hesiod's description of

Zeus' climactic engagement with the Titans is particularly noteworthy. The scene is replete

with repetitive images of fire, lightning, thunder, rain, flames and extreme heat. Zeus

emerges as not only the god *of* these elements and phenomena, but as the phenomena

themselves. While this is not surprising in and of itself, Hesiod's description provides an

overpowering picture of total chaos and near-apocalyptic imagery.[461] The repetition of

words describing Zeus' lightning and thunder have the effect of underscoring his repeated

actions against the Titans, leaving the impression that these are formidable opponents and

Zeus' might is awe-inspiring both in terms of concentrated power and destructive qualities.

Moreover, although this scene is often described as Zeus' *aristeia*,[462] the emphasis lies not

---

[458] O'Hara (1994) 222 notes the validity of modern conflation and follows Hardie (1986) 85 who
justifies it because ". . . ancient indifference to the distinctions is plain" in Roman literature; and
Gregory (1999) 103 also observes "a tendency in Greek literature to conflate the two groups."

[459] For the most comprehensive discussion of the Gigantomachy see Vian (1952) who makes a
clear distinction between the two battles (esp. 16-19).

[460] For a discussion of these particular scenes in the *Theogony*, see Mondi (1986) and Blaise and
Rousseau (1996). On the Titanomachy more generally, see Mondi (1985) and Clay (2003) esp.
100-128; from a psychoanalytic perspective see Sussman (1978) and Caldwell (1989) 146-170.

[461] See Appendix A for the complete text of the excerpt.

[462] See, for example, Mondi (1986) 27 who refers to this description as "conventional."

on the god himself, but upon his weaponry: it is his lightning and the resulting fires which cause the most damage and which become emblematic of the Titans' defeat and Zeus' victory.[463] It is also this scene which provides the paradigmatic model upon which future opponents of the Olympian order will be based, both in terms of imagery and thematic concepts.

The majority of the Titans, once vanquished, were imprisoned in Tartarus, where they were to remain for eternity.[464] This was not, however, to be Zeus' last battle for sovereignty. According to Hesiod, Gaia gave birth to one further potential rival to Zeus, her last child Typhoeus. In retribution for Zeus' defeat of the Titans (Gaia's husband and siblings), Gaia mated with Tartarus to produce Typhoeus as a challenge to Zeus' mastery over the elements and, in particular, that of fire.[465] Once again, the scene depicted by Hesiod (*Theog.* 820-869) is full of destructive imagery, but there is a crucial difference – Typhoeus too is associated with fires and flames and the now one-on-one combat between Zeus and Typhoeus is no longer one-sided (as it seemed to be when Zeus fought the Titans).[466] Zeus' fires on their own are not enough to award him victory and he must leave

---

[463] This is not to ignore the important role of the Hecatoncheires in the final battle, but I would disagree with Mondi (1986) 31 that their rocks are the sole contributing factor to the Titans' demise. Furthermore, Mondi's assertion that "the Titans are not ultimately scorched by lightning" during the final action at 713-720, completely ignores the impact of the preceding passage containing Zeus' *aristeia*.

[464] Zeus did free a select few of the Titans in return for their "allegiance" (including the Hecatoncheires) and in two fragementary plays (*Prometheus Unbound* and Cratinus' *Wealth-Gods*) the chorus is made of freed Titans. I would like to thank my external examiner for bringing these two plays to my attention.

[465] This is only one version of the Typhoeus myth: Apollodorus (1.6.3) locates the Typhonomachy after the Gigantomachy as the final opposition to the new Olympian order and the *Homeric Hymn to Apollo* (305-09) makes Hera, not Gaia, the progenitor of Typhoeus.

[466] Although Sussman (1978) 69 notes that "Zeus' fires have shape and form" whereas Typhoeus' fires are "formless and undefined."

Olympus (where he and the other gods were based against the Titans, who were stationed on Mount Othrys, *Theog.* 632-33) and face Typhoeus, not from long-range but in hand-to-hand battle (πλῆξεν ἀπ' Οὐλύμποιο ἐπάλμενος, 855).[467] In this scene the emphasis is not just on Zeus' weapons, but on the way he wields them and the close proximity with which he must engage his enemy, underscoring how close he came to defeat (noted earlier at 836-38).[468]

According to Hesiod (*Theog.* 882-85), it was Zeus' defeat of Typhoeus that led the other gods to urge Zeus to take up the "kingship" of Olympus. Apollodorus (1.2.1) places this event after the Titanomachy (not after the Typhonomachy) and has Zeus, Poseidon and Hades cast lots for their dominions, in contrast to Hesiod's depiction of the gods' insistence at Gaia's bidding to proclaim Zeus their ruler. In either scenario, however, it was only after Zeus was granted sovereignty that the Gigantomachy was fought. According to Apollodorus (for Hesiod does not describe this war between the Olympians and the Giants who had formed an uprising), this war was initiated by Gaia because of the Titans' defeat at the hands of the Olympians. The Gigantomachy was fated to end when a mortal or demi-god was enlisted to aid the gods (Heracles according to Apollod. *Bibl.* 1.6.1, or Heracles and Dionysus according to a scholiast of Pindar, schol. Pind. *Nem.* 1.101). In order to fulfil the prophecy, Zeus sent Athena to enlist Heracles and it was his arrival at Phlegra which precipitated the end of the war. The details of the war as provided by Apollodorus are few and brief: the individual celestial participants and their quarry are

---

[467] Apollodorus 1.6.3 provides a similar account of hand-to-hand combat, but differs substantially in other aspects of the battle.

[468] For discussions of the Typhonomachy in Hesiod see Blaise (1992) and Goslin (2010); Yasumura (2011), esp. 117-131, offers some interesting insights into the version given in the *Homeric Hymn to Apollo*; and Ballabriga (1990) offers an interpretation based on the version provided by Apollodorus which sees Zeus nearly defeated by Typhon and in need of rescue and rehabilitation by Hermes and Aigipan.

presented as a catalogue with the added information that the remaining Giants were killed by Zeus' lightning and all were shot by Heracles' arrows (1.6.2). It was this battle in particular which flourished in Athens on both vase-imagery and on large-scale monuments such as the Parthenon.[469]

In each myth, the Titans, the figure of Typhoeus and the Giants serve as adversaries of Zeus and his "new order" in order to underscore the future futility of such attacks. But there remains a fundamental difference: the Titanomachy also represents the tensions between father and son and the end of a cyclical battle where the son's role and purpose is to replace his father. After the Typhonomachy, it is agreed and, even encouraged, by the other gods that Zeus should rule, a decision which is the first step toward unopposed sovereignty. The defeat of the Giants is only possible because of Zeus' earlier victory and his ability to garner support from the other gods.[470] Had he not already established himself as the god with chief authority, it may not have been possible for him to recruit the necessary allies or attain the combined force required for victory. The Gigantomachy represents a final battle between the established order and forces of chaos or even invaders with illegitimate designs for seizing control of the cosmos.[471] Thus, while each of the adversaries of Zeus is a paradigm for futile future attacks, they nevertheless

---

[469] Moore (1995) 633: "The Gigantomachy is one of the most important myths depicted in Greek art, especially in the sixth and fifth centuries B.C. Representations begin soon after the Panathenaic Games in honor of Athena were reorganized and several of the earliest illustrations appear on vases dedicated on the Acropolis." Sanford (1941) 55: "The gigantomachy was an integral part of the Athenian religious tradition. Not only were this and the related conflicts chosen as the subjects of the metopes of the great temple of Athena, with the Amazonomachy on the goddess' own shield, but the gigantomachy itself was embroidered on the magnificent peplus (*sic*) presented to Athena at the Panathenaia – the great civic festival . . ."

[470] As Mondi (1985) 333 notes in his discussion of Hesiod's *Theogony*, "lines 881-85 leave no doubt that in the traditional Titanomachy it is the victory over the Titan generation which *first* establishes Zeus in power" (emphasis in the original).

[471] O'Hara (1994) 219.

also signify quite different dynamics between the opposing sides. For instance, references to each of these battles in later literature (or even as artistic decoration and imagery) may not only symbolize "order versus chaos," "civilized versus barbarian" or "defenders versus invaders" *et cetera*, but also ideas such as "legitimacy versus illegitimacy," "Golden Age versus Silver or Iron Age" and even "old versus new." Any of these ideas (or others) can be imputed to these myths and will then resonate differently depending on the context – and it is precisely the differences between the two separate battles which will determine which one an author or artist will recall or emphasize and how an audience member or viewer will respond and interpret the scene.

It is also of relevance that the Titanomachy declines in importance during the sixth and fifth centuries while literary and artistic representations of the Gigantomachy begin to flourish after the mid-560s.[472] The upsurge in the retelling of the myth (ascribed to the re-organization of the Panathenaia) was likely responsible, at least in part, for the eventual conflation of the two battles.[473] Thus one must tread with caution when assessing references to the Titanomachy in particular, for it may well be that the Gigantomachy is in fact the main reference. However, because of the rarity of references to the Titanomachy, the more likely it becomes that a secondary reading of the text or scene does in fact contain a reference to its "original" myth. This becomes especially true when turning to the Roman materials, for their reception of the Greek myths had had that much more time to become

---

[472] Ferrari (1994) 223.

[473] Vian (1952) 173 suggests Euripides is the first to conflate the two groups (citing *IT* 224 and *Hec.* 472 as evidence, the latter discussed further below), a view which has gained much currency but which, until recently, has not been seriously challenged. Stamatopoulou (2012) provides a compelling argument which would see Euripides as purposely "confusing" the Titans and Giants for thematic purposes rather than unknowingly or carelessly conflating the two groups.

interchangeable. Thus, it is with this is mind that references to the Titans in Euripides'

Hecuba and Seneca's *Agamemnon* and *Hercules Furens* will be examined.

Euripides' Titans: *Hecuba*, the Peplos of Athena and a "Living Death"

In the extant corpus of Euripidean tragedy there are only two references to the race

of Titans to be found and both are made in connection to the *peplos* of Athena: *Hec.* 466-

74 and *IT* 221-24. Only the lines from *Hecuba* contain an explicit mention of Zeus and

these are sung by the chorus of captive Trojan women as they imagine their futures after

the capture of Troy. The passage from *Hecuba* (as well as that in *IT*) has attracted attention

precisely because Euripides utilized the Titanomachy instead of the Gigantomachy as the

image woven into Athena's peplos. As Stamatopoulou has noted, "the depiction of the

Gigantomachy on the Panathenaic *peploi* is unanimous" – the only exception to be found

is Euripides.[474] The fact that the real ritual peplos given to Athena during the Panathenaia

depicted the Gigantomachy has led scholars to the conclusion that Euripides is merely

conflating the two cosmogonic wars; however, Stamatopoulou has offered a new

interpretation which sees Euripides as using the Titanomachy in order to distance the

Trojan chorus from reality and suggests that an Athenian audience would understand the

"mistake," not as conflation, but as an inherent part of the chorus' (mis)understanding of

Athenian life.[475]

Thus, if we take the chorus' reference to the Titans as such (and not as a confused

reference to the Gigantomachy), their reference to Zeus evokes the Hesiodic narrative of

the Titans' eventual demise:

> ἢ Παλλάδος ἐν πόλει
> τὰς καλλιδίφρους Ἀθα-

---

[474] Stamatopoulou (2012) 72.

[475] Stamatopoulou (2012) 78.

ναίας ἐν κροκέωι πέπλωι
ζεύξομαι ἀρα πώ-
λους ἐν δαιδαλέαισι ποι-
κίλλουσ' ἀνθοκρόκοισι πή-
ναις ἢ Τιτάνων γενεάν,
τὰν Ζεὺς ἀμφιπύρωι κοιμί-
ζει φλογμῶι Κρονίδας; (*Hec.* 466-74).

The lightning which was so prevalent in Hesiod returns here as the weapon that Zeus used long ago to lay low the Titans. Not only does the chorus' confusion about the participants depicted on the peplos emphasize Athena's absence from the image,[476] but it stresses the climactic moment of Zeus' *aristeia*. The ten-year Titanic war becomes symbolic of the ten-year Trojan War; however, the Titans not only symbolize the fallen Trojan men but also the women themselves. The language the Trojan women use to describe the fate of the Titans is ambiguous: they do not die but are put to sleep (κοιμίζει) – they endure a "living death," much as the Trojan captives must now face a living death as slaves.[477] The fate the women imagine they will weave into the fabric is, in fact, their own. Unknowingly perhaps, the women imagine embroidering their fate into the history of Athens as well as into the larger cosmogonic myth.

Zeus' importance as the one who wields the weapons which ultimately lay low the Titans (and not the Hecatoncheires) also implies his support in the Trojan War as though he is responsible for the resulting Greek victory and Trojan defeat. By extension, the women are also suggesting their fates have been decided by Zeus' will. This is not to suggest that the women should be seen in opposition to the gods, but rather, by placing themselves, even symbolically into the position of fallen Titans, they are accepting their defeat as total and complete with no possibility of escape. The idea that the women will

---

[476] Stamatopoulou (2012) 76, because Athena had no part in the Titanomachy.

[477] Meagher (2002) 125, referring to Cassandra's preference of death at Neoptolemus' hands, rather than enduring a "living death" as a slave.

endure a "living death" continues throughout the ode, especially when they sing of exchanging their current home for place in Hades' halls (481-83). As the Titans were laid low and imprisoned, so too will be the women of Troy. Euripides' choice of the Titanomachy here encapsulates the futures the women will face far more effectively than any reference to the giants could possibly accomplish; and Zeus' role in each war is clearly underscored.

Seneca's Titans I: *Agamemnon* and the Cyclical Nature of Revenge

There is only one mention of Titans in Seneca's *Agamemnon* but it is full of symbolic potential. During the second choral ode, which is a prayer of thanksgiving to the gods for Agamemnon's victory, the chorus invoke Phoebus to sing of the time when the Titans were vanquished by Jupiter's lightning, *cum Titanas fulmine victos / videre dei* (334),[478] or when the Giants created a staircase of mountains piled on top of mountains,

> vel cum montes montibus altis
> super impositi
> struxere gradus trucibus monstris (*Ag.* 335-37).

By using the non-specific term *monstris*, it is unclear whether the chorus are confusing the Titans with the Giants or referring to two separate and distinct events. A superficial reading of the chorus' suggestion would highlight the futility of attacking the gods and Jupiter in particular, for it was specifically the lightning bolt which overcame the Titans and which, one may infer, halted the attempts by the Giants. Both events are used to illustrate the superiority of the gods and the destruction that awaits those with aggressive or exalted and haughty designs.[479] In the context of the play, this suits well as a

---

[478] If the text of MS E is secure; MS A: *fulmine misso / fregere dei*, Tarrant (1976) 238-39. Tarrant has opted to retain E as has Fitch, but in either scenario the general sense remains the same.

[479] Although Tarrant (1976) 238 gives primacy to the mountains here and not to the motif of the giants.

commentary on the preceding scene where Aegisthus and Clytemnestra plot their usurpation of Agamemnon's authority in retaliation for his slaughter of Iphigenia, his conduct at Troy (described as *spiritus tumidos*, 247) and his assumed future tyrannical behaviour at Mycenae (*veniet tyrannus*, 252).

The reference, then, to Titans and Giants is a commentary on both Agamemnon as deserving of the destruction which will be later enacted and also on Aegisthus and Clytemnestra for attempting a similar course. If one reads the song of the Titans on a more symbolic level it also speaks of the cyclical effects of such attacks. The Gigantomachy was a one-time affair; the Titanomachy (although it was only one battle) symbolizes the potential for never-ending conflict between generations of the same family. As Boyle notes, the *Agamemnon* is nothing if not a play concerned with the cyclical nature of revenge, "an alternating cycle of blood,"[480] although one might say "an alternating cycle of *familial* blood." The Gigantomachy does not add that level of symbolism, but the Titanomachy certainly does.

The emphasis on the lightning bolt as the definitive element in defeating the Titans is also reminiscent of Zeus' *aresteia* in the *Theogony*. It was Zeus' full barrage of thunder and lightning against the Titans which played a decisive part in their defeat. The chorus' memory of this particular event not only symbolizes the effort needed in order for the god to successfully attain his supremacy, but also Jupiter's eventual absolute victory. It was Jupiter who was ultimately victorious against the Titans and it will be Jupiter and his chosen representative who will become victorious in the play. The god's involvement is clear throughout: Priam fell before an altar of Jupiter, giving Agamemnon mastery over Troy; Agamemnon will do the same while "honouring" the same deity. It will take both Clytemnestra and Aegisthus to overpower Agamemnon and, although the text provides no

____

[480] Boyle (1983) 200.

definitive future for the usurpers, Orestes is spirited away by Strophius under the protection of the god Jupiter (935-39). Thus, even though Jupiter's role in the play is somewhat elusive, there is nonetheless a sense of his involvement during the course of events.[481] The ten-year Titanic battle and eventual victory is played out by the characters of the play with the Jovian supremacy hinted at in the final scene. The Titans remain emblematic of overt usurpation but also of eventual futility, as in the prophetic words of Cassandra to Clytemnestra: *Veniet et vobis furor* (1011) and so too will defeat.

Seneca's Titans II: *Hercules Furens* and the Nature of Succession

In Seneca's *Hercules Furens* there are two further references to Titans and each is specifically associated with Jupiter, underscoring the significance of this early cosmogonic event. Juno is the first to bring the episode into the drama while she is plotting how to hinder her step-son's supposed ambitions to usurp his father's place as sovereign of the heavens. She briefly entertains the idea of bringing the Titans out of Tartarus[482] as her allies in her endeavour, recalling how they earlier had attempted to hinder Jupiter's authority: *Titanas ausos rumpere imperium Iovis / emitte* (*HF* 79-80). There is clearly conflation at work here, for it was the Giants who had initially banded together to challenge Jupiter's rule, but it was certainly the Titans who acted to defend their right to reign. As Fitch notes, "conflation of Jupiter's foes is common in Augustan and later poetry;"[483] however, here it is only the reference to the Titanomachy which works well thematically.

Juno essentially wants to re-create and re-live the earlier cosmic strife with herself taking the role of Gaia in order to re-establish herself as both the legitimate wife of Jupiter

---

[481] Davis (1993) 210-11.

[482] Fitch (1987) 144.

[483] Fitch (1987) 144-45.

and also as a "king-maker" as Gaia's role had been.[484] But, if the Gigantomachy was meant to be understood as the underlying frame of reference (with Titans=Giants), Juno would be placing Hercules in the role of Jupiter as though he is already victorious and Jupiter would lose his place as sovereign. If, on the other hand, we take Juno's label of Titans at face value and the Titanomachy as the frame of reference, their release on her orders brings to mind an earlier release of primordial gods in order to win a war. In Hesiod we learn that Zeus had liberated his father's brothers from their bonds in Tartarus and in exchange they were indispensable in defeating Kronos and the Titans (*Theog.* 501-05, 651-53).[485] Juno's desire to see the Titans released so that they might aid in her war against Hercules is an attempt to re-stage the Titanomachy in order to "save" Jupiter's sovereignty from a potential usurper, thereby reclaiming her honoured place in the heavens. The liberated gods, however, fought *for* the usurper, not against him; this will be realized by the "mad" Hercules when he imagines that they will rally under his leadership against his father's imperium.

There is one further underlying motif behind Juno's reliance on the Titans for support. In the *Homeric Hymn to Apollo*, Hera calls upon Earth and the Titans to assist her in producing a child who will be strong enough to challenge Zeus as Zeus had challenged Kronos (335-39). The Titans are inherently connected to the theme of pitting sons against their fathers and Juno's ultimate abandonment of the idea in favour of summoning furies who will act on her behalf is sensible when considered *in toto*. The Titans would prove to be poor allies for Juno, for, if she had acted on her first impulse and released them, she

---

[484] Yasumura (2011) 83; see also Chaudhuri (2008) 65 who interprets Juno as being aligned with the earth and as "mother of the Giants."

[485] As Yasumura (2011) 104-05 explains: "The reciprocity engendered by this event (liberation of the gods as a gift, and then their helping Zeus in exchange) is decisive for Zeus, because the aid of the older gods is indispensable for the victory over the Titans."

would, in effect, have undone the basis upon which Jupiter's kingship was formed and created a war[486] which Hercules could potentially have won. After all, she acknowledges that Hercules has defeated those imprisoned in Tartarus before. Thus, while Seneca (through Juno) has only briefly mentioned the Titans (with some conflation), the images and motifs which are associated with them are intrinsically woven into his larger discussion of the complicated father-son relationship which exists between Hercules and Jupiter.

Juno's initial instinct to call upon the Titans also foreshadows the second reference made to them in the play when Hercules' mind has been taken over by furial madness. The hero believes that he should be awarded his apotheosis, but recognizes Juno's unwillingness to allow his deification and thus threatens to unchain Saturn from his imprisonment and lead the Titans to war against his father:

> vincla Saturno exuam,
> contraque patris impii regnum impotens
> avum resolvam. bella Titanes parent
> me duce furentes . . . (*HF* 965-68).

It is now Hercules' turn to relive the early cosmogonic strife as he imagines himself waging war against Jupiter, echoing Juno's earlier fears that her step-son would become a usurper.[487] As Hercules continues to imagine the war being played out he turns from leading the Titans to defending himself against the Giants and eventually to sacrificing his own children. Fitch understands "such confused leaps of thought" as a portrayal of madness and symbolic of the forces of reason against unreason.[488] But what Hercules is playing out is an imagined version of the next chapter of the cosmogonic history. His

---

[486] Chaudhuri (2008) 74: For Juno "to resort to the aid of the Titans and Typhoeus implies a disturbing and dangerous desperation."

[487] Chaudhuri (2008) 100.

[488] Fitch (1989) 369.

leadership of the Titans corresponds to his imagined usurpation of Jupiter; upon seeing the Giants, Hercules now envisages himself *in place of* Jupiter and now must defend *his own* realm. His dispatch of his own children corresponds to the early pattern of eliminating one's children in order to retain his newly-won authority. Because all of this occurs while Hercules is under the Furies' "spell" as it were, his imaginings do not necessarily correspond to the hero's actual desires or reality. But Hercules *is* playing out precisely the scene which Juno originally contemplated but ultimately abandoned because the outcome would displace Jupiter rather than protect his sovereignty. Having the scene play out under the Furies' madness illustrates Hercules' potential to rival Jupiter but ultimately serves Juno's will by having the hero succumb to the primordial instinct to eliminate his sons in order to retain his own imperium.

Seneca's Titans are thus more than mere glosses on a theme of chaos versus reason; they are intimately connected to the themes of his plays and illustrate both the cyclical effects of revenge and the tensions that exist between fathers and sons. Although some aspects of Seneca's depictions of the Titanomachy may be heavily influenced by earlier conflations with the Gigantomachy, there nonetheless remains a clear resonance with Hesiod's description of the Titans. It is that early generation of gods which underscores most clearly the themes of Seneca's *Agamemnon* and *Hercules Furens*, themes which would not be served nearly so well by reference to the Giants, the race to which I will now turn.

Heracles/Hercules and the Gigantomachy: Whose War?

Given the popularity of the Gigantomachy during the fifth century at Athens, it is unsurprising to find references both to the event and to the participants in several plays of Euripides (*Heracles, Ion, Phoenissae* and *Bacchae*), two of which give special emphasis to

Zeus' role in the war. In both *Heracles* and *Ion*, Zeus is mentioned specifically as one of the gods who fought in the war and *Ion* even provides details about his opponent Mimas (215). References to the Giants in *Heracles* are more frequent than in the other plays and also have the most relevance to the present investigation of Zeus.[489] References to giants also occur in three of Seneca's plays (*Oedipus*, *Hercules Furens* and *Thyestes*), although again their relevance to Jupiter is limited. Only those references in *Hercules Furens* and *Thyestes* have any direct correlation to Jupiter, but in each play the allusions offer perceptive insights into the themes that Seneca is presenting. Whereas the Titans were used, more often than not, in both Euripides and Seneca to emphasize the ultimate authority of Zeus and Jupiter, the Giants are used to underscore more clearly the gods' weaknesses and reliance on either other gods (or mortals) or their weaponry (rather than on their might alone), corresponding rather well to Hesiod and Apollodorus' earlier depictions of the Titanomachy and Gigantomachy.

As with the Titans, conflation also occurs when discussing the Giants of the early cosmogonic period. The Gigantomachy generally refers to the war fought between the gods and the Giants at Phlegra; however, there is another set of giants who are often included in the Gigantomachy, but who (in all likelihood) did not participate in it.[490] These other giants are specifically named (Otus and Ephialtes, the Aloidae) and once attempted to build a staircase to Olympus to challenge the gods by piling mountains on top of one

---

[489] Although *Phoenissae* also contains a single reference to the giants (127-30), the allusion is not related to the gods or to Zeus; instead, it is concerned with themes which will be of more concern when discussing Capaneus and Zeus (pp. 265-71).

[490] In a tentative outline of the Gigantomachy, Yasumura (2011) 56 suggests that Otus and Ephialtes did, in fact, participate in the war by binding Ares (*Il.* 5.385) before their attempt to reach Olympus on their mountainous staircase.

another.[491] This was not a war as such, but rather an act of hubris and was duly punished by the gods in one form or another.[492] Often, however, these staircase-building giants are brought into the Gigantomachy in later (particularly Roman) literature as though their attempt to reach Olympus was part of the larger battle with the result that conflation of the two events becomes commonplace.

The Giants and specifically those directly involved in the Gigantomachy, are referenced several times throughout the *Heracles*; on each occasion, the reference is made in conjunction with a remark relating (directly or indirectly) to the relationship between Heracles and Zeus, highlighting both the thematic interest in the father-son relationship and the implications of having Heracles fight alongside Zeus as his son and protégé. Their close relationship is underscored early on in the play when Amphitryon swears by Zeus' name that Heracles is the god's son and specifically mentions the aid Heracles gave Zeus during the Gigantomachy:

> Διὸς κεραυνὸν ἠρόμην τέθριππά τε
> ἐν οἷς βεβηκὼς τοῖσι γῆς βλαστήμασιν
> Γίγασι πλευροῖς πτήν' ἐναρμόσας βέλη
> τὸν καλλίνικον μετὰ θεῶν ἐκώμασεν (*Her.* 177-80).

---

[491] The mountains they use are consistent (Olympus, Ossa and Pelion), but the order in which they are used to build the staircase varies from author to author: see Apollod. 1.53; Quintus Smyrnaeus 1.516; Hyg. *Fab.* 28;

[492] There are many versions of their punishment(s) and the gods involved vary depending on the account. What seems to be consistent, is that the idea of Jupiter (or Zeus) instigating the punishment is a Roman idea – he does not seem to be implicated in any of the Greek sources who discuss these particular giants: Homer suggests Apollo was responsible for their demise (*Od.* 11.305) as does Pausanias (9.29.1); Apollodorus provides a story of Artemis tricking them into spearing each other, while Diodorus (5.51.1) suggests they died in a battle, quarrelling with each other; Hyginus (*Fab.* 28) notes two versions, one suggesting Apollo killed them for attempting to build their staircase, the other that Apollo killed them for assaulting his sister Diana. It is only when turning to Roman sources that Jupiter is the one to dispatch the giants: Virg. *Georg.* 1.276; Ovid *Met.* 1.151.

Not only did Heracles join the war against the Giants, but he did so as Zeus' partner and in the god's chariot.[493] It was their combined efforts which ensured victory for the gods and defeat for the Giants. Amphitryon's example is, however, somewhat double-edged: he is using Heracles' involvement in the war as proof of his descent from Zeus, but the very idea of Zeus requiring the aid of a mortal in order to become victorious over foes who are themselves immortal (being born of Gaia), seems to undermine the force of what he is arguing. It certainly seems to elevate Heracles to the stature of the gods, but at the same time, Amphitryon seems also to be highlighting the weaknesses of the gods and Zeus in particular. Either the Giants are such a force to be reckoned with that victory can only be achieved with every divine or semi-divine being fighting together against them, or Zeus is not so powerful that he can be successful without his son's assistance. Whereas the Titans were used to illustrate Zeus' absolute authority, references to the Giants seem to highlight his reliance on others and, in particular, on his battle-partner and offspring Heracles.[494]

A similar sense is achieved later in the play when Heracles is off-stage during his "mad" scene and committing his atrocities against his family. It is reported by the messenger that Athena or her phantom appears in the house in order to stop Heracles from killing his (foster) father and the imagery employed compares Athena's stoning of Heracles to a similar event in the Gigantomachy:

τί δρᾶις, ὦ Διὸς παῖ, μελάθρωι;
τάραγμα ταρτάρειον ὡς ἐπ' Ἐγκελάδωι ποτέ, Παλλάς,
ἐς δόμους πέμπεις (*Her*. 907-09).

---

[493] Bond (1981) 114.

[494] Although such co-operation from Heracles could be symbolic of the mortal race opting to work together with the gods in order to maintain cosmic stability. But such an interpretation still requires Zeus to rely on the subordination *and* support from humans in order for his rule to be successful.

Enceladus was one of the few named Giants of the Gigantomachy and was known as the giant whom Athena had stoned to death. That she appears in order to stop Heracles from committing parricide is itself somewhat unsurprising given her traditional role as the hero's protectress, but that she uses a similar technique in stopping him is quite suggestive. Such an analogy implies that Heracles' actions have gone beyond that which is acceptable behaviour[495] for Heracles is acting in a manner befitting the Giants and thus worthy of divine punishment; but such an image also suggests that Heracles is of such a stature that it takes Athena's entrance and her use of force to stop him. It is presumably on Zeus' orders that Athena comes to Heracles' aid (and acts as a foil to Iris and Lyssa who act as Hera's representatives[496]). Only another divine child of Zeus is capable of stopping Heracles' actions and once he is cast as though a Giant, it would be understood that the hero is now an immediate threat and must be challenged and defeated in one way or another.

It is fitting that the final reference to the Giants in *Heracles* returns full-circle to their initial mention. Amphitryon once again confirms that Heracles went to Phlegra to fight on behalf of and alongside the gods:

> ἐμὸς ἐμὸς ὅδε γόνος ὁ πολύπονος,[497] <ὃς> ἐπὶ
> δόρυ γιγαντοφόνον ἦλθεν σὺν θεοῖ-
> σι Φλεγραῖον ἐς πεδίον ἀσπιστάς (1190-92).

There are two important differences to note. The first relates to the way in which Amphitryon introduces Heracles at this time: earlier he called Heracles a son of Zeus, but here Amphitryon introduces the hero as his *own* son, although he maintains that Heracles fought and won against the Giants. The second item of importance is that we have confirmation that the Giants have been killed. This piece of information is significant

---

[495] Papadopoulou (2005) 126.

[496] Papadopoulou (2005) 125.

[497] See Willink (1988) 86-88 for a discussion of the thematic import of this word.

symbolically, for the earlier references to the Giants described them as active opponents (as though they are presently a threat) rather than enemies already defeated. Here, the Giants are confirmed as dead – they no longer pose any such threat – in contrast to the Titans, who are almost always described as being struck down (and thus on the defensive), rather than "actively" fighting. Heracles, like the Giants, was still actively fighting monsters earlier in the play and only now at the end when he is himself "defeated" do we also hear that the Giants are defeated too. Heracles is both a Giant-killer and a Giant himself. Only when this last "giant" (which is what Heracles had become) was defeated by Athena,[498] is Zeus once again assured of his sovereignty. The Giants of this play then symbolize both Zeus' own weakness and his reliance others (both Heracles and Athena), but their defeat is also symbolic of Zeus' level of security: only after they are truly defeated is Zeus truly safe and it is this motif which Seneca brings out more fully in his own tragedies.

Seneca makes use of the other (staircase-building) Giants in his *Thyestes*, but in his *Hercules Furens* he refers twice to the Phlegraean race of Giants. In much the same way as Euripides emphasizes the father-son relationship Seneca too uses the Gigantomachy to raise the issue of Hercules' paternity. However, he differs from Euripides in one significant way insofar as he questions the extent to which Hercules was involved in the war. In Euripides, Heracles and Zeus were (more or less) depicted as equals, for although Heracles was enlisted to aid the gods, Zeus remained an integral force in the war. In Seneca, on the other hand, the gods, including Jupiter, seem absolutely unable to take a stand against their opponents and Hercules is not so much aiding the gods as he is becoming their entire defensive force:

> post monstra tot perdomita, post Phlegram impio
> sparsam cruore postque defensos deos

---

[498] Hamilton (1985) 22.

nondum liquet de patre? (*HF* 444-46).

The Giants are even more aggressive than depicted in Euripides, but it is also made very clear that Hercules had no difficulty defeating them (and seemingly defeating them single-handedly). Amphitryon's question about whether there should be any doubt as to who the hero's father is, is again somewhat ironic. The doubt that arises is not so much whether Hercules is Jupiter's son, but rather why the gods and Jupiter in particular need such a defender. Jupiter's reliance on his son is exaggerated even more in Seneca and Hercules becomes a replacement for his father from early on in the cosmogonic history, foreshadowing the events that will follow when Hercules imagines that he actually will assume Jupiter's role.[499]

The second reference found in *Hercules Furens* is during the "mad" scene when Hercules believes he is leading the Titans to war against Jupiter; but he also mentions that he sees the Giants armed and prepared for war:

> Quid hoc? Gigantes arma pestiferi movent.
> profugit umbras Tityos, ac lacerum gerens
> et inane pectus quam prope a caelo stetit!
> labat Cithaeron, alta Pallene tremit
> marcentque Tempe. rapuit hic Pindi iuga,
> hic rapuit Oeten, saevit horrendum Mimas (*HF* 976-81).

Hercules is reliving the early cosmogonic war and the Giants are alive once again. The language suggests that Hercules is not attempting to lead these Giants into war, but rather that they are attempting to war with him.[500] The language also suggests that such a breach of the natural law (escaping the underworld and attacking the heavens) has a profound effect on the environment and nature. It is precisely this idea of breaking natural

---

[499] Littlewood (2004) 35 briefly discusses this statement in terms of Amphitryon's agon with Lycus and how Amphitryon "allows even the Olympian order to be subsumed in a cyclical struggle of power."

[500] Rose (1985) 119.

boundaries which is so adversarial, but it is exactly what Hercules accomplished when he too escaped the underworld and (imagined that he) attacked his father's domain. What is somewhat different in this version of the myth is that Seneca is presenting the Giants as having seized particular mountain peaks as if they are each going to attack from their own particular vantage point. This is very reminiscent of the Titanomachy when the gods were assembled on one mountain whereas the Titans were assembled on another (and conflation is clearly at work, for Tityos was a Titan and not a Giant). But Seneca is clearly referencing the Gigantomachy, for Mimas was one of the few named Giants from the war and specifically the named foe of Jupiter (Eur. *Ion* 215).[501] Not only are the Giants "active" opponents once more, but those enemies of Jupiter, which Hercules had vanquished long ago, are once again preparing for war. The correlation between victor and vanquished that was apparent in Euripides is not present in Seneca;[502] rather, Hercules is confronting every opponent that his father faced but, unlike his father, he does so without the aid of his own son. The supposed weakness of Jupiter in having his son help defend his realm is now shown to be a sign of prudence. Hercules cannot live up to the task at hand on his own, confirming both the need to rely on the strength of others and the importance of maintaining a father-son relationship (the first lesson Hercules eventually accepts, the second he learns far more painfully).

The Giants of Seneca's *Thyestes*: Re-Living Enemies of the Past

Seneca makes far more use of the "staircase Giants" in his *Thyestes*, although he does introduce them by way of a conflated reference to the Phlegrean Giants. As in *Hercules Furens*, Seneca depicts these Giants as more "active" in their descriptions. They

---

[501] Fitch (1987) 372-73.

[502] *Contra* Chaudhuri (2008) 107-08 and n. 74.

are mentioned first by the chorus after they notice strange phenomena occurring and the sun retracing its steps; they begin to wonder if the Giants have returned: *numquid aperto carcere Ditis / victi temptant bella Gigantes?* (805-06). These lines are very reminiscent of *HF* 976-81, especially when the chorus goes on to ask about the mountains:

> numquid struitur
> via Phlegraeos alta per hostes
> et Thessalicum
> Thressa premitur Pelion Ossa? (*Thy.* 810-12).

The general theme of the returning (once-conquered) Giants remains the same; however, here the use of the staircase Giants provides a somewhat different resonance. In *HF* the Giants were attempting to station themselves on individual mountain tops as the Titans had once done; here, it is imagined that they are attempting to reach the heavens and attack Jupiter at close range and in his own domain. This image is well-suited to a play whose antagonist also reaches the heavens to supplant Jupiter.[503] Although the attack by the Giants is not happening (either on-stage or in someone's frenzied mind) and it is only one possibility for explaining cosmological events, it nonetheless offers insights into how the chorus is responding to the events of the play. Atreus' acts have disturbed the natural laws in much the same way as the Giants (and as Hercules) had disturbed them. The chorus, by comparing the consequences of Atreus' transgressions to that of re-emerging Giants, suggests not only that Atreus should also be considered a "Giant" in the same way, but also that he should now suffer a similar punishment.[504]

---

[503] Tarrant (1985) notes that the imagery of Jupiter vanquishing the Giants was popular in Augustan poetry and was symbolic of Augustan triumphs. The inversion here of Giants returning to wage war on their conqueror could thus have political ramifications and indicate a "negation of Augustan confidence in the stability of the regime." The stability of the Olympian order is certainly being questioned here and will be discussed throughout chapter 9.

[504] Tarrant (1985) 207; Davis (1989) 432.

This similar punishment is precisely what Thyestes wishes for when he prays to Jupiter to avenge his own act of filial cannibalism. When he finally understands what Atreus has done and what he himself has consumed, he asks for Jupiter's thunderbolts:

> manuque non qua tecta et immeritas domos
> telo petis minore, sed qua montium
> tergemina moles cecidit et qui montibus
> stabant pares Gigantes, hac arma expedi
> ignesque torque (*Thy.* 1081-85).

Thyestes too references the Giants when he requests Jupiter's bolts of lightning, as though he understands that the awful deeds committed were gigantomachic in nature. He also reinforces the earlier statement that the Giants were once defeated, but attacks worthy of their name can still be perpetrated. This recurring idea that defeated Giants can return is of importance and significance for Jupiter, for it suggests that not only is the underworld a place from which evil(s) can be released (and indeed the Fury attests this idea well), but also that it is no longer an appropriate location for sending hubristic individuals. If the gates of Dis can be breached and Jupiter can no longer punish those who transgress his laws by sending those implicated there, chaos will ensue. Indeed, such chaos occurs in this play and Jupiter's bolts of lightning which Thyestes so fervently prays to receive are no longer effective.[505] Jupiter can no more blast Thyestes with his fires than he can truly defeat Giants, or those who behave in gigantomachic fashion. "Giants" will continue to wage war and will eventually succeed in their attacks.

---

[505] Davis (1989) 434.

Seneca's Typhoeus: Jupiter's Demise?

Typhoeus is mentioned very infrequently in the tragedies of Euripides and Seneca, occurring once each in Seneca's *Thyestes* and *Medea*.[506] As Zeus' final foe before gaining absolute supremacy, Typhoeus represents the god's most impressive and difficult enemy, as well as the turning point for his sovereignty. Typhoeus appears in *Thyestes* during the same catalogue of possible causes for the cosmic disruption identified by the chorus. Just as they wonder if the Giants are preparing for war, so they wonder if Typhoeus has escaped his imprisonment: *num reiecto / latus explicuit monte Typhoeus?* (*Thy.* 809-10). In this particular example, there is little difference between this monster and the Giants whom the chorus fear have re-emerged. Typhoeus' inclusion in the list of monsters, who were formerly imprisoned but who are now feared to have escaped, only intensifies the sense of chaos and cosmic disruption.

The second example found in *Medea*, however, does offer some further insights. Typhoeus is mentioned by Medea when she is preparing the poison to use against Creusa and Creon. She prays to Hecate and gives her an offering which includes the limbs of Typhoeus: *tibi haec Typhoeus membra quae discors tulit, / qui regna concussit Iovis* (*Med.* 773-74). Unlike the other monsters who are mentioned, Typhoeus is not only defeated here (and thus "passive"), he (or at least a portion of his parts) is being offered to another deity as though Typhoeus is Medea's to offer. That she only offers his *membra* suggests either that she has dismembered him somehow (for it is generally presumed that he is imprisoned whole), or that he has willingly offered himself up, or has been "defeated" again, in order

---

[506] The sole reference to Typhoeus in Euripides is found in *Heracles* where the hero is defeating a three-bodied Typhon (1272); but this is likely either a conflation of two distinct beasts, or a reference to another serpent-like monster, rather than the formidable opponent of Zeus.

that Medea can use him to successfully call upon her goddess to aid her.[507] But we are left wondering how she could possibly have obtained this particular monster, or even parts of him, since he was such a formidable opponent to Jupiter, a fact which is also highlighted. The one enemy who posed the greatest threat to Jupiter has become, through Medea's agency, a mere set of limbs with which to please a goddess much humbler than Jupiter. Such a drastic change in Typhoeus' status signals the potency of Medea's magic and the potential for her to become a threat herself to Jupiter – an idea that will be more fully discussed below (chapter 9, pp. 283-315).

Thus, although Typhoeus either does not appear or is infrequently mentioned in the plays of Euripides and Seneca, these two images (and the latter in particular) are powerful enough on their own to highlight significant motifs in their respective texts. Typhoeus is such an emblematic symbol of the early cosmogonic opposition to Zeus (and Jupiter) that such a drastically different depiction will resonate with the audience on several levels.[508] His initial defeat by the Olympian order secured and crystallized the kingship for Jupiter. That such an enemy is "defeated" a second time by a mortal woman with magic suggests that perhaps the time has come again for Jupiter to (re)earn his hard-fought sovereignty, for it is clear that a new weapon has been honed to defeat even the toughest of opposition. Medea has reduced Typhoeus from the near-equal of Jupiter to a pile of (severed) limbs – he no longer holds the position of most feared "monster." Others (including Medea) will now take his place.

---

[507] Hine (2000) 189 suggests the *membra* are in fact snakes' bodies and that Medea's use of them is "suitably grandiose and subversive;" Ogden (2013a) 18 similarly states that only the greatest "cosmic" dragons are good enough for her purposes."

[508] A recent and thorough discussion of Typhon in Greek and Roman literature is found in Ogden (2013a) 19-38.

Overt Threats: Capaneus and Ajax

After the defeat of the Giants and other gigantomachic figures, Zeus is assured of his position and metes out justice through intermediary figures, rarely involving himself *directly* in the punishment of mortals.[509] There are, however, a small number of exceptions to this general rule, including two men who figure prominently in our tragedies. Capaneus, one of the famous "Seven" who besieged Thebes and Ajax ("the lesser" of Locria), a participant in the Trojan War, can be singled out for their theomachic personalities. Unlike the early cosmogonic monsters the Titans and Giants, Capaneus and Ajax cannot truly be called usurpers, for they do not launch a real attack on the heavens, but they do threaten the gods and boast of their own incredible prowess, believing themselves to be invincible to divine wrath. Neither man can make good on their threats against the gods but, like the Giants and the Titans, their open hostility to the gods earns them celestial displeasure and, more specifically, a *personal* response from Zeus and Jupiter. It is this personal response that is worth investigation, for Zeus and Jupiter do not often involve themselves directly with meting out punishments; when they do it is no insignificant episode. That these gods involve themselves personally with Ajax and Capaneus suggests that their boasts and hostility are thus far more threatening than one might initially assume.

As similar as these two figures are to each other, however, their stories also contain some notable differences. The punishment that both men receive is the same one levelled against Zeus' early foes, but the method in achieving that punishment is markedly different. Zeus takes on Capaneus directly while Ajax meets the god's lightning through Athena. The weapon is the same, but the extent of Zeus' personal participation is lessened.

---

[509] Generally, Zeus and Jupiter only involve themselves when the cosmic order is in jeopardy: mere hubris, while worthy of punishment, is not necessarily worthy of either god's personal attacks. Their fires and bolts are reserved for those exceptional cases where the perpetrators endanger the god's own status or the cosmic balance.

When considering their representation by Euripides and Seneca, further distinctions can be made, at least in the case of Ajax. Euripides only promises this punishment for Ajax; we are not provided the pleasure of seeing or hearing about its fulfilment during the course of the play. We can be guaranteed that it will happen as Athena and Poseidon discuss, but that is all. Seneca, on the other hand, delivers to us the specifics of how Ajax met his death through a messenger speech demanded by Clytemnestra. Athena remains the force behind Zeus' thunderbolt, but here we are afforded the luxury of hearing about her "in action" and witnessing (second-hand) the struggle of Ajax to overcome the gods' will. The perspective of the scene is thus very different in Euripides than it is in Seneca (divine *versus* human) and this allows for a more balanced interpretation of this mythological event. Although his endeavour to stand out against the gods does not earn him a direct meeting with Zeus himself, Ajax is nonetheless a threat, albeit a "lesser" one than Capaneus, and earns his title as a (very) unsuccessful theomachic enemy of Zeus and Jupiter. But it is Capaneus to whom I will turn first.

Zeus and Capaneus in Euripides' *Phoenissae*

As discussed in chapter 7, Zeus is not merely an ancestor of Thebes in Euripides' *Phoenissae*, he is also an active participant in the Theban war as his thunderous fury strikes out at Capaneus for his impious outbursts against him. The story of Zeus and Capaneus is a favourite amongst the poets, for it demonstrates quite dramatically the force of the gods and the punishment awaiting those who transgress divine laws and those who believe themselves to be of a higher station than they really are.[510] Euripides does not

---

[510] In tragedy Capaneus appears in Euripides' *Phoenissae* and *Supplices* (not under investigation here) and is mentioned in his *IA* (246), in Aeschylus' *Septem* (423, 440) and Sophocles' *OC* (1319); there is no mention of this figure by Seneca, although he does receive extended treatment by Statius (*Theb.* 10. 827-939). See Chaudhuri (2008) esp. chapters 2 and 3 for a thorough

disappoint and includes Zeus' display of divine punishment during the first messenger speech. Anticipation of this scene, however, is heightened early on in the play through Antigone during the *teichoskopia* scene.[511] When the pedagogus explains to the maiden which one of the generals has uttered disrespectful words against the city, Antigone's response is to pray to Nemesis and Zeus.[512] She hopes that Capaneus' desires to overtake her city and enslave its population are not met with divine favour:

> ἰὼ Νέμεσι καὶ Διὸς βαρύβρομοι βρονταὶ
> κεραύνιόν τε φῶς αἰθαλόεν, σύ τοι
> μεγαλαγορίαν ὑπεράνορα κοιμίζεις (*Phoen.* 182-84).

Nemesis and Zeus are invoked to punish Capaneus' hubris and Antigone is very specific in calling upon Zeus' thunder. She is asking for the god to appear as a force of retribution rather than any other potential manifestation (Zeus as a saviour, for example, would have been just as appropriate, for Antigone fears the women of Thebes may be taken as slaves, 190-92[513]) and this is underscored by her simultaneous invocation of Nemesis, a goddess *par excellence* of punishment.[514] Antigone's prayers will, of course, be answered and Capaneus will be struck down with the thunderbolt of Zeus (following mythological and literary precedent). Ominously perhaps, her prayer immediately follows the first reference to Capaneus in the play and is important not only as a precursor to the events which will follow, but also because Euripides has subtly differentiated him from his fellow captains. Antigone has been asking about each general and Capaneus is the only one in this instance

---

discussion of Statius' Capaneus and his literary predecessors (esp. Ovid, pp. 259-63); see also Ripoll (2006) 253-54.

[511] See Burgess (1988) and Scodel (1997) for discussions of the teichoskopia scene.

[512] As Nau (2005) 139 remarks, these are "very apt" deities for Antigone to address.

[513] Luschnig (1995) 194.

[514] Amiech (2004) 282.

to be identified solely by his hubristic *nature* and not by his armour or weaponry.[515] All that is said of his *actions* is that he is measuring the walls (180-81), as though he need neither armour nor weapons nor even an army to become a threat. It is Capaneus' μεγαλαγορίαν ὑπεράνορα which will earn him a very specific response from Zeus: κοιμίζειν (184). This is the same word used in Euripides' *Hecuba* of the Titans who were depicted as laid low on Athena's peplos (*Hec.* 473-74) and is made use of here in a similar context. It is the first clue among many that Capaneus ought to be seen as more than a one-dimensional character: he is being specifically associated with Zeus' traditional enemies (both the Titans and the Giants) and is inherently dangerous. It will be no surprise that he is afforded divine response worthy of the god's oldest foes. Antigone's prayer that his boasting be punished will be an accurate assessment of Capaneus' character and the two deities invoked here foreshadow well his impious behaviour toward the gods.

When we finally hear what exactly Capaneus is boasting about in the (first) messenger speech, we become aware of how right Antigone was to call down Zeus' lightning bolt in order to punish this transgressor. Not only does Capaneus believe he will topple the towers of Thebes, something that will not transpire, but that he would do so even if it were against the will of the gods and Zeus specifically:

> μηδ' ἂν τὸ σεμνὸν πῦρ νιν εἰργαθεῖν Διὸς
> τὸ μὴ οὐ κατ' ἄκρων περγάμων ἑλεῖν πόλιν.
> καὶ ταῦθ' ἅμ' ἠγόρευε καὶ πετρούμενος
> ἀνεῖρφ' ὑπ' αὐτὴν ἀσπίδ' εἱλίξας δέμας,
> κλίμακος ἀμείβων ξέστ' ἐνηλάτων βάθρα (*Phoen.* 1175-76).

---

[515] Hippomedon is carrying a shield of bronze and is likened to an earth-born giant; Tydeus carries barbarian weapons, his army using light shields and javelins; Parthenopaeus is followed by a mass of soldiers; Polynices is wearing golden armour; Amphiaraus rides on a chariot carrying sacrificial victims to satisfy the earth's thirst for blood. See Nau (2005) 127-33.

As Mastronarde rightly notes, the use of σεμνὸν is used to enhance the impiety of this blasphemous remark and, as discussed in chapter 1 (pp. 24-25), can be used to refer to the *most holy* aspect of something divine.[516] Capaneus' boasting is part of the traditional myth and Euripides is following Aeschylus in his presentation of a boasting madman (*Sept.* 422-36), but he seems to be particularly blasphemous in this presentation. The latter poet provides far more detail than the former about Capaneus, but by now Euripides has at least informed us of Capaneus' shield.[517] In furthering his association with Zeus' early enemies, Capaneus' shield depicts a giant unearthing the city of Thebes from its foundations and carrying it off on his back (almost a mini-Atlas figure,[518] yet another Titanic reference); we are also told that he is likened to the god of war himself, Ares (*Phoen.* 1129-33). The emblem on Capaneus' shield does not correspond, however, to the threats he makes against the city: he wants to raze the city to the ground, not pick it up by its foundations and, as Luschnig has noted, it is the Thebans who do this in order to combat the enemy not vice versa.[519] The motif of the Argives as Giants, on the other hand, does correspond well to the events at Thebes and this is especially true of Capaneus. The imagery is reminiscent of the Gigantomachy as is the result: Capaneus' impious behaviour toward Zeus earns him the same punishment as the god meted out to the Giants.[520] Furthermore, the inclusion of the ladder[521] in the description of his actions emphasizes Capaneus' desire to rise to the

---

[516] Mastronarde (1994) 476.

[517] For discussions of the shields in Euripides see Harrison (1992) and Fernandelli (2000), both in relation to Statius; Hilton (2011) 28-33 and appendix C, in relation to Aeschylus' *Septem*; see also Kamerbeek (1948) 280 and Chaudhuri (2008) 53.

[518] Nau (2005) 140.

[519] Luschnig (1995) 93.

[520] Nau (2005) 140.

[521] The imagery of the ladder has met with some interest, with scholars proposing very different interpretations for its meaning: for example, Feingold (1968) 95 sees implicit sexual imagery

level of the gods as if re-enacting the actions of another set of Giants, the Aloadai, who were also met with Zeus' anger.[522] Thus, Capaneus' assault on Thebes has little to do with Thebes itself; it is merely a means to an end. His desire to breach the walls against even divine will is a direct challenge to the gods: he is testing them to see how far he can go.

The messenger continues his description of the events and we are told that Zeus does directly intervene to punish Capaneus for his outrageous blasphemies:

ἤδη δ' ὑπερβαίνοντα γεῖσα τειχέων
βάλλει κεραυνῶι Ζεύς νιν· ἐκτύπησε δὲ
χθών, ὥστε δεῖσαι πάντας· ἐκ δὲ κλιμάκων
[ἐσφενδονᾶτο χωρὶς ἀλλήλων μέλη,
κόμαι μὲν εἰς Ὄλυμπον, αἷμα δ' ἐς χθόνα,
χεῖρες δὲ καὶ κῶλ' ὡς κύκλωμ' Ἰξίονος]
εἰλίσσετ', ἐς γῆν δ' ἔμπυρος πίπτει νεκρός (*Phoen.* 1180-86).[523]

Zeus never appears in "person" in tragedy and this direct intervention (a physical manifestation of the god, which is readily identified as Zeus) is as close as the god comes to taking part in the action of any play (the parallel scene in Aesch. *Sept.* 423-46 only imagines what will take place, rather than describing it after the fact). The result of such action suggests several items of importance: the first is that Zeus does see, hear and take an interest in human affairs (at least in terms of the world of the play); secondly, the god does answer prayers, as Antigone had earlier prayed to him and this is his answer; third, Zeus requires respect and will punish anyone who is impious toward him. Where there were only implicit hints at the god's presence and interest in Thebes elsewhere in the play, this

___

associated with the device while Nau (2005) 141 interprets the ladder as underscoring Capaneus' villainous attitude.

[522] If there is an implicit reference to these two particular giants, there may be further parallels with Eteocles and Polynices. The pair of giants were only defeated when Artemis changed into a deer and ran between them, at which time they both hurled their weapons, but instead of striking the deer, killed each other. The motif of fratricide is further embedding itself in the imagery and an earlier prayer to Artemis by Antigone to stop Capaneus (192) may be relevant here.

[523] Kovacs (2002) has reinstated the bracketed text, but treats it as potentially spurious.

show of power and vengeance provides positive evidence for Zeus' will and influence. Although only part of this passage is considered authentic, it nonetheless presents a vivid image of the futility of opposing the will of the gods – not only will Capaneus suffer Zeus' anger, but so too will the house of Laius for their own acts of disobedience. The bracketed part of the passage could also suggest the metaphorical re-planting of the Sown-men who will manifest themselves in the guise of Eteocles and Polynices, thus hinting at the continuation of the cycle of vengeance (but this, of course, can only be speculation). Zeus' swift response is both an assurance of divine authority and a safeguard against a new army led by this pseudo-Giant.

The final episode connected with Capaneus and Zeus is the result of this display of arrogance and deserved retribution. Zeus' action prompts an immediate response from the Argive army and is interpreted by Adrastus as an omen of the god's will, inducing him to retreat; it is also interpreted by the Thebans (as a whole) as a sign from Zeus that the god is on their side:

> ὡς δ' εἶδ' Ἄδραστος Ζῆνα πολέμιον στρατῶι,
> ἔξω τάφρου καθεῖσεν Ἀργείων στρατόν.
> οἱ δ' αὖ παρ' ἡμῶν δεξιὸν Διὸς τέρας
> ἰδόντες ἐξήλαυνον, ἁρμάτων ὄχοι
> ἱππῆς ὁπλῖται, κἀς μέσ' Ἀργείων ὅπλα
> ξυνῆψαν ἔγχη· (*Phoen.* 1187-92).

This simultaneous interpretation of Zeus' action is significant for two reasons: the first because, as Craik notes, Zeus' punishment of Capaneus was personal and did not necessarily reflect the god's anger at the Argive army as a whole, although that is precisely how Adrastus views it.[524] Similarly, it was not necessarily a show of support for the Thebans, although that is their interpretation. This in itself implies fallibility on the part of mortals to interpret correctly the will of the gods, unless they are diviners of some sort.

---

[524] Craik (1988) 237.

This leads to the second reason why this episode is of importance: during the *teichoskopia*, the old man tells Antigone that the Argive army comes with dikē on their side (154-55), something the above passage clearly does not indicate.[525] The old man presumes he can understand the will of the gods and the workings of dikē, but he will be shown to be mistaken in his belief and thus the interpretations of Adrastus and the Thebans are no more likely to be correct. In the event, the Thebans do win and the Argives lose, but victory will come only at the cost of Menoeceus' self-sacrifice and a fratricide, which leads to a suicide and an exile, as well as further hubris against the gods when Polynices is left unburied. The meaning of victory and dikē is muddied indeed.

Zeus, Ajax and Euripides' *Trojan Women*

The one other Greek tragedy in which Zeus comes very close to making a personal appearance but does not manifest himself in even quite the same fashion as in *Phoenissae*, is *Troades*. Although it will happen outside the text as it were, Zeus is again mentioned as participating in the destruction of a particular individual, this time in the person of Ajax. In the prologue's dialogue between Athena and Poseidon, the two gods discuss the future demolition of the Greek fleet as it sails away from Troy.[526] Athena explains to her uncle her plans for the Greeks and her father's promised participation:

> καὶ Ζεὺς μὲν ὄμβρον καὶ χάλαζαν ἄσπετον
> πέμψει δνοφώδη τ' αἰθέρος φυσήματα·
> ἐμοὶ δὲ δώσειν φησὶ πῦρ κεραύνιον,
> βάλλειν Ἀχαιοὺς ναῦς τε πιμπράναι πυρί (*TW* 78-81).

---

[525] Similarly, the scene between Polynices and Eteocles (446-637) would also suggest Polynices has the more "just" motivations; however, as much as dikē may attend Polynices, it does not necessarily attend the army that has followed him.

[526] See Dunn (1993) for a discussion of some of the peculiarities of this prologue; see also O'Neill (1941); Luschnig (1971); and Goff (2009) 38-42.

Zeus' participation in this episode is, in some ways, very different from that in *Phoenissae*: there, it was instantaneous death for Capaneus. Here, Athena has gone to her father for his aid and has asked for his help in his guise as a god of weather, not justice. Athena has been the one slighted by the Greeks and it thus falls to her to demand retribution. Zeus is participating here for very different reasons. Capaneus posed a threat to Zeus' established authority and needed to be eliminated. Ajax, although a transgressor of divine law does not constitute the same threat and thus does not warrant the same punishment. That being said, Ajax is representative of Greek dishonour: his own actions at the temple of Athena and his peers' implicit approval of his treatment of Cassandra are breaches of supplicatory laws, not to mention a display of disrespect for his daughter. Zeus, as god of suppliants, should be no less involved in their punishment than Athena, whose temple was profaned. Ajax, at least in this particular version, is thus a threat only so far as he is an example of hubris.

Of more interest is the focus on the lightning bolt of Zeus. Zeus will not be the one to wield it against the Greeks; instead he has promised to hand it over to his daughter to use as her weapon of choice. Although Zeus is intimately connected with thunder and lightning, it is no surprise that he should give up his weapon to Athena, for she is in many respects a double of her father.[527] What such an exchange symbolizes is something greater however; Zeus' transfer of his lightning bolt to Athena not only symbolizes the great trust he places in his daughter and their likeness to each other, but it also clearly implies his approval of her intentions to destroy the Greek fleet insofar as her use of his weapon to do so becomes an extension of his own displeasure at the Greeks' behaviour. Athena has asked Poseidon to take part as a favour to her and he grants it due to familial courtesy, not out of any particular grudge against the Greeks.[528] Zeus, on the other hand, will act of his

---

[527] Yasumura (2011) 86-96.

[528] Lloyd (2009) discusses the divine and familial discourse between Athena and Poseidon.

own accord in creating a tempest *as well as* in tandem with Athena through her use of his weapon.

The emphasis on the transference of power from Zeus to Athena is strengthened when Poseidon concedes to help his niece. He agrees to partake in her plan for vengeance and instructs her to go to Olympus to accept Zeus' lightning:

> ἀλλ' ἕρπ' Ὄλυμπον καὶ κεραυνίους βολὰς
> λαβοῦσα πατρὸς ἐκ χερῶν καραδόκει,
> ὅταν στράτευμ' Ἀργεῖον ἐξιῆι κάλως (*TW* 92-94).

In this divine perspective the emphasis is placed on the complete barrage of natural elements that will be deployed against the Greeks. Although we have heard the reason for Athena's anger (that Ajax dragged Cassandra from her temple by force and the Greeks made no reparations, 70-71), it has been eclipsed by the utter devastation that Athena has planned for the Greek army. The brief, two-line reason for her contempt is followed by twenty-three lines of future destruction (75-97[529]). We will be ignorant of the Greek response to the disaster which will befall them, ignorant too of Ajax's personal response (which elsewhere is as hubristic as that of Capaneus). We are left only with the image that the two gods paint for us. Athena first: Zeus' storms, rain and wind will be unleashed; then will come the lightning bolt which will strike the ships afire; finally, Poseidon's swells and eddies will reveal the carnage. Then Poseidon: the entire Aegean will be in confusion; beaches and reefs will be full of death; and finally, the transfer of the lightning bolt to Athena from Zeus' hand is commanded. The awesome might of the gods is depicted well and the two leave no doubt as to the destruction that will come. But Poseidon brings us abruptly back to the fact that this still requires Zeus' lightning bolt and only when Athena acquires it, will any of it come to pass. The lightning bolt is thus not only an instrument of revenge and punishment, but it is also the symbol of Zeus' authority over life and death (as

---

[529] On this scene, see O'Neill (1941) 316-18.

discussed in chapter 1, p. 37). Without the transfer of Zeus' lightning, Athena will not have

the destructive capability she envisions nor will Poseidon grant his aid. His directive for

Athena to go to Olympus and specifically to take the lightning bolt from Zeus' hand is

both a command to seek her father's approval (and thus ensure that Poseidon's own

participation will also be approved) as well as to seek his authority. The transfer of his

lightning bolt is also a transfer of his power and a symbol of Zeus' imperium. Although the

Greeks will meet Zeus' wrath through Athena, they will nonetheless meet his wrath and it

will be no less destructive than if he had wielded the weapon himself.

Jupiter, Ajax and Seneca's *Agamemnon*: A Delusional "Theomachist"

The divine prophecy of Euripides' *Troades* is thoroughly fulfilled in Seneca's

Agamemnon when the messenger is ordered by Clytemnestra to speak openly about the

fate of the Greek fleet on its way home from Troy. Although Eurybates hesitates to speak

ill-omened words on the day of Agamemnon's return and thus on a "festive" occasion (*Ag.*

416-18), he does give in to Clytemnestra's demands. Eurybates provides a human

perspective on how the ships and soldiers were doomed by the gods during one fateful

night and an incredible storm. His report of the sea-storm, positioned in the very centre of

the tragedy, has attracted scholarly attention due to its length (at over 150 lines it is

Seneca's longest messenger speech) and elaboration on a scene with no clear extant

source(s).[530] As Baertschi notes, "the storm . . . is portrayed in exhaustive detail" and

deserves special attention.[531] Although Baertschi's focus is on the epic nature of the

messenger speech and the figure of Eurybates, she also argues for a heightened sense of

pathos and suspense through the use of *ecphrasis* and the depiction of Ajax. While

---

[530] Baertschi (2010) 254; see also Tarrant (1976) 248-49 for an outline of the speech.

[531] Baertschi (2010) 254.

Baertschi offers a very thorough analysis of the scene, I wish to examine her conclusion here:

> The last line of the narrative (*Ag.* 556) . . . "[he] lies conquered by earth and fire and sea" . . . stresses the cosmic dimensions of Ajax's *hybris*. His impious acts have violated the natural order and destabilized the universe, and it therefore takes the joint collaboration of all three elements, earth, fire and water, to eliminate him and re-establish order.[532]

According to Baertschi, Ajax's hubris consists of his blasphemies against the gods and his rape of Cassandra at Athena's temple (not mentioned, "but certainly present in the audience's memory").[533]

Not every scholar has interpreted Ajax in this scene as a deserving victim of the gods. Some would rather see him, for example, as a beacon of light struggling against the malevolence of divine forces.[534] While I believe this particular view of Ajax's defiance is unwarranted, it nevertheless illustrates the potential for a multi-faceted interpretation of the soldier's struggle against the gods. I would posit instead that Ajax, very much a hubristic character, is not the cosmic disruptor that Baertschi would make him out to be. A review of the divine forces at work and Jupiter's involvement in particular, suggests instead that Ajax is not simply suffering for his current outbursts (which seem to be delusional rather than theomacic) but rather *as one among the Greeks* for their conduct at Troy.

Eurybates' account of the sea-storm is preceded by a choral ode, the themes of which are intrinsically related to those found in the herald's description. Most significantly for the present discussion, the chorus is invoking several divinities, none of whom are likely to be favourably disposed to the royal household on whose behalf they seem to be

---

[532] Baertschi (2010) 266.

[533] Baertschi (2010) 265.

[534] Wilson (1985) 153; see also Boyle (1997) 40: "In his defiant struggle, refusal to be subdued, heroic resistance, courage and challenge in the face of hostile, apparently perverse gods (532-56), Ajax of Locris . . . dramatises the spectacular paradox of the greatness of impotent humanity."

praying.[535] Even though the chorus is singing a hymn of thanksgiving for Agamemnon's return they are also singing and invoking deities in their capacities as avengers: Apollo is a *victor* (*Ag.* 323) armed with arrows (324) who once sung of the destruction of the Titans and of the Giants' attempt to attack the heavens (334-339); Juno too is a *victrix* (347) who rules over war and peace (345); Minerva, daughter of the Thunderer (*magni nata Tonantis*, 356) is remembered for her attacks against the Trojan towers and characterized by her spear (357-58); Diana is also a *victrix* for her triumph over Niobe (375-76); and finally Jupiter is invoked as the one who exercises his authority by lightning bolt and whose nod makes the world tremble (381-85). The chorus is thankful for the (presumed) renewal of peace, but their invocations underscore the power and authority of the gods and their inherent nature as the ultimate victors. The Trojan War was not won by the Greeks but by the gods.

The introduction of Jupiter into Eurybates' narrative is influenced by this choral ode and its depiction of the god as the ruler over all (*Tuque ante omnes / pater ac rector fulmine pollens*, *Ag.* 382-83), "anticipating the fact that Jupiter sanctions the storm described in Act 3 (528-29)."[536] We are being prepared for an act of retribution on Jupiter's behalf that is both deliberate and unmerciful, leaving an impression of the god's total and complete supremacy. Eurybates emphasizes the destructive elements of nature, the winds at war with each other (474-78), the sea smiting the heavens (471) and finally fires falling from the clouds: *excidunt ignes tamen / et nube dirum fulmen elisa micat* (494-95). This is not a direct reference to Jupiter, but Seneca will make clear in less than forty lines (and has already hinted), that the god is in fact the cause of the storm. Here we are presented with the full barrage of Jupiter's "natural" attributes and the dangers presented

---

[535] See Davis (1993) 208-211 for a discussion of the potential for irony throughout the ode.
[536] Davis (1993) 210.

when one dishonours the gods. The fire, lightning and clouds are presented in a very negative light and this heightens the destructive nature of Jupiter's wrath, as well as illuminating the dire situation in which the Greeks have found themselves and the futility of attempting any kind of appeasement. There is nothing that one can do other than accept one's fate and any other action, as will be made evident through the figure of Ajax, will produce nothing positive.

It has been noted that sea-storm imagery in Senecan tragedy is usually associated with vengeance[537] and this storm is no exception as nature and the gods literally battle against the Greeks. There is also an argument for seeing some irony in the depiction of the lightning in particular, for as destructive as this celestial phenomenon is for the Greeks, the soldiers are almost comforted by its presence (496). Because darkness had enveloped their senses in such an unnatural way, the light emitted from the lightning was wished for, ruinous though it proved to be.[538] Another argument suggests that the lightning presented here is merely a conventional part of traditional sea-storm imagery. Tarrant notes that lightning becomes commonplace after Virgil, contrasting Latin practice with Greek where in Homer (*Od.* 12.415, 14.305) and Euripides (*Tro.* 80-81) lightning is clearly presented as "the weapon of the gods."[539] While this may be true, there is nothing to say Seneca did not take advantage of both traditions, for Jupiter is certainly involved in this storm and this lightning is a prelude to his vengeance.

The storm is atonement for the destruction of Troy (577) and Seneca makes explicit the divine forces behind it:

---

[537] Baron (1972) 70, as cited in Wilson (1985) 145; see also Shelton (1983) 168-69.

[538] Wilson (1985) 151.

[539] Tarrant (1976) 269; I would suggest lightning is the weaponry of Jupiter (and Zeus) specifically and when used by another deity (usually Minerva/Athena) it is an extension of his authority and imperium.

> fulmine irati Iovis
> armata Pallas quidquid haud hasta minax
> haud aegide et furore Gorgoneo potest,
> hoc igne patrio temptat . . . (*Ag.* 528-31).

Tarrant believes that the inclusion of Jupiter's anger is not accounted for,[540] and yet the god's anger seems warranted for the disrespect shown to his altar (448) and ultimately to the god himself (as discussed in chapter 7, pp. 224-25). Although Jupiter is not the focus of the Ajax episode (that role belonging to Pallas), he does "open" the divine element, as he is given primary position in the line and the narrative alludes to him several times. The significance here lies in the *irati*, an unusual epithet for the god, especially in verse.[541] Seneca uses the word to emphasize Jupiter's lack of control over his emotions and to signal that this storm is not concerned about fate or cosmic justice, but rather with a personal grudge against the army as a whole.

As in Euripides, it is not Jupiter himself who attacks the Greeks; instead, Pallas has gained access to Jupiter's weapons so as to carry out this mission. Although this action in itself is not an innovation, the fact that Pallas must use Jupiter's arms, because her own weapons are not powerful enough, does seem to be an interesting added detail.[542] Pallas' weaponry is listed in order of destructive power, with Jupiter's lightning bolt the most potent, thus importantly assuring the fury of the Gorgon cannot achieve what Jupiter is able to achieve. This also underscores Jupiter's superiority to Pallas, as the verb *tempto* suggests either that she could fail in her mission to destroy the Greeks, or that she may fail at using Jupiter's fire – and this despite the fact that most would know that she does succeed in eventually destroying the army, including the obstinate Ajax.

---

[540] Tarrant (1976) 275.

[541] *Iratus Iuppiter* found in Cic. *De Off.* 3.102.7; *iratum Iovem* in Seneca the Elder *Controv.* 10.5.6; *irato Iove* occurs in Seneca's *HF* 932, Seneca the Elder's *Controv.* 10.5.1, 10.5.6, 10.5.24; *Iovem iratum* occurs in Cic. *Ep. ad Fam.* 7.12.2; *Iuppiter iratus* occurs in Petronius *Sat.* 44.5.2.

[542] Tarrant (1976) 276.

When the other Greeks have conceded defeat, Ajax continues to fight against his

imminent fate and Pallas continues to harry her target:

> vela cogentem hunc sua
> tento rudente flamma perstrinxit cadens.
> libratur aliud fulmen: hoc toto impetu
> certum reducta Pallas excussit manu,
> imitata patrem (*Ag.* 533-37).

Pallas' first attempt to destroy Ajax is obviously unsuccessful, for a second bolt is needed

with which she imitates her father and achieves her goal. This "imitation" of Jupiter

suggests that the god never misses and thus Pallas would be mimicking his ability to

launch bolts "on target;" equally, such imitation could also refer to Pallas mirroring

Jupiter's destructive nature and his provision for vengeance without mercy. Again,

although Jupiter is not the *immediate* source of the divine wrath, by continually alluding to

him, even obliquely, Seneca intimates that Jupiter approves and supports the actions of the

other divinities, especially his daughter. He does not need to be physically present during

the action for Pallas is in control of the Greek homecoming and is able to carry out his

plans.

Even after this last attack, Ajax continues to taunt the gods, believing that he has

defeated the gods and conquered heaven:

> tandem occupata rupe furibundum intonat:
> "Superasse me nunc pelagus atque ignes iuvat,
> vicisse caelum Palladem fulmen mare" (*Ag.* 544-46).[543]

If the text is sound, and most editions insert both lines of text, we are presented with quite

a boast from Ajax. He takes on supernatural qualities here, as *intonat* is often associated

with Jupiter and *furibundum* evokes images of the Gorgon's fury. Wilson argues that Ajax

---

[543] If the latter two lines are sound. Suspicion abounds especially with regards to this
catalogue of dangers, which includes the accusative *Palladem*, the sole instance of this
form in the Latin corpus.

is here meant to be a positive image in light of all the other Greeks who perish as cowards and Seneca is dwelling on his manner of death and response to fate.[544] While Jupiter is not specifically mentioned, Ajax is of the belief that in conquering *caelum* and *fulmen*, he is essentially defeating the god. He is clearly mistaken in this belief for the absence of Jupiter's personal response to this "challenge" shows that Ajax is not a "real" threat to the heavens, like the Giants or Titans, he is merely one more Greek atoning for his behaviour at Troy. His death is not due to truly theomachic behaviour as Baertschi would have it; instead, he is paying the price for past actions as well as his past and present hubris.[545]

Ajax shows no fear of anything natural or divine and indeed invites Jupiter to strike him down himself, but he receives no Jovial response:

> tene horream
> aliena inerti tela iaculantem manu?
> quid si ipse mittat? (*Ag.* 550-52).

One may be inclined to see Ajax as threatening Jupiter and, indeed, Ajax does believe that he is launching a challenge against the god; but Jupiter's lack of response reinforces the fact that Ajax's threat is an empty boast. Jupiter seems only to take (vengeful) action himself, without the use of an intermediary, when the cosmic order or his regime is under threat, as with the Gigantomachy or Titanomachy. By deputizing other deities, Jupiter is emphasizing the fact that he does not feel a need to be involved, for the other gods are capable of restoring and keeping order on his behalf. Ajax then is boastful and deserving of punishment, but should perhaps be seen as an *exemplum* of the Greeks and their hubris. Unlike Capaneus who had an army of soldiers ready for battle, Ajax is depicted alone, his fellow shipmates now praying to the gods for mercy – there is no substance or foundation to his threat. Jupiter's presence, although not physically manifest in this scene, is felt

---

[544] Wilson (1985) 153.

[545] Lefèvre (1973) 82.

through the continual allusions to his elements of power and this is enough to illustrate his authority and complete superiority.

Concluding Remarks

The themes of the Titanomachy and Gigantomachy are prevalent in both Greek and Roman literature, but references to either event are comparatively sparse in Euripides and Seneca. But when references to each do occur, they underscore particular motifs that are associated with each one: the cyclical and generational pattern of violence in the Titanomachy and the fight to hold onto sovereignty against forces of chaos in the Gigantomachy. Euripides only twice refers to the Titanomachy, but such usage, I would argue, is intentional and highlights the potency of Zeus' thunderbolts as weapons against the Titans. Both cosmogonic wars are used by the playwright primarily to underscore the supremacy of Zeus and the defeat of all those who would venture against him. Seneca, on the other hand, makes more extended use of both wars, but such references serve to emphasize Jupiter's potential to *lose* his domain, rather than accentuate his supremacy. The Giants and Typhoeus in particular are emblematic of Jupiter's rather insecure position. He may be the lord of Olympus still, but he may not be forever.

The figures of Capaneus and Ajax are moulded on these Titanic and gigantomachic beings and receive similarly harsh treatment from Zeus and Athena. The extent to which Zeus is willing to involve himself personally in punishing acts of hubris has a correlation to the nature of the hubris committed. Capaneus receives Zeus' thunderbolts from the god's own hands indicating the seriousness of Capaneus' crimes. Such involvement also showcases Zeus' might and continued interest in maintaining cosmic balance. The thunderbolts levelled against Ajax are the same weapons Zeus used against Capaneus, but they are issued instead from Pallas' hands. The force behind the punishment is no less, but the presence of Pallas instead of Jupiter, demonstrates the level of concern the god has for

Ajax's crime. He realizes the man is no threat to his own *imperium* and can thus leave the

punishment to his "double" Pallas.   In this respect, Zeus and Jupiter are rather similar and

they intervene only when required; such requirement seems to be a veritable threat to their

own stability or to the cosmic order. Otherwise, they make use of other deities when

needing to punish mortals, preferring to stay more aloof whenever possible.

There are two characters who do go beyond the mere threats of Ajax and Capaneus, although neither *overtly* expresses a desire to undermine or expel Zeus or Jupiter. Seneca's Medea, through language, imagery and associations, is progressively shown to model herself on and mimic the god Jupiter. She does not explicitly profess any aspiration to challenge the god's will, but she is successful in destabilizing the cosmos and does become a successful threat to his supremacy. Seneca's Atreus, however, succeeds even where Medea fails to go: although he again does not express any overt designs to overthrow the gods, this is precisely what he accomplishes. By the end of the play Atreus has emptied the heavens of its inhabitants as he himself takes their place. Jupiter is shown in each of these plays to be ineffectual in meeting the challenges presented by each of these theomachic individuals. Although Medea does not launch a *direct* challenge to Jupiter, her departure at the end of the play suggests that if she were to launch such a challenge, she has the potential to be successful. Atreus succeeds even here and Jupiter cannot thwart his usurpation of the heavenly throne. It is in these two plays especially that Seneca portrays Jupiter at his weakest and most vulnerable state and one from which the god cannot recover.

Covert Threat: Medea

Like Ajax and Capaneus, Medea may be characterized as a threat to Jupiter in Seneca's *Medea*; but unlike them, she never *directly* attacks, undermines or suggests that she wishes to challenge Jupiter's will. Furthermore, unlike Ajax and Capaneus, who are ultimately unsuccessful in the endeavours to test the god's supremacy and omnipotence, Medea is quite successful in at least matching the authority of Jupiter and becoming a true threat to his world order and sovereignty. Although Medea never attempts to complete her usurpation of Jupiter's position, it becomes clear by the end of the drama that she could successfully challenge Jupiter's will and potentially overturn his cosmos. Medea does not seem to have any designs to go this far with her abilities, but their potential to wreak such chaos is enough to warrant labelling her a "threat" and a successful one at that. We are relieved, I think, at the end of the play when Medea departs into the ether that she does not attempt any further havoc than that created in Corinth, for it seems the longer she remains on earth (or in the play) the more unstable and uncertain things become. Although her opposition to Jupiter is secondary to the satiation of her anger toward Jason, it is nonetheless present and nonetheless worrisome.

Medea's opposition to Jupiter, which builds over the course of the play, can be illustrated through the various articulations of her inherited divinity (her descent from both Sol and Oceanus provide two impressive divine relatives upon whom Medea can model her actions) and her gradual usurpation of Jupiter's own attributes (the use of lightning and fire, the ability to grant life or death and the *auctoritas* to enable her will to be done). Throughout the play, the qualities that Medea exhibits, either inherited or learned, and the actions she takes, place her in opposition to the gods and to Jupiter in particular. Her choices and the consequences of those choices reinforce the threat that Medea really is, but it is not until it is too late that her audience, both in the play and beyond, realize the full extent of her capabilities and the harm that she could bring to the larger world should she choose to do so.

Divine Heritage I: "Granddaughter of the Sun:"[546]

The fact of Medea's *inherited*, rather than *inherent*, divinity[547] would not, on its own, necessitate Medea's opposition to Jupiter; indeed, it would almost necessitate an

---

[546] Title of Luschnig's 2007 monograph.

acceptance of his divine order and sovereignty over it. The importance of her (inherited) divinity lies instead in its enabling quality – it is precisely because of her genealogy and descent that Medea can achieve her goals and have the ability to accomplish what she does. The emphasis on *inherited* divinity is of importance, for Medea is not divine in and of herself (at least not until the end, when she experiences an apotheosis of sorts, appearing in place of a *dea ex machina*) and thus her acts remain in the human realm; it is as a mortal woman that she punishes Jason and gradually augments her own abilities until they match those of Jupiter.[548] Medea's descent from Sol provides her with three relatives who aid in this gradual divinization and who offer her (either "genetically" or through example) paths and abilities which enable her to effect the outcomes she desires: the most significant and important is Sol, her paternal grandfather and the one from whom Medea seeks assistance; the second is Phaëthon, her cousin and a parallel counterpart who offers a negative example of how to assert one's divine affiliation; finally there is her father Aëetes, whose relationship to Medea, although literally abolished in his death, nonetheless provides

---

[547] Littlewood (2004) 149: "The theme of the human inheritance of divine power is introduced at the opening through the Argonautic myth, but in the subsequent lines it is Medea who gradually assumes divine power."

[548] The status of Medea as mortal, semi-divine or fully divine by the end of Euripides' *Medea* is explored by several scholars, e.g. Cunningham 1954; Collinge 1962; Knox 1977; Cowherd 1983; Worthington 1990; Konstan 2007, based on imagery which is common to both plays (the escape in the chariot, Medea's descent from Sol/Helios, her ability to murder her own children). Seneca's Medea, however, differs significantly from her Euripidean counterpart and studies discussing the divinity of Seneca's Medea are relatively few. The most obvious departure in Seneca's characterization is in Medea's magical abilities, which Seneca chooses to highlight and put on display and which are often used to define Medea as a witch, rather than a goddess. The most prominent advocate for Medea's divinity in this play is Nussbaum (1997); Schiesaro (2003) and Littlewood (2004) also see Medea as embodying divine elements, although neither believes her to be a goddess of any description. The most recent and persuasive arguments for Medea's divinity can be found in Walsh (2011) 80-131.

Medea with a past life in a symbolic "golden age." Together these relations of Medea guide her actions and offer her a way of moving forward after Jason. The separation of Medea from Jason results in a loss of identity for Medea and her divine relations offer (what seems to be) the only possible identity left for her to assume.[549] Unfortunately for Jupiter, this movement toward Medea-as-deity results in a new threat to his cosmos and one which he may not be able to thwart should Medea choose to exercise her capabilities to their full extent.

The importance of Medea's descent from Sol is apparent very early in Seneca's play. The loss of Medea's identity as Jason's wife and earlier as her father's daughter, leaves the heroine with few male relatives from whom she can gain validation. Sol, as Medea's closest male relative, is naturally the one to whom she first turns and her prayer to him at the beginning of the play indicates the importance she will now place on this relationship:[550]

> spectat hoc nostri sator
> Sol generis, et spectatur, et curru insidens
> per solita puri spatia decurrit poli?
> non redit in ortus et remetitur diem?
> da, da per auras curribus patriis vehi,
> committe habenas, genitor, et flagrantibus
> ignifera loris tribue moderari iuga . . . (*Med.* 29-34).

This introductory appeal to Sol not only emphasizes Medea's divine inheritance as the granddaughter of the Sun, but it foreshadows her exit in a chariot at the end of the play. This appeal for a chariot also introduces the first symbol upon which Medea's thematic characterizations and associations all hinge: the chariot not only links her to Sol but also to

---

[549] The theme of "identity" in Seneca's *Medea* has long been recognized and general discussions of the topic can be found in Henry and Walker (1967); Guastella (2001); Fitch and McElduff (2002); Benton (2003); Roisman (2005) esp. 82-86; and Walsh (2011).

[550] See Walsh (2012) chapter II and esp. 85-87 for a discussion of this particular entreaty to Sol.

Phaëthon, her element of fire and, her chthonic familiars, the serpents (which also link her to her other grandfather, Oceanus, discussed below, pp. 296-301).

In the play, as in the myth, Sol as Medea's grandfather is of paramount importance. Even before her direct appeal to him for assistance (33), she includes him in her list of deities by whom Jason swore his marriage pledges, as the god who "divides the day" (*dividens orbi diem*, 5) and will grant her the one day she needs to accomplish her deeds (298).[551] Medea traces her lineage back to him once again during her conversation with Creon: *quondam nobili fulsi patre, / avoque clarum Sole deduxi genus* (209-10). The light of the Sun is Medea's heritage and she sees herself as not only inheriting his nobility and divinity, but also his light: she herself shines and she repeats this to Creon a few lines later, *decore regali potens / fulsi* (217-18). Her description not only foreshadows the deaths of Creon and his daughter, whose fortunes will also be reversed (*rapida Fortuna ac levis / praecepsque regno eripuit, exilio dedit*, 219-20), but she also blurs the meaning of the Sun's light. On the surface she is presenting herself as a descendent of pure (i.e. good) light, but underneath that surface is lurking the more threatening undertones of his fire, his heat, his destructive element. These are the qualities she inherits; these are the qualities she will use to her advantage and to Creon and Creusa's demise.[552]

That Medea places her descent from Sol above all else is further demonstrated by her determination that her children, as relatives of Sol, should not mix with those of lesser status, principally those related to Sisyphus, the ancestor of Creon and Creusa (512). In order to ensure such mixing never happens she uses the gifts Sol gave to her father Aeëtes, a robe and a necklace, with which to conceal a heaven-wrought concoction of fatal fire

---

[551] Although expunged from the current texts, line 768 would reinforce the idea that Sol (or Phoebus) halts the day for Medea: *die relicto Phoebus in medio stetit*, or conversely, that Medea has successfully halted the day through her magic and arts.

[552] Fyfe (1983) 82.

(570-74). Medea equips her sons with the precise items Sol presented to her family as proof of their divine heritage: it is as though Medea herself is now bestowing upon her children their own gifts of lineage. But theirs will not be so pure, for the robe and necklace must first be anointed with death (*sed ante diris inlita ac tincta artibus . . . flamma iam tectis sonet* (576-78). Medea's children inherit, not Sol's gifts, but her perverted version of them: death and destruction; their fate is sealed in this bestowal. The last image of Sol is an appeal by the chorus for him to hide the sunlight, echoing Medea's first reference to him as the god who apportions daylight (5):

> Nunc, Phoebe, mitte currus
> nullo morante loro,
> nox condat alma lucem,
> mergat diem timendum
>   dux noctis Hesperus (*Med.* 874-78).

They do not wish him to see the destruction that awaits the last members of this "noble" line. This is, in fact, the last image of Sol in the play, for when Medea exits in the chariot at the end of the play she is not escaping because Sol has saved her by sending her his personal chariot. The chariot in which she will escape is not Sol's horse-drawn chariot, but rather one led by a team of fiery-snakes, perhaps indicating that this chariot is her own. Equally, Sol cannot hide from the destruction of Corinth, of his great-grandsons or the achievement of his granddaughter. Medea has ensured that the daylight he apportions to the world is enough for her and he must witness her triumph as she had predicted he would.

Chariots of Fire: Medea and Phaëthon

The image of the chariot is an important one throughout the play and became an important aspect of Medea's myth since its appearance at the end of Euripides' tragedy as her mode of escape to Athens. The main difference in Seneca's version is that Medea escapes not to Athens, but into the heavens (*caelum*, 1022) and, as Jason says, to a place where there are no gods (*nullos . . . deos*, 1027). The escape in the chariot is significant in both plays, but that significance is muddied by the supposed granting of Sol's personal vehicle to Medea as she requested at the outset of the play (29-34, quoted above, p. 286). Medea does ask for her paternal or ancestral (*patriis*, 32) chariot and this must mean that she wishes, as her cousin did, to drive the sun-chariot and to take the reins of the fiery horses which lead it.[553] The problem, however, is that this is not how she escapes. She does take off in a chariot, but it is not led by the horses of the Sun. Instead, twin serpents are yoked to her chariot (*gemini colla serpentes iugo*, 1023), an image that is not at all reminiscent of Sol. This image of Medea flying into the heavens on a winged chariot is an image of her apotheosis; she is joining the ranks of divinities,[554] each of whom has their own personal chariot.[555]

But these book-end images of the chariot are enhanced by the other story of a descendant of Sol wishing to drive his chariot. The story of Phaëthon is significant, not only in terms of its relevance to Medea and her mode of escape, but also to the Argonautic expedition and the other themes of importance throughout the play. It is brought to the forefront in the third ode where the tale of his quest for divinity provides an *exemplum* of

---

[553] Assumed by Fitch and McElduff (2002) 28 n. 26.

[554] Knox (1977) 212: "But supernatural winged chariots . . . are properties, in Greek mythology, of gods . . ." Although Knox's comments are made in the context of discussing Euripides' *Medea*, they nevertheless can be applied to Seneca's play here.

[555] Sol's chariot is always drawn by horses, fiery though they may be, and, indeed, his team is considered to be the first use of the quadriga (Hyg. *Astronomica* 2.13). Each divinity has its own chariot, drawn by its own set of animals: Ares has a four-horse chariot, as does Zeus; Artemis has a four-hind chariot; Poseidon's chariot is drawn by four fish-tailed horses; Demeter's chariot is drawn by snakes as is the chariot of Triptolemus, Hades' by four black horses, Dionysus' by tigers. Medea's use of a serpent-drawn chariot fits the divine pattern well.

those who seek to transgress natural boundaries and of those who seek to attain a higher

status than that allotted to them:

> ausus aeternos agitare currus
> immemor metae iuvenis paternae
> quos polo sparsit furiosus ignes
> > ipse recepit (*Med.* 599-602).

The figure of Phaëthon in this play is widely recognized as an analogy to Jason and his

crew: where Phaëthon attempted to conquer the skies, the Argonauts attempted to conquer

the sea; Phaëthon paid with his life first and the Argonauts, save Jason, have also paid with

theirs.[556] But Phaëthon does not only parallel Jason and his fellow crew members – Medea

too will fly in a winged chariot, effectively re-treading the path that he took and she too

will leave part of the world aflame.[557] The difference of course is that where Phaëthon

failed, Medea will triumph. Phäethon provides Medea not only with an exemplum and

model to follow, but a model which failed, showing her the potential for disaster.

Unfortunately for Jason, Creusa, Creon and the Corinthians, disaster is exactly what

Medea is looking to accomplish.

Phaëthon was struck with one of Jupiter's bolts before he could cause any more

damage to the earth as he fell aflame from Sol's chariot. Medea not only pays heed to his

story and thus makes use of her cousin's misfortune in a psychological way, but she also

takes advantage of the physical remains of his downfall. Medea literally uses the flames

from his body to her benefit: in her incantation to Hecate, Medea takes precisely the "ever-

---

[556] Bishop (1965) 314; Fyfe (1983) 89-90; Henderson (1983) 100-01; Davis (1993) 88; Littlewood
(2004) 148-71; Walsh (2012) esp. 52-60. For a discussion of Phaëthon in Senecan tragedy in
general, see Littlewood (2004) 103-71.

[557] As Littlewood (2004) 157 aptly comments: "Through the double identifications with the figure
of Phaëthon Medea and the Argonauts resemble each other; through the double identification
Medea recalls the crime for which the Argonauts die."

living flames of lightning" (*vivacis fulgura flammae*, 826[558]) from Phaëthon's body, as if usurping the lightning that brought him down will enable her to recreate the fire he had caused. Medea remembers and utilizes the myth of Phaëthon to provide herself with a precedent and a reason to call upon the Sun in the manner that she does. She traces her cousin's path once more, but now she is mindful of his mistakes and with his ashes she will triumph.

A key difference in the two requests to Sol for his chariot is that Phäethon wished to drive it as proof of his descent from Sol; Medea will only receive her own chariot after she proves her worthiness to drive it. She was already granted gifts from Sol to prove her divine lineage (the robe and necklace), thus the chariot is either an unnecessary third object as evidence of Sol's ancestry, or it is being used for an altogether different purpose. Although Medea mimics Phaëthon in many ways in order to achieve her revenge, and her request to Sol suggests a further parallel, Medea's abrupt departure *upward* through a path to heaven (*patuit in caelum via*, 1022) in a chariot drawn by serpents, suggests a clear departure from her model. Although she will leave Corinth in flames, she herself will be heading in the opposite direction: toward the gods and toward her own divinity.[559]

"Fire is her Patrimony, as Snakes are her Familiars"[560]

The final image of Medea departing in her chariot includes two further elements of intrinsic importance to her characterization: fire and serpents. The flame which Medea imposes upon Corinth is a heaven-wrought destruction, not willed by the gods, but rather

---

[558] The notion that Phaëthon's body was still smouldering is present in Euripides' fragmentary *Phaëthon* and may have inspired Seneca's imagery: cf. *Phaëthon* 215: ἀτμὸν ἐμφανῆ <φλογός>.

[559] Henry and Walker (1967) 178.

[560] Nussbaum (1997) 219.

by Medea herself. The climax of Medea's use of fire occurs during her incantation where she provides details about the nature of the fire she will use against the royal household. The fiery mixture not only includes the flames of her cousin Phaëthon but also the fire of Prometheus, which he stole from Jupiter and now pays for with his liver, as well as a sulphuric fire given to her by Mulciber:

> Ignis fulvo clausus in auro
> latet obscurus,
> quem mihi caeli qui furta luit
> viscere feto
> dedit et docuit
> condere vires arte, Prometheus.
> dedit et tenui
> sulphure tectos Mulciber ignes,
> et vivacis fulgura flammae
> de cognato Phaethonte tuli (*Med.* 820-27).

Thus, not only does Medea have an inherited ability to manipulate fire, but she is also equipped with heaven-wrought fires and flames, gifted to her (by Prometheus and Mulciber) or taken by her for her own use (from Phaëthon). The result is a devastatingly fatal fire of ultimately divine origin. It is of little wonder that neither Creusa nor Creon survive the onslaught; however, Medea's manipulation of this heavenly fire suggests an ability on her part to punish mortals with the same degree of intensity as a goddess[561] and even to match Jupiter's fires, for her combination of flames includes his own fire augmented by that of another deity.

The scene is emblematic of Medea's sorcery and is used by Seneca to illustrate her magical prowess, but as a whole it receives little attention from scholars who interpret it as nothing more than a way to differentiate Seneca's Medea from that of Euripides.[562] But to

---

[561] For a discussion of Medea exhibiting goddess-like qualities, see Walsh (2012) 80-131.

[562] Guastalla (2001) 209 is less dismissive, but nevertheless views the scene as constructed "according to the literary taste of his own times" rather than interpreting it with any thematic implications.

pass over the scene without seeing anything more than Medea's witchcraft at work would be to miss the cosmic significance of the elements Seneca has her use.[563] A witch she might be, but no ordinary witch. None but she could have access to ashes from Phaëthon's body, or the fire of Prometheus, who *taught* her how to use it. Not only does fire course through her body as a descendant of Sol, but she surrounds herself with it, she becomes it.[564]

Fire as an element and as an image is present throughout the play[565] from the very beginning through to the end. But it is not only fire that Medea is attuned to; the serpent or snake is also present and paired with the first image of fire:

> nunc, nunc adeste, sceleris ultrices deae,
> crinem solutis squalidae serpentibus,
> atram cruentis manibus amplexae facem . . . (*Med.* 13-15).

Fire and snakes have long been recognized as associated in Latin poetry[566] and Seneca's *Medea* is no exception. In this initial image of fire and snake, the two are condensed into the figure of the Fury, a figure that Medea herself becomes over the course of the play. It is, however, before and during the incantation scene that the image of the snake becomes

---

[563] For example, Roisman (2005) 85 offers at least a surface interpretation of the scene: "This emphasis on Medea's . . . witchcraft serves two functions. First it enables Seneca to show the means by which Medea accomplishes her vengeance. . . The other function of Medea's 'witchness' is that it . . . epitomizes his heroine's superhuman evil." Roisman does not, however, discuss in detail the use of the divine sources of fire, which would enhance her argument of Medea's "evilness."

[564] Pratt (1963) 216: "Fire is so much identified with Medea . . ."; Fyfe (1983) 83: "Medea is presented in part as an elemental force working directly on Creusa, Creon and Corinth"; Berry (1996) 11: "the fires of her anger – her primary weapon and the source of her power."

[565] See Henderson (1983) 99 for a catalogue of fire imagery.

[566] The first significant work on the pairing is Knox (1950); in Seneca's *Medea*, see Nussbaum (1997) esp. 234-40.

the dominant figure itself rather than the person who wears or associates with them. She

begins by calling the snakes of the natural world:

> tracta magicis cantibus
> squamifera latebris turba desertis adest.
> hic saeva serpens corpus immensum trahit
> trifidamque linguam exertat et quaerit quibus
> mortifera veniat; carmine audito stupet,
> tumidumque nodis corpus aggestis plicat
> cogitque in orbes (*Med.* 684-690).

But these earthly serpents are not strong enough for her purposes; she must look to heaven

(*caelo petam venena*, 692) for appropriate monsters. Thus, she calls on more other-worldly

snakes:

> huc ille vasti more torrentis iacens
> descendat anguis, cuius immensos duae,
> maior minorque, sentiunt nodos ferae
> (maior Pelasgis apta, Sidoniis minor),
> pressasque tandem solvat Ophiuchus manus
> virusque fundat; adsit ad cantus meos
> lacessere ausus gemina Python numina,
> et Hydra et omnis redeat Herculea manu
> succisa serpens, caede se reparans sua.
> tu quoque relictis pervigil Colchis ades,
> sopite primum cantibus, serpens, meis (694-704).

The majority of these snakes took on Olympian deities as their prey; the final serpent, the

one who guards the fleece, is perhaps the most dangerous, being the sacred animal of

Mars. That Medea is able, by her chanting, to mesmerize such a beast is no mere feat. Such

a tale is reminiscent of Hermes lulling to sleep Argus (Ov. *Met.* 1.668-723), another beast

whom none could put to sleep, except for a god. Medea's magic, or innate power over

Mars' sacred serpent suggests she can rival the gods themselves.

In fact, Medea is not yet through with her use of serpents; there is one final snake

for her to offer up in order for her to complete her ritual. To Hecate she sacrifices the limbs

of Typhoeus, Jupiter's most powerful enemy:

Tibi haec cruenta serta texuntur manu,

                    novena quae serpens ligat,
            tibi haec Typhoeus membra quae discors tulit,
                qui regna concussit Iovis (*Med.* 771-76).

Medea began with snakes of the earth and she ends with the earth's most powerful

chthonic progeny. How she acquired his limbs is not stated, but her wish to use Typhoeus

as part of her weapon against her enemies suggests she is taking on his own attributes. She

is simultaneously proving her control over such a creature (assimilating herself with

Jupiter) and using Typhoeus' power to augment her own (placing herself in opposition to

Jupiter). Medea's control over both snakes and fire may be part-and-parcel of a witch's

repertoire, but the specific details Seneca provides suggest Medea is something far more

powerful.

The importance of Medea's relationship to Sol is underscored throughout the

tragedy, for it is precisely this relationship which Medea uses to construct her identity, or

at least one aspect of it. But the significance of Sol as Medea's grandfather is far greater

than just being a divine ancestor: it is through the chariot which Medea requests from him

that the heroine's multi-faceted characterization is articulated. The chariot is the symbol

through which Medea's celestial inheritance (in its many forms) is brought together. Not

only is the chariot a symbol of Medea's eventual apotheosis, granting her a status and

ethereal access equal to that of the gods, but it is also the symbol of fiery destruction,

notably through the exemplum of her cousin Phaëthon. It is both a symbol of immortality

and flaming cosmic ruin. But this is not all. The most significant visual clue to the

chariot's meaning is embedded in the team which is yoked to the chariot and pulls Medea

into the heavens: fire-breathing serpents. The element which brought Phaëthon down is

that which will carry Medea away; but the horses are replaced with the ultimate chthonic

symbol: the snake. Such creatures are at home with Medea. They symbolize fertility, but

also the early creative powers of Gaia: it was a serpent, Typhoeus, which offered Jupiter the ultimate test as he battled for cosmic power. And once again the serpents have arisen, but this time under the imperium of a woman with the knowledge of the past and the ability to forge a new future.

Divine Heritage II: Granddaughter of the Ocean:

Medea's descent from Sol is a clear and important part of the heroine's mythic identity; however, it is only one of her two illustrious lineages. The ancients knew the rest of Medea's genealogy even though it is rarely mentioned: her mother was an Oceanid goddess of knowledge named Eidyia, who was born of Oceanus and Tethys (Apollon. Rhod. 3.268; Hes. *Theog.* 960; Ps.-Apollod. *Bibl.* 1.9.23). Such a genealogy, descended from Titans on both sides of her family, is significant for Medea and indeed for the play as a whole.[567] But Medea's maternal ancestry is often neglected and even ignored, despite the fact that it has a significant "presence" in the very fabric of her myths: her descent from Helios/Sol or even her status as niece of Circe, receives far greater attention. Yet as a granddaughter of Ocean, it should come as no surprise that Medea is the first maiden to travel across the seas; as a daughter of a goddess of knowledge, Medea's characterization as someone who is clever and can match wits with men makes perfect sense. Whether or not the authors of her myths were consciously creating a Medea-story that included these details because of her ancestry cannot be known: but these details are an intrinsic part of her identity and I would argue it is at least partially because of this genealogy that she is constructed as she is. Further details borne out of Seneca's play, such as Medea's presentation as the price or "dowry" for the Argonautic voyage; her clear associations with water imagery; the importance of Prometheus (another of Medea's cousins) in her

---

[567] It may also be significant that Eidyia, Medea's mother, is the *youngest* of the Oceanides (Apollon. 3. 244-245), replicating the notion that the youngest child poses the greatest threat.

achievement of success, strengthen this argument and point toward a Medea who is constructed to be as powerful and deific as her Titanic ancestry could make her.

Medea's descent from Oceanus is not mentioned by Seneca, but this ancestry remains present throughout the play, potentially from the first few lines. Medea's opening monologue has her call on several deities including the "master of the sea" (*dominator maris*, 4):

> quaeque domituram freta
> Tiphyn novam frenare docuisti ratem,
> et tu, profundi saeve dominator maris (*Med*. 2-4).

It is generally understood as a reference to Neptune,[568] but the epithet would work equally well for Oceanus, especially given Medea's ancestry. This is the sole extant use of the word pair *dominator maris* and the closest parallel, *dominator freti*, is found in Seneca's *Phaedra* (1159). That both *freta* and *maris* appear in Medea's prayer may suggest the two are not meant to be understood as synonymous.[569] Both can mean "the sea" but the former can also indicate smaller portions of it, such as straights and channels.[570] If one accepts *dominator maris* as an epithet of Oceanus, Medea's prayer has her call on both of her

---

[568] Costa (1973) 62: "Neptune and the Sun are invoked because the former allowed Jason to sail over his waters to Colchis and the latter was M.'s grandfather." A reference to Oceanus here would create a prayer to both of Medea's grandfathers, not only producing a nice parallel, but also suggesting that Jason's voyage in the Argo and abandonment of Medea wrongs Oceanus twice over.

[569] Certainly Fitch's translation (344) would suggest a slightly different semantic range for the two words: "and you who taught Tiphys to bridle the novel ship that would tame **the seas**; and you ferocious tamer of **the deep sea**."

[570] *fretum* appears again during the first choral ode when they ask for the gods who rule heaven and sea to be present (57); the context here would indicate Neptune is being summoned. Indeed, Neptune was conceived of, in early Roman cult, as a fresh-water deity rather than a god of the seas, Dumézil (1996) 389.

grandfathers, her closest male relatives, to witness her plight and furthermore, it introduces Oceanus into a narrative with which he is closely associated.[571]

Moreover, when Medea speaks of her own ancestry to Creon (which begins with her descent from Sol) she defines her origins through reference to water boundaries:

> quodcumque placidus flexibus Phasis rigat,
> Pontusque quidquid Scythicus a tergo videt,
> palustribus qua maria dulcescunt aquis,
> armata peltis quidquid exterret cohors
> inclusa ripis vidua Thermodontiis,
> hoc omne noster genitor imperio regit (*Med.* 211-16).[572]

Such a description is unsurprising given Medea's foreign identity, but such an emphasis on watery regions, specifically in the context of her genealogy, ties the heroine to water thematically as well as ancestrally.[573] But Medea's watery heritage is not only illustrated through her ties to physical watery locations, but also iconographically. The snake, or serpent, with which Medea is clearly associated is likely inherited from none other than her maternal grandfather, Oceanus, whose artistic representation is of

a half-man, half serpent divinity.[574]

Oceanus even appears twice in Seneca's play by name, the first during the second choral ode, whose theme is the Argonautic voyage and the cosmic implications of its

---

[571] Another such reference to Oceanus may be found in the third choral ode where the Corinthians ask the "gods of the sea" to spare Jason: *Parcite, o divi*, 595; *Iam satis, divi, mare vindicastis*, 669. The references are both oblique in terms of their intended recipients and they could merely be gods in general. If specific deities were in fact understood to be the referents, Neptune and Oceanus would be the most logical choices.

[572] *genitor* could here also indicate Oceanus himself as Medea's progenitor, although the context would suggest Aeëtes is the referent.

[573] Medea is also constantly compared to the sea or as having "watery" characteristics: 388, 392,406, 411-14; 586-89; 762-66; 940-43; see Henderson (1983) *passim*.

[574] Beaulieu (2012) 4860 notes this serpentine depiction became common in the Hellenistic period and throughout the Roman period.

success.[575] The ode begins by describing the first oceanic voyage and ends with what has sometimes been viewed as a prophetic description of the new world:

> Venient annis saecula seris,
> quibus Oceanus vincula rerum
> laxet, et ingens pateat tellus,
> Tethysque novos detegat orbes (*Med.* 375-78).

Oceanus and Tethys, one of the earth's primordial couples, are mentioned here in a very cosmic way: they once created all the world's waterways (symbolized by the Oceanides and the Flumina/Potamoi) and they will once again open new worlds after this conquest by the Argo. Medea's role in this cosmic turn of events is made clear in the preceding stanza when the chorus reflect on the "rewards" of Jason's quest:

> Quod fuit huius pretium cursus?
> aurea pellis
> maiusque mari Medea malum,
> merces prima digna carina (361-63).

Medea is compared to the sea as a destructive (elemental) force, but she is also described in a very mercantile fashion as though she herself was "bought" through the Argonautic expedition. Throughout the play Medea is very concerned with her dowry[576] and places much emphasis on its return: this particular ode highlights the transaction between Jason and the seas and one might go so far as to suggest that between Jason and Oceanus. Medea is not only the "prize" but also the "price" in both a destructive sense (in that she becomes a tool for the revenge for the conquest of the sea) and in a contractual sense (in terms of Jason and Medea's marriage).[577] Although Seneca does not emphasize the relationship

---

[575] This particular ode in conjunction with the ode following it have been the subject of much scholarly discussion; see e.g. Bishop (1965); Lawall (1979); Segal (1983) 237-42; Fyfe (1983) 86-91; Henderson (1983) 100-11; Davis (1993) 78-93; Benton (2003); and Littlewood (2004) 151-60.

[576] See especially Abrahamsen (1999) for a discussion of the dowry as an important theme.

[577] Bishop (1965) 314; Littlewood (2004) 153-54; Walsh (2011) 121.

between Oceanus and Tethys and Medea, the ode itself is very much concerned, first with the process of the Argo breaking the established covenants of the known world through its conquest of the sea (*bene dissaepti foedera mundi / traxit in unum*, 335-36), here clearly symbolized by Oceanus and Tethys; and secondly, with the acquisition of the latter's granddaughter, whose presence in her new surroundings will be catastrophic. There is a parallelism established between the Argo's intrusion into Medea's homeland (which is described using motifs of the golden age[578]) and Medea's intrusion into the Greek world. With the desecration and destruction of the Colchian lands (and thus a movement from a "golden age" to an "iron age")[579] there is a displacement of Colchians themselves (embodied by Medea) who now need to establish a place of their own once again.[580] It is clear that Medea cannot stay in Corinth, or indeed in any Greek (i.e. Roman) city and thus her eventual movement toward the ether as the only place left for her to inhabit.[581]

The second appearance of Oceanus in the text occurs during Medea's incantation scene as she assembles her offerings to Hecate. Medea proclaims her power over the weather (usually the prerogative of Jupiter) and her control over the ocean: *egique ad imum maria, et Oceanus graves / interius undas aestibus victis dedit*, 755-56. Oceanus has

---

[578] Candida nostri saecula patres / videre, procul fraude remota. / sua quisque piger litora tangens / patrioque senex factus in arvo, parvo dives, / nisi quas tulerat natale solum / non norat opes (*Med.* 329-34).

[579] Ovid (*Met.* 1.89-150) offers a description of the "ages of man" similar to that of Hesiod, but with minor variations which parallel well the themes of Seneca's *Medea*: e.g. in the Golden Age, Ovid explains that there were no need of laws, for crime and punishment were unheard of (90-2); men knew of only their own shores (96); and food was plentiful with no need to work the soil (102-04). In contrast, Ovid's Iron Age is characterized by the lack of truth and *fides* (129); the navigation of the sea (132-34); and war and familial strife were rampant (142-46).

[580] Medea's Nurse, in fact, earlier makes this explicit: *abiere Colchi* (164).

[581] One may compare this displacement of Medea to that of Juno in Seneca's *Hercules Furens*. The goddess complains of the intrusion into the heavens by the conquests of Jupiter and thus makes her presence known in the mortal world, again with disastrous consequences.

"consigned his waves to the interior," as Medea has conquered his tides, suggesting that she now fully embodies the power of seas, but also that she is now in control of her emotions which have until this point been in flux. The end of this stanza emphasizes Medea's control over the watery elements both physical and metaphysical: *sonuere fluctus, tumuit insanum mare* (765). The "waves have sounded" and the "unsound sea has swelled." Seneca's use of the perfect tense here denotes a completed action – the waves are now done sounding and the sea now finished swelling, neither will do so again. The inclusion of *insanum* to describe the sea also suggests that Medea's earlier *insanitas* (*insanit*, 383) is now over as well.[582] Only once more will Medea be likened to the sea (941) and it will be a conflict within her of two different waves, rather than a conquest over Oceanus as in her incantation.

Medea and Prometheus: Images of a Golden Age

The second of Medea's cousins to appear in the tragedy is Prometheus (his mother was an Oceanid, just as Medea's mother was). Unlike Phaëthon, whose myth is recognized as an important parallel to Medea and Jason, Prometheus' significance has been underestimated.[583] He appears by name twice during the incantation scene, but his image is invoked periphrastically much earlier. When Medea is first contemplating her revenge against Jason she wants to keep the image of the Caucasus in her mind and her words suggest that Prometheus' punishment is the object of her image:

> per viscera ipsa quaere supplicio viam,
> si vivis, anime, si quid antiqui tibi
> remanet vigoris. pelle femineos metus,
> et inhospitalem Caucasum mente indue (*Med.* 40-43).

---

[582] Littlewood (2004) 59-60.

[583] The best discussion of Prometheus' relevance in *Medea* is Walsh (2011) 117-31.

The Caucasus is the location of Prometheus' punishment, although it may also be an inhospitable region which invokes fear. But even more important than the mention of Prometheus' place of agony, is the reference to the punishment itself: *per viscera*. Just as it was through Prometheus' liver that Jupiter tortured his enemy, it will be through Medea's *viscera* (1013) that she punishes Jason. The children she has already borne to Jason and any that may yet be born will die by the sword, providing the potential for a recurring punishment should Medea have any further children. When the Caucasus is next mentioned (much later in the text) it is followed immediately by Prometheus' name (*Caucasus Promethei*, 709) as though to signal the important relationship between the two words. Prometheus' recurring punishment provides Medea with yet another mode of action to adopt and adapt in both its metaphor of place (the guts) and of time (repeated punishment).[584]

Prometheus is mentioned twice during the incantation scene: first by the Nurse as she describes the various items Medea is gathering for her concoction and then by Medea herself in reference to his theft of Jupiter's fire. Medea uses both a plant which bears the blood of Prometheus[585] (*quae fert . . . / sparsus cruore Caucasus Promethei*, 708-09) as well as his stolen fire. Much like Medea's use of Phaëthon's ashes after his downfall, which she makes use of to augment her own powers, her use of a plant bearing Prometheus' blood suggests she is again attempting to extract his "essence" for her own purposes. Prometheus was able to match wits with Jupiter and to bring about civilization through his theft of Jupiter's fire – but he was not able to escape the wrath of Jupiter and

---

[584] Walsh (2011) 69-70 discusses Medea's act of taking a sword to her own *viscera* in terms of the symbolic penetration of the female body by the male. Although she does not link the two figures in this way, Prometheus' own torment by Jupiter is similarly symbolic of the god "feminizing" the Titan as further humiliation.

[585] This plant may be identified as mandrake, a hallucinogenic plant with a history of use in witchcraft, specifically for making love philtres.

thus suffered for his crime. Medea, on the other hand, is as capable as Prometheus at matching wits and has abilities to match his own. She too "steals" fire in the form of Phaëthon's ashes (826-27, burnt by Jupiter) and is given fire by Prometheus (again from Jupiter):

> Ignis fulvo clausus in auro
> latet obscurus,
> quem mihi caeli qui furta luit
> viscere feto
> dedit et docuit
> condere vires arte, Prometheus (*Med.* 820-24).

Medea's fire is thus no less stolen than it had been originally, but the intention for it has changed drastically. Prometheus used it in order to provide mankind with the tools for civilization (cooked food, metallurgy *et cetera*); Medea will now use it to destroy the very foundation of civilization, in both the political and domestic spheres.[586] She wreaks havoc on the Corinthian monarchy, killing the current ruler along with his daughter and his heirs, thus causing total ruin on the political front. The murder of her sons and future children ensures that the symbol of marriage and the family unit, upon which society is based, is also utterly destroyed. Although Medea blames Jason for the violation of their marriage pact,[587] their divorce is not quite enough to shatter the foundation of society, but her own actions against their sons certainly qualifies. Thus, while Prometheus provides a precedent for the theft of fire, Medea repeats the action with opposite intentions and results. Medea symbolizes the end of civilization, or at least, the end of the Olympian order of civilization.[588]

---

[586] Walsh (2011) 124.

[587] Recent discussions of the theme of marriage in *Medea* can be found in Abrahamsen (1999) and Guastella (2001); see also Walsh (2011) 17-79 *passim* for the theme and importance of gender.

[588] In this respect, Walsh (2011) 121-23 argues that Medea is another Pandora, in terms of Medea's ambiguous status as both a "prize" and a "reward" as well as her part in the destruction of mankind.

In the figure of Medea the elements of fire and water are combined, but they are embodied in a woman who is wholly of Titanic origin. The gods she emulates are not the celestial deities, but rather the chthonic ones – the Furies, Persephone and even Gaia. Medea harkens from a land which is, or was, before the voyage of the Argo, a remnant of the Golden Age, the Age of the Titans. That race was known for fathers killing, or attempting to kill, sons in an effort to remain in power; known also for mothers who had to choose between husbands and sons. Had Medea been male, she would have fit the pattern well: she killed her father and brother in an attempt to create a new life for herself; she then killed her sons in an attempt to hurt their father and regain control. Of course Medea is not male, but this Golden Age is also not necessarily the same Golden Age as that of her ancestors. Like Jupiter, who learned from his own father's and grandfather's mistakes in order to supplant them,[589] so too did Medea. Instead of following in their footsteps, becoming a passive partner in order to create a new order with Jason, she became the active partner and achieved success where none of her ancestors had before: the sons she bore did not survive to claim her place and, by destroying Creusa, she ensured that Jason could not replace them either. She has become equal to Jupiter, not only as an elemental force, but also as the most clever and knowledgeable Titan, the last of their race.[590]

The Last of the Titans? Medea versus Jupiter

The preceding discussion, which focused on Medea's ancestry, emphasized both her inherited qualities and the familial exempla whom she emulated and highlighted the real and potential destruction of Corinth and the wider cosmos. Both halves of her divine

---

[589] Yasumura (2011) 84.

[590] The notion that Medea is a Titan has only been tangentially suggested by Berry (1996) 12 who refers to her as a "self-empowered Titan Fortuna." He is not arguing, as I am, that Medea should be interpreted as belonging to the race of Titans herself.

ancestry are fused together and the combination produces disastrous results, not just for the mortals who surround Medea, but also for the gods and Jupiter in particular. Medea is able to challenge the gods in three distinct ways: through her embodiment of fire and water and usurpation of Jupiter's prerogatives; the use of her voice as an instrument of immense *auctoritas*; and ultimately to act as a *theomacha* by her opposition to the current divine order. It is precisely because of her knowledge, abilities and emulation of her family members that her challenge to the divine order becomes possible. The only reason she is not successful (as Atreus is in *Thyestes*), is because we are left only with the image of Medea riding into the ether: we have no idea what will happen after she arrives.

The Fusion of Fire and Water: An (Un)natural Combination

As embodied in Medea, the fusion of fire and water, two disparate elements, becomes a cause for concern, a heralding of disaster. But such a combination is not unique to her; Jupiter too enjoys and offers to mankind the benefits (but also the consequences) of both elements. As the god of weather and rain, Jupiter is intrinsically related to the element of water, but in this case, in a positive sense, for rain was needed for a good harvest. As the god of lightning, Jupiter was also intrinsically related to the element of fire, for thunderbolts not only could cause fire, but were believed to be made of fire (Sen. *NQ* 2.21.2-4).[591] Thus Jupiter too can be said to embody both elements. The important distinction, however, between the two is that the duality of Jupiter's elements represents both advantages and disadvantages; whereas the fusion of the two elements in Medea produces only destruction for those she wishes to attack. In Seneca's play this motif appears early as Medea reflects on Jason's impending marriage and wonders how he could proceed with a new marriage knowing the dangerous consequences of her crimes: *merita*

---

[591] Jupiter also produced fire/flames as portents, for example in Virg. *Aen.* 2.681-86.

contempsit mea / qui scelere flammas viderat vinci et mare? (120-21). Medea's crimes have already subdued the individual elements of fire and water and in doing so, she has embraced them as a part of who she is: *hic mare et terras vides / ferrumque et ignes et deos et fulmina* (166-67). It is at this point that Littlewood argues for Medea's gradual assumption of celestial authority,[592] setting herself up to become divine by the end of the play.[593] Such an argument is very persuasive given Medea's genealogical history, but Littlewood does not press the issue or stress the cosmic implications of what a divine Medea could accomplish. Medea's self-identification with the sea and fires (*mare* and *ignes*) is understandable, but she then goes on to include lightning and divinity as part of who she is. Such a statement should not be taken as merely rhetorical or even an exaggeration. It is foremost a threat (to her mortal enemies as well as to "the powers that be"), but it is also a prophetic and true statement of *what* Medea is and will be. The gods that she claims as part of her identity would be Sol and Oceanus, but the lightning can only belong to Jupiter. It is through her use of Jupiter's lightning that Medea will be able to assume its power too and with it, the ability to truly challenge its rightful owner.

Jupiter's fires may also be referenced in terms of the force of Medea's emotions. The second Argonautic ode begins with a description of the intensity of Medea's burning hatred after being abandoned in marriage:

> Nulla vis flammae tumidive venti
> tanta, nec teli metuenda torti,
> quanta cum coniunx viduata taedis
> ardet et odit (*Med.* 579-81).

The flames and wind may be oblique references, but they are quite compatible with Jupiter's lightning and his control over the weather. The comparison the chorus makes suggests there is no force of nature which could possibly match Medea's own personal

---

[592] Littlewood (2004) 149.

[593] Littlewood (2004) 15.

fiery hatred toward Jason. The implication is such that Jupiter's lightning bolts would be less potent than any fire Medea could create (and such a feat seems plausible after Medea concocts her heavenly-wrought fire-potion). But the chorus take the idea even further three verses later: *caecus est ignis stimulatus ira / nec regi curat patiturve frenos* (591-92). Although they are clearly referring to Medea here, there is an undertone which suggests they are again comparing her to Jupiter, himself often criticized for his careless use of thunderbolts and for blindly throwing them at undeserving mortals.[594] The implicit comparison between Medea and Jupiter is unsettling, not least because of her potential inherited power, but also because it hints at the presence of a force in the world capable of overturning Jupiter's world-order – and such hints only become more serious as the play progresses.

The most potent expression of Medea's fiery capabilities is delivered by the messenger when describing the effects of her deadly potion on the palace and its inhabitants. Not only does the fire she creates seem to be under her control but it does not follow the rules of nature – the rules which Jupiter maintains:

> Avidus per omnem regiae partem furit
> ut iussus ignis ....
> ....
> Et hoc in ista clade mirandum accidit:
> alit unda flammas, quoque prohibetur magis,
> magis ardet ignis; ipsa praesidia occupat (*Med.* 885-86, 888-90).

Even the language the messenger uses to describe what has happened suggests a god was involved, for he says the event is "miraculous" (*mirandum*). That the fire and water again combine as one highlights Medea's perversion of nature and the dangerous side effects of

---

[594] E.g., Ovid *Pont.* 3.6.27-32: *Iuppiter in multos temeraria fulmina torque / qui poenam culpa non meruere pati*; or, *Oct.* 245-46: *Pro summe genitor, tela cur frustra iacis / invicta totiens temere regali manu?*

the two elements joined as one.[595] Although Jupiter also encompasses both fire and water,

natural law, *his law*, states that water ought to extinguish fire. Medea's ability to overturn

this basic principle spells disaster for Corinth and for the wider cosmos.

Such a feat is not the first time she has disrupted Jupiter's world-order either.

During Medea's incantation, she enumerates the various ways in which she has taken

control over natural laws, those which should be the domain of Jupiter:[596]

> et evocavi nubibus siccis aquas
> egique ad imum maria, et Oceanus graves
> interius undas aestibus victis dedit;
> pariterque mundus lege confusa aetheris
> et solem et astra vidit, et vetitum mare
> tetigistis, Ursae. temporum flexi vices:
> aestiva tellus horruit cantu meo,
> coacta messem vidit hibernam Ceres.
> violenta Phasis vertit in fontem vada,
> et Hister, in tot ora divisus, truces
> compressit undas, omnibus ripis piger (754-64).

Not only has Medea subdued the tides of Oceanus, but she has forced dry clouds to

produce rain, a clear encroachment into Jupiter's domain and an abrasive challenge to his

authority. Such a challenge to Jupiter would not normally go unnoticed or unpunished.

That Medea is successful and that her powers continue to grow suggests an impotency on

the part of Jupiter to thwart her actions. And it is not only Jupiter's domain into which she

advances: Ceres too has felt the touch of Medea's magic. Such a compendium of violations

against natural law may be part of a traditional view of witchcraft; but as Medea is so

much more than a mere witch, her ability to transform the seasons and completely confuse

---

[595] Henderson (1983) 99.

[596] Cf. Sen. *Phaed.* 960-61.

night and day should not be taken lightly, especially as the latter is indicative of the worst kind of impiety.[597]

Voce non fausta

Medea's voice, what she says and how she uses her words, are significant not only for achieving her revenge, but also for the fear they generate in the rest of the characters in the play.[598] They wish her to be a silent figure, matching her status as a foreign and "barbarian" woman. It is as if they have all read the other "Medeas" and comprehend her ability to match words with deeds: Medea's threats are not idle and when she speaks things *happen*. Such a character trait is usually associated with those in power – emperors, kings, gods – and Medea's ability to use her voice with such *auctoritas* is a further demonstration of her subtle and yet successful challenge to Jupiter. Hers is the voice we hear first as she speaks the opening prologue, invoking the gods above and praying to the gods below. This scene was discussed earlier (in chapter 2, pp. 83-85) with respect to the furies, but it is worth noting again the way in which Medea subverts audience expectation through her choice of words. Of the upper deities she requests nothing; rather she directs words of ill-omen (*voce non fausta*, 12) to those who dwell in the depths of the earth: Chaos, unholy spirits of the dead, Dis, Proserpine and the Furies. These deities are requested to bring death upon Creusa, Creon and the entire royal lineage while *she* is to grant Jason the gift of life.[599] Both of Medea's prayers will be answered in full which suggests either the

---

[597] The sun re-tracing its course, as in the myth of Atreus and Thyestes discussed in chapter 3 (106-11), is a cosmic reaction to mortal behaviour. That Medea can force such a reaction strongly suggests that her abilities far outweigh that of a normal witch and should be seen as an attack on the divine order.

[598] See Fyfe (1983) *passim* for brief remarks about the theme of speech throughout the play.

[599] Benton (2003) 275 emphasizes the fact that Medea's existence was based upon an identity built around Jason and her revenge is a way to make him experience a similar loss. Thus, in granting

legitimacy of her request or the authority inherent in her words. Any doubt about the outcome of her request is addressed by her series of rhetorical questions to which one can only answer "yes" (*Med.* 28-31). What Medea has said will eventuate and we are guaranteed the efficacy of her prayers.

The choral epithalamium for Jason and Creusa provides a parallel to Medea's opening invocation to the gods,[600] and consequently some scholars have argued about whether one prayer garners more sympathy from the audience than the other and which is the more powerful. Hine has argued persuasively that Medea's prayer subverts the wedding ceremony and the audience would see Medea as having the upper hand. Her prayer *voce non fausta* would be considered an intentional challenge to conventional piety and even a single word of ill-omen would disrupt a religious ritual.[601] Indirectly, Fyfe's observations that the chorus unintentionally acknowledge Medea as Jason's lawful wife (*coniugis*, 103; and again at 581, *coniunx*) and that they feel a need to placate the gods (*placet*, 62) further suggest that Medea has a stronger claim on the gods and thus a more powerful prayer.[602] The chorus also ends their prayer with a wish that Medea depart in silent darkness (*tacitis eat illa tenebris*, 114),[603] a foolhardy hope that will be proven naïve, for Medea is anything but silent after hearing their epithalamium. It is thus precisely because Medea voiced her inauspicious prayer that the wedding hymn is doomed to failure and the wish for Medea to be silent is understandable. The fact that Medea speaks immediately after the chorus members voice their hope for her silence proves how

---

Jason his life, she is granting him an existence predicated and constructed by his relationship with her.

[600] Hine (1989) 413.

[601] Hine (1989) 414-15.

[602] Hine (2000) 111.

[603] Motto and Clark (1988) discuss this particular phrase.

ineffectual their wishes are; indeed, the only prayers addressed to the gods that will be answered are those voiced by Medea.

Even Medea's Nurse is aware of the power and destruction of Medea's voice. After Medea's outburst following the epithalamium, and with her heart set on vengeance, she decides that Creon should be the target of her rage and her Nurse immediately begs her to be silent (*sile, obsecro*, 150). Medea rebukes her, but the Nurse continues, slowly realizing that silence will not protect her (*vix te tacita defendit quies*, 158). After Medea exclaims that she intends on taking revenge by way of delays before she departs, the Nurse tries once more to control her words (*compesce verba*, 174). Delaying tactics are nothing new to Medea: whilst escaping from her father, Medea murdered her own brother to delay her pursuers. Her expressed desire to use delaying tactics yet again invites those who know Medea's past to fear yet more deaths as part of her plan. And so it is because the Nurse knows what such delays bring, that any mention of further delays compels her once again to silence her mistress. Her attempts are futile and while this is the last time that the Nurse tries to curb Medea's anger and voice, she is not the last to try.

It is during Creon's initial monologue that Medea is again urged to keep quiet, even before the two actually meet. Creon describes Medea as seeking closer speech (*propius affatus petit*, 187) and he orders his servants to keep her quiet (*iubete sileat*, 189).[604] After an initial repartee, Medea declares that Jason should depart with her, but Creon retorts that her voice comes too late (*vox sera venit*, 198). Medea taunts him with being unjust and he gives in to her, leading to a long defence speech. One hundred lines after Creon's initial declaration that Medea leave his kingdom, the king returns to the issue and requests again that she leave, asking why she is contriving delays with speech (*quid seris fando moras?* 281). Medea's words are bound up once again with the idea of delays, suggesting that she

---

[604] Fyfe (1983) 81.

is plotting the imminent murders and Creon is obviously wanting her to cease her speech. She persists however, using her sons as an excuse, and Creon is eventually persuaded to give her the one day's grace which will lead to his death.

Jason, too, understands the power of Medea's voice,[605] twice urging her to curb her tongue; the first is after she accuses him of desiring power and he wishes to cut short their long conversation (*longa colloquia amputa*, 530); the second comes after Medea's prayer to Jupiter to strike one of them down and Jason implores her to speak quietly (*placida fare*, 538). It is only when Jason speaks of their sons as the sole reason for his being that Medea pretends to acquiesce to his request and asks that her words should be forgotten (*haec [verba] irae data / oblitterentur* 556-57). Jason does as requested and expels her previous words from his mind (*Omnia ex animo expuli*, 557) and thus his fear as well. Medea, having ensured that Jason no longer worries, is now able to use her voice to carry out her revenge. She calls upon Hecate (*vocetur Hecate*, 577) and prepares for the incantation scene which will combine the powers of her voice with her magical abilities.

Just prior to Medea's incantation, the Nurse describes Medea's preparations and comments on the effectiveness of her speech: the world trembles at her first words (*mundus vocibus primis tremit*, 739). This seems very reminiscent of Jupiter's nod and how the world trembles upon its appearance, a common motif since Homer (for example, *Il.* 1.530, where Zeus grants Thetis her request and at his nod all of Olympus shakes), as well as Jupiter's weapons in Seneca's *Hercules Furens* (*cuius excussis tremunt / humana telis*, 517-18). Even Jupiter's ability to shake the world is now lost to Medea's first words. Her first words of the play invoked the *di coniugales* (1) and her first words of the incantation invoke the silent dead and the gods of the dead (740). The world trembles

---

[605] Fyfe (1983) 79.

when Medea calls upon the gods and with good reason. She is harnessing their powers and she is the one instilling fear in the world, attempting her own version of justice.

The incantation scene demonstrates the full extent of Medea's powers. That so much time is given to witnessing Medea make her invocations and chant her magic (over 100 lines) should be taken as an indication of the importance of this scene.[606] When Hecate's rites are mentioned in Medea's opening speech, they are explicitly referred to as silent (*tacitis sacris*, 6). Here, however, there is nothing silent about them and the fact that Medea is voicing these rituals aloud must have made an impact on the audience. Either Medea is subverting yet another ritual by performing it contrary to tradition, or she is making the ritual even more powerful through the use of her voice. This scene could have been reported by the Nurse (who does report the initial preparations), but the choice to have Medea physically perform and voice everything makes this scene that much more powerful. And when Medea is finished, she asserts as much: *Parata vis est omnis* (843). It is at this point that Medea has her sons called in order to carry out the deaths of Creon and Creusa.

Medea's ability to speak and cause things to happen is matched by a motif of other characters and creatures being silent, or having ineffectual voices. This motif is carried throughout the play: Orpheus and even his lyre falls silent (*Orpheus tacuit torpente lyra*, 348); the Argo loses it voice (*vocem perdidit Argo*, 349); the Sirens were nearly compelled to follow Orpheus (358-60); the dead are also silent (*vulgus silentum*, 740). The winds are also referred to as being silent (*siluere venti*, 627; *tacente vento*, 766), as if nature itself fears Medea's voice, when at 766-67 the woods lose their shade at the bidding of her voice (*nemoris antiqui domus / amisit umbras vocis imperio meae*). Medea's powers are

---

[606] Pratt (1983) 87-89 offers a brief discussion of the scene and Seneca's attention to detail in creating it.

articulated through her words and because she is known to match words with deeds, everyone and everything fears her voice and not without reason.

Medea Theomacha

There are also other indications in the text to support the idea that the gods in general are concerned about Medea, as they should be. There are frequent suggestions that her attack is not only aimed at Jason and the Corinthians, but that the cosmos at large is also a target.[607] In conversation with Medea, Creon states that she actually worries the gods (*sollicita deos*, 271) and her Nurse believes Medea to be impious: *magnum aliquid instat, efferum immane impium* (395). Such statements are not made lightly and given Medea's background, they are fully justified. Medea even asserts that she will attack the gods and shake the world (*invadam deos / et cuncta quatiam*, 424-25). The cosmos seems again to be in her mind when she tells her Nurse that she will not be at peace unless everything is in chaos:

Sola est quies,

mecum ruina cuncta si video obruta;
mecum omnia abeant. trahere, cum pereas, libet (*Med.* 426-28).

Medea is essentially wishing to send the world back into the primal state from whence it originated. She is repudiating the current world order and will only have peace if chaos is restored, a paradoxical desire. Even if we had serious reservations about her ability to accomplish this, such a desire is highly disconcerting, especially since Medea is aggressive toward the heavens, as the Nurse later claims (*aggressam deos / caelum trahentem*, 673-74). If one is sensitive to such sentiments throughout the play, this aggression would seem to come to a head when the chorus states that Medea threatens even the king (*regi minatur ultro*, 856). In context, they are referring of course to Creon, but it is not inconceivable that

---

[607] Henry and Walker (1967) 71.

she should threaten the king of heaven too.[608] She will stop at nothing to achieve her goals, even abandoning shame and piety (*fas omne cedat, abeat expulsus pudor*, 900).[609] All that Jupiter and his divine order are meant to represent, all that he is meant to protect, Medea is renouncing. In this respect she resembles most clearly the figure of Atreus in *Thyestes*, although in that play it is a Fury who first forsakes the Olympian order and eventually succeeds in forcing the gods from heaven. Perhaps Medea will be successful after all, for Jason's last words (indeed the last words of the play) claim that there will be no gods wherever she is going: *testare nullos esse, qua veheris, deos* (1027).

Covert Usurper: Atreus

Seneca's Atreus qualifies as a theomachist not because he *sets out* to challenge the gods or Jupiter, but because his triumph over Thyestes is considered a success on both a personal and cosmic level.[610] The conflict between the two brothers can be interpreted variously: on the surface it is a quest for revenge and an attempt to solidify one's family line, each moving forward (through the guarantee of Atreus' paternity) and looking back (by duplicating past events, both brothers prove their descent from Tantalus). On a secondary level, fraternal strife, especially over a throne, is often indicative of foundation myths and such a contest between Atreus and Thyestes, especially when it involves the destruction of the heirs of one's enemies, is suggestive of a "new order" in Argos (even if it is merely a re-establishment of an existing city). On a third level, this idea of a "new order" coupled with the overt reaction to the play's events from the cosmos (symbolized by the Sun's disappearance) suggests that Atreus has not only ended his previous reign as co-ruler with his brother and is looking forward to a new sole monarchy, but he has also

---

[608] Hine (1989) 419.

[609] Cf. *Thy.* 47-48a: *et fas et fides / iusque omne pereat.*

[610] Morford (2000) 165.

achieved a new order in the cosmos.[611] He has displaced the gods and has himself taken their place. Atreus has become a theomachist not by directly challenging Jupiter like the Giants or Ajax and Capaneus (although the Gigantomachy is an important touchstone at the end of the play, discussed further below, p. 331), but rather by following a Medea-like path to its ultimate end. Through his accumulation and conferment of "knowledge," his absolute perversion of ritual and his newly re-established role as dispenser of "justice," Atreus not only proves his "worthiness" as the epitome of the Tantalid line, but he truly inherits his family's throne and takes his place as Jupiter's heir.

Knowledge is Power: The Pursuit of Omniscience

Seneca's play begins with Tantalus, accursed ancestor of Atreus and Thyestes, Jupiter's own son, as the ghost through whom the actions, deeds and interpretations of the play must be filtered. Although he appears physically in the prologue only, the audience is continually reminded of his presence throughout the play both through allusions (53, 242, 626, 717-18 and 1011) and through his namesake who leads Thyestes into Argos against his will.[612] He has been summoned from the depths of the Underworld by *Furia* who uses Tantalus for her own ends (discussed more thoroughly in chapter 2, pp. 86-89): she wishes him to infect the house of Pelops, to bring strife on his descendants and to continue fulfilling the curse on his line. Not only does nature begin to react immediately to his presence on earth (106-21), but we are told that he will be forced to watch the banquet that he himself will propel to its fruition (63-66).[613] That he, or rather his ghost, should be the one to do so is most appropriate given both his current punishment (being unable to be

---

[611] Agapitos (1998) 233.

[612] As Boyle (1983b) 220 states, "he has dominated the play."

[613] See Shelton (1975) for a discussion of the temporal sequences in the play, including the presence of Tantalus at the feast.

sated by food, he must be filled with the deaths of family members) as well as his original sin (offering a feast of human flesh to the gods). But the idea of food and feasting, hunger and thirst, is not the only reason for Tantalus to be the most apt ancestor for Atreus to emulate.

Although the impious feast is certainly one of the transgressions for which Tantalus is being punished it is clearly not the only one. Instead, we hear first that his overly-loquacious tongue is the reason for his current predicament: *ingenti licet / taxata poena lingua crucietur loquax* (*Thy.* 91-92). Although Tantalus does not provide specifics, it is understood that he is referring to his inability to keep the secrets of the gods to himself: that is to say, he was given divine knowledge and attempted to share it with mortals. By alluding to this specific transgression rather to than the banquet, Tantalus makes it clear that it is not the latter sin for which he feels the most regret; instead, he mourns the fact that he could have had a share in immortality and become heir to Jupiter had he been able to cope with the knowledge he had been given and not attempted to confer it onto others. When he did so, he not only violated the trust he had been given but he had also attempted to take on divine attributes by disseminating their secrets.

Tantalus' second transgression, the feast, is also clearly important as the exemplar for Atreus' banquet but it too carries with it connotations of having or withholding knowledge. As Boyle notes:

> The cooking and serving of one's children's flesh to test the omniscience of gods seems gruesome index of perverse ambition, a hunger for knowledge, superiority, power, for which the everlasting frustration of corresponding bodily appetites seems not only fitting punishment but emblem.[614]

Tantalus' attempt to deceive Jupiter and the other gods was clearly a test of their omniscience: he wanted not only to deceive the gods and undermine their divinity (by

---

[614] Boyle (1983b) 199.

forcing them to eat human flesh instead of ambrosia and essentially degrading them, bringing them "down" to his level), but also to acquire a kind of power over them by illustrating superior knowledge that they, he presumed, did not have. The original sin was thus an attempt to overthrow his enemies through deception, by withholding knowledge and by degrading them through an act of bestiality. It was not merely the feast itself, but the way it was (mis-)represented.[615] Atreus thus not only resembles Tantalus in the preparation of the feast, but also in the way that he attempts to (re)gain control and power as monarch.[616] Where he differs from his ancestor is in his success – he initially takes the place of Tantalus, with Thyestes standing in place of the gods; but when he is able to reveal the knowledge of the feast to his brother, the hierarchy is inversed and he himself takes the place of the gods and of Jupiter specifically.[617]

Both sins have their place in Seneca's plot: the feast is the most obvious, but the idea of hidden knowledge and whether or not it should be shared is of no less importance. When Atreus confers with his *satelles*[618] about sending his own sons Agamemnon and Menelaus to retrieve Thyestes, his decision about whether or not to tell them is influenced by their own questionable status. In order for Atreus to be certain about his own heirs, his own heirs must be made knowledgeable (*consili Agamemnon mei / sciens minister fiat, et fratri sciens / Menelaus adsit, Thy.* 325-27) about what he is keeping hidden (*occule*, 333). Their ability to partake of and conceal Atreus' secrets is analogous to Tantalus' own

---

[615] One might also compare the feast to an even earlier sacrificial meal, the fat-covered bones Prometheus offered to Zeus: what one sees is not necessarily what one receives.

[616] For a discussion of the different concepts of "king" introduced throughout the play, see Rose (1987); Davis (1989) 426-29.

[617] Lefèvre (1981) 33.

[618] See Mader (1998) for a discussion of the *satelles*-scene; see also Kovacs (2007) for a discussion specifically concerning the concept of power as the ability to make people want what they do not want (*quod nolunt velint*).

experience of divine knowledge; however, once again his descendants are able to succeed where he himself had failed. Atreus, in both his own attempts to conceal and confer knowledge on others begins to resemble divinity.

The importance of knowledge comes to the fore in the final scene when Thyestes has at last been "enlightened" by Atreus through the double-*anagnorisis*. Atreus takes great pleasure in being the one to confer the "knowledge" of the feast on his brother (*discutiam tibi / tenebras*, 896-97[619]). Atreus first reveals the dismembered heads of Thyestes' sons and forces Thyestes to recognize who and what they are – not merely a cognizance of his sons' deaths, but a realization that he had begotten the very instrument of his downfall. Atreus understood exactly where his brother's weakness lies; now Thyestes also recognizes the place where Atreus could and will hurt him the most. Nevertheless, Thyestes' retort that he now recognizes his brother (*Agnosco fratrem*, 1006) is only partially true. Certainly his original instincts about him were correct, but at this point he only *thinks* he knows who his brother is, for he is as yet ignorant of the whole truth. Thus, when the assertion is made that he recognizes his brother, it only serves to underscore Atreus' complete control over the events and his brother. Full recognition still remains and it will be recognition not only of who and what Atreus is, but of who Thyestes is as well.

Atreus then reveals the full horror of what has transpired: the murder of the boys, the cooking of their limbs and the feast presented and consumed. Both Meltzer and Mader

---

[619] Mader (2003a) discusses the relationship between knowledge/ignorance and clarity/darkness and the idea that in this play darkness protects Thyestes from the truth and total ruin. He suggests (219) that Atreus' statement that he will "disperse the shadows" means both "I will dispel your ignorance" and "I will enlighten you" literally bringing Thyestes out of the unnatural darkness that has descended upon him and as well as figuratively shattering the shadow of ignorance that is currently shielding him from the truth.

have interpreted Atreus' disclosure of this knowledge as "divine revelation."[620] Thyestes'

horror and comprehension of what he has just done is what Atreus had been waiting for; as

Mader says, he is anticipating the *process* whereby Thyestes comprehends his actions,

rather than the actions themselves.[621] Thyestes now knows and understands who they both

are as descendants of Tantalus (*stare circa Tantalum / uterque iam debuimus*, 1011-12).

But this is still not enough for Atreus; he remains dissatisfied. This dissatisfaction is partly

due to his insatiability, but also because Thyestes was not aware of his actions as he was

feasting; both he and his sons were *nesciens* (1065, 1066) of the meal as he was eating.

Atreus furthermore accuses Thyestes of planning too late a similar feast for an

"unknowing" (*inscio*, 1107) brother. Such emphasis on the dichotomy between the

knowing Atreus and the unknowing Thyestes underscores their power imbalance and the

distance that has been created between them. Atreus' preoccupation with his own

knowledge in comparison to others speaks to his own sense of self-divinization and the

realization of the "successful feast." Atreus succeeded where Tantalus did not; he proved

his omniscience over his brother thereby "winning" the right to rule.

Thyestes' participation in and completion of the original Tantalid feast not only

places him in the position of the "ignorant"[622] but he also becomes a second Kronos/Saturn

figure in a new succession myth for the cosmic throne. In an effort to maintain control of

the cosmos, Kronos had swallowed his children whole to avoid usurpation by his own son.

Thyestes' seduction of Aërope and theft of the ram were similar attempts to eliminate his

---

[620] Meltzer (1988) 314; Mader (2003) compares Atreus' revelation to that of Athena at *Il.* 5.127-28
and Venus at *Aen.* 2.604-06 and refers to Atreus as a "self-styled *divus*" (221).

[621] Mader (2010).

[622] Agapitos (1998) 251 discusses the *anagnorisis* in terms of a ritual initiation "which demands
two conditions: active Atreus as omniscient initiator desires to "grant" vengeance (*qua*
knowledge), which he views as a process; passive Thyestes as doubting initiate desires to acquire
power (*qua* knowledge), which he perceives as a state of life."

potential fraternal rival. And now Atreus has provided Thyestes with precisely the scenario

which would guarantee that he will remain the *paterfamilias* of his own line by eliminating

his own sons. He becomes another Kronos-figure through the eating of his children, but

because they were dismembered before being consumed and because the gods have fled

(1020) there is no chance for them either to escape on their own or to become whole again

as the gods had done with Pelops. Atreus remembers the history of succession well and

uses it to his own advantage. When Atreus triumphs over Thyestes he regains the certainty

of his own paternity, his marriage and the right to the Argive throne. Thyestes' unwitting

participation in the feast ensures that even though he may now be a *paterfamilias* without

heirs, his failure to accumulate knowledge and his undertaking of impious actions ensure

that he can never attain the cosmic throne that Atreus has cleverly achieved through his

knowledge of the succession myths and the perversion of mortal, natural and divine

boundaries. The feast thus not only facilitates the degrading of Thyestes to a bestial

level,[623] but also the apotheosis of Atreus as a now perverted-divine being. The gods have

no place in such a world and thus disappear into the unnatural night: "the gods' withdrawal

from man's world is accompanied by the dramatization of their impotence.[624]

Achieving Divinity: Apotheosis and Ritual Perversion

The first hint of Atreus' divinity comes ironically from the mouth of the young

Tantalus as the youth attempts to persuade his father to accept the offer of kingship from

his uncle. He insists that: *Nec abnuendum est, si dat imperium deus, / nec appetendum est.*

frater ut regnes rogat (471-72). Although young Tantalus does not *intend* to refer to

Atreus as a divinity, the connection he makes between god-given imperium and his uncle's

---

[623] See Boyle (1983b) esp. 209-13 who discusses of the theme of man-as-beast in the context of
Thyestes.

[624] Boyle (1983b) 219.

offer suggests quite plainly that Atreus is taking on divine qualities. Atreus-as-*deus* is more than a mere suggestion that, as monarch, he has the ability to offer kingship and bestow power upon Thyestes. It is the first step toward Thyestes' downfall and Atreus' assumption of divine office. The events that transpire after Thyestes' accepts the crown from his brother are all under Atreus' gaze and are "acted out" according to his plan.[625] Atreus-as-*deus* will eventually manifest himself more fully at the end of the play, but his arrival later is foreshadowed by this seemingly innocent remark which tells the audience most clearly under whose auspices this play is truly being performed.

That Tantalus should allude to a god bestowing imperium upon a mortal is significant in one other important way: during the next choral ode there is an allusion to just such an event occurring.[626] The chorus is addressing Atreus and they believe that he should fear the wrath of the god who gave him his own power:

> Vos quibus rector maris atque terrae
> ius dedit magnum necis atque vitae,
> ponite inflatos tumidosque vultus (*Thy.* 607-09).

Although it is not made explicit, it is clear that the god to whom the chorus is referring must be Jupiter, the only god who could grant Atreus such a dominion.[627] What is striking about this particular passage, however, is the fact that it contains the only instance of this specific designation (*rector maris atque terrae*) for Jupiter in the entire Senecan corpus. *Summe caeli rector* appears later as Jupiter's rightful title (1077), but *rector* in combination with *maris* is unique. As master of earth and sea, Seneca is explicitly

---

[625] Schiesaro (2003) 55-58 and 133-138 provide a thorough discussion of the idea of Atreus as meta-poetic director. See also Mowbray (2012) 124-30 for her analysis of Atreus as a type of avenger-*vates*.

[626] See Davis (1989) for a discussion of the role of the chorus in *Thyestes*.

[627] The chorus is addressing Atreus, but the plural *vos* (and later *vobis*, 610-11) suggest that they are also including other tyrants or kings (Emperors?) who have been granted similar power by Jupiter.

separating him from his more usual mastership of the heaven or sky. This unusual title could be meant to signify his rule over the whole world and provide polarity, signifying a domain from heaven to sea;[628] however, because of the singularity of the epithet there is likely more underlying Seneca's choice of words. On their own, one may be inclined to think at first of Neptune rather than of Jupiter, for he is the master of the sea *par excellence* and he has connections to land as the "earth-shaker." But Neptune does not have a place here and it seems that his brother has usurped his epithet.[629] No longer perceived as master of the heavens by the chorus, Jupiter no longer retains his usual abode or his title; his realm has been downgraded to that of the earth and sea.

The remainder of the choral phrase provides further clues as to what Seneca has in mind: *ius dedit magnum necis atque vitae* implies that Jupiter has given Atreus the authority to give or take life (a prerogative enjoyed by the Greek Zeus), and so the god cannot punish Atreus when he kills Thyestes' children and takes this bestowed imperium to a whole new level. The effect of having an Atreus-as-*deus* who takes on Jovian characteristics is such that there can only be one ultimate power: Ateus' ascent to divinity and specifically to a Jovian divinity, must entail a descent or downgrading of Jupiter to a point where the two are no longer in conflict. Such a descent can in fact be traced in the play until the god is understood to have left the drama and the mortal world of Argos for good when he is reduced to a comet which departs at lines 698-99 during Atreus' sacrificial act.

It is through a messenger-speech that the sacrifice is brought to life, as it were, for the audience, but immediately before describing how Atreus slaughters his nephews, the Messenger notes the various unnatural portents that occur. He explains how the grove

---

[628] Tarrant (1985) 177.

[629] For example see Ovid *Met.* 11.207 for Neptune as *rector maris*.

trembles and the earth shakes (*Lucus tremescit, tota succusso solo / nutavit aula*, 696-97)
— one wonders if this is Jupiter's final protest as master of earth and sea — and then he
describes the comet: *e laevo aethere / atrum cucurrit limitem sidus trahens* (698-99). Stars
and celestial phenomena are explicitly linked to the gods throughout the play,[630] and this
particular celestial event is highly significant. A *sidus* was traditionally believed to be a
shooting star or comet and it was this type of omen which presaged the death of Julius
Caesar (Verg. *G.* 1.488, Luc. 1.526-9) and was commonly believed to portend disaster,
death or a change in government. The ancient authors seem to agree for, according to
Rogers,

> "Seneca seems to regard comets as, generally speaking, omens of grave
> import . . . Pliny regards a comet as a terrifying omen . . . and like
> Calpurnius Siculus he interprets the one after Caesar's death as forecasting
> the bloodshed of the civil wars . . . For Suetonius and Dio the comet of 54
> was clear omen of Claudius' imminent death . . . Finally Tacitus . . . counts
> the comet of 64 as one among a series of prodigies foretelling of impending
> disasters, and states that a comet was always expiated by Nero with noble
> blood (Tac. *Ann.* 15.47)."[631]

These post-Augustan authors all seem to share a common perception of comets as
harbingers of disaster and, in particular, of a change in leadership; indeed Tacitus
explicitly states that the public believe this to be true (*Ann.* 14.22). The comet seen in our
play might well be taken as an indication of Atreus' resumption of the Argive throne;
however, Thyestes has been in exile and while his return is based on the premise that he
will co-rule with his brother, it is a premise based on a ruse and will not come to pass. But
there certainly is a change of leadership in this play and it certainly does involve Atreus. In
a provocative move, Seneca uses the comet to represent not the death of Atreus, but rather

---

[630] The chorus refers to stars as *turba deorum* (843) and *sacris...astris* (844). For a discussion of
the gods as stars see: Davis (1989) 433-34 and (2003) 68-69. See also O'Brien (2001) for a
discussion centered on the "star-chorus" at 848-74.

[631] Rogers (1953) 243-44.

the simultaneous "abdication" of the cosmic king Jupiter and the apotheosis of Atreus to

the vacated throne of the god. Jupiter, of course, cannot truly die, but he does officially

leave the drama, the city of Argos and, indeed, the world of *Thyestes*, giving up his place

to his final heir.

That Tacitus should also mention Nero's expiation of comets through blood

sacrifice may be coincidence when referring to a play which presents a comet followed by

the sacrifice of three noble youths and it may well have made some in the audience uneasy.

But regardless of any contemporary sentiment, the sacrifice is a central concern for

Seneca. Several scholars have noted how Atreus completes the murder of his nephews in a

very ritualistic manner as a sacrifice to himself and to his *impiae . . . irae* (*Thy.* 712-13).[632]

The perversion of ritual practice has generally concentrated on the aspect of human

sacrifice, which is of course the core of the scene.[633] But it has also been noted how Atreus

occupies each and every role that would normally be meted out for such a sacrifice: he is

priest, diviner, the one offering the sacrifice and the one receiving it.[634] The only role he

does not play is that of the sacrificial being itself. Taking on these multiple roles has

greater significance however, than merely dominating the action and ensuring it is

accomplished to his satisfaction. To take the second pair as an example, by placing himself

in the position both to offer and to receive sacrifice ensures that Atreus receives the "gifts"

at both ends as it were. As Boyle states, "the distinctions the sacrifice implies are

dissolved."[635] A proper sacrifice would normally entail an offering by the propitiator to a

deity either in thanks or in order to receive a boon of some description (or perhaps in

appeasement). If successful, the deity would presumably assent to the demand, but would

---

[632] Lefèvre (1981) 34-35; Meltzer (1988) 324; Morford (2000) 172.

[633] For example, Meltzer (1988) 325

[634] Agapitos (1998) 250-51.

[635] Boyle (1983b) 213.

in any case receive the pleasures of the sacrifice. Atreus, by assuming both positions, ensures that as recipient he will, regardless of the outcome, receive some pleasures of the sacrifice and as "propitiator" will receive what he desires: assurance of his lineage, revenge on his brother and surpassing the crimes of his ancestors (this time "getting it right").

Although the aspect of human (and familial) sacrifice is the most horrendous aspect of the ritual scene, it is not the only perversion to occur. Atreus' occupation of each side of the sacrifice distorts the meaning and viability of the ritual's use. Now that a mortal has become the recipient of divine sacrifice (the first instance in the play of a mortal intruding upon the divine world in the play) the gods can no longer receive their dues as they should. It is at this point that Atreus-as-*deus* comes into realization. The Fury had earlier demanded that there no longer be anything *fas* in the world (*et fas et fides / iusque omne pereat*, 47-48a): the destruction of the institution of sacrifice ensures not only that the Fury's demands come to fruition, but that *nefas* will surely fill the void where all that was *fas* had been.

Seneca also makes it quite clear that such grandiose sentiments on the part of Atreus are not mere exhortations of a megalomaniac, but rather, they are indications of a truth that is not readily acceptable and yet glaringly obvious. As Atreus re-enters the drama after the Messenger speech and ensuing choral ode, he announces his identity not as brother of Thyestes or even as king of Argos but instead as an equal to the gods and one who has achieved revenge, his kingdom and his inheritance:

> Aequalis astris gradior et cunctos super
> altum superbo vertice attingens polum.
> nunc decora regni teneo, nunc solium patris.
> dimitto superos . . . (*Thy.* 885-88).

The banquet has not even occurred and yet Atreus is assured of his identity once more and of his triumph over Thyestes.[636] Such assurance arises from his assumption of divine attributes and apotheosis during the sacrifice.[637] Atreus' adherence to every aspect of the ritual ensured that its inherent structural integrity remained, but his perversion of the various roles involved also ensured that its meaning has been forever altered. Sacrifice, prayers and offering can and will continue, but the recipients are no longer the celestial deities. Atreus-as-*deus* is manifest and he has come to collect his first-offerings.

It is with Thyestes' belch (911-12) that Atreus is "officially," as it were, the new cosmic king.[638] He himself knew it before and now it is plain for all to see. Thyestes' indulgence in the banquet not only completes the sacrificial meal and the final element to the ritual, but it also confirms Atreus' triumph and victory over his enemy, the erasure of his rival's line and proof of his ability to dismiss the gods, take their place and ensure their impotence for justice. Jupiter can do nothing now to stop Atreus, can do nothing to aid Thyestes and can no longer reside in his rightful place in the heavens. As Thyestes exclaims, *fugere superi* (1021), and prayers will be futile for they will only serve the interests of Atreus, the newly-established *deus*: *vobis vota prospicient mea* (1076).[639]

---

[636] Agapitos (1998) 235 suggests that the identity Atreus is now assured of is Atreus-as-mythological exemplum much like Medea when she reaffirms her identity (*Medea nunc sum*, *Med.* 910).

[637] Davis (1989) 433: "The metaphor of touching the stars is a common means of suggesting the achievement of success in Roman literature. It has connotations of apotheosis." Morford (2000) provides a detailed study of this passage.

[638] Meltzer (1988) 314: "He [Atreus] interprets signs as diverse as his brother's belch and the darkness which replaces daylight as confirming his omnipotence." See also Mader (2003b) for a brief discussion of the importance of this specific scene.

[639] Again, there is a double-meaning in the use of *vobis* here: in a literal sense, Thyestes is addressing the deities of the Underworld, but equally (and ironically) he is also addressing Atreus as a new *deus*.

Dispenser of Justice: Jupiter's Heir

Atreus, having claimed his status as a *deus*, takes his place as Jupiter's successor. Specifically, he takes upon himself the role of "dispenser of justice and punishment." In other words, he takes the place of Jupiter as cosmic moderator and source of order. Although Atreus' revenge is of a very personal nature, it nevertheless has cosmic implications in the way it was conceived and carried out and this is aside from the very overt reaction of the cosmos which plunges the world of the play into unnatural darkness. That Atreus had designs all along to become Jupiter's replacement is clear from his very first scene as he contemplates his revenge. He sees himself as meting out a very Jovian punishment to Thyestes for the plans he has to take back the kingdom:

> regna nunc sperat mea:
> hac spe minanti fulmen occurret Iovi,
> hac spe subibit gurgitis tumidi minas
> dubiumque Libycae Syrtis intrabit fretum,
> hac spe, quod esse maximum retur malum,
> fratrem videbit (*Thy.* 289-94).

Two implications are immediately apparent upon hearing/reading these lines. The first is that Atreus believes his brother's crime is worthy of Jupiter's thunderbolts, the god's most severe punishment and, furthermore, that Atreus believes his mode of revenge to be equal to the god's in severity. Secondly, due to the very obvious absence of Jupiter's thunderbolts (especially when requested by Thyestes at 1089-90), Atreus' revenge does indeed become the equivalent of Jupiter's lightning. Thyestes' crimes, moreover, also fit well the Jovian model for deserving such retribution: those brought low by Jupiter's bolts are those who overtly covet his place in the cosmos (or wish to overturn his rule), or they are those who strive to upset the balance/equilibrium he has created. Thyestes is guilty on both counts. He seduced Aërope and took the golden ram into his possession in order to become the ruler of Argos and, incidentally, to become "heir" to Jupiter. He also partook of a sacrilegious meal which blurred the boundaries between man and beast and between life and death. That he was an unwitting participant does little to alleviate the effect of these crimes.

There is one final point to mention with respect to Atreus' comparison to Jupiter in this speech. He ends his threat of punishment within the context of Thyestes meeting other dire fates, which he would not survive, and then reaches his climactic point: that the worst fate and *maximum malum* (293) for Thyestes will be to see his brother. Such a belief in the severity of his own methods of revenge, suggests not just that Atreus is equal to Jupiter in his ability to inflict punishment and mete out justice, but that he is in fact a greater threat to Thyestes than Jupiter could ever be.[640] As the *maximum malum* in the world, Atreus is usurping Jupiter's position as an arbiter of "justice" and retribution, ensuring that any future decisions about what will be considered proper behaviour will be his to make as well as any decisions concerning the penalty for those who transgress *his* laws.

The most poignant moment for Jupiter's demise comes with Thyestes' appeal to the god during the final exchanges in the play. Having finally become "enlightened" by Atreus as to the fate of his sons and his own transgressions which have caused the Sun to turn back its course in horror and the gods-as-stars to flee their abodes in heaven, Thyestes makes a final plea to Jupiter to strike him down and be punished for his *scelera*. The passage is worth quoting in full:

> Tu, summe caeli rector, aetheriae potens
> dominator aulae, nubibus totum horridis
> convolve mundum, bella ventorum undique
> committe et omni parte violentum intona,
> manuque non qua tecta et immeritas domos
> telo petis minore, sed qua montium
> tergemina moles cecidit et qui montibus

---

[640] As Agapitos (1998) 234 states (quoting Seidensticker 1985): "Atreus lives in a world of comparisons with the 'comparative of surpassing' as his guiding principle."

> stabant pares Gigantes, hac arma expedi
> ignesque torque. vindica amissum diem,
> iaculare flammas, lumen ereptum polo
> fulminibus exple (*Thy.* 1077-87).

Thyestes begins by using (what he assumes remains to be) Jupiter's rightful title as *caeli rector*. The epithet harkens back to the earlier instance of *rector* (607), used by the chorus to describe Jupiter as master of earth and sea. Here the epithet is used in conjunction with the sky, Jupiter's natural element and abode and the target of Atreus' ultimate desire. When Thyestes insists that his subsequent pleas will be of interest to his brother (1076), he speaks a truth of which he is wholly unaware. Atreus, having usurped Jupiter's role as arbiter of justice and having succeeded in dethroning him, inadvertently and unintentionally has become the object of Thyestes' prayers. It is Atreus who is now *caeli rector* as he exclaimed at the beginning of the Act (885-92) and thus while Thyestes *believes* that he is calling upon the sovereign god to relieve his suffering, he is in fact calling upon his brother, who now has gained these titles.

That the audience should understand this invocation as a reference to Atreus is emphasized by the very Roman colouring of the phrase which follows it: *aetheriae potens dominator aulae*. Seneca's choice of *dominator* is intriguing in itself, for it is not a word often used by earlier authors. It is first attested in Cicero (*de Nat. Deor.* 2.4) as an epithet of Jupiter and one which carries with it a cosmic importance, one transcending mere government. Aside from one other use by Maecenas,[641] there is no other example of it until Seneca, where this is one of seven instances.[642] The prevalence of the term by Seneca and its obscurity in other sources suggests that Seneca is being very selective here. When compared with his other usages it carries connotations of malevolence and thus should be taken as such here. In conjunction with the term *aula*, we are presented with a reference to

---

[641] *Appendix Vergiliana*, 1.87

[642] *HF* 1181, *Med.* 4, *Phaed.* 1039, 1159; *Ep. ad Luc.* 107.11.1; *e Clea.* 1.

the overlord of a grand palace;[643] in the context of the play this can only mean Atreus (whose palace was earlier referred to as an *aula*, 697) even though Thyestes includes the descriptor *aetheriae*. This additional descriptor serves, instead of reinforcing Jupiter's authority, to underscore emphatically that which Atreus has achieved. It is he who is in control of Jupiter's heavenly palace following the god's abandonment of it.

As Thyestes continues his (misguided) plea to Jupiter, he begs that the world enshroud his crime and that he be punished by the god. But he wishes not to perish by natural phenomena (as if a victim), but to be struck as though he were a threat, as the Giants were when they attempted to reach heaven:

> manuque non qua tecta et immeritas domos
> telo petis minore, sed qua montium
> tergemina moles cecidit et qui montibus
> stabant pares Gigantes . . . (*Thy.* 1081-84).[644]

As mentioned already, Thyestes was attempting to wrest the Argive throne from Atreus as well as become Jupiter's heir. These offences coupled with his breach of nature's boundaries (the feast) renders him a threat equivalent to that of the Giants. Thyestes' wish that Jupiter treat both brothers as if Giants, the traditional enemies of the gods and Jupiter in particular, reinforces the idea that both brothers attempted an attack against Jupiter, Atreus by successfully attaining the heavens and Thyestes because of his violation of nature.

Thyestes continues his appeal for Jupiter and now asks: *vindica amissum diem* (1085). This motif of the retreating sun is an important one and was introduced by the Fury in the prologue when she demanded: *nox alia fiat, excidat caelo dies* (51).[645] The Fury hints at the fact that this is not the first time that the sun had fled the sky. Jupiter bade the

---

[643] See Faber (2007) for a discussion of the thematic importance of the palace throughout the play.

[644] See Faber (2007) 431-32.

[645] *alia* found in manuscript *E*; *alta* and *atra* also possibilities.

sun and stars to retrace their steps when Atreus ascended the throne to give proof of his right to rule (Apollod. *Ep.*2.12). Now, at the Fury's instigation the sun has indeed left for a second time,[646] here to give Atreus *her* "blessing" to rule, a twist on the earlier tradition and one which further highlights Jupiter's impotency. The idea of the "lost day" or "lost light of day" also seems to have Promethean undertones to it. Jupiter has lost that which separates men from gods and which is now in Atreus' possession. Unlike Prometheus, he has thoroughly succeeded in undermining Jupiter's order and has forever more blurred the distinction between the celestial and the mortal.

As poignant as this speech of Thyestes is for the utter reversal of Jupiter's fortunes, it is in the final lines of the play that we are provided with the most powerful summation of Atreus' cruelty, despotism and divine affinities. Thyestes' final utterance is to call upon the avenging gods to take revenge on Atreus, leaving his punishment in their hands: *Vindices aderunt dei: / his puniendum vota te tradunt mea* (1111-12). As Atreus is now among the ranks of such avenging gods and, for all intents and purposes, their leader, Thyestes has consigned such punishment for Atreus, in very dark ironic fashion, to Atreus himself.[647] His brother's response is to undertake such punishment and to twist it to his own purpose. In very Jovian fashion, he leaves the punishment of Thyestes to his children to carry out, effectively cursing his line (as gods generally are wont to do). Atreus embodies the very qualities one would expect of the gods and Jupiter in particular, but his intentions and actions speak to his very *human* essence. There is little that is truly *heavenly* about Atreus, but much that can be called godly.

---

[646] There is a second "double night" to which this may also be referring: famously Hercules was conceived when Jupiter delayed the rising of the sun. Here the Fury is declaring that a great evil will be conceived – one to rival Jupiter's other son and which will ascend to heaven.

[647] Morford (2000) 171: "Now, in the final scene of the play, Atreus proves that he has displaced the gods. He has transcended the *vindices dei* to whom Thyestes appeals (1110). *He is the deus vindex* . . . [emphasis in original]."

In Medea and Atreus Seneca presents us with two mortals who embrace chthonic as well as heavenly powers in order to achieve their aims, which simultaneously render them equals to, and challengers of, Jupiter and his world-order. Jupiter does not make much of an appearance in Seneca's *Medea*, but such lack of Olympian authority is consistent with the increase in chthonic powers with which Medea begins the play. Medea is shown throughout the play to capitalize on her own inherited divinity and begins a process of deification: her departure at the end of the play is the culmination of such a process and indicates her complete apotheosis. Medea's assumption of divine authority corresponds to an eventual impotency on the part of Jupiter to thwart her plans or punish her crimes. Medea assimilates herself to Jupiter and eventually takes on his epithets and symbols of authority. Jupiter does not and cannot curb Medea's power, becoming idle throughout the course of the play. Rather than an indication that Medea poses no threat to his imperium, Jupiter is almost transformed into a frozen spectator who must watch her enact a ceremony of impending doom. That Medea triumphs at the end is indicative, not of Jupiter's support, but of his ineffectuality in maintaining order. Jason's words at the end of the play that she will meet no gods wherever she goes, could easily be understood as renunciation of the ether by the divine order and Medea's usurpation of the realm.

In a similar way, Atreus also triumphs over Jupiter, but in *Thyestes* such a triumph is complete and without question. Jupiter is not only reduced to a spectator, but one who will not stay in the heavens and who essentially abdicates his place.[648] Atreus' victory is

---

[648] Although the events of *Agamemnon* follow those of *Thyestes*, the latter play is generally accepted to be the later play and so the more positive role of a Jupiter who protects the young Orestes in *Agamemnon* is not necessarily in conflict with a Jupiter who abdicates authority to Atreus in *Thyestes*. In fact, such contrasting visions of the god may be a further indicator of the

not only over his brother, but over Jupiter as well. Seneca's Jupiter in this play is shown to be even less responsive than in *Medea* and leaves a very discomforting vision of the supreme god. The acts of men in the human world have become so atrocious that Jupiter and the rest of the gods have abandoned their traditional place and role as guardians of mankind. Jupiter, the one god who should be the most supportive of kings, leaves the world of the play; we are not convinced he could ever return. Such a depiction is nowhere to be found in Euripides' tragedies or in those of Sophocles or Aeschylus either. It is clearly a product of the Imperial age and one which bodes ill for those of Seneca's contemporary Rome.

relative dating of the two plays; the more positive portrayal occurring earlier in Seneca's *oeuvre*, the more negative portrayal occurring at a later, more turbulent, period of the author's life.

I set out in this dissertation with a number of aims in mind, the foremost among them to offer a more detailed analysis than has hitherto been attempted of passages concerning Zeus and Jupiter within the tragedies of Euripides and Seneca. Such a study, on this scale, is a first. The preceding discussions, I believe, have highlighted both the significance of Zeus and Jupiter within their respective tragedies and the potential for further investigation in the same vein. The scope of my study, although broad, has been necessarily restricted by the parameters of a PhD dissertation; however, the tragedies that I have covered and the themes that I have discussed together suggest that the present study is more than a mere sum of its individual "Parts."

I began this investigation with a number of questions in mind concerning the tragic representation of Zeus and Jupiter by Euripides and Seneca. Throughout the last nine chapters, I believe I have gone some way toward answering those questions and interrogating the similarities and differences that exist between the two playwrights' conceptions of their respective deities. I would like to revisit those questions and offer some final remarks about what I have achieved throughout this study.

I set out to answer a seemingly straightforward question concerning the function of Zeus and Jupiter in the plays of Euripides and Seneca: whether references to either god could have an impact on the interpretation of a given play or add resonance to any themes therein. My individual investigations of Zeus and Jupiter within the plays presented here demonstrate quite clearly that references or allusions to each god within a play can usually be identified as illustrative of specific themes and motifs of significance. My aim has been to identify why particular mentions of Zeus and Jupiter are relevant and how they are used by each playwright. Such interpretations of Zeus- and Jupiter-passages or allusions are not the only ones possible, but they do illustrate the underlying importance of reflecting on each passage. Rather than dismiss allusions that seem to convey no more than a poetical *topos*, every mention has the potential to enhance our understanding of a play's thematic interests.

My second set of questions regarded the broader notion of representation: how is Zeus portrayed by Euripides and Jupiter by Seneca? My thematic discussions have proved that the answer is far more complex than the simplicity inherent in the question. I began by taking the ideas associated with Zeus (fate, justice, the cosmos) and his Homeric status as "Father of Gods and Men" and examining the depth and complexity of such connections within the tragedies of Euripides. Certainly, Zeus' associations with fate and justice remain operative within the Euripidean corpus and the god is understood to be particularly concerned with each concept. Although never used explicitly, the Homeric image of Zeus' scales can be applied well to Euripides' Zeus as a metaphor for his interest in maintaining balance in the world and his jurisdiction over life and death. But Euripides also questions Zeus' "justice" by highlighting the incongruity between the divine and mortal conceptions of what that justice entails. Euripides' mortal characters cannot see a larger cosmic picture and, by necessity, must operate in "shades of grey" as opposed to living by Zeus' "black and white" rules of conduct, which are eventually borne out in each instance. Such a "black and white" vision can also be seen through Zeus' representation as a deity of natural law. The forces of nature are under his guidance and can be used to demonstrate his will (as in his support of Atreus' kingship), or to punish mortals who have transgressed his laws (as in the case of Capaneus). Zeus is interested in the affairs of men insofar as mortals help (or hinder) his cosmic duties, but he is less invested in the day-to-day affairs of everyday individuals. Such intervention, when required, is usually deputized to other deities, who carry out his will.

As for Seneca's Jupiter, he remains invested in the maintenance of cosmic balance and is similarly concerned with notions of justice; but his relationship to other deities associated with these concepts suggest a Jupiter who is far less secure in his position as the ultimate authority. He is portrayed as a god who comes into conflict with goddesses of justice and retribution as well as Natura herself. Seneca's Jupiter, far from being an unassailable unifier, is beset by deities (and even mortals) who attempt to undermine his will. Such impressions are borne out by my investigations of Zeus and Jupiter's relationships with the other Olympians. While Zeus is portrayed as coming into conflict with his sister-wife Hera, she is not ultimately endeavouring to overthrow her husband's sovereignty, but rather to re-assert her own godhead and ensure her own *timē* is respected. Zeus maintains his *auctoritas* with his wife, as well as with his male siblings, Hades and Poseidon. The three male Olympians work together under Zeus' rule, without the need for any conflict. Jupiter is less lucky in this respect, for he is represented as nearly interchangeable with his nether-brother; while he still has autonomy in his own realm, he must respect the same autonomy of his brothers in order to avoid any friction. Jupiter is portrayed with considerable power but is far less secure in retaining that power.

Indeed, this insecurity on the part of Jupiter is the key difference between the Euripidean and Senecan conceptions: Zeus, for all that he may be questioned and criticized, is never shown to lose his *auctoritas*; Jupiter, on the other hand, is challenged in *Medea* and supplanted in Seneca's *Thyestes*. Such a loss of power is significant and demonstrates a drastic shift from Euripides' conception of Zeus. It is in this area in particular that one can see how consistent, or not, each playwright's vision of their god can be. Euripides seems to have a rather consistent conception for Zeus, although he can still mold his myths to present a particular theme (as he does with Eros and Aphrodite). Seneca, on the other hand, is somewhat less consistent, although Jupiter's insecurity can be found in varying degrees throughout the corpus. The presentation in *Thyestes*, but also in his *Medea*, does suggest a shift from other, perhaps earlier, plays. The degradation that Jupiter endures at Atreus' hands suggests that *Thyestes*, at least, represents a bleaker vision for Jupiter than is seen elsewhere.

The final set of questions I posed in my introduction referred to broader implications of such representations of Zeus and Jupiter in their respective tragedies. Such inferences, by necessity, must be tentative in nature. Approximately 500 years passed after the plays of Euripides were written and originally performed for Athenian audiences by the time Seneca penned his tragedies for Roman consumption. Fifth-century Athens could not have been more different from Imperial Rome in the first century C.E. But the two playwrights (and nations) shared a common literary and mythological culture, which can clearly be seen at work in Seneca's reception of Greek and Euripidean tragedy. That the two tragedians offer broadly similar conceptions of Zeus and Jupiter also speaks to this shared literary culture, but the specific differences which have been highlighted (especially with regard to Jupiter's insecurity), speaks to the political realities of each playwright's time.

Euripides' portrayal of Zeus suggests a playwright who is invested in maintaining the political hierarchies of Athens in order to retain social stability. He suggests that doubt in, or mistrust of, the gods by mortals is undermined by mortal reliance on divine assistance: criticisms of Zeus only highlight the dependency of mankind on his favour. If individuals are to rely on the divine, they need to accept that their own lot is only one (small) part of a larger cosmos and that mortal and divine notions, of fate and justice in particular, are not synonymous. This difference in perception may be applied also to the *demos* and politicians of Athenians: first, it requires political cohesion in order to maintain social stability; second, those who rely on their superiors ought to accept their position and understand in relation to the wider mechanisms of state; third, the ideals of the *demos* and those of the men in charge will not always coincide, but such differences are inevitable and not necessarily detrimental.

The rather more unsettling depiction of Jupiter by Seneca indicates the playwright's uneasiness with relying on the gods at all. The presence in Seneca's life of a formidably powerful emperor surely resonates with his depictions of Jupiter, a similarly powerful deity; however, the insecurity that attends the god could very well reflect the potential for usurpation of the Imperial office. Seneca is less ready to advocate for Jovian interest and success in providing assurances to mortals. While the god ought to be the one to support the Imperial office, and thus all Romans, Seneca suggests Jupiter is just as likely to abandon the person of the emperor and leave Rome to its own demise if he is not appropriately honoured. The ascendancy of the mortal king and simultaneous descent of the divine king speaks to Seneca's own lived experience and offers little comfort to those who look to the gods for stability in an unstable world.

Both Euripides and Seneca offer their own conceptions of what the ultimate deity is and what he should do, as well as how mortals ought to interact with him and with each other. They offer both positive and negative examples of such interactions as models for individuals to use in navigating hierarchical relationships, both mortal and divine. In this way, the models of each author still provide *exempla* for similar relationships today. There is certainly scope for further exploration of their roles in tragedy, both Greek and Roman, but also of their broader significance in Greek and Roman society and its lasting effects. While this study of Zeus in the plays of Euripides and of Jupiter in those of Seneca is a first, my hope is that it will not be the last. Both Zeus and Jupiter held much esteem in their respective societies, but modern scholarship has done them only minor justice. It is my final aim that with the present study further justice may be done and that it leads to even more discussions worthy of the Father of Gods and Men.